Ecology, Economy and State Formation in Early Modern Germany

This is an innovative study of the agrarian world and growth of government in early modern Germany through the medium of pre-industrial society's most basic material resource, wood. Paul Warde offers a regional study of south-west Germany from the late fifteenth to the early eighteenth century, demonstrating the stability of the economy and social structure through periods of demographic pressure, warfare and epidemic. He casts new light on the nature of 'wood shortages' and societal response to environmental challenge, and shows how institutional responses largely based on preventing local conflict were poor at adapting over time to optimise the management of resources. Warde further argues for the inadequacy of models that oppose the 'market' to a 'natural economy' in understanding economic behaviour. This is a major contribution to debates about the sustainability of peasant economy and society in early modern Europe, to our understanding of the growth of the state, and to new ecological approaches to history and historical geography.

PAUL WARDE is Lecturer in History at the University of Cambridge.

Cambridge Studies in Population, Economy and Society in Past Time 41

Series Editors

RICHARD SMITH
Cambridge Group for the History of Population and Social Structure

JAN DE VRIES
University of California at Berkeley

PAUL JOHNSON
London School of Economics and Political Science

KEITH WRIGHTSON
Yale University

Recent work in social, economic and demographic history has revealed much that was previously obscure about societal stability and change in the past. It has also suggested that crossing the conventional boundaries between these branches of history can be very rewarding.

This series exemplifies the value of interdisciplinary work of this kind, and includes books on topics such as family, kinship and neighbourhood; welfare provision and social control; work and leisure; migration; urban growth; and legal structures and procedures, as well as more familiar matters. It demonstrates that, for example, anthropology and economics have become as close intellectual neighbours to history as have political philosophy or biography.

For a full list of titles in the series, please see end of book.

Ecology, Economy and State Formation in Early Modern Germany

Paul Warde

University of Cambridge

CAMBRIDGE UNIVERSITY PRESS
Cambridge, New York, Melbourne, Madrid, Cape Town, Singapore, São Paulo

Cambridge University Press
The Edinburgh Building, Cambridge CB2 2RU, UK

Published in the United States of America by Cambridge University Press,
New York

www.cambridge.org
Information on this title: www.cambridge.org/9780521831925

First published 2006

Printed in the United Kingdom at the University Press, Cambridge

A catalogue record for this book is available from the British Library

ISBN-13 978-0-521-83192-5 hardback
ISBN-10 0-521-83192-X hardback

Contents

Figures

Maps

Tables

Acknowledgements

Much of this work has depended on the expertise, goodwill, generosity, hospitality and friendship of others. First of all, entitlement to financial assistance made the whole project possible. For this I am grateful to the Economic and Social Research Council, The Deutsche Akademische Ausstauschdienst, the Centre for History and Economics at King's College, Cambridge, the Ellen MacArthur Fund for Economic History of the Faculty of History, Cambridge, and Fitzwilliam College and Pembroke College, both of the University of Cambridge. These last two have provided, beyond financial support, a congenial, rewarding and supportive atmosphere in which to pursue both research and teaching.

The archives I have consulted in Germany have been unfailingly helpful as well as treasure-houses of documentation. I am particularly indebted to the expertise and willingness of the staff of the Hauptstaatsarchiv Stuttgart. In Bietigheim I have enjoyed the assistance of Stefan Benning, and in Markgröningen, Petra Schad. The town archive of Leonberg, great swathes of which still remain to be thoroughly examined, has been unstinting in its support and facilitated a stream of demands and requests. I am very grateful to the archivist there, Bernadette Gramm, for her help and good company. The Landesbibliothek Baden-Württemberg, the Universitätsbibliothek Tübingen, and the Universitätsbibliothek Hohenheim have all been of assistance. Valuable material was also obtained by the good offices of Reinhold Schaal, Winfried Schenk, Verena Winiwarter, Volker Trugenberger, and Stefan Brakensiek. Closer to home, the staff of the University Library, Cambridge, especially those of the map room, and the British Library, have unflappably processed and answered many queries.

In Cambridge, the Centre for History and Economics and the Cambridge Group for the History of Population and Social Structure have provided wonderful academic homes, and many good times. I am grateful to all of my colleagues in these research centres, and I heartily wish them the continued success that their efforts and achievements richly deserve. It is always difficult to do justice to individual contributions to another's work, but over the years I have benefited in many ways through seminars, conversation, or having research material made available from the following and more: Bob Allen, Mark Bailey, Stefan Brakensiek, Per Eliasson, Rüdiger Glaser, Bernd-Stefan Grewe, Steve Hindle, Astrid Kander, Christian Keitel, Erich Landsteiner, Jack Langton, Andreas Maisch, Paolo Malanima, Tine de Moor, Craig Muldrew, Sheilagh Ogilvie, Elke Osterloh-Gessat, Ulinka Rublack, Reinhold Schaal, Winfried Schenk, Erik Thoen, Volker Trugenberger, Nadine Vivier and Jan Luiten van Zanden. Emma Rothschild, Miri Rubin and Tony Wrigley have been generous with their support and advice. A special mention has been earned for Chris Briggs and Leigh Shaw-Taylor, both for innumerable and mostly merry conversations and arguments around the themes of this book (among other things), and equally their hawk-like attention to, and honest critique of, failings of both substance and style in my work. I have enjoyed and benefitted from what I can remember of meetings of the Agrarian History Group in Cambridge! The anonymous referees of the book manuscript provided penetrating, very detailed and very helpful criticisms of drafts.

This project was conceived many waxings and wanings of the moon ago in conversation with Bob Scribner, whose industry in the archive, breadth of interest and support were of crucial importance to it all. Some years after his all-too-early death, I hope that this book has finally, through many detours, borne the fruit of those conversations, and bears in some way the touch of his inspiration. More recently I have had the very great fortune to enjoy the supervision and good company of Richard Smith, and the cohort of students to whom he has so generously leant support at the Cambridge Group for the History of Population and Social Structure. His polymathic range of interests and enthusiasms, not least for football and television, but stretching to most aspects of a peasant society that one could conceivably discuss, has shaped much of the thinking I have done in recent years, and it has always been a pleasure.

My work in Germany has been made possible by periodic invasions of the domestic space of Elisabeth and Sieger Hörrmann, and, more recently, Mechthild Vollmer, Johannes Knoblauch and Flora. I am immensely grateful to them and it has been great fun. Joanna Thompson has lived with this work for as long as she has lived with me. I hope now to demonstrate to her that the two can, in fact, be separated. She of course receives the greatest thanks, and, perhaps, the most benefit from the appearance of this book!

Glossary

Allmend	Common land
Amt	Administrative district
Auchtwiesen	Meadows set aside for special grazing
Beisitzer	Resident household head without membership rights in village or town commune
Bürger	Member of a village or town commune
Bürgermeister	Village mayor and chief financial officer
Bürgerschaft	The collective members of the village or town commune
cordwood	Relatively small diameter wood often used for fuel and measured out in 'fathoms' or 'cords'
Dorfgericht	Village court
Ehrbarkeit	'Notables', the leading non-noble members of village and town society
Etter	Wall or fence surrounding the village
faggot	Bundle of very small diameter wood (in modern terms, under 7 cm in diameter) usually used as fuel
fathom	Volume measure for wood
Flecken	Settlement
Fleckenbuch	Book of village ordinances and regulations
Flur	Cultivated ground
Flurzwang	Mandatory collective regulation of cropping patterns
Forstamt	Forest district
Forstknecht	Forest warden
Gaabholz	Grant of wood by communes to their members
Gemeinde	The 'commune', often used with the narrow sense of the communal authorities
Gerechtigkeit	Right, usually used for a right considered defensible or established in law
Gericht	Court of law

Heimburg	Village mayor
Hochwald	Woodland consisting only of stands of mature timber trees
Hof	Large tenant farm or manor
Holzgaab	The giving out of the *Gaabholz*
Holzmangel	Wood shortage
Hube	Tenant farm, usually smaller and of later origin than a *Hof*
Hut	Forest ward, patrolled by a warden
Inwohnerschaft	The inhabitants of a settlement
Klafter	Volume measure for wood, fathom
Landschaft	The Estates with the right to sit in the *Landtag*
Landtag	Territorial assembly or diet of Württemberg
Markgenossenschaft	Corporate group of commoners having use-rights to a resource
Markung	Jurisdictional unit of village or town government
Most	Sweetened grape juice
Nahrung	Subsistence
Notdurft	Needs, basic requirements
Oberrat	Supreme Council in Stuttgart
Ordnung	Ordinance
Pfleger	Overseer, guardian, warden
Rat	Council
Richter	Juror
Scheffel	Volume measure for grain
Schultheiß	Ducal bailiff, chief village official, and head of village court
Schütz	Field warden
Söldner	Smallholders providing corvée labour with their hands
Steuerbuch	Register of tax liabilities and payments
staddle	Young tree preserved to grow into mature timber
standard	Mature timber tree surrounded by underwood
Untergang	Boundary commission
Vogt	District Governor
Vogtgericht	District court
Weistümer	'Manifests', documents recording village regulations and field orders
Zahlmeister	Ducal official responsible for sheep
Zelg	One of the large open fields
Zwing und Bann	The jurisdictional power exercised by village or town authorities

Currencies, weights and measures

Land

1 *morgen* = 0.3316 hectare

Volume (wood)

1 *Klafter* = 3.386 m^3
1 *Klafter* = 6 × 6 × 4 Württemberger cubic feet (144 ft^3)

Volume (grain)

1 *Scheffel* = 8 *Simri* = 177.2 litres = 1.7 hectolitres

Volume (wine)

1 *Imi* = 16.7 litres
1 *Eimer* = 2.939 hectolitres
16 *Imi* = 1 *Eimer*

Currency

1 *Gulden* (fl.) = 60 *Kreuzer* (kr., x.)
1 *Batzen* = 4 *Kreuzer*
1 *Ort* = 15 *Kreuzer*
6 *Pfennig* (d., pfg.) = 1 *Schilling* (s., ß)
20 *Schilling* (s., ß) = 1 *Pfund* (lb) = 43 *Kreuzer* (kr., x.)

Abbreviations

fl.	*Gulden*
HABW	Historische Atlas Baden-Württemberg
HStAS	Hauptstaatsarchiv Stuttgart
KSL	Königliche statistische Landesamt
STABB Bh	Stadtarchiv Bietigheim-Bissingen
StAL	Stadtarchiv Leonberg
StAM	Stadtarchiv Markgröningen
StAR	Stadtarchiv Renningen
SWG	Sammlung der württembergischen Gesetze
WSL	Württembergische statistische Landesamt
x.	*Kreuzer*

Introduction

I will begin with two stories, stories that seem to provide contradictory accounts of the powers of the early modern state over the lives of its lowly subjects. Sometime in the late 1540s, a forest warden, a lowly paid official who was responsible for enforcing forest laws on the ground, was walking on patrol in an area of meadow in the wooded hills to the north-west of Stuttgart. 'Young Hans' was about thirty-five years old and had only recently begun what would be a long career as a warden. On the meadows he ran into his neighbouring warden, one Martin from Rutesheim. Hans commented that he hadn't seen Martin in a long while, and they agreed to go and have a drink of wine together, almost certainly the locally produced white wine, in the nearby village of Weilimdorf. On the way they ran into the swineherd of Weilimdorf with his pigs on the 'wasted meadows'. The name was somewhat misleading, as the pasture there was in fact quite good owing to its open canopy and protected status. 'Horstus Leckher', Hans said to the swineherd, 'I have forbidden you more than once' to be taking his herd into the meadows. As he told the swineherd he would do, Hans went to the house of the ducal bailiff and village headman (*Schultheiß*) of Weilimdorf to complain. The *Schultheiß*, however, was not at home, and so Hans dropped the matter and we may presume went off for his drink with Martin. This was not the only time that Hans had cause for complaint. Both he and Gall Schlecht, who had earlier been the field warden of the village and who by the 1570s was the swineherd, testified that Hans regularly came knocking at the door of the *Schultheiß* to tell him to keep the village herdsmen out of the meadows. However, although within his power, Hans never fined anyone for these transgressions. And thirty years later in the 1570s, villagers were still letting their cows, sheep and pigs go where they wanted. They had done so in the 1530s along with many other villages, coming to blows with men from Stuttgart in 1536 who temporarily gaoled herders they felt were in 'their' woods. And they were doing much the same, and still squabbling, in the 1610s.[1]

The second story is rather different. On the Friday after Ascension 1563, Martin Schütz's wife was returning home from the shepherd's house in the village of Dürrmenz at about ten in the evening. This woman, whose first name we do not know, was about forty, of pious repute, and often visited the sick. She and her husband were 'hard-grafting true workers and day-labourers', with eight children to support. On this night the shepherd's house was the scene of a traumatic deathbed, and as she reached her own dwelling, Schütz's wife let out a lament. 'O God, O God, what wretchedness and misery is on this Earth, what must a person suffer until he comes away from this Earth, O God do not forsake us.' Suddenly, an angel stood beside her. 'O wife, what lamentations have you?' 'I ask God the Almighty', she replied, 'that he will send his Holy Spirit to us to shine his light upon us, that we may bear the wretchedness and misery of the world with patience.' 'O you wealthy', answered the angel, 'O you wealthy and your unrepentant hearts, how are your hearts set so hard against the poor. God is angered.'[2]

This was remarkable enough. But the angel continued to appear, even after the authorities came to hear, quite by accident, of the apparitions. The angel appeared when she was laying her young child down to sleep in the afternoon; when she was cutting fodder for livestock with other wives and children in the village woodland; when she was churning butter. Soon the tales spread. Over the border in Baden, a woman was heard to claim that the 'angel woman' would preach of a prophecy and the pastor would record it. Hundreds of people flocked to the village from neighbouring communities, 'like the Catholics go on pilgrimage' (these villages were nominally Lutheran). Her husband 'was not pleased by these matters'.

The government moved swiftly to interrogate the woman. Senior theologians pored over the angel's comments. Was he a phantasm, a ghost, an evil spirit, or least likely, the real thing? The village headman (*Schultheiß*) sought, with some success, to stem the flow of people seeking the 'angel woman'. Locally, social tensions were high. Hailstorms had caused crop damage, only a year after a great hailstorm had struck the vineyards of Stuttgart and led to the burning of eleven alleged witches. The angel seemed to want to stir up the poor against the rich. Officials reached back into their archive to re-examine an earlier case in the village of Burckach where a young boy had been

---

[1] HStAS A368 Bü 12.
[2] This and the following passages draw on the testimonies in HStAS A206 Bü 3618.

'visited' by an 'angel' in his bed at night. Eventually, having uncovered a previous history of family visions, the government concluded that the angel was mere fantasy and commanded the woman to speak no more of it. Schütz's wife, perhaps fortunately, disappears from the record.

A state that interrogates young boys about their night-time visions? Where theologians dissect the comments of an angel as relayed by the village do-gooder? Such things were not just peculiarities of more modern forms of surveillance and regulation. But was this the same world where for decade after decade villagers and indeed village officials flouted the instructions of the agents of central government who lived and drank among them? Of course, these stories tell of very different things. Despite the extraordinariness of the second story, both to contemporaries and to us, students of the early modern period are far more likely to know of the second kind of tale than the first. In the instance of the angelic apparition, the machinery of government seems pervasive, all-interrogative. Yet students of the early modern world often tend to think that the state was, by later standards, quite weak. In other words, that the regular flouting of laws characterised long centuries of their existence. The first story rings truer to this viewpoint than the second, and was certainly a far more frequent occurrence, although it is less well known. One can, however, find books and articles that argue for the strength or weakness of the state in any early modern century we care to choose. Part of this apparent confusion lies in a categorical elision, a collapsing of the multiplicity of governmental action into one. It is surely permissible for 'the state', a mighty and highly diverse beast, to be good at some things and bad at others; it does not function equally well in all walks of life, as we well know today. Yet this situation has also arisen because studies of the operation of the state have tended to focus on things that we, in a world of abundance, term 'immaterial': authority, divinity, sovereignty or community. There is no disputing the centrality of these and other related issues. At the same time, however, the exercise, application or appropriation of these ideas was linked to very material things: fodder for cows, sheep and pigs; the holding of property; hail; death at the end of a wretchedly hard life. The relevance and power of the immaterial rested upon its intersection with the material realities of existence. This is a book about the state and the material world.

There have been plenty of books written about the influence of the state on the material world. There have also been plenty of books written about how the material world shaped different types of states.[3]

---

[3] To pull a couple from a potentially large selection, Scott, *Seeing like a state*; Wittfogel, *Oriental despotism*; see the discussions in Ellen, *Environment, subsistence and system*.

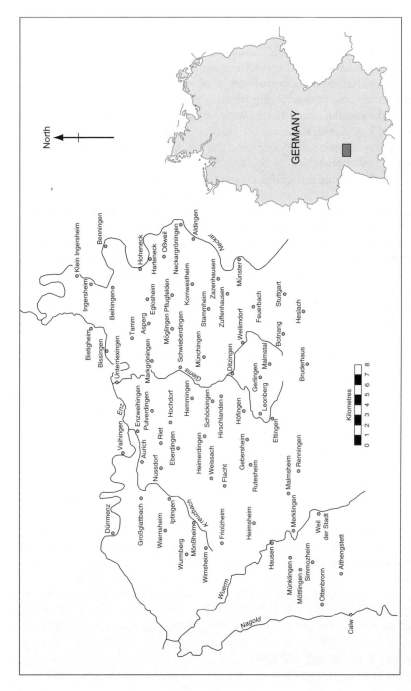

Map I.1 General map of area

This work thus falls into at least two very well-established traditions, which is by no means a bad thing. It has been rarer however to set these issues together in a study of the constant and dynamic interaction of all levels of government and material resources, at least in the early modern period. This will hopefully provide a fresh perspective not just on what the state did, or how it was constrained, but how it was *formed*. The reader should perhaps be warned that there will be more heard about flocks than heavenly hosts. Angels seem to have said what large numbers of people already thought; but sheep did their own thing, and their influence is thus deserving of explanation.

The arena for this investigation will be the forest district (*Forstamt*) of Leonberg in the Duchy of Württemberg, lying to the north-west of Stuttgart, from where the two stories above have been taken (see map I.1). In 1600 this region, which stretched from the foothills of the Black Forest in the west to the narrow valley of the Neckar in the east, was home to around thirty thousand souls. It was a land of nucleated villages and undulating hills of Muschelkalk, with pockets of clay and loam, rising from the east to the west. On the southern fringes of the region stood a massif of sandstone hills that formed a horseshoe around the city of Stuttgart, home to some ten thousand souls at most. The *Forstamt* had a scattering of small towns, none holding more than two thousand inhabitants at any point, and some less than half this size. These semi-urban centres were often barely distinguishable from the largely agricultural villages that dotted a landscape of open fields, riverbank meadows, woodland and vineyards. Most small towns, however, were centres of local government. The region was divided into various smaller districts (*Ämter*), binding the small towns into a unit with a couple of or a dozen of the surrounding settlements, with each district ruled by a local governor, the *Vogt*, who resided in the town. Thus there was an *Amt* Leonberg, centred on the small town of that name, as well as the much larger *Forstamt* Leonberg, so named because the ducal forester happened also to live in Leonberg. Why is a forestry district the unit of analysis? This is because wood was the most important raw material of this society, and a matter that the state concerned itself with greatly.

Why wood?

This book is a study of the use of wood and the management of its source, woodland. There was basically no item, or economic or social activity, in early modern central Europe that did not involve wood in its production, transportation or environment. Wood provided, literally, the framework for everyday life. Werner Sombart's comment that the pre-industrial era was above all the 'wooden age' is rightly celebrated and repeated.[4] Yet despite this, detailed studies of the wood economy and society's relations with it have remained, for the most part, far from the mainstream, and some countries have produced no major studies in recent years at all.[5] Estimates of levels of wood consumption and wood production are few and far between, a situation unimaginable in the case of foodstuffs. Wood was everywhere tangible and discussed in early modern Europe, and thus a study of any of the elements in the title of this book – ecology, economy, state formation – invites an understanding of what was going on with this material. Equally, any study of wood can become an avenue to understanding much of the needs, tensions, conflicts and attitudes of the day. Of the four very basic necessities of life, food, clothing, heating and housing, the latter two directly concerned wood, and almost solely wood, in this era. As people heated food and baked bread, it also intimately concerned the first, and one cannot even make clothing without spindles, distaffs and looms.

Sombart used the expression the 'wooden age' to distinguish the pre-industrial and industrial eras. As he saw it, the Industrial Revolution was characterised to a large degree by a *relative* decline in the importance of wood as an energy source and as a raw material.[6] There have been many characterisations of the Industrial Revolution, but a recent and forceful one has made much the same argument in more sophisticated, and wider, terms. The Industrial Revolution was above all a shift from an economy based on *animate power* (plants and animals) to one based on *inanimate power* (above all, types of fossil fuels and engines). Tony Wrigley has attractively characterised this as the shift from an 'organic economy' to a mineral-based energy economy.[7] Central to this process is a move away from a world based around the natural growth cycles of organic matter to one that can exploit the stored up 'capital' of fuels that do not have to be reproduced, for at least as long as stocks last. This last strategy has undoubtedly fuelled massive and unprecedented

---

[4] Sombart, *Der moderne Kapitalismus*, Bd. II.2, p. 1138.
[5] Recent years have seen renewed interest in *forest* history, in part propelled by scholars beyond Europe, but less interest in *wood*. See Agnoletti and Anderson, *Methods and approaches*; Kirby and Watkins, *Ecological history*; Petterson, *Skogshistorisk Forskning*; Watkins, *European woods and forests*.
[6] In absolute terms, the consumption of wood has generally continued to expand. *Per capita* consumption of wood in Germany today however is probably a little lower than in the early modern period. For current consumption, see Schmidt, *Der Wald in Deutschland*, pp. 3–4; for a wide-ranging global study, see Williams, *Deforesting the earth*.
[7] Wrigley, *Continuity, chance and change*; Wrigley, 'Energy constraints'.

economic growth both in terms of the overall size of the economy, and *per capita* income.

If this energy revolution is key to the Industrial Revolution, then we must understand why it took place. This book will certainly not answer that question, which has already been the cause of large and heated debate. In the English language, the proposition of John Nef in 1932 that a 'timber famine' produced a price situation favourable to the adoption of coal as a major fuel, perhaps as early as the sixteenth century, is the starting point for all discussion.[8] Most countries on the continent, but most notably France and Germany, have seen similar historiographical debates devoted not only to the transition to coal use (which came as late as the second half of the nineteenth century or even early twentieth century in many parts of Europe), but the development of modern forestry.[9] The latter was traditionally seen as an initial and necessary solution to 'wood shortage' (*Holzmangel*) before cheap transport, above all railways, allowed the switch to fossil fuels. Often the debate has been couched in unhelpful terms. 'Timber', as it is usually understood to mean large pieces of mature wood, is not at the heart of the issue because it was not used as fuel. Similarly shipbuilding, which is often blamed for deforestation, consumed only a tiny part of aggregate demand, and then for particular types of unusually shaped timber.[10] Numerous studies, of both the iron industry and of price series, have since sought to refute the 'timber famine' thesis and argued instead that the move to coal was an autonomous innovation, a technological change that was not connected to incipient shortages.[11] Certainly contemporaries worried about shortages of wood, but, it has been argued, this was largely a rhetorical ploy designed to ensure that others were barred access to the resources that particular interests wanted to exploit on as favourable terms as possible.[12]

---

[8] Nef, *The rise of the British coal industry*; Hammersley, 'The charcoal iron industry'; Hatcher, *The history of the British coal industry*, pp. 5–55; Hatcher, 'The emergence of a mineral-based energy economy'; Allen, 'Was there a timber crisis?'

[9] For a small selection of this very extensive literature, see Williams, *Deforesting the earth*, pp. 168–209, 276–301; Woronoff, *Forges et forêt*; Radkau, 'Wood and forestry in German history'; Schäfer, '*Ein Gespenst geht um*'; Ernst, *Den Wald entwicklen*; Schmidt, *Der Wald in Deutschland*; Sieferle, *The subterranean forest*; Kjaergaard, *The Danish Revolution*.

[10] For example, Rackham, *Trees and woodland*, pp. 94–7; Grove and Rackham, *The nature of Mediterranean Europe*, pp. 167–8; Eliasson and Nilsson, 'Rättat efter skogarnes auftagende'.

[11] Allen, 'Was there a timber crisis?'; Hammersley, 'The charcoal iron industry'.

[12] Radkau, 'Zur angeblichen Energiekrise des 18. Jahrhunderts; Radkau, 'Das Rätsel der städtischen Brennholzversorgung'; Allmann, *Der Wald*; Schäfer, '*Ein Gespenst geht um*'.

The 'shortage' debate is to some extent a red herring. If some of a resource still exists, then that resource is only in short supply if people are not prepared to pay the cost of getting it to the consumer. It is another way of saying that it is too expensive. A frequently employed argument in eighteenth-century Germany was that wood was wasted because it was too cheap, basically meaning that some consumers disliked the fact that other consumers got it for less. Of course, a product can be in short supply if we expect it to come from a particular geographical unit, such as a local woodland, principality, nation-state or even continent. It is always *relative* to a particular unit that circumscribes how far we think it is reasonable to go to get the product. If the expense becomes very great, then it can have an unsettling or even catastrophic effect on economic and social relations. Much of the debate about 'wood shortage' has really been about how large an area historians have circumscribed as being a reasonable and affordable supply zone in their analysis, although they rarely state this in simple terms.[13]

Part of the purpose of this study has thus been to understand the *flows* of the resource and the *position* from which particular consumers have viewed its availability. This requires an understanding of how wood was produced (and thus woodland ecology); the state of the economy; the property relationships determining access to the resource; particular forms of demand for wood; and its expense in particular places, at any one time, relative to other commodities. One can still talk about shortages, but only in this carefully specified sense. In order to do this I have chosen an area of early modern Europe that might be characterised by its lack of peculiarity. The region of Württemberg that I have chosen to study was largely agrarian, though with a little proto-industry. The region subsisted from arable farming, viticulture, some dairying and sheep farming. It was not heavily wooded but neither was it short of woodland. It was not far from a major source of timber and fuel in the Black Forest, and lay adjacent to what, for the day, was a medium-sized city. Middling trade routes crossed the territory, but it had none of the advantages for transporting goods of maritime regions. In other words, the *Forstamt* Leonberg experienced much the same cluster of fortunes as many other inland regions of the continent, with no factors that would obviously skew its resource consumption in a particular direction by making that consumption, in early modern terms, especially expensive or cheap. It is precisely these regions

[13] Schmidt, for example, basically accepts the rhetoric of small and fragmented early modern principalities being natural units of supply despite his careful attempts at quantification. Schmidt, *Der Wald in Deutschland*.

which generated the great bulk of consumer demand for basic commodities in early modern Europe, and which are almost systematically ignored by many economic historians. Württemberg's history during this period was, however, far from banal. It was often far more dramatic, and indeed calamitous, than any of its inhabitants could have possibly wished.

We need to know more about pre-industrial wood use, not only in understanding the societies of the time as precursors to the Industrial Revolution, but also their internal dynamics in their own right. Wood here is the prism through which many aspects of social interaction and economic practice can be observed. Major regulation of wood at the level of the state began in Germany, and much of Europe, during the sixteenth century, but the processes that drove this regulation are more often assumed than proven. The period before the eighteenth century has rarely been a matter for consideration even by forest historians, with whom German language studies have been unusually well endowed. Still less have economic historians focused rigorously on such issues of resource management in this period. It is true that fuel often took up at most 5 per cent of household incomes (drawing on data from large cities) and perhaps as little as 2–3 per cent of total income.[14] Yet coal took up as little as 1 per cent of National Product in eighteenth-century England, and it is rather difficult to write an economic history of England in that period without putting coal somewhere near the heart of the story.[15] This study hopes to contribute a large amount of empirical evidence at a fairly fine-grained scale – but at a scale large enough to permit comparative observations. It is a study of wood, but one that seeks to situate wood near the heart of a larger story of ecological, economic and social development. To comprehend this story I have chosen to focus on three areas of study: ecology, economy and state formation. The background and uses of these fields of investigation in relation to this work now require more detailed elucidation.

Ecology

In the last two decades 'ecology' has become one of those 'good words' that must always represent some useful and progressive insight. It has proven to be a flexible creature, emerging in all kinds of academic, political and everyday talk. Of course like any overly useful concept, such ubiquity can be its downfall – how can we tell that it gives any real

[14] Troeltsch, *Die Calwer Zeughandlungskompagnie*, pp. 234–5; see also chapter 5.
[15] Hatcher, *The history of the British coal industry*, p. 551.

additional insight into issues, or generates any problems genuinely deserving of solution? The term *Ökologie* was created by Haeckel in 1866, with partly mystical connotations of holism and interconnectedness. The ecological sciences, particularly those relating to biology and behaviour, have latched on to the importance of the interconnections between factors often traditionally isolated for study whilst largely discarding the mysticism.[16] Ecology has hence become particularly associated with the 'natural world'. A Chicago School of 'social ecology' emerged in the 1920s, and the concept took firm root in anthropology, most famously in the work of Julian Steward.[17] History has preferred the term 'environment' for its intellectual encounter with the natural world, at least in Europe. Interest in human–environment relations have been largely mediated via historical geography and historians such as Fernand Braudel and his generation of the *Annales* School in France, and W. G. Hoskins and 'local history' in England.[18] 'Environment' has also been the preferred term for the many who have wrestled with the question of the relationship between a population and the resources available to it derived from the work of Malthus and, to some degree, Ricardo. 'Environmental History' has, however, only recently emerged as an explicit sub-discipline of the historical sciences, first in North America and then in Europe.[19] Extremely diverse in character, it has no more methodological implications than an interest in the relationships between humans and the non-human world in which they find themselves.[20]

Ecology has both a broader and more precise meaning. One might say that by operating at a higher level of abstraction, 'ecology' permits models that can be fitted to more kinds of problems than describing a relationship between 'people' and their 'environment', though the latter is usually a helpful distinction. 'Ecology' describes the

---

[16] Mensching, 'Ökosystem-Zerstörung', p. 15; Ellen, *Environment, subsistence and system*; Moran, *Ecosystem concept*.

[17] Steward, *Theory of culture change*; Steward, *Evolution and ecology*.

[18] Braudel, *The Mediterranean*; Hoskins, *Making of the English landscape*, to name just two of many books in these traditions.

[19] The American Society for Environmental History was founded in 1976, the European Society for Environmental History was formally instituted as late as 2001. The field has matured to produce some first broad syntheses. See Hughes, *Environmental history of the world*; Radkau, *Natur und Macht*; Simmons, *Environmental history*; Worster, *Wealth of nature*; Myllyntaus and Saikku, *Encountering the past in nature*; Siemann, *Umweltgeschichte*; Delfort and Walter, *Storia dell'ambiente europeo*; Quaternary and Holocene studies also make use of the term 'environmental history'.

[20] Though there are of course trends and basic questions that have been repeatedly investigated. For some statements of these approaches, see Worster, *Rivers of empire*; Worster, 'Transformations of the earth'; Sörlin, *Naturkontraktet*; Cronon, *Uncommon ground*. See also note 19.

interconnectedness of elements, in other words, their interaction and operation as a *system*. Ecological sciences examine the repeated and patterned interrelations of elements within a system, indeed the very things that define them as a 'system' as opposed to the 'environment' in which the system resides. Some recent work on German and Swiss agrarian history, for example, views the transition to a 'modern' agriculture, largely during the nineteenth century, as a systematic change, partly predicated on energy flows related to the 'energy revolution'. The repeated application of fertiliser obtained from waste products within the system, for example, was almost completely superseded by the use of chemical fertilisers. In this case it is perhaps not very enlightening to say that 'humans' have changed their 'environment', as what has in fact taken place is a shift in the chemicals accessible as nutrients by plants, both forms of which were mediated by human action.[21] The profound character of this shift is only apparent however in the overall interrelationship of the elements that make up the system. Ecology refuses then to draw in advance any particular lines around the object of study because it is examining patterned behaviour and relationships, which may well transcend traditional boundaries such as that between 'man' and 'nature' or 'humans' and the 'environment'. There are good reasons, however, for treating people themselves as bounded systems at times, not least in everyday life. We should note at this point that 'repeated', and 'patterned', by no means necessarily mean 'predictable' and 'inevitable'. Recent systems theorists have tended to find quite the opposite even within bounded, limited and observable systems. An obviously patterned and iterative, yet relatively unpredictable, system is the weather, one that had a profound influence on early modern life. It can be seen however that there is something distinct about the approach of 'ecology', and this study tries to operate in the spirit of that approach.[22] 'Ecology' also has a more precise usage defined clearly by Ellen:

Ecological production may be defined as the creation of organic materials resulting in species and population reproduction. It is not to be confused with *economic* production, which is the creation of value in order to reproduce social and economic foundations.[23]

---

[21] Pfister, *Bevölkerung*, pp. 126–9; Winiwarter, 'Landwirtschaft'.

[22] See Lenk, 'Bemerkungen zur Methodologie'; Prigogine and Stengers, *Order out of chaos*; Wolf, 'Simplicity and universality'; Geisel, 'Chaos, randomness and dimension'; Medio, *Chaotic dynamics*. For a discussion of systems theory in a sociology context, see Luhmann, *Social systems*.

[23] Ellen, *Environment, subsistence and system*, p. 130.

Of course economic values have to be explained as a consequence of ecological flows, while ecological flows are often the result of choices made in accordance with economic values. Yet this seems a useful methodological distinction that helps us understand how the economy is embedded in wider ecological processes. This approach will be manifest at first in chapter 1, which seeks to model the operation of the agricultural systems that generated food and structured the landscape of early modern Europe.[24]

My use of the term 'ecology' seeks on one level to avoid constantly recreating a division between the human world and its natural 'environment'. One could as easily say that what mattered more was the farming unit or collectively managed land of the village, together with its human, animal and plant inhabitants, as opposed to the 'environment' of other villages, international monetary trade or the tax state. 'Environments' were not constants determined by soil and climate on which humans acted. Ecologists have tended to abandon the idea of a 'climax community' of plant and animal species that would inevitably emerge in a given environment were it not disturbed by humans. Palaeoecologists, who study the long-term development of plant communities, are now able to tell us that given places usually have had varied and quite distinct communities of plants at different points in time. At different times the configuration of plant and animal species in an area may be quite divergent, as a result of the 'availability' or proximity of colonising plant and animal species, and humans, and all of their actions. Hence it makes more sense to speak, as some have done, of a much wider woodland ecology (in the case of woodlands) or 'historical ecology'.[25] All species, like humans, have their struggles, migrations and settlement patterns.

However, in the pre-industrial period, all ecologies were subject to one overwhelming constraint. This constraint is the availability of solar energy. Given that species can only store energy for a fairly small amount of time, and until the advent of large-scale fossil fuel cannot tap into previously stored energy, the operation of any system or ecology tends to be constrained by the amount of solar energy reaching the land surface on which it exists. In fact, nearly all of this energy is

---

[24] Erik Thoen and others in the CORN (Comparative Rural History of the North Sea Area) network have employed the related, but not identical term 'agro-system'. See Bavel and Thoen, *Land productivity*.

[25] Grove and Rackham, *The nature of Mediterranean Europe*, pp. 45, 72–106; Moreno and Poggi, 'Storia della risorse boschive'; Kirby and Watkins, *The ecological history*. 'Historical ecology' as a field has also been popular with Scandinavian scholars and had some influence in Spain.

dissipated and only a tiny proportion is used productively.[26] This forms the basis of what Wrigley calls the 'organic economy',[27] or the 'photosynthetic constraint', as the availability of energy to other species is to some extent determined by the efficiency of plants in converting solar energy into growth via photosynthesis, although in most parts of the Earth animals absorb far more energy from heat directly from the atmosphere.[28] We thus have the Industrial Revolution stated in terms of energy flows. It is the escape from this photosynthetic constraint. We have already seen from the previous section how essential was the history of wood use, and indeed the ecology of wood use, to this dramatic and unprecedented development. Thermal energy from burning wood in fact provided the single biggest source of energy to humans in pre-industrial northern Europe.[29]

Integrity and disturbance

There are two significant concepts – one from more philosophical ecological thought, and one from the discipline of 'landscape ecology' – that are worthy of further elaboration. They are worth a special mention because they underline approaches to causation taken in this work. The concepts are 'integrity', and 'disturbance'.

To use Regner's definition, 'A ... system exhibits integrity if, when subjected to disturbance, it sustains an organizing, self-correcting capability to recover toward an end-state that is normal and "good" for that system. Other end-states than pristine or naturally whole may be taken to be normal and good.'[30] This allows us to define and examine pattern and process without falling into the trap of trying to represent an 'apogee' or a 'perfect' system. In practice most systems survive, or to put it another way, exhibit integrity, because they demonstrate a degree of flexibility and variation in the way they work. Without this leeway it would also be very difficult to explain how systems change. Social and natural systems are generally not like machines where the removal or alteration of one component causes the entirety to stop working. However, the social sciences have had a tendency to develop 'machine-like' models or 'ideal types' which then present us with the often

---

[26] Smil, *Energy in world history*, p. 12.
[27] Wrigley, *Continuity, chance and change*; Wrigley, 'Energy constraints'.
[28] Wrigley, 'The classical economists', p. 33. Heat energy, of course, cannot be converted or metabolised like food into the nutrition necessary for human survival. Malanima, 'The energy basis', p. 56.
[29] Malanima, 'The energy basis', pp. 54–5.
[30] Cited in Westra, *An environmental proposal for ethics*, p. 29.

insurmountable difficulty of trying to explain why one leaps from one system to another without an 'exogenous' push, an unexpected shove from outside. In emphasising the capacity to organise as the centre of concern, rather than smoothness of operation, the 'integrity' approach moves away from the often narrow functionalism of ecosystem studies.

A 'disturbance' is 'an event that significantly alters the pattern of variation in the structure or function of a system'.[31] A 'disturbance regime' is a pattern of events or systematic behaviour that re-configures another system such that its organising capacity is impaired, though not necessarily destroyed. The disturbance regime may be a vector of change, whilst having its own 'integrity' that may or may not be altered by the event. This language is somewhat abstract, but both terms allow us to think about process and stability – or 'dynamics' – without constructing ideal types, where the transition from one ideal type to another must be explained. This last problem has usually ended with a rather clumsy formulation of 'co-existence' of different stages in history, or 'uneven' development, such as in (but by no means only in!) classical Marxism.[32] There is also the danger of positing a stable village, characterised by a rigid social and familial order, unsullied by the pressures of market exchange, a 'traditional' or 'pre-industrial' society that is undone by the 'disturbance' of modernity, capitalism or commercial exchange, all familiar stories in earlier historiography. It would be somewhat akin to the 'discrete society' marvellously described in the lands of the monastery of Ottobeuren in southern Swabia by Govind Sreenivasan, although in Sreenivasan's model this is but a fleeting phase that is soon undone by demographic and economic pressures internal to that world.[33] But as we shall see, a society that displays 'integrity' is not necessarily 'discrete'. 'Integrity' in some areas may be maintained by flows and exchange in other areas. We must now also turn to examine what was indeed a key unit of early modern life in central Europe, the village.

Understanding the village

In early modern historiography, approaches drawing on ecological thinking have usually taken the village or the manor as the unit to be

[31] Forman, *Land mosaics*, p. 38.
[32] This somewhat teleological formulation which presupposes 'modernity' as contrasted with other elements that are identified as merely archaic has crept into many fields, not least the study of the history of everyday life. See Lüdtke, 'Introduction. What is the history of everyday life?'
[33] Sreenivasan, *The peasants of Ottobeuren*, chs. 2 & 4.

analysed. Historians engaging in such 'village studies' have been most influenced by the discipline of anthropology, above all cultural and social anthropology rather than studies more directly concerned with the natural world and energy flows. Given the prevalence in pre-industrial societies of forms of collective management of resources, anthropologists have sought to investigate the relationship between the nature of the resources required, and the reproduction of the community and the social order, in fairly narrowly delineated spaces and small communities. The necessity of living within the 'photosynthetic constraint' has been frequently posited as the basic reason for village communal organisation and the consequent ordering of the landscape and society. The work of Robert Netting on the Alpine village of Törbel has been most influential among European scholars interested in these questions. Scandinavian historians have also drawn on a strong anthropological and ethnographic tradition to develop an explicitly 'ecological' approach, understanding the development of local settlement and societies as an offshoot of local resource endowments. It is perhaps no surprise that the scholars most interested in such endeavours have studied regions traditionally viewed as 'marginal' where uncultivated land and 'natural' resources played a large part in the local economy.[34]

In the 1970s these anthropological studies fitted well with a rising interest among historians in historical demography. The village, where records of baptisms, marriages and burials were preserved, appeared to offer the ideal unit for the rigorous empirical investigation of demographic trends and their relations with social structures, the economy and environment.[35] One discovery of such studies turned out to be that early modern peasants were in fact more mobile and less bound to the local soil than had been expected. However, the need to collectively manage village agriculture was viewed as the basic reason underlying communal identity and local institutions. Equally, the disappearance of the need to collectively manage the landscape in those areas that saw the early successful introduction of a 'modern', private-property-based agriculture has been presented as the explanation for the need to

---

[34] Netting, *Balancing on an Alp*; Löfgren, 'Peasant ecotypes'.

[35] For a selection of the studies in northern Europe influenced by these trends, many of which did not appear until the 1990s: Wrightson & Levine, *Poverty and piety*; Skipp, *Crisis and development*; Beck, *Unterfinning*; Sabean, *Property*, Sabean, *Kinship in Neckarhausen*; Christiansen, *A manorial world*; Medick, *Laichingen*; Schlumbohm, *Lebensläufe*; Jeggle, *Kiebingen*; Kaschuba and Lipp, *Dörfliches Überleben*; Imhof, *Die verlorene Welten*; Fertig, *Lokales Leben*; Hagen, *Ordinary Prussians*. It should be noted that these by no means inaugurated the village study, which was already a feature of the historiographical landscape in England, Hungary and Italy.

develop in turn new and more 'modern' forms of collective institutions such as welfare provision.[36] In this last case it is argued that traditional communal management and reciprocal relationships within kin groups and between households had previously provided an adequate resolution to potential problems such as infirmity, crop failure and rare cases of indigence. Private-property regimes, in contrast, tended to systematically throw up casualties of the system and leave little room for the accidents of life, which in turn required collectively sponsored welfare provision. The wealth of information that has been produced by the 'village study' has perhaps not yet been fully digested by historians, and very few works on the agrarian economy remain uninfluenced by this tradition of interrelating environmental, demographic and social issues.

The 'adaptability' thesis

However, most of these historians were not specifically interested in the ecologies of agricultural practice, landscape management or energy flows in their own right. They were simply seen as the necessary condition for the social structures and demographic behaviour that were fully worthy of empirical investigation (and, of course, these things were and are essential!). However, following a path trodden first by ethnographers of late nineteenth- and twentieth-century villages, and exemplified by Netting's work on Törbel, some recent work has attempted to provide a more rounded view of the village or agrarian ecology. Notable among these is the work of Rainer Beck on the village of Unterfinning in Bavaria. Influenced by the modelling of the natural sciences, but also the traditions of writing on Alpine environments, Christian Pfister and mostly recently Verena Winiwarter and Christoph Sonnlechner have sought to provide models of the flow of resources and energy within pre-industrial agrarian economies that include both naturally occurring processes and social systems, and the interactions between the two.[37]

The strength of these last approaches has lain in the fact that they rest upon sound foundations of empirical data, unlike some of the modelling of village societies by economists. Secondly, they have sought to introduce a more comparative approach, in the case of Pfister between Swiss grain-growing regions, viticulture regions and Alpine, pastoral

[36] Schofield, 'Family structure'.
[37] Beck, *Unterfinning*; Pfister, *Bevölkerung*, Winiwarter and Sonnlechner, *Der soziale Metabolismus*; see also Bayliss-Smith, *Ecology of agricultural systems*.

communities. However, the increased tendency to compare *single villages* is equally prey to the danger of building 'ideal types', where from the beginning of the study a village is taken to 'stand' for a particular type of community. It has become clear in undertaking this work, as others have also noted, that such an approach is flawed and leads to the peculiarities of single communities being projected onto regions. To avoid this danger, I have adopted a regional approach, taking in a relatively large number of communities subject (for that part of the world) to relatively variant local environments.

In his ground-breaking work on Swiss agrarian history, Chistian Pfister postulated that the key problem for the pre-industrial agrarian economy was the 'manuring-gap' that could not be bridged in the agrarian economy.[38] What he meant by this was that the nutrients extracted from the soil by growing crops had to be replaced in a large part by the nutrients from the manure produced by livestock fed elsewhere. With the technology and organisation of the time, however, there was barely ever enough manure because the animals were too poorly fed, but insufficient crops or pasture could be spared for the animals because they were needed for humans and next year's seed. Productivity faced severe limits, and variability in harvests necessitated various 'buffering' strategies designed to deal with disturbance. The answer was to avoid risk, and opt for crops that were not necessarily very productive, but that were relatively reliable. In this world, crises were essentially 'exogenous' and agrarian fortunes 'tied to climate both in [the] short and long term'.[39] The assumption here is that early modern communities were basically adapted as well as they could be to the local environment. As an economic historian has recently put it, the economy was subject to the doctrine of 'exhausted opportunities'.[40] People had basically tried all reasonable options and this was the best that they could get.

Recent economic history has demonstrated clearly, however, that even without changes in technology, agricultural regimes could in certain circumstances significantly raise productivity.[41] It is equally well known that subsistence crops unsuited to local conditions were grown in many environments in early modern Europe because of the lack of the infrastructure necessary to trade between regions or even villages. The ability of localities to overcome this problem has been attributed to two main factors. Gradual rises in productivity and

---

[38] Pfister, *Bevölkerung*, pp. 126–9.   [39] Ibid., pp. 49–60, 145.
[40] See Grantham, 'Contra Ricardo'.
[41] See the essays in Bavel and Thoen, *Land productivity*.

changing terms of trade encouraged investment, especially encouraged by urban growth, opened access to markets, reduced the cost of trade and permitted specialisation. In some cases specialisation reaped much higher physical productivity, as well as financial returns, from the soil. Alternatively, it has been argued that the very institutions that were supposedly best adapted to the local ecology and provided a rational underpinning to the village community were in fact the very things preventing economic progress. Only the removal of these institutions allowed growth, suggesting that before agrarian modernisation, communities were often poorly adapted to the possibilities of local resource use.[42] This was the basic argument of much contemporary literature during the period of late eighteenth- and nineteenth-century enclosure and agricultural change. Of course such arguments can and have been combined. One can argue that exogenous changes or 'disturbances', or sufficient development within local 'agro-systems', can change conditions to the degree that the previously existing and successful institution is no longer rational. It is not difficult to see that both proponents and opponents of the 'adaptability thesis', as I term it here, operate with a form of environmental determinism. Within a given technology and set of institutional parameters, we would expect the local economy to be largely dependent on its 'resource endowment' and climate.

Determinism tends to be a dirty word these days but with a current understanding of systems and the interaction between humans and the environment there is no reason why it should be so. However, what will become clear in this study (as in many others) is that the local environment, the 'opportunities', is not in fact a pre-determined given but is part of the process of human history. Or, conversely, human history is but a part of the process of the development of local ecology. Chapters 1, 4 and 5 of this book are devoted to examining this process, though its thread runs through all aspects of the study. I believe it best to examine ecological relations on a regional level in order to pick out what was 'patterned' behaviour and relationships, and what was not. Equally, one could test comparatively to what extent communities attempted to adapt to changing circumstances. Chapter 1 will deal most explicitly with the 'village' and the flows of resources within that setting, particularly of nutrients and labour within the local agricultural economy. Chapter 4 will examine the woodland ecology and the demands placed upon it. Chapter 5 will attempt to aggregate flows

---

[42] This is a frequently encountered argument, but for a recent systematic restatement, see Hopcroft, *Regions, institutions and agrarian change*.

within and beyond the entire region of study. In doing so it attempts to provide a model of thinking about ecological history, a model of, as I term it, 'the two ecologies'. These are basically an ecology of 'integrity', and an ecology of 'disturbance', or as I will later call them, a 'territorial' and a 'transformatory' ecology. Historians are perhaps far less inclined to privilege single forms of explanation (environmental, institutional, mental, class struggle, and so on) than they used to be. Is there, however, a way usefully to combine different approaches without simply saying change is the result of an ill-defined 'mix' of factors? My argument is that tracing the 'integrity' of, and 'disturbance' to, systems of resource flows, is one of the most useful tasks historians can undertake. It is precisely because the *results* of ecological interaction can only be determined empirically that ecology should be historical. But it is also the case that ecological thinking provides a promising avenue for the synthesis and testing of other forms of explanation that can be applied to the historical record.

Economy

Much of the discussion in the previous two sections belongs in some sense to the staple fodder of economic history. Obviously this book is about the economy, and to a large extent, the very traditional concerns of 'political economy' that from its beginnings manifested a strong concern with the interactions of human welfare, 'natural' conditions and the institutional control of resources. The study of the economy hardly needs any introduction. Chapter 2 addresses many of the classic interests of economic history, such as the distribution of wealth, changes in *per capita* income, and the relative importance of different sectors of the economy. Although Württemberg is not short of studies of its economic and social history, most of the output has been focused on particular settlements, industries or the state management of the economy. This volume hopes to contribute in a small way to a more synthetic economic history of the region.

There are, however, wider issues at stake that deserve some more expansive discussion. Economics is to a large extent about the measurement of flows – of goods, resources, cash, migrants, expertise, information, and so on. It is rare however, that economic historians attempt to measure a large number of these flows at any one time. There are good reasons for this, of course. It is very time-consuming, and very difficult to do accurately, even where good data is available. Many historians of agrarian societies, moreover, have not even agreed which flows are important. They divide (crudely expressed) into those who, firstly, see peasant societies as, by definition, being composed of largely subsistence agriculturalists who are largely immune to price shifts and economic cycles. Secondly, there are those who prefer to use price data and consider monetary flows, relative prices and terms of trade as the best explanatory tools to understand the whole economy, even the subsistence sector. One group thus examines the flows of resources within the household, farm or collectively managed village economy, while the other tends to concern itself with commerce. Again very crudely expressed, it is an analytical division between those who study calories and those who study cash.

Markets and the 'natural economy'

A frequently encountered way of conceptualising these themes is to differentiate between the 'market' and the 'natural' economy. There is an enormous literature on these distinctions that can only briefly be glossed here. The 'natural economy' is generally considered to be one that operates on the basis of semi-autonomous, subsistence-orientated peasant households obtaining most of the necessities of life directly through their own labour. Exchange does occur on a local basis, and occasionally through wider trade, in these communities. However it is orientated towards obtaining the 'use value' of the goods being exchanged. Farmers with ploughs, for example, make the equipment available to ploughless smallholders who will in turn provide some harvest and threshing labour to the larger farms in a reciprocal exchange. There is no attempt to extract additional 'value', or obtain the benefits of unpaid labour that can be used for other purposes ('profit', in Marxist terms), in this system. Exchange is nearly always 'in kind' where the use values articulated in the exchange are transparent to all.[43]

---

[43] This rather simplistic model will ignore many variations, not least arguments about the importance of 'semi-proletarians' with access to small amounts of land in discussions of merchant capitalism and proto-industrialisation. This model is strongly influenced by Marxist thought and the work of Russian agronomist A. V. Chayanov. Chayanov, *The theory of peasant economy*; Ellis, *Peasant economics*, pp. 51–2; Harrison, 'The peasant mode of production'; Langton and Höppe articulate a similar argument in terms of time-geography. Langton and Höppe, *Peasantry to capitalism*, p. 46; Cancian, 'Economic behaviour in peasant communities'; Beck, *Naturale Ökonomie*; on the historiography and problems of assuming an undifferentiated 'household', see Sabean, *Property*, pp. 88–100; Bois, *The crisis of feudalism*, p. 136. Braudel devotes some time to these distinctions: Braudel, *The wheels of commerce*, pp. 59–60, 224–5, 249–65. Recently, Sheilagh Ogilvie has argued against the worth of distinguishing a 'non-market' *mentalité* or non-marketised exchange relations in early modern Europe. Ogilvie, 'The economic world'.

In the terms of this argument the 'market economy' would be connected
to a very different regime, governed by commercialisation, the use of
money in exchange, and dependency on others for both the hiring out of
one's labour power or sale of products, and the purchase of the necessities
of life. In market exchange there is no direct relationship between the 'uses'
of goods being exchanged; generally speaking money (or more likely the
promise of money through a credit mechanism) changes hands in return
for labour in a production process or consumer goods. Given the uneven
distribution of wealth and power, it becomes possible for the powerful to
set the terms of exchange and thus accumulate wealth, first and foremost in
the form of cash that can then be invested in other sectors of the economy
to generate more wealth. They will direct this capital towards areas of the
economy where relative scarcities are such that the difference between the
cost of selling and the price of the good sold is maximised. Indeed, the price
of the good will be expected to include a profit approximating to the
average rate of profit for investors.[44] Hence commercialisation and the
development of 'impersonal' relations of exchange will tend towards
the accumulation of capital, and eventually an economic system that
prioritises that accumulation above all else ('capitalism'). The potentially coercive nature of such exchange relationships is disguised by the
fact of formally freely contracted exchange relations, and the unequal
nature of exchanging parties is disguised by the impersonal form of the
transaction.[45] It almost goes without saying that such a model is usually
seen as one with no direct regard for the resources being exchanged and
hence no regard for the environment that reproduces them. Some of those
scholars who always conceptualise exchange along market lines would
argue however that there is no real difference between these two modes
of operating. The 'natural' economy is simply one aspect of a universal
set of economic behaviour where cash exchange is avoided because the
terms of trade are too unfavourable to the peasant who has other options.

Pleasing as these two models may be, and at times very useful, it is
not apparent that they really work as general explanations of behaviour
among the early modern peasantry. They can provide useful entry
points to our understanding of economies, but we shall see that the

---

[44] On the difference between this and the situation of peasants or 'petty commodity
producers', see Milonakis, 'Commodity production'.

[45] This is not quite the same as 'directing productive effort to where the greatest relative
scarcities are indicated by the highest prices.' Langton and Höppe, *Peasantry to capitalism.*
pp. 1–2. For an accessible account of the form of capitalist exchange relationships, see
Zanden, *The rise and decline of Holland's economy,* pp. 5–7. It must also be stressed that
many different forms of accumulative economies can exist. For example, see Pratt, *The
rationality of rural life,* p. 154.

systems of flows are generally too complex to be satisfactorily placed within any one model. They also imply, as do economists more generally, that behaviour is patterned because it is the result of conscious choices by rational individuals assessing how to manage resource scarcities. This is a pleasant and necessary conceit for us all to make daily life bearable, but its real applicability is rather difficult to test. The patterns that do emerge in economic behaviour, and some suggestions for explanations, are presented in chapters 1, 2 and 5. Above all chapter 5 will examine how the results of this study can be set against the traditional concerns of those analysing 'peasant economies'.

State formation

State formation has become a concept regularly employed and widely understood not just in the historiography of early modern Europe, but as a 'mainstream' issue in the historiography of most human societies of the past few millennia.[46] The early modern period has long been seen as crucial in the fashioning of the modern state, or 'state formation' as it is increasingly called. The latter concept seeks to draw attention to the fact that declaring the existence of the state as a legal entity (with an abstract character that went beyond the mere assertion of lordship), or promulgating rules and laws to which the subjects or citizens of a state were supposed to adhere, was not enough. States required infrastructure, sometimes institutional, sometimes physical, sometimes in terms establishing the legitimacy among its subjects of acting in particular roles, to have a realistic prospect of even vaguely matching up to the claims to authority put forward. Thus establishing the idea and effectiveness of the 'state' basically meant having people on the ground who could reasonably order others to do things. The larger this body of people became, the more they became associated with a 'machinery' of government, an abstract structure called the 'state' in English but initially '*Wesen*' in German. This began to detach the notion of 'domination' or 'lordship' (*Herrschaft*) from simply being the top–down exercise of one's will over another, the personalised authority exemplified in medieval feudal relationships. To run a 'state' one needed many intermediary office-holders who performed duties, for the most part because they thought it was a reasonable thing to do.[47] One did not obey, or even

---

[46] For a short bibliography of the literature, see chapter 3.
[47] This story is exemplified in the work of Gerhard Oestreich, whose notion of 'social disciplining' is based on the shift from feudal oaths of fealty to more modern contractual relationships that stress the obedience of the subject in a tightly regulated and

become the forest warden, because of who the person of the forest warden was, 'Young Hans' or 'Martin from Rutesheim'. One obeyed him because obeying forest rules was generally agreed to be a sensible thing to do.

This does not mean that the fundamental nature of authority, especially royal or princely authority, was not underpinned by violence. The vicious treatment meted out to particular forms of crime, or the bloodletting that could follow open rebellion, are adequate testimony to this. Thus the arguments of some historians, that relations of power and authority are always reciprocal, can only be agreed with under the proviso that there is nearly always a weaker side that labours under a greater burden of fear and resentment. However, much of the expanded activity of the state, and its apparently growing authority during the early modern period, did not come from a greater drive to 'discipline' and 'control', but rather the co-option of previous forms of government. What perhaps defined the state above all else was its assertion, or more precisely the assertion in the sets of rules that underpinned the state's authority, that it was the fundamental regulator of society. Over time, many other forms of authority, whether guilds, private associations, village communes and town governments, and even princely rulers, gradually conceded that the right to regulate, or oversee regulators, lay with the state. Thus the real achievement of 'state formation' was to instil an acceptance that the state should involve itself in all those things that people generally thought ought to be done. Some theoretical perspectives, perhaps still underdeveloped in early modern historiography, have also argued that the state could not possibly have done this without broader shifts in the nature of power during the period. Rather than asserting the 'negative' right to prohibit, power 'becomes a matter of obtaining productive service from individuals in their concrete lives', a 'positive and technical' generation of the *desire* for an effective state.[48] Of course, people no more agreed with the manner in which the state might go about this than they agreed with each other about the manner in which any aim should be accomplished. But since the early modern period, movements against the very being of what could recognisably be called the state have been few and far between, and their political success has been negligible.

self-disciplined society working for the common good. Oestreich traces this development over the entirety of the early modern period, with roots in the secularization of society as a reaction drawing on classical and late medieval humanist thought against the religious divides of the sixteenth and early seventeenth centuries. Oestreich, *Geist und Gestalt*, pp. 178–97.

[48] See Foucault, *Power/Knowledge*, pp. 119–25. The idea of class domination of the state apparatus, and hence its utilisation by particular social groups, was of course a commonplace of Marxist writing and fed into this more sophisticated conceptualization of power.

The sixteenth and seventeenth centuries in particular provided these means for the expansion of state authority, though the real impact of innovation is still hotly debated by historians of Europe. After 1500, regulation and the promulgation of territorial laws, especially under the influence of Roman law, provided the legal grounds for action. The increasingly expensive wars of the seventeenth century provided the greatest impetus towards the creation of a 'tax state' that moved beyond the princely rulers' earlier reliance on more limited personal finance. Taken together these breakthroughs provided the underpinnings of the self-consciously interventionist and modernising state of the eighteenth century, whether in its 'absolutist' or 'enlightened' guises.[49] Across the entire period, a gradual accumulation of local loyalty, integration of village powerbrokers into the machinery of government, and the 'social disciplining' of personnel to conform to centrally determined norms, bound the ambitions of 'the centre' and those of the 'locality' (or at least those who wielded influence locally) into a coherent unit that expected both to act to resolve problems, and was expected by its subjects to provide solutions.[50] In turn, it was the state that was granted a fundamental role in regulating the flows of and accumulation of resources in the early modern world. This could be done, as in the case of the 'Enlightened' state of the eighteenth century, through attempts to dissolve the local authority that collectively managed village agriculture. It could be in managing state forests and guaranteeing subsistence rights for welfare reasons. Or it could be in providing the legal infrastructure and guarantees that allowed people to trade with confidence, or created monopolies to the benefit of some and exclusion of others. Obviously it could put those in position of state power in an ideal situation to direct those flows for their own benefit, although equally making them theoretically subject to the standards and rules they laid down for the population more generally. A fashion for writing economic history as fundamentally about the history of states is returning, though in the guise of writing about 'institutions'.[51] This trend will be incorporated into this work, seeking to establish the driving forces behind the regulation of resources in the *Forstamt* Leonberg, the personnel who undertook such regulation and the attitudes of all those caught up in such actions.

---

[49] For Germany, see Wilson, *Absolutism*, pp. 17, 36; Strauss, *Law, resistance and the state*, pp. 61–5, 85.

[50] Hindle, *The state and social change*, pp. 17–19; Braddick, *State formation*; Oestreich, *Geist und Gestalt*, pp. 178–97; Raeff, *The well-ordered police state*; Münch, 'The growth of the modern state'.

[51] For example, Epstein, *Town and country*; Epstein, *Freedom and growth*; Hopcroft, *Regions, institutions and agrarian change*; North and Thomas, *The rise of the western world*.

The state is dealt with most directly in chapter 3, and the effects of its regulation on the woodland are measured in chapter 4.

A short history of Württemberg: population and politics

Württemberg was the largest and most influential state of south-west Germany in the early modern period. It was, however, tiny by European standards, occupying a mere 2 per cent of the surface area of the Holy Roman Empire of the German People, and was inhabited by only a slightly higher proportion of its population.[52] Strategically placed, potentially threatening, but in practice often exposed and under-resourced, Württemberg's history is one of ambition and catastrophe. The Counts of Württemberg were already pre-eminent nobles among the numerous nobility of the region in the fourteenth century. Local warfare, judicious purchases and marriage alliances consolidated their power on either side of the Neckar valley in the century after the Black Death. Their territory remained fragmented, however, with no major urban centres. Unlike the leading local rivals, the Habsburgs, the Counts of Württemberg had no great territories beyond the region from which to draw support and expertise. However, under the rule of Eberhard the Bearded, who reunited the temporarily split territories of the patrimony, Württemberg's status led to its ruler's elevation to a Dukedom, and the territory to a Duchy, in 1495.[53] As we will see, Württemberg, while influential in the region, was also unusual. From an early date, the nobility enjoyed no formalised intermediary role in government and thus in this polity the Duke alone was in a position to combine formally lordly and state power, or put another way, the functions of landlordship and the judiciary. This gave an unusual amount of influence to other local authorities such as communes and district governors in comparison to neighbouring polities.

The long sixteenth century: growth and retrenchment

The forceful and sometimes unstable personality of Duke Ulrich (ruled 1498–1519, 1534–50) defined much of Württemberg's history in the first half of the sixteenth century, twinned with the contemporary princely imperatives of the expansion of the principality and the style of a Renaissance ruler. The rapidly expanding expenditure under his

---

[52] Hippel, 'Historische Statistik', p. 52.
[53] For general political histories of Württemberg, see Mertens, 'Württemberg'; Grube, *Der Stuttgarter Landtag*; also the *HABW*.

rule prompted innovatory attempts to raise revenue and, in turn, the 'Poor Conrad' rebellion of 1514. Andreas Schmauder has recently argued that the rebellion of 1514, although triggered by fiscal pressures, had genuinely revolutionary potential, spurred on by a network of sworn rebels seeking a fundamental realignment of the fortunes of the rich and the poor under the name of 'Poor Conrad', a symbolic moniker for the ordinary man.[54] But this radical movement failed. Its leaders mostly fled, and many were executed, but the rebellion left its mark in political practice and stands as the founding event of a 'whiggish' tradition of Württemberger constitutional history. Seizing on the weakness of the Duke, who took time to assemble military forces to enforce his rule, the urban 'notables' of the Duchy obtained a calling of the Duchy's Estates, a consultative institution that had frequently been convened over the previous half century during periods of political uncertainty. In return for the right to the freedom to migrate, and to have grievances aired, the Estates agreed to underwrite Ulrich's debts in the 'Tübingen Contract'. This document has long been seen as a charter for Württemberger constitutionalism amid a sea of princely autocracy. Württemberg's Dukes could only rule by virtue of a contract freely entered into by its Estates and witnessed by the Emperor as guarantor. In fact the Estates only sporadically enjoyed the 'rights' enshrined in the Contract while the dukes continued to make financial demands and go their own way. The events of 1514 did, however, permit the establishment of a parallel administration of the Estates to manage financially general taxation and formulate some policy, and it strengthened an already established tradition of consultation with urban notables represented in the Estates. Württemberg's political body was henceforth woven of more strands than could be found in many of its neighbours. These strands did not, however, include the nobility as a body incorporated directly into the state. With little interest in contributing to the burden of payments by the Estates, they did not turn up to a diet of 1515. The long-term and unforeseen consequence of this was that they and their admittedly relatively small lands did not become formally incorporated into the growing state, though numerous local nobles served the Dukes in some form of official capacity and occupied most of the higher tiers of the administration.[55]

Ulrich did not however rule for long. The murder of the husband of his lover, followed by an ill-judged annexation of the city of Reutlingen,

---

[54] Schmauder, *Württemberg im Aufstand.*
[55] On the administration of this period, and especially elite participants, see Vann, *The making of a state*; Marcus, *The politics of power.*

brought about invasion by the Swabian League, a loose confederation (of which Württemberg was a part) binding together the numerous polities of the region. The only power prepared to handle the Duchy's extensive debts were the Habsburgs, who purchased the territory in 1520. Though classically seen as centralising and authoritarian rulers, their legacy to Württemberg was rather different. Efforts were made to extend and improve legislation, but largely under the auspices of local bureaucrats, as the nominal ruler, Ferdinand of Austria, was occupied elsewhere. As was often the case in early modern Europe, his subjects resented 'foreign' rule while in practice his administrators were given a fairly free hand to govern. These tumultuous years of Reformation saw the Peasants' war of 1525 sweep the Duchy, to be crushed militarily at Böblingen in May of that year.[56] A series of poor harvests prompted the first attempts at legislation for poor relief. In 1534, a newly Lutheran Ulrich, capitalising on an alliance with fellow convert Philip of Hesse and exploiting the Habsburgs' preoccupation with the Ottoman threat, re-conquered the Duchy.

The energy of Ulrich and his capable son Christoph, allied with a trend towards expanding state power and the implementation of the Reformation, left deep marks on the Duchy. By Christoph's death in 1568, legislation had established a state Church and system of visitations, schooling in the vernacular was on the way to becoming widespread, and major legislation had codified the tax, property, poor relief and inheritance systems. The great monasteries of the region had become Protestant seminaries, and their incomes were devoted to the state. This process was not without its setbacks. The defeat of the Protestant Schmalkaldic League by Charles V in 1546 saw the occupation of the land by Spanish troops and the imposition of the 'Interim', a religious settlement that was little more than a stop-gap en route to the return of Catholicism. But by 1552 Christoph was secure enough to shake off its terms and build a securely Lutheran state.

The entirety of this period saw the population grow, although it is difficult to be precise about numbers. Tax records leave us fairly extensive information on households, but not on the size of those households. Karl-Otto Büll has estimated from tax records of 1544 that the population stood at around 208,000. It may have been a little higher than this, but certainly not much; von Hippel estimates around 226,000.[57] This

---

[56] Maurer, 'Bauernkrieg', to choose one of numerous local accounts. More general literature on the Peasants' war has tended to focus on the ecclesiastical lordships of the southwest or on Franconia.

[57] Hippel, 'Historische Statisitk', p. 57.

was after a period of growth that was already certainly under way in the final quarter of the fifteenth century. Limited data suggests fairly rapid growth between 1525 and 1545, but after mid-century the situation changed.[58] Climatic downturn from the middle of the 1560s struck at food supplies and the economy, resulting in the most catastrophic dearth period of the age in the early 1570s. Far more influential demographically, however, was the repeated occurrence of plague. Plague epidemics are detectable more widely in Württemberg in 1541–3, 1551, 1555–6 and 1564–5. It struck Leonberg in 1572, 1576, 1584–6, 1594, 1596–7, 1608–9 and 1611–12, and the mid-1620s. The town of Bietigheim suffered in the mid-1560s, especially in 1607, and in 1626–7. These epidemics often carried away a fifth or a third of the population.[59] The result of these 'exogenous shocks', which accounted for far more than any other form of mortality, was a population in the *Forstamt* Leonberg that lay only 12 per cent higher in 1598 than it had been in 1544. However, 1598 stood immediately after yet another benighted period of dearth and plague, and was at the bottom of one of the 'troughs' in this population rollercoaster. Population recovery was rapid, and it is likely that the entire century from the late 1550s to the 1630s saw a see-sawing of population, with growing numbers from very high fertility levels regularly culled by epidemic disease.[60] Certainly the pre-Thirty Years' War average age at

---

[58] Data survives for twelve settlements in the district of Leonberg for both 1525 and 1544. Estimates can only proceed on the basis of household numbers, not their size. Ernst, 'Geschichte', pp. 336–7; HStAS A54a Amt Leonberg.

[59] Benning, 'Eine Stadt', pp. 11–12; Trugenberger, 'Der Leonberger Raum', p. 85.

[60] This process makes absolute population levels difficult to determine, because we would expect quite large fluctuations in household size depending on whether we are dealing with the period immediately before or after an epidemic. As we only have figures for households, it makes the size of the multiplier required to establish the true level of the population rather uncertain. Benning chooses 5.1 for pre-war Bietigheim; much higher than the figure of 4.1–4.4 for male-headed households and 2.3–2.9 for female-headed households found by Ogilvie in the district of Wildberg in 1626, 1717 and 1722, with little variation over the century. In the district of Leonberg, 'soul-tables' recorded all communicants in 1654, 1676 and 1703. Comparing the figures from the first and last dates with household numbers in 1655 and 1708 yields a multiplier of 3.9 and 5 respectively. Maisch provides figures only for the 1760s and 1770s, ranging from 3.8 (district of Nagold) to 4.2 (Herrenberg). Benning's high figure for the early 1630s may however come from people seeking shelter in the town during the war years. There will, then, be some margin for error in these figures. Benning notes household numbers in Bietigheim leaping from 223 in 1598 to 284 in 1602, which must have come in part from in-migration. Neither my data nor Ogilvie's finds any strong demographic patterns predicated upon proto-industry or viticulture, though farmers' households tend to be a little larger. Benning, 'Eine Stadt', p. 13; Ogilvie, *State corporatism*, pp. 234–8, 289; Ernst, 'Geschichte', pp. 336–7; HStAS A368L Bü 136; Maisch, *Notdürftiger Unterhalt*, p. 32.

first marriage was low, lying in the early twenties. Maisch's and Benning's work shows baptisms peaking in Württemberg at some time between the 1590s and 1610s, when crude birth rates may well have been over 50 per 1,000 in some settlements, but they generally fell at around 40 per 1,000 or less in the pre-war decades. However, plague meant that crude death rates stood at over 60 per 1,000 in some short periods of years, double what might have been expected without these 'exogenous shocks'.[61] Consequently parts of Württemberg witnessed a classic 'high pressure' demographic regime of high fertility and mortality with relatively low overall growth. Apparently high fertility rates suggest that emigration may also have been a factor.

We do not have exact population figures for the whole of the *Forstamt*. There were 4,146 taxpayers surveyed (covering nearly the entirety of the region) in 1544–5. Extrapolating this out over the missing settlements suggests that there may have been around 24,000 inhabitants in the region. In 1598 there were around 27,000, based on a survey recording 4,630 households which again did not quite cover the entire region. The early seventeenth century, despite continued plague, appears to have brought continued growth, with the households' numbers recorded in 1629–34 suggesting a total population of around 35,000.[62]

The reign of Ludwig (1568–93) was in many ways one of quietude in Württemberger politics. Ludwig's successor was the forceful and autocratic Friedrich, but his administrative energy and centralising tendencies did not survive his death in 1608. By this time, as the population began to rise rapidly again, all of Germany was slipping towards religious war as the patched-up deals of the sixteenth century began to become unravelled. Conflict began in earnest in 1618, and the Leonberg region lost its first casualties when the local militia were mauled by Croatians fighting for the Catholic Imperial forces near Ölbronn in 1622. This fell in a period of dizzying and disruptive price inflation triggered by economic dislocation, but above all manipulation of the metal content of the currency. By one report, children played with handfuls of coins in the street,

---

[61] Benning finds a crude mortality rate of 31 per 1,000 in 'normal years' (i.e. non-plague) for the period 1586–1629. Benning, 'Eine Stadt', p. 12; I have made my own calculations from Maisch's data, and the parish records of Rutesheim. Deaths appear generally to have been under-recorded. Maisch, *Notdürftiger Unterhalt*, pp. 31–3, 54–8; Gemeinde Rutesheim, *Heimatbuch Rutesheim* (1970), pp. 182–5.

[62] The 1598 survey was explicitly conducted to record numbers of households ('citizens and inhabitants'), while the 1629–34 data comes from tax records. There are records from sixty-one settlements in 1598 and fifty-eight in 1629–34. The population estimates assume a low figure of 4.25 persons per household. HStAS J1 Nr.141g; A261 Bü 421, 727, 891, 998, 1126, 1470, 1634; Hippel, 'Historische Statistik', p. 53; Benning, 'Studien zur frühneuzeitlichen Seuchengeschichte', p. 91.

it had become so debased.[63] Government re-established monetary order in 1623, but military and quartering burdens steadily increased. A wave of Imperial victories saw the Duchy effectively occupied by 1629 and the re-Catholicisation of the monasteries.

The century of iron

In the next four years, however, the region saw a catastrophe the like of which has never been visited on it before or since. Emboldened by the Swedish invasion of Germany, Duke Eberhard III led the Duchy into a new Protestant alliance that was crushed by Imperial forces at the battle of Nördlingen on 6 September 1634 (Gregorian calendar). Pursued by Catholic forces, the Swedes and Protestant armies fled westwards. On 28 August 1634 (Julian calendar, which is used in Württemberg and for the most part in this book), three gunshots from lookouts on the Asperg announced their arrival and the coming conflagration. By 12 September, the fortress, that as ever acted as a magnet for plundering forces rather than a defensive bastion for local communities, was fully invested by Imperial troops. The siege lasted until 28 July 1635, when the garrison and sheltering peasants surrendered with honour. In the meantime, however, hundreds had died in the fortress from influenza-type diseases, and thousands more had died from plague throughout the region. Several villages were rased to the ground by marauding troops; in places the entire stock of horses was killed or requisitioned; most land went uncultivated, and in the following years a few people even starved to death.[64] Although the duke recovered his Duchy in 1638, repeated march-pasts and quartering of armies proceeded with brutality from all sides in the conflict until the end of the war in 1648. Reliable population figures from the mid-1650s indicate that the population of the *Forstamt* Leonberg was around 60 per cent lower than it had been in 1634.[65]

The 1640s however already saw a vigorous government response, the re-establishment of functioning authorities and reform of the education system. The population began to recover, standing around 40 per cent larger in 1676 than in 1654, and at twice the level of 1654 by

---

[63] Ginschopf, *Chronica*, p. 124. On the events of the Thirty Years' War, see Ernst, 'Geschichte', p. 386; Trugenberger, 'Der Leonberger Raum', pp. 116–20; Niklaus, 'Dreißigjähriger Krieg', *HABW*, VI, II.

[64] Burckhardt, *Eglosheim*, pp. 139–45.

[65] This is based on the fall in household numbers in sixty settlements. Households may also have been smaller than in the pre-war period. HStAS A261 Bü 421, 727, 891, 998, 1126, 1470, 1634.

1703.[66] This is despite mortality crises that struck in the 1670s, the mid-1690s and after the *grand hiver* of 1709. The extremely high levels of mortality generated by plague retreated, but crisis was still brought by dysentery, typhus and even hunger. Mortality rates seem to have been in the low 30s or high 20s per thousand outside of crisis years, and fertility probably remained high, at least in the high 30s to low 40s per thousand. Despite a lower incidence of extreme mortality crisis, this record of continued growth does not sit entirely easily with a rise in the average age at first marriage, which was notably higher in the post-war period and continued to rise. The number of women who never married rose significantly into the eighteenth century. As yet the data from different settlements does not give a very consistent picture. The pre-war population was probably not reached until the 1720s.[67]

The latter part of the seventeenth century and early eighteenth century continued to be marked by conflict and invasion. Successive Dukes of Württemberg sought to raise taxation levels gradually and develop military power as the south-west remained a strategic crossroads in struggles between the Habsburgs, French armies of Louis XIV, and the wider span of international alliances involving the Dutch, British and other German states.[68] Most mortality crises were associated in some way with the fortunes of war. French forces repeatedly extorted vast sums of money from the Duchy and occupied the region in 1675, 1693 and 1707. However, supposedly 'friendly' troops from other German states, and Marlborough's army in 1704, brought their own exactions. The Treaty of Utrecht ending the war of Spanish Succession would bring some respite. Württemberg remained, as we shall see, a poor corner of Europe, with only a few industries of regional importance and an agriculture vulnerable to climatic fluctuation. A series of hard years for viticulture in the late 1730s and the coldest winter of the millennium in 1740 became the trigger for widespread migration, in part to the Americas, from south-west Germany.[69] As a consequence the population of many settlements stagnated again, though as ever it is difficult to weight the 'push' factor of

---

[66] These figures are based on the district of Leonberg only, covering seventeen settlements. 'Soul-tables' recorded 4,000 souls in 1654, 5,541 in 1676 and 7,786 in 1703. Ernst, 'Geschichte', pp. 336–7.

[67] Crude rates are estimated from data provided by Andreas Maisch and Rutesheim registers. His figures on mortality show a marked retreat in summer and early autumn mortality peaks after the war. Maisch, *Notdürftiger Unterhalt*, pp. 31–3, 54–8, 64; Gemeinde Rutesheim, *Heimatbuch Rutesheim* (1970), pp. 182–5.

[68] Accounts of these processes are provided in Wilson, *War, state and society*; and Carsten, *Princes and parliaments*.

[69] Glaser, *Klimageschichte*, pp. 176–80; Fertig, *Lokales Leben*, pp. 298, 358; on local effects of the 1730s crisis, see Benning, 'Überfluß und Mangel'.

communal restrictions on marriage and limited economic opportunities against the 'pull factor' of New World opportunities, which after all also succeeded in drawing many migrants from far more successful economies.

This short history should constantly be borne in mind. The book deals with the issues outlined in this introduction in a largely thematic way. Yet although the population levels and political structures of the Duchy were in many ways similar in the early eighteenth century to the late sixteenth century, many things were profoundly different. The demographic regime, insofar as we can currently tell, had altered quite markedly, although vital rates had not perhaps shifted so much as the retreat of plague and changing marital behaviour might suggest. Over the period, the pressures and balances between resources and population had also radically altered. Climate change, too, was measurable and significant. Early eighteenth-century Württemberg was in many ways similar to the Duchy in preceding centuries, but not because of long-lived stability or a homeostatic, self-regulatory economic and demographic regime. This book aims to discover, as far as is possible, what, if any, form of 'regime' existed.

1   The peasant dynamic

Dynamism is not a concept commonly associated with the peasant. A 'peasant' after all is certainly not 'modern', and as modernity is almost defined by its dynamism, its relentless adaptation and its ingenuity, a peasant by definition can partake of none of its qualities without ceasing to be himself. Country air makes one slow and cautious, tied to the bounty of the soil and the grind of seasonal tasks, where one remains caught in the grip of voracious landlords. The 'peasantry' are often not so much defined by their particular qualities as by a 'lack': a lack of resources, flexibility, information, knowledge, certainty, markets, freedom or imagination, and consequently their only virtue can be to disappear on acquiring some or all of these.[1] Their rebellions are understandable but pig-headed and backward-looking. Although Marx's comments on the 'idiocy of rural life' and the inability of the French peasantry to act as effective political agents are much maligned today, they retain the salient point that under no model of social change ever applied to Europe can the peasantry, as a peasantry, be a vehicle for sustained progress.[2] Their historical mission is to cease to be, and as they generally chose not to accept this, then other exogenous forces must be the agents of their destruction.

In the lands of the middle Neckar and the Black Forest we can clearly identify a peasantry from at least the thirteenth century, that cannot reasonably be said to have disappeared until some decades into the

---

[1] See a standard set of definitions in Scott, *Peasantries*, especially pp. 2–3; Ellis, *Peasant ecomomics*, p. 4.

[2] This does not preclude the notion of a 'peasant road to capitalism', in which endogenous changes cause the dissolution of the peasantry. A very few exceptions, such as work on early modern Norway, postulate a diversification of rural activity where peasant farming was combined with fishing and resource extraction. Marx and Engels, *Communist manifesto*, p. 84; Marx, 'Peasantry'; see also citation in Chayanov, *Peasant economy*, p. xviii; and the discussion in Hoppenbrouwers and van Zanden, *Peasants into farmers?*; also the comments in Farr, 'Tradition', p. 17; Söderberg and Myrdal, *Agrarian economy*, p. 22.

nineteenth. Six hundred years is no trifling period of time. Of course this was a period of great change, whether almost imperceptible on a daily basis (the great increase in livestock size, or the variation of the climate) or perplexingly rapid (the collapse of the old Church order during the Reformation, or the catastrophic losses inflicted on the land in the 1630s). Yet we can also discern behind these what Emmanuel le Roy Ladurie memorably called the 'immense respiration of a social struc-ture'.[3] A dynamic, in other words, but an enduring one. The core of agricultural methods and tasks, the institutions and powerbrokers did not alter fundamentally between the time when they came clearly into view around the tail end of the fifteenth century, and the great age of Reform around 1800.

'Institutions and powerbrokers' are mentioned here not simply because they kept a peasantry 'in their place', maintaining them as peasants, but because the 'peasant dynamic' in fact entailed a political economy of its own, a system in which they themselves were partici-pating elements. Respiration, after all, is not ossification; it is expansion or contraction according to the circumstances of the moment, the reflected or unreflected relationship of a species with its environment. To see the peasantry either as dyed-in-the-wool conservatives, or much-maligned modernisers, where the constraining force in both cases is the dead hand of feudalism, is to some extent to miss the point.[4] Peasants themselves reproduced themselves as peasants, admittedly under constraints, like all social groups. A better question would be, what constellation of circumstances and forces made it so that the peasantry reproduced itself while shaping the political economy of Württemberg for six long centuries?

By our standards, much was lacking for the peasantry of early modern Württemberg. Take Heinrich Zimmermann, the inventory of whose possessions was drawn up on 4 April 1720, after his death. A carpenter in the poor village of Gebersheim, he held a few plots of land (as did many artisans) and the tools of his trade: a couple of axes, a hatchet, an 'iron' for measuring corners and a couple of panniers. At his house and barn (actually half of a building for each) he had a cow and a rooster, and a few stored crops, hay, curds and some wine. His house contained three bedsteads, two chests, a table, chair, several stools, a bread mould

---

[3] Ladurie, *Peasants of Languedoc*, p. 4.
[4] For the side of the debate that sees the peasantry as essentially constrained by 'exo-genous' institutional rather than 'inner' or 'cultural' forces, see Ogilvie, 'The economic world'.

and a bin for flour. For reading matter, two hymn books and a prayer book. There were twenty-two items of clothing and linen in the household.[5] And that was it. Heinrich was by no means among the poorest, but life was spartan, even at the end of the period under investigation here. Few possessions came in from outside, although most 'consumer' items (if such necessities can be called that) did so, because Gebersheim was dependent for many things on the wider world. But nearly anything of any great value came from Heinrich's peasant holding or was probably produced in the village itself.

The American anthropologist George Foster has spoken of a peasant society as one moulded by the 'Image of Limited Good'. The 'image' is that the welfare of oneself, and one's community, is dependent on a fixed set of naturally given resources. These resources do not have to be employed in the same way over time, but there comes a point where higher consumption cannot be supported by increasing production, and the only means to achieve this consumption is to take a share of the resources that had previously gone to someone else. In an economist's terms, the marginal returns to increased inputs into production are very low or negligible, and lower than the returns to efforts to redistribute the production of the community as a whole in one's own favour. Fortune is not simply something achieved through one's efforts, but achieved to the detriment of others.[6] The land is capable of supporting only a limited amount of material wealth, or has a 'carrying capacity', as an ecologist would put it.

Added to this was the fact that whilst resources might be relatively fixed, the income flows they generated were not. They could be highly variable. Agricultural production in particular varied according to the weather, and consequently, because demand for other products tended to depend on what was left over after everyone was fed, demand for manufactured products was equally subject to the harvest, or put another way, that year's weather. It was difficult for peasants to accumulate consumer goods because in good years food was cheap and brought them little income. In bad years they both could suffer a shortfall in food themselves, and could not easily borrow from those working in manufacturing who suffered exactly the same kind of problems. Caught in this bind, peasants tended to look to 'outsiders' for succour in times of hardship, such as lords, rulers and divine powers. Yet because of this dependency on powerful 'outsiders', these powers became an

---

[5] HStAS A584 Nr.1061. I am grateful to Andreas Maisch for making this data available.
[6] Foster, 'Image of limited good'.

integral part of 'peasant political economy', a political economy defined not so much by lack as by limits, as any political economy is. This situation of course left peasants open to exploitation too.

It is these limits which are the key to our understanding of peasant economy in early modern Europe. After all, one could as well define the peasantry as those who did not live in the Land of Cockaigne as define them as a group that lacked the benefits of modern markets in factors of production.[7] Limits were, and are, in contrast, very real. The political demands of peasants, even in a 'revolutionary' moment such as the rebellion of 1525, were always carefully constructed delimitations of rights, obligations and responsibilities. Peasants faced not only 'risks' inherent to all economic behaviour, but well-defined 'hazards' in a particular ecology that required management. Although historians have tended to speak of peasants as having a general 'risk aversion', this is rather easier to assert than to prove. What we can and should examine is the response to particular hazards such as variable weather, disease or currency manipulation by government. Peasants, like any other social group, strove to bring order to their world, or to put it another way, sought to reduce the complexities of everyday life. Such complexities pertained not so much to the agrarian 'system' as a whole, which was very simple by our standards, but the unpredictable consequences of choices, and the difficulty of making choices, at each stage of the production process.[8] Hazards could not be eliminated, but by reducing the possible ramifications of making the wrong decision, or of coming into conflict with others, peasants could narrow down the reasons for failure to a few variables. This could easily involve scapegoating of natural forces, divine wrath or personal failings. In turn, the material base for reproduction had a social dimension comprising two main strands. Firstly, the aforementioned dependency on extra-village institutions. Secondly, in the articulation of a 'moral community' of householders, the group of consumers that drew their sustenance

---

[7] See this form of definition in Scott, *Peasantries*, pp. 2–3; Polanyi, *The great transformation*, pp. 65–76.

[8] This analysis is influenced by Luhmann. It does not, as a consequence, start out from the assumption of the reality or non-existence of a 'peasant *mentalité*', but addresses each sphere of peasant activity on a case-by-case basis. Nor does it accept Ogilvie's argument that 'mainstream economics . . . regards *all* economic agents as seeking to obtain the lowest possible risk for the highest possible return', refuting the thesis that there can be a distinct 'risk-minimising' approach to economic behaviour. Ogilvie's definition appears to this author to collapse categories into meaninglessness, where it would be impossible to distinguish the motivating factors behind economic choices. See Luhmann, *Social systems*; Ogilvie, 'Economic world', p. 431.

from the locally delimited stock of resources. In articulating the moral community, peasants simultaneously erected an ever-contested alignment of 'insiders' and 'outsiders', or respectively those 'insiders' to whom a multiplicity of moral criteria applied (and could be disciplined for failing to live up to expectations), and those who were viewed simply as opposing agents in a transaction (and could be safely blamed, or cheated).[9]

The following sections, and much of the rest of the book, will seek to unravel the dynamics of this political economy, and the strategies by which different sections of the 'peasantry' sought to secure themselves a living, avoid hazards and maintain some kind of order. In doing so, I hope an empirically grounded definition of the Württemberger peasantry will emerge, a group that thus far and contrary to frequent historical practice have only been very loosely defined as agriculturalists who see their welfare as being rooted in the immediately available resources of their locality. The next two chapters begin by considering the very notion of access to resources encapsulated in ideas of 'ownership' and 'property'. The kinds of solutions and conflicts that resulted will be examined in the context of the ordering of household, village space and the management of the landscape, before a more detailed examination of the parameters and possibilities of the rural economy. This will make clear that peasants were exposed both to limitations imposed by local resource endowments, and seasonal, annual and long-term variations in their productivity. But if an understanding of the ecology of the agricultural system is essential to comprehending this peasant world, it will also be seen that environmental change and ecological sensibilities on the part of the peasants are not sufficient to explain changes in that world over time. Peasant economic life partook of various social and legal institutions, in part set up to deal with ecological hazard, but equally to manage the disputatiousness that arose between peasants amid the effort of getting by or getting ahead. These institutions, explored in this and the following chapter, shaped their behaviour and their long-term fortunes. Of course manufactures, marketing and long-distance exchange beyond the immediate world of the village were also necessities, if not everyday ones for most. These must be drawn into our discussions, which means examining the relative fortunes of town and countryside and the variation in the whole economy of the region and over time. By the close of chapter 2, it should

[9] See Bailey, 'Peasant view', pp. 299–321.

be clear what was desired, what worked for particular groups, and what became untenable or generated conflict.

Making space

To comprehend a world profoundly worried with the scarcity of resources, and where those resources largely grew on the land, a starting point is to comprehend how that land was organised and conceptualised. By the late fifteenth century, and in most places considerably earlier, there was no part of Württemberg that lay unclaimed and unregulated. Most land fell within a *Markung*, the jurisdictional bounds of the village or municipal authority, and was subject to its *Zwing und Bann*, the power of the village authority to bind or loosen, to command and forbid.[10] Those areas of land lying outside *Markungen*, usually more rugged or swampy woodland, were directly subject to lords who owned the soil. Of course in an age where map-making was rudimentary and in any case rarely employed, the precise definition of boundaries was often a matter for dispute. A combination of the memory of man and physical markers from fences to rivers, streams, ditches, marker stones, pathways or prominent trees had to suffice. This privileged 'local knowledge' and the role of testimony, sometimes even in contradiction to the written word which itself was often unenlightening. Cadastres of ground-rents, for example, generally defined position relative to other plots of land and physical features, rather than the precise course of boundaries. The government did not attempt systematic survey of boundaries until 1707, and detailed mapping had to wait until the nineteenth century.[11]

What is striking when one delves into the records of rural life is the *materiality* of the manner in which the landscape was defined and regulated, a materiality born of everyday use and interaction. There was little need for most villagers to squabble over boundaries that they defined by their own activity over the year. It has been noted many a time that the peasantry of early modern Europe did not have a 'modern' concept of property, of 'absolute' ownership, and instead ordered their world through use and the exercise of *use-rights*. But the distinction here is perhaps of degree rather than kind, because 'property' is always a type of claim to use that requires the consensus of one's neighbours, a social fact. The kinds of uses to which land was subject, the physical form of the landscape and the material basis of its utilisation, had at

---

[10] For more detailed explanations, see Bader, *Dorfgenossenschaft*, pp. 90–102.
[11] Ernst, 'Geschichte', p. 283.

least as large a role to play in the development of property relations
during this period as abstract, legalistic concepts of ownership. Hence
the right to the fruits of a tree, to pasture one's livestock on the fallow or
waste grounds, or lordship or 'rights to the soil' or even mineral wealth,
entailed variant forms of expression and regulation ('property rights')
precisely because they pertained to distinct material conditions.

The main distinction that is made regarding property rights is
between *dominium directum* and *dominium utile*. The first pertained to
a direct right to the soil itself, the 'ground', though not necessarily what
grows out of it or lies beneath it. This 'use' is the form of property right
most familiar to us today and lay at the core of lordship in western
Germany, though it was not the only significant form. By *dominium
directum* we may understand 'landlordship' or '*Grundherrschaft*', a right
that proved fundamental because in the long run it was able to gather
up and absorb most of the other kinds of property claims that pertained
to the ground that it embraced. It thus became a generalised right to use
a defined space, as we would recognise property denoting today,
although we are in fact far more circumscribed in what we can do
with our property than some historians seem to realise. *Dominium
utile*, on the other hand, was a right of use or usufruct that pertained
to particular resources in a given area, such as the right to farm the land
in a form of tenancy. The returns from *dominium directum* over the
ground were easily measured in the form of rent, a form that more
material, but less easily comparable, 'uses' (such as wood-gathering or
pasturage) eventually succumbed to. But we are getting ahead of ourselves; the last major 'use-rights', known in Roman law as *Servituten*,
were not dissolved in Württemberg until 1873.[12] These two distinct
forms of property rights were rather tidy legal fictions, however, and
quotidian practice was considerably more hazy, if not confused. But in
the sixteenth and seventeenth centuries, broadly speaking, *dominium
directum* belonged to the lords, and *dominium utile* was exercised by
their subjects.

In the absence of reliable mapping, the overlapping of various rights
could cause difficulties especially when a period of neglect was followed by a period of intensification of land use, such as in the late
fifteenth century or after the Thirty Years' War. Woodland was a landscape type particularly exposed to this development, as the marker
stones or trees that defined areas of property easily became overgrown
or mistaken, especially in less-frequented areas. Such a dispute over the

---

[12] Schlitte, *Zusammenlegung der Grundstücke*, p. 1190.

location of a boundary between some ducal woodland and the private woodland that lay in the hills between Stuttgart and Leonberg in 1527 led to a very simple sketch map of the district that may well be the first of its kind from all of Germany.[13] The case required the testimony of numerous witnesses who attempted to recall the various (and apparently unrecorded) transactions that this patch of land had been subject to stretching back into the 1480s.[14]

Most problems, however, were more prosaic. Nothing perhaps expresses the materiality of property relations better than an ordinance from Hemmingen that ordered that if a tree cast a shadow on the neighbour's land (presumably retarding the growth of his grass), that neighbour could take a third of the fruit! Or from next-door Gebersheim, where, once it could no longer be uprooted with two hands, a fruit tree became the protected property of the commune. The latter of course acted as an incentive to good husbandry, but one can only imagine the struggles inspired between the determined farmer and the equally obdurate sapling. A more devious way of dealing with such unwanted intrusions, that appears occasionally in the court record, was to knock a couple of nails into the young tree and watch it wither.[15]

In many ways this was an efficient and cheap means by which to regulate space. People had rights to material rather than to 'areas', although with most usages the definition of some kind of permitted 'area' was concomitant to defining the use. This meant however that as uses of different parts of the land varied over the year, and between years, methods of management and defining space had to alter as was appropriate. As we shall see, this saved on either the amount of supervision or monitoring of boundaries required, or the immense effort of constantly shifting fencing to demarcate changing land use. This was not, by later standards, a very productive economy, and until the eighteenth century the costs of investing to alter the complex system of overlapping rights to different materials on the same area of land were possibly not balanced by the productivity gains of doing so. The rights themselves were in fact very simple and readily comprehensible; if my tree damages your pasture, you can have some of the produce of my tree. All that remained was for communal authorities or lords to set the levels of compensation that should ensue. We must now examine how this system operated in practice. I will begin at the focus of most wood consumption – the home and the hearth – and move outwards

---

[13] Hagel, *Stuttgart*, pp. 33–4.   [14] HStAS A368 Bü 5.
[15] HStAS A583 Bü 262; A584 Bd.832; A227 Bü 1143.

towards the boundaries of the village's land where the woods tended to lie. Having established the parameters of the landscape, we can proceed to examine the productivity of the system and its response over time to the challenges faced in Württemberg's turbulent history.

Inner space

Nucleated settlements predominated across the region and across the period, consisting of dwelling houses surrounded by barns, stables and a scattering of trees. Settlements of any size were surrounded by an *Etter*, a wall that might be a palisade, or a smaller fence, of stone or even a hedge. This was an important legal boundary akin to the town wall, which served as a regulatory barrier to prevent further expansion into the village fields, and allowed the closing of gates and control of movement during the hours of darkness.[16] Trees, orchards, gardens and barns could in practice lie either side of the *Etter* but for the most part dwellings were all within. To our eyes the village interior would have seemed a pleasant, tree-lined and often carefully tended space in contrast to the relatively barren open, fenceless and hedgeless fields that lay beyond. Most villages were dominated by a church. Many settlements also enjoyed various buildings under communal control, such as a town hall, a meat store, bathhouse, bakery, smithy, a poorhouse and communal granary, some of which were leased out but remained the property of the village commune. The need for access to waterways and wells would have bound most villagers into a collective daily routine, where the watchmen of Renningen, for example, were responsible for breaking the ice at dawn after a cold night. In this village, where water was in short supply, obtaining it was a collective spectacle as well as experience. Petitioners for a new well in the 1590s described pregnant women and servants, eager to get to the old well first, slipping in icy conditions, and horses falling over each other in the effort to get a drink![17]

Dwelling houses were half-timbered, but increasingly, as the period wore on, provided with a stone lower storey, especially after the Thirty Years' War. Many urban houses had been constructed this way in the fifteenth century. The lower storey was generally not a living space but sunken stables, stalls or storage space, from which the warmth of the animals rose into the rest of the house. A few houses had wine-cellars. Generally those with farming interests had a small yard with a barn and

---

[16] See Bader, *Das mittelalterliche Dorf*, pp. 74, 112–16; Ernst, 'Geschichte', p. 284.
[17] HStAS A572 Bü 69; A206 Bü 1002.

stalls at the back away from the street. Larger farmsteads might have a kennel, washhouse and large threshing floor too, and every house that could kept its dungheap, the key to sustaining fertile farming land. From 1495 onward rural buildings were never supposed to be more than two storeys high, but in larger settlements this was often honoured in the breach.[18] Thatched rather than tiled roofs remained the rule in the countryside until the eighteenth century, although attempts were made to enforce a transition to tiles after the Building Ordinance of 1565 in some places.[19]

Rooms increasingly made their appearance during the sixteenth century, especially after developments in construction that facilitated increased prefabrication of storeys that could be stacked atop each other. This previously urban style was prevalent in rural building after about 1550. It allowed the construction of houses and barns in specially designated areas outside of the settlement, the frame then being transported into place, and frequently the displacement of whole buildings large distances.[20] The hearth or the oven was the 'soul of the chamber' – effective in retaining and radiating heat by evening time but leaving houses bitterly cold at waking time. Stoves generally seem to have been fired from the kitchen, with a back-stove built through the wall into the main living chamber, or where the heat simply filtered through a wattle-and-daub wall. Smoke, with guards against sparks, was led through an outlet in the kitchen ceiling to disperse in the attic, where it could also keep pests off any crops stored above.[21] The light and heat of the fire was supplemented by tallow candles and oil-lamps, though we still do not know how often these remained unlit and families had to go without. In parts of Germany, lighting the fires in April or September was considered unusual and the mark of a cold snap.[22] Inventories, such as Hans Zimmermann's cited above, suggest that furnishing was simple and limited and decoration rare. The 'prophet' Hans Keil of Gerlingen, who had broadsides of religious, newsworthy or fantastical events nailed up around the house in 1648, was something of a rarity.[23] Rising population during the sixteenth century seems to have led to more rooms and

---

[18] The town of Leonberg made stone lower stories mandatory by the 1580s. HStAS A572 Bü 41; Assion and Brednich, *Bauen und Wohnen*, pp. 184–6, 192, 196–7; Gromer, *Bäuerlichen Hausbaus*, p. 53; Schröder, *Weinbau und Siedlung*, p. 121.

[19] Elke Osterloh-Gesaat, personal communication. HStAS A206 Bü 1536.

[20] Gromer, *Bäuerlichen Hausbaus*, p. 53; Benning, 'Eine Stadt', p. 34.

[21] See the account of nineteenth-century life in Malmsheim by Häfner, cited in Assion and Brednich, *Bauen und Wöhnen*, p. 190; Gromer, *Bäuerlichen Hausbaus*, p. 55.

[22] Glaser, *Klimageschichte*, pp. 143, 156, 167.

[23] For a discussion of Geil's case, see Sabean, *Power in the blood*, pp. 61–93.

more families per building that may have assisted heating, rather than a proportionate expansion in the number of buildings.[24]

Of course not everybody lived in rural villages. In 1624, around the peak of population, Johann Öttinger recorded the settlements of Württemberg in some detail.[25] At this point the *Forstamt* Leonberg contained five small towns, fifty-three villages under Württemberger jurisdiction and a handful more subject to the minor nobility, several sheep stations and leased-out demesne farms, a few castles (which were mostly fortified manor houses rather than fortresses), over forty mills of various kinds and scattered houses for forestry officials. The only sizeable populations outside villages were in the towns, although this distinction was a fluid one; many villages were larger than the smallest towns, and only Leonberg and Markgröningen could boast large fortifications, regular markets and princely residences. Even these centres housed less than 1,500 people. Slightly larger towns such as Vaihingen an der Enz, Bietigheim, Marbach and Weil der Stadt all had parts of the *Forstamt* in their hinterlands, and the *Forstamt* boundary ran along the walls of the capital, Stuttgart, yet even this 'city' housed less than ten thousand people during the period. Urban buildings were far more likely to have stone ground floors, large cellars and several storeys, especially along central arteries and around squares; but otherwise they differed little from rural counterparts.

This was a wooden world, urban and rural, and with little else to decorate it save for a few bits of furniture, and glass or linen for the windows, both interior and exterior took on the texture of whatever wood a household could avail itself of. The half-timbering of the exterior belonged to oak, but interiors were increasingly given over to pine, which the work of Jutta Hoffmann shows to have been an ongoing process from 1400 right until the nineteenth century. However, building techniques showed a considerable refinement in large houses in the years 1500–50, and this is probably reflected in an increase in the use of pinewood for interiors and less reliance on massive timbers.[26]

The inner space, even that of the 'home' (though we should remember that homes were often shared spaces and contained lodgers and servants as well as a 'nuclear family'), was subject to extensive regulation by local and state authorities. This ranged from the 'reformation of manners' and upkeep of morals to extensive measures to prevent fire, and at least theoretically strict planning rules that dictated where

[24] On interiors more generally, see van Dülmen, *Kultur und Alltag*, pp. 11–23, 56–68.
[25] HStAS J1 Nr.141g.
[26] Hoffmann, 'Jahrringchronologien', p. 98; Gromer, *Bäuerlichen Hausbaus*, p. 53.

malodorous industrial processes should be sited, or how much wood one was to be allowed for a particular building. Rules on building were enforced by the municipal court and a carpenter engaged by the authorities. In a world where resources were perceived to be scarce, the form or decoration of one's home or farmstead were not simply matters of taste, but 'luxury', 'superfluity' or 'need' to be balanced against the overall needs of the community.

Making the *Markung*

The heart of the *Markung* was the *Flur*, the cultivated ground. This was dominated in most places by the 'open fields' of the arable land, large expanses in which the actual plots of individual farms were scattered in small narrow strips. These strips were organised in blocks (called 'furlongs' in English), usually with an identifying name. In turn the blocks were parts of large fields, from three to six per village, called a *Zelg* or *Ösch*. Meadowland used for growing hay and math tended to cluster around streams and valley-floors, and vineyards usually made use of slopes less suitable for the cultivation of cereal crops. Smaller garden plots tended to cluster near the village. Although these often were used for more intensive cultivation, such as of dye-crops, flax, hemp or vegetables, 'garden' here pertains to a legal right for the land to be exempt from communal regulation, rather than necessarily indicating anything about its use. There were however also gardens owned by the village commune. *Egarten* were plots temporarily cultivated but left for long periods as rough pasture, usually where the ground was too poor to bear frequent cultivation. More often than not these bordered on woodland and might be the result of fairly recent clearances.

The proportion of the *Markung* that each land use took up varied considerably over the region, a reflection not only of ecology, but the demand for land generated by the local social structure and economy. Indeed, the area under cultivation varied very considerably too from over 98 per cent of the *Markung* in Ditzingen to as little as 7 per cent in Botnang around 1630.

Much of the uncultivated land was wooded, and to some degree these figures are an index of the extent of local woodland, but there were areas of open pasture too, increasingly large as one moves to the west of the region. The line between pasture with scattered trees and 'wooded' land could be somewhat hazy. Fairly complete figures for the extent of land under varying types of cultivation survive from 1629–34, 1655 and from the first half of the eighteenth century. That they tally reasonably well speaks in favour of the accuracy of the earlier

Table 1.1 *Proportion of the* Markung *under cultivation, 1629–34*[a]

Place	% Markung cultivated	% Markung uncultivated
Aurich	50	50
Bietigheim	62	38
Bissingen	50	50
Botnang	7	93
Ditzingen	98	2
Eltingen	N/A	N/A
Enzweihingen	54	46
Feuerbach	40	60
Gebersheim	55	45
Gerlingen	25	75
Groß Ingersheim	76	24
Heimerdingen	46	54
Heimsheim	62	38
Hirschlanden	75	25
Höfingen	65	35
Klein Ingersheim	38	62
Kornwestheim	91	9
Leonberg	N/A	N/A
Markgröningen	64	36
Möglingen	N/A	N/A
Mönßheim	20	80
Münchingen	53	47
Münklingen	47	53
Münster	18	82
Nussdorf	28	72
Oßweil	60	40
Renningen	36	64
Riet	40	60
Rutesheim	47	53
Schwieberdingen	38	62
Tamm	65	35
Weilimdorf	63	37
Zuffenhausen	56	44

Note: [a] The figures for cultivated land derive from the area taxable as arable, vineyard or meadow in the years 1629 to 1634, and are thus not records of the area actually cultivated in those years. The area of the *Markung* can only be taken from surveys taken at the beginning of the twentieth century, which will introduce some inaccuracies into the data. Broadly speaking, however, these reflect local conditions in the early seventeenth century. Boundaries of the *Markung* have been taken from data of 1907.

Sources: HStAS A261 Bü 421, 727, 891, 998, 1126, 1470, 1634; KSL, *Württembergische Gemeindestatistik.*

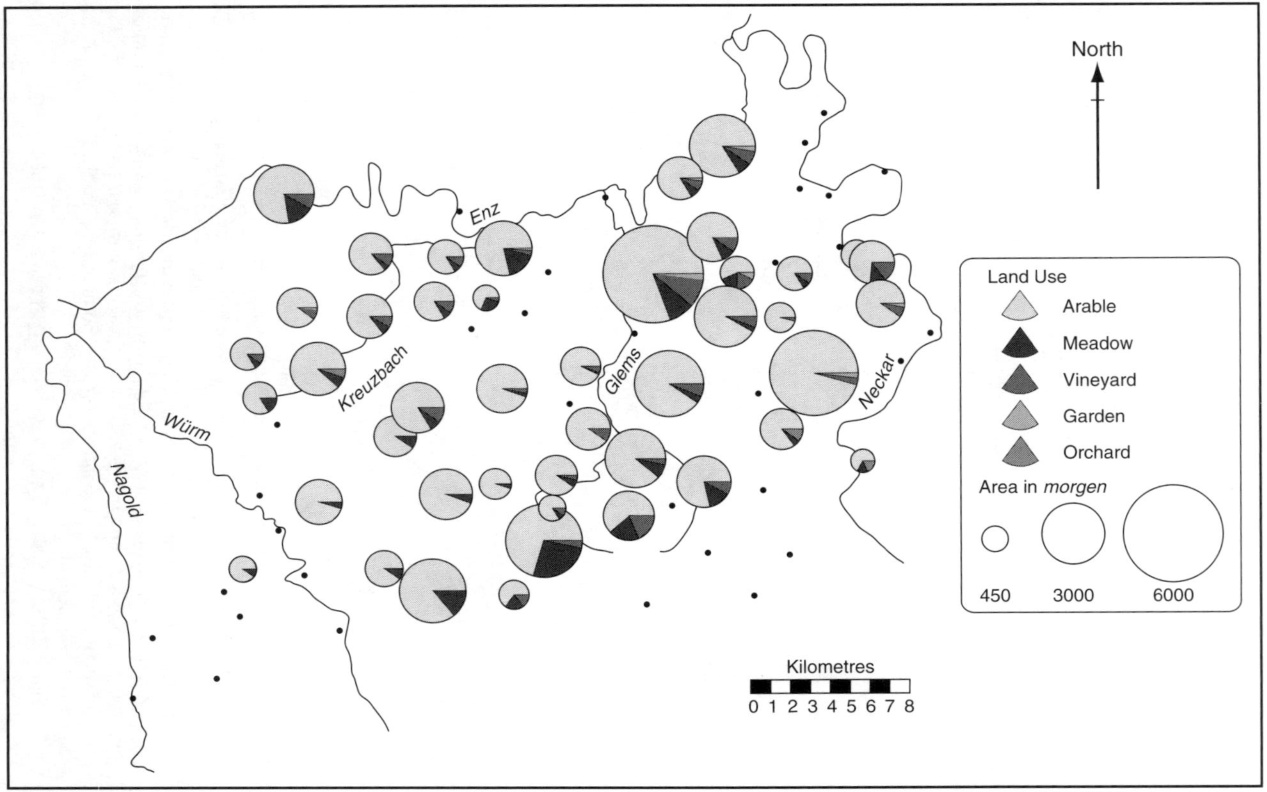

Map 1.1 Land use, 1713

assessments. For some individual plots, and holdings of landlords in a particular village, it is possible to take this analysis back into the fifteenth century, without, however, being able to speak confidently of the division of cultivated space as a whole. Map 1.1 indicates that arable land was the most important land-use everywhere, with only a few areas with damper valley-bottoms devoting considerable amounts of space to meadows. Vineyards were entirely absent from the more elevated south-west of the region, and were a more significant land-scape element around settlements with steep slopes that could be so utilised (see map 1.1). This is particularly clear on the flanks of river valleys such as at Aurich, Riet and Münster, but vineyards were also significant on the hillier land near Stuttgart.[27]

Land-use changed over time, of course. Thanks to the careful work of Volker Trugenberger, it is possible to trace these processes reliably back to the beginning of the sixteenth century for the entire *Markung* of the town of Leonberg. Here the area of vineyard expanded from 173 *morgen* in 1528 (10 per cent of the total) to 293 *morgen* in 1575 (16 per cent of the total). This was the great age of vineyard expansion that saw it reach its maximum extent across southern Germany. By 1629 this had fallen back to 261 *morgen*. However, it was little different even as late as 1730. In fact, despite worsening terms of trade, viticulture remained prominent in the landscape in the early eighteenth century. With the demographic losses of the Thirty Years' War both the area of arable and vineyard showed a considerable contraction. Meadows that were more dependent on favourable ecological conditions and less labour-intensive to work remained stable. These losses were made up by the first decades of the succeeding century.[28]

The patterns found in Leonberg are mirrored more widely, but again we find considerable local variation. The proportion of cultivated land devoted to particular uses can be compared between the cadastres drawn up by the Austrian government in the 1520s, and taxation records from 1629–34. Unfortunately the former only comprise those properties where the Dukes of Württemberg were landlords, and it may well be that in individual settlements those lands that they happened to own did not mirror the general breakdown of land use. For example, if we compare the distribution of the uses of cultivated land for the village of Höfingen from the year 1629 with the same distribution for ducal property only in that village in 1523, we find that ducal lands at the earlier date made up 69 per cent of the arable land at the later date,

[27] Calculated from data in HStAS A261 Bü 421, 727, 891, 998, 1126, 1470, 1634.
[28] Trugenberger, *Zwischen Schloß und Vorstadt*, p. 50; HStAS A261 Bü 1126, 1128, 1134.

Table 1.2 *Proportion of cultivated area under each land use*[a]

Place	Vineyard			Meadow			Arable		
	1520s	1634	ca 1730	1520s	1634	ca 1730	1520s	1634	ca 1730
Asperg	0.25	N/A	0.20	0.18	N/A	0.22	0.57	N/A	0.58
Aurich	N/A	0.16	0.06	N/A	0.09	0.08	N/A	0.75	0.86
Bergheim	0.01	N/A	N/A	0.08	N/A	N/A	0.92	N/A	N/A
Bietigheim	0.11	0.10	0.07	0.10	0.07	0.09	0.80	0.84	0.84
Bissingen	0.00	0.08	0.06	0.08	0.11	0.12	0.92	0.81	0.82
Botnang	N/A	0.31	N/A	N/A	0.23	N/A	N/A	0.45	N/A
Ditzingen	0.01	0.04	0.03	0.11	0.05	0.08	0.88	0.91	0.88
Dürrmenz	N/A	N/A	0.08	N/A	N/A	0.15	N/A	N/A	0.78
Eglosheim	0.08	0.05	0.05	0.14	0.10	0.13	0.78	0.86	0.83
Eltingen	0.02	0.03	0.04	0.23	0.23	0.26	0.75	0.74	0.70
Enzweihingen	N/A	0.13	0.07	N/A	0.12	0.13	N/A	0.76	0.80
Feuerbach	N/A	0.26	N/A	N/A	0.17	N/A	N/A	0.57	N/A
Flacht	N/A	N/A	0.02	N/A	N/A	0.05	N/A	N/A	0.93
Gebersheim	0.00	0.04	0.02	0.02	0.05	0.04	0.98	0.91	0.94
Gerlingen	0.12	0.19	0.19	0.19	0.16	0.17	0.69	0.65	0.64
Groß Glattbach	N/A	N/A	0.10	N/A	N/A	0.06	N/A	N/A	0.84
Groß Ingersheim	0.10	0.12	N/A	0.07	0.05	N/A	0.83	0.84	N/A
Hausen	N/A	0.00	N/A	N/A	0.09	N/A	N/A	0.91	N/A
Heimerdingen	0.03	0.04	0.03	0.05	0.03	0.03	0.92	0.93	0.94
Heimsheim	0.00	0.01	0.01	0.07	0.04	0.05	0.93	0.95	0.94
Hemmingen	0.02	0.07	0.04	0.03	0.04	0.04	0.95	0.89	0.92
Hirschlanden	N/A	0.02	0.04	N/A	0.02	0.02	N/A	0.97	0.94
Hochdorf	0.00	N/A	N/A	0.03	N/A	N/A	0.97	N/A	N/A
Höfingen	0.01	0.06	0.04	0.05	0.05	0.06	0.94	0.90	0.90
Hoheneck	N/A	N/A	0.22	N/A	N/A	0.02	N/A	N/A	0.76

Iptingen	N/A	N/A	0.07	N/A	N/A	0.08	N/A	N/A	0.85
Klein Ingersheim	N/A	0.15	N/A	N/A	0.07	N/A	N/A	0.78	N/A
Kornwestheim	N/A	0.01	0.01	N/A	0.02	0.03	N/A	0.96	0.96
Markgröningen	0.12	0.10	0.10	0.05	0.07	0.07	0.83	0.82	0.83
Merklingen	N/A	0.01	N/A	N/A	0.10	N/A	N/A	0.89	N/A
Möglingen	0.09	0.04	0.04	0.06	0.03	0.03	0.85	0.93	0.93
Mönßheim	0.09	0.08	0.06	0.09	0.15	0.08	0.82	0.77	0.86
Mottlingen	0.00	N/A	N/A	0.09	N/A	N/A	0.91	N/A	N/A
Münchingen	0.01	0.04	0.04	0.04	0.03	0.04	0.95	0.92	0.91
Münklingen	0.01	0.03	0.03	0.07	0.16	0.10	0.92	0.81	0.87
Münster	N/A	0.48	0.17	N/A	0.11	0.14	N/A	0.41	0.68
Neckarweihingen	N/A	N/A	0.13	N/A	N/A	0.12	N/A	N/A	0.75
Nussdorf	N/A	0.16	0.12	N/A	0.04	0.04	N/A	0.81	0.84
Oßweil	N/A	0.01	0.01	N/A	0.03	0.05	N/A	0.95	0.93
Pflugfelden	0.00	0.01	0.01	0.01	0.02	0.03	0.98	0.97	0.97
Renningen	0.00	0.01	0.01	0.12	0.11	0.14	0.88	0.88	0.86
Riet	N/A	0.37	0.28	N/A	0.06	0.07	N/A	0.57	0.65
Rutesheim	0.00	0.01	0.01	0.08	0.05	0.05	0.92	0.95	0.94
Schwieberdingen	0.00	0.07	N/A	0.04	0.03	N/A	0.96	0.90	N/A
Simmozheim	N/A	0.00	N/A	N/A	0.06	N/A	N/A	0.94	N/A
Tamm	0.02	0.07	0.10	0.07	0.04	0.09	0.91	0.89	0.81
Warmbronn	N/A	N/A	0.11	N/A	N/A	0.26	N/A	N/A	0.63
Weilimdorf	N/A	0.08	0.08	N/A	0.04	0.13	N/A	0.88	0.78
Weissach	N/A	N/A	0.05	N/A	N/A	0.09	N/A	N/A	0.86
Wiernsheim	N/A	N/A	0.02	N/A	N/A	0.07	N/A	N/A	0.91
Wimsheim	N/A	N/A	0.01	N/A	N/A	0.16	N/A	N/A	0.91
Wurmberg	N/A	N/A	0.02	N/A	N/A	0.14	N/A	N/A	0.83
Zuffenhausen	N/A	0.11	0.09	N/A	0.07	0.06	N/A	0.82	0.85

Note: [a] The figures from the 1520s refer only to ducally owned property.

Sources: HStAS A261 Bü 413, 421, 727, 728, 891, 905, 998, 1003, 1004, 1126, 1128, 1134, 1160, 1177, 1183, 1470, 1634, 1635, 1641.

73 per cent of meadowland but only 16 per cent of vineyards. This could have been caused by a precipitate rise in vineyard acreage, but is likely to have stemmed to a large extent from the Dukes owning a relatively small proportion of the acreage of vineyard, but a majority of the arable and meadowland, already present in the 1520s. This difference between the ducal ownership of vineyards and other forms of land use holds among nearly all of the settlements for which we have data. Generally speaking, it was not unusual for the ducal properties in the 1520s to comprise more than half of all land under cultivation in the 1620s, but in the case of vineyards the proportion was much less, rarely more than a third. However, the evidence and contemporary comment all suggests a steady rise in the acreage of vineyard at least until the latter part of the sixteenth century.[29]

We can be far more confident about land-use change over the following century, because we are comparing like with like, allowing for the probability of some inaccuracies in measurement. A comparison of 1629–34 with data from the first half of the eighteenth century, spanning the period from the 1710s to 1730, also encompasses two eras with roughly similar population levels so we can see how the post-war reconstruction of Württemberg differed from its experience in the early seventeenth century.[30] We have data from thirty-seven places for both the seventeenth and eighteenth centuries, about half of the settlements of any size in the region.

This displays a marked, though not universal, decline in the proportional area of vineyard. The greatest difference is to be found in those areas previously highly dependent on commercialised viticulture. Thus in villages such as Aurich, Riet and Münster, arable agriculture has become far more important in relative terms by the eighteenth century. Vineyards have also nearly entirely disappeared from the ecologically unfavourable western and central districts of the *Forstamt*, areas where the wine was 'almost nothing more than vinegar', according to a report of 1731.[31] But in the south-east, its extent remained virtually unchanged, or even expanded. Thus decline was not universal, rather vineyards had become largely confined to those settlements that displayed a high value per acre of vineyard in the tax returns of the eighteenth century, and dwindled elsewhere.[32]

[29] HStAS A261 Bü 727, 891, 998, 1126. The 1520s data has been obtained from Schulz, *Altwürttembergischer Lagerbücher*. The calculations are my own.
[30] HStAS A261 Bü 413, 421, 727, 728, 891, 905, 998, 1003, 1004, 1126, 1128, 1134, 1160, 1177, 1183, 1470, 1634, 1635, 1641. Schulz, *Altwürttembergischer Lagerbücher*.
[31] HStAS A368L Bü 136.
[32] This contrasts with the district of Brackenheim, where viticulture, although central to the economy, was in decline by the early eighteenth century. Döbele-Carlesso, *Weinbau*, p. 44.

Many settlements also display a relative shift towards meadowland at the expense of arable. It should be remembered, however, that we are dealing with relative proportions of the cultivated area, not absolute acreages. This preference for meadow – most noticeably in Weilimdorf – may have arisen soon after the end of the Thirty Years' War. However, the variation is mostly explained by fluctuation in the proportion of the *Markung* cultivated rather than actual conversion. Indeed, the post-war period was one of general absolute expansion, and some of viticulture's relative decline should be attributed to vigorous growth of the arable land. This expanded by some 7 per cent between 1630 and the end of the seventeenth century and by even more in the north-west corner of the *Forstamt*, where it could as much as double in size. Overall, this expansion continued right up until 1713, with another 9 per cent again being added to the area of land taxed as arable. This advance was also most marked west of the Glems. By 1730 however this most recent gain seems to have been lost again. This may well have been because the 1713 figures exaggerated the area actually under cultivation, but some of the abandonment seems to have been recent, with the land either lost altogether or being cultivated only occasionally. Certainly the extensive 1204 *morgen* that Mönßheim 'added' to its arable land in the post-war period, an expansion of 60 per cent, corresponds exactly to that area recorded as *Egarten*, or only occasionally cultivated, in 1730.[33] It may be that this land, and other apparently 'new' arable in this region, was always cultivated occasionally but did not feature in previous tax returns. Indeed, Heimsheim explicitly left this kind of land out of its returns on 1629 because it argued that it would make their assessment unfeasibly high.[34] Formally, when uncultivated, *Egarten* reverted to being communal property used as common pasture, and hence was not taxable. Meanwhile, meadowland expanded by up to a factor of three (in the case of Weilimdorf), but commonly within the range 25–75 per cent. Thus a somewhat more favourable meadow-to-arable ratio was to be found in the early eighteenth century than was present a century earlier, despite the expansion of the arable. Only a couple of places show an actual fall in the cultivated area since before the Thirty Years' War. Thus we cannot speak of a 'fixed' endowment of cultivated resources over the period. There were clearly variations not only in the area of cultivated land, but perhaps more significantly, in the way that land was utilised over time and most importantly of all in

---

[33] HStAS A261 Bü 1134.   [34] HStAS A261 Bü 1126.

terms of any agricultural 'system', the balance between different forms of cultivation.

Surveys of woodland area survive from 1523 onwards, and even earlier in the case of woodland that was leased out by the Duke as a part of farm tenancies, and was thus recorded as private by the forestry administration. The 1523 survey covered only ducally owned woodland and even then, it seems, with many gaps. Further surveys of 1556, 1583 and 1682 are far more comprehensive.[35] The boundaries recorded in the maps of the 1680s appear to tally well with those noted in writing a century earlier, or indeed throughout the eighteenth century, with only minor changes.[36] Roughly speaking, however, about a third of the western half of the *Forstamt* was wooded and about a fifth of the east, though with significant local variation. Some documentary evidence shows clearances during the sixteenth century, mostly for vineyard, but probably not on a scale that would have greatly altered the total extent of the woods. There is no evidence that the expansion in the cultivated area after the Thirty Years' War was at the expense of woodland. It is more likely that open pasture, which had been more extensive in the west of the region, was brought under the plough, if only occasionally.

A 'poor recycling technology'

This phrase of Christian Pfister's encapsulates the efforts of the peasantry to manage the dilemmas of the 'agrarian system' of the age. Within the world of the 'limited good' or the 'photosynthetic constraint', survival depended to a degree, where long-distance trade was weakly developed, on the successful and sustainable recycling of nutrients within the local ecology. This was not a simple task. To survive, at a very basic level, families needed food and fuel. Food could come in the form of vegetable and cereal matter, and animal products, most significantly dairy products, to provide the semblance of a balanced diet.[37] Wood housed the family and provided the material for a material culture, but at a fundamental level was required for heating and cooking. One could not go on forever, however, extracting

---

[35] These are discussed further in chapters 2 and 4.

[36] Although the boundaries appear unchanged over time, estimates before 1682 give much lower figures for woodland area. Consequently we can place little reliability on the earlier estimates. In some cases it seems that the area of 'productive' woodland was noted, that is, woodland deliberately coppiced for the production of fuel and fencing, rather then the wooded area as a whole.

[37] For a detailed breakdown of the diet of Bavarian peasants, see Beck, *Unterfinning*, pp. 151–2, 520.

nutrients or calories from the system and expect them to be replaced, especially in an era of increasing demand. Contemporaries were well aware of the need for 'recycling', most importantly to replace soil fertility via the transfer of biomass from pasture to the cultivated land via the medium of their livestock's manure. Although this was not the only manner in which soil nutrients could be replenished, it also sped up the general decomposition of other organic matter, and remained the critical variable from the viewpoint of humans. Cultivation also tended to make soils more acidic over time, which in some places meant that more alkaline materials, usually marl, had to be dug into the loam to keep a balance that crops could tolerate. However, marling, in turn, could accelerate the uptake of nutrients from the soil and hence also accelerate exhaustion. Different soils could bear very different rates of exploitation, but some marling and manuring was an essential component of farming in this region.[38]

This biomass transfer could only prove sustainable if the extent and productivity of the arable land was held in balance with the extent and productivity of the source of manure, the pasture. If, in response to the demand for food, the cultivated land expanded too far into the pasture, then the area of the latter would be diminished, and endangered by overgrazing, leading to degradation and a lack of nutrients. Part of the solution was to extend grazing into the woodland. At the same time, to allow for grass growth in the woodland, tree-cover had to be widely enough spaced to permit sunlight to reach the forest floor. In turn, this jeopardised the size of wood yields, although saplings themselves needed the light provided by the demise of older trees in the canopy to develop. Allowing grazing animals into the woodlands threatened the regeneration of the tree-cover, as the very young saplings were vulnerable to being grazed and killed for the first few years of life.

Seasonal change generated further dilemmas. Hay meadows were an important source of protein-rich fodder, and were protected from grazing for several months of the year (usually mid-spring until midsummer) to allow for a lush growth. This hay, sometimes with a second crop of math in September, was not consumed immediately because it was required to tide animals over the winter when grass growth stopped and there was insufficient fodder on the open pastures to see livestock through the cold months. Yet in storage, this hay lost considerably in protein content, never mind the potential ravages of mould and pests. Even with the hay, however, the livestock had to be sent out early onto

---

[38] See Shiel, 'Improving soil fertility'; Newman and Harvey, 'Soil fertility'; Winiwarter and Sonnlechner, *Soziale Metabolismus*, pp. 20–1.

the open pastures after winter, cropping the grass too early so that they were not able to get the best out of it. While communal herding saved labour, it by no means allocated the energetic resources of the area effectively.[39] Peasants could not utilise all of the calories and nutrients that their land actually produced because of the uneven distribution of that production over the year.

In turn, communities of peasants feared loss of their precious bio-mass altogether, whether in sales or transfers outside the *Markung* to bring profits, or to the farmsteads of peasants who might hold land in one village's fields but actually reside somewhere else. One could portray this concern as proof of an 'ecological' consciousness on the part of peasant communities. To some degree it was. Equally, however, it could pertain to more obviously economic considerations, especially on the part of lords. To export hay, straw or manure, produced by the careful management and allocation of village resources, could be viewed as an attempt to cash in on that management without having to pay the full costs of capital depreciation caused by the loss of biomass.

To cope with these dilemmas, peasants managed resources via the institution of the village commune. The records of communal regula-tion came increasingly to be written down during the sixteenth century. As only a few of these 'village ordinances' or 'village books' have survived, it is difficult to tell how extensive the regulation really was, for there is a danger in inferring too much from a self-selecting sample of survivals. Rules banning the export of material such as wood, hay and straw, however, were relatively common in the south-west of Germany.[40] Similarly, many places limited livestock numbers to pre-vent overgrazing. The ducal government required communes to inform them of the number of grazing animals from 1552. Grazing rights were legally vested in the commune, rather than individual households. The tools for this regulation were various, perhaps the most frequent being to limit free grazing rights to those animals that one could 'overwinter', usually meaning provide with winter fodder from one's own holding. Another tool was simply to set a maximum number of livestock that could be grazed, often differentiated according to the size of the farm enterprise. These were not always absolutes. Leonberg, for example, seems to have allowed extra animals into the herd for a set payment per beast. However, in 1579, when peasants in Renningen felt their pasture was being overgrazed, they even complained of households grazing

---

[39] See Christiansen, *A manorial world*, p. 149.
[40] Warde, 'Common rights'; Ernst, 'Geschichte', pp. 286–7.

'oxen and sheep, with which they might very well do without'! Animals often, though not always, had to be pastured either in a communal herd under the supervision of a collectively employed herdsman, or kept in particular allotted spaces, saving both labour and preventing individuals from sneaking extra beasts onto the pastures.[41]

These kinds of rules could certainly operate against rapid commercialisation of resources, as locals were prevented from selling them off, whether directly (straw or wood, for example) or in 'processed' form as fattened beasts or dairy products. Of course there was a market for animals, but it was limited to a scale of operation seen as appropriate for a largely self-supplying household. However, such regulation does not necessarily demonstrate an anti-market *mentalité*, as those who saw themselves as the owners of the capital asset embodied in the precious local biomass, whether village communes, municipalities or lordships, were often happy to engage in sales when it suited them. Regulation was a collective response to a specific problem of biomass retention. The commune of Gebersheim, for example, was quite happy to permit the sale of wood within the commune 'as expensive as one can', even when export was banned.[42] These rules should probably not be reduced to an origin in 'environmentalist' or 'economic' attitudes. They were part and parcel of a general need to ring-fence resources and maintain productivity in an era of limited capital for investment, to sustain a workable system with considerable flexibility in access to land and resources over the year, and to define that system against an environment which threatened to destabilise its functioning.

The ability of the commune to determine access times to, and allocation of, many of the village's resources, prevented any one individual from 'free-riding' or undermining the system with their own choices as to how to use resources that were generated, to some degree, by collective endeavour. As a collective 'pact' it could assist greatly in reducing labour costs by providing collectively financed monitors and supervisors of the system. To some extent the opportunity costs of individual households were subordinated to a wider 'good' that judged a potential failure of the system in the long term to be the greater cost. Yet this was not a permanent battle between private vices and public virtues, or vice

---

[41] The expression from Renningen runs, 'ochsen und schaafvieh ... deren sie gar wohl entbähren mögen.' STABB BhB A1678; B545; HStAS A348 Bü 5; A572 Bü 41, 69; Warde, 'Common rights'; Maisch, *Notdürftiger Unterhalt*, p. 93.

[42] HStAS A584 Bd.832; for other examples, see HStAS A59 Bü 13a; A227 Bü 1130, 1143; A368L Bü 136; A557 Bü 145; A572 Bü 41, 56, 69; A583 Bü 261; StAL Höfingen Fleckenbuch. The commune of Malmsheim banned even internal sales, however. Ernst, 'Geschichte', p. 287.

versa, but a set of ongoing arguments about the complexities of choices and their potentially chaotic ramifications. Regulation was not against commercialisation in itself, and nor was it necessarily in favour of equality. The measure by which equality was established was in any case always contested, as will be discussed later. Rather, regulation simplified choices, and established who could make what choice and who could object to it, in a system where land use and rights changed over the year and there was a high potential for an uneven distribution of benefits and costs as a consequence of individual actions. One would not expect such a system to operate smoothly or consistently over time, and this was indeed the case. Interests often diverged, sometimes strikingly so, and I do not wish to minimise the friction between lords and peasants, and between peasants and peasants. It is the course of such ramifications and friction that will occupy most of the rest of this book.[43] Any assessment of these strategies and achievements must begin with the most basic food crop of all: cereals.

Corn – the *'mal nécessaire'*[44]

Cereal crops were the indisputable kernel of the rural world. It was not that they were always, everywhere, the main source of income, but rather were the main source of food, increasingly so during the sixteenth century, the 'century of grain'. They were 'the basis of all human society, the greatest wealth of the state and the necessary means of the preservation of life,' as the field orders of Weil der Stadt in the eighteenth century put it.[45] In the *Forstamt* Leonberg, grain-growing meant the production of spelt and oats as the main crops, with smaller amounts of rye, wheat, lentils, einkorn, barley and peas also grown. The region was dominated by the 'three-course rotation'. On one field, the main food crop was planted in the autumn. In most of Württemberg this was spelt, a hardy variety of wheat. It was sometimes mixed with a little rye, partly because feudal payments in kind still demanded it, but also because rye had other useful properties, such as providing strong

---

[43] This is the classic 'tragedy of the commons' problem as formulated by Garret Hardin. Elinor Ostrom has opposed Hardin's model by pointing to various examples of successful collective management of 'common pool resources' that suppressed free-riding. The literature on these issues is now very extensive. Hardin, 'Tragedy of the commons'; Ostrom, *Governing the commons*; dealing with these matters in early modern European history, see de Moor, Shaw-Taylor and Warde, *Management of common land*; Demélas and Vivier, *Les propriétés collectives*.

[44] Mulliez, 'Du blé, "mal nécessaire" '.

[45] Ernst, 'Geschichte', p. 372. On the 'century of grain', see Militzer, *Getreidebaus*.

Table 1.3 *The three-course rotation*

	Field one	Field two	Field three
Year one	Spelt	Oats	Fallow
Year two	Oats	Fallow	Spelt
Year three	Fallow	Spelt	Oats

straw for binding vines to stakes or thatching, and protecting the spelt from the wind.[46] The second field lay bare until the spring when the spring-sown or summer crop was sown. This consisted largely of oats, which were primarily used as horse fodder but could also be used as a foodstuff to prepare gruels in poor households. Barley and peas were also grown, and peas especially could be sown late, if sufficient seed was available, when it became clear that the other crops were damaged. This happened in Gerlingen's fields in the spring of 1643, when frosts assaulted the rye, beans and early-sown peas.[47] The third field lay fallow and open to grazing by the communal herd. After the harvest in August, the previous year's winter-crop field would lie bare until it was sown with oats in the spring; the spring-crop field would lie fallow for a year; and the fallow field would be sown soon after with the new winter grain. Hence the uses of the fields were rotated over a three-year cycle. This varied the nutrients extracted from year to year and gave some fourteen months respite during the fallow period, which allowed soil fertility to recover and gave the peasants time to work it over to remove weeds.[48]

The plots of individual peasant households were scattered throughout these fields in small parcels, rarely more than half a hectare in extent and often considerably smaller. The 424 *morgen* holdings of Jerg Minner of Kornwestheim, for example, possibly the wealthiest farmer (and a

---

[46] This wheat variety was more demanding of nitrogen than any other crop, as well as being critical for food, and hence went first in the rotation. Campbell, *English Seignorial Agriculture*, pp. 218–20; Beck, *Unterfinning*, p. 104; Fél and Hofer, *Bäuerlicher Denkweise*, p. 60; Döbele-Carlesso, *Weinbau*, p. 62.

[47] The crops sown can be found in tithe accounts and the extensive surveys of crop reserves taken in 1622–3, as well as account books of municipalities and institutions. HStAS A237a Bü 580, 586, 601; A302 Bd.7046, 7048; A572 Bü 55; StAL Armenkastenrechnungen; StAM Spitalrechnungen; HStAS A237a Bü 580, 586, 601; A572 Bü 55.

[48] The classic view of the reason for fallowing is to allow for the 'recovery' of soil nutrients, but this view is by no means universal. Braudel, for example, attributes the fallow period largely to the necessity to clear weeds through ploughings. Braudel, *The identity of France. Volume Two*, p. 341.

tradesman and lender) in Württemberg at his death in 1599, were divided into no less than 160 parcels.[49] Various explanations for this practice of scattering have been advanced. These range from the random accretions of centuries of partible inheritance, to a deliberate 'rationality' that sought to minimise the risks that farmers faced by not concentrating all one's holding in one place, and thus making it subject to one soil-type and micro-climate and vulnerable to pest attack.[50] This attractive argument, however, is stymied by the fact that it appears that few peasants held their parcels of land equally distributed between the three fields although it may have been an ideal.[51] Holdings showed considerable variation, to the point that they might not have any land at all in one field. If this was where the winter grain, the main food crop, was to be sown that year, then they would have to seek their subsistence elsewhere.[52] The variation in yields from year to year caused by this was far higher than the risk-minimising effects of scattering the small parcels. We must then doubt whether the latter can really be explained by a deliberate policy rather than the difficulties of being able to consolidate one's land by finding enough ready sellers and buyers prepared to go through with the necessary transactions. In any case, one could rarely work more than half a hectare at the most in any single day, so the scattering may not have had so much practical importance to the peasants. Nevertheless, the balks and headlands that surrounded the plots and gave space to turn the plough had to be carefully regulated by communally appointed overseers to prevent encroachment or disputes. Equally, to prevent people trespassing on others' land and damaging their crops, the time at which harvesting could begin was set by village officials. As we shall see, the reciprocities of labour and equipment involved made this, to some extent, a 'collective' enterprise in any case.

A petition from farmers in the district of Marbach just to the east of the Neckar from the year 1647 furnishes us with a rough breakdown of the

---

[49]   Boelcke, 'Bäuerlicher Wohlstand', p. 255.
[50]   See for example, Campbell and Godoy, 'Commonfield agriculture', p. 102; McCloskey, 'The open fields of England'.
[51]   Some demesne holdings or large and probably long-enduring impartible farms did have their holdings evenly scattered in this region of Württemberg. Karl Siegfried Bader pointed out the lack of evenness in plot scattering as early as 1973. See Bader, *Rechtsformen*, p. 97.
[52]   So much is clear from examining and mapping the layout of thirty-four holdings recorded for taxation purposes in the settlements of Hoheneck, Neckarweihingen and Backnang in 1607. It is also clear from a far larger sample I have assembled of post-harvest crop stores from 1,236 households in settlements in Württemberg in 1622 that plots were frequently far from evenly spread in the three-field system. HStAS A237a Bü 580, 582; A314 Bü 6; A359 Bü 6.

costs of arable farming. According to them, the seed took up 16 per cent of the costs of cultivation, although for the most part peasants would have provided this themselves. Reaping, the other end of the process, accounted for 10.5 per cent of costs, carting 6 per cent, threshing another 10.5 per cent and the preparation of the ground the remaining 58 per cent. If we reduce this to the labour of a peasant on his own plot, providing his own seed and buying in carting when necessary, then reaping and threshing each took up 13 per cent of his labour on the arable respectively, and ploughing, sowing, harrowing, manuring and weeding about 74 per cent.[53] The pre-harvest work on a *morgen* of land took up between about twenty-five and twenty-seven 'labour-days' (the amount of labour one man could provide in a normal working day).[54] These estimates are broadly in line with the accounts kept by (admittedly unusual) farmers elsewhere in northern Europe such as Rienck Hemmema in the Netherlands or Robert Loder in the English Midlands.[55] The same work was not applied every time in the cropping cycle, however, as fields were generally manured only once every six years.[56]

These figures suggest that provision of the necessary labour power for careful cultivation, if those days could be evenly spaced out over the year, was easily available in the early seventeenth century.[57] Activity was not, however, equally spaced over the year, and neither was the distribution of landholding nor the equipment to work it. The fields

---

[53] HStAS A230 Bü 97. Georg Fertig's work on the demesne of Cathrinenthal, not far from the *Forstamt* Leonberg, reckoned that threshing costs took away some 8 per cent of the harvest. Fertig, *Lokales Leben*, p. 305.

[54] This is a rough estimate, but the figure would not deviate far from this. It is based on the tillage costs of 5 fl. 32 x divided by a daily wage of 0.2 fl. As the data comes from a petition complaining about the situation of farmers employing labour in a time of high wages, it is unlikely to underestimate money costs. Some of the costs may also have been the provision of draught power, so, if anything, less labour-days would in fact have been required. HStAS A237 Bü 97.

[55] Fussell, *Robert Loder's farm accounts*, p. xviii; Gorbonzoon, *Rienck Hemmema*; Slicher van Bath, 'Robert Loder en Renck Hemmema'. They also bear comparison with data assembled by Rainer Beck and Michael North in Bavaria and Prussia. It might be noted, however, that this is a considerably higher labour input than that given by Bob Allen for English farms. Allen based his calculations on figures from the late eighteenth century, when the productivity of labour in English agriculture and the quality of tools was very much higher than at earlier dates. Allen, *Enclosure and the yeoman*, p. 57; Beck, *Unterfinning*, p. 587; North, 'Lohnarbeit'.

[56] See the tax laws in Reyscher, *SWG*, Bd.XVII, p. 359.

[57] Independent calculations by myself and Wolfgang von Hippel on Württemberg and regions within it, based on the size of the population and weighting for age, suggest that around a third of available labour power would have been needed in arable agriculture outside of the harvest time. In the latter, nigh on all available labour would have had to be employed. Viticulture, dairying and livestock all used considerably less. However,

had to be worked, 'as the daily needs required, appropriate to each place, the time and weather'.[58] Harvesting efforts, that might take three to five 'labour-days' per *morgen*, had to be completed swiftly when the crop was in the right condition. If it was allowed to become damp, sprouting could occur and mould set in, and the summer months often saw the highest precipitation and were prone to storms. One did not have to possess a very large holding before most households would require extra-familial labour. Even the apparently more sedate pace of other kinds of work, such as ploughing or weeding, could be subject to pressures to speed efforts forward. Many arable farmers did not have a plough, and would have to borrow or hire one; draught livestock were (relative to the number of users) in short supply, and the weather and pests governed when work had to be completed.[59]

This must have been a considerable incentive for many households to retain servants, guaranteeing their labour when required, despite the costs of keeping them over the year. As landholding and arable farming remained fairly widespread among the population, such problems were not so easily solved by simple recourse to free labour and equipment markets. At the critical junctures, there might not be enough to go round without some kind of co-operation, servants aside. This was sometimes explicitly laid out in village or municipal field orders. Bietigheim's statutes stipulated, for instance, that the tenant farmers were obliged to plough, harrow and perform carting for the cotters and artisans, while the cotters and day-labourers were obliged in turn to work for the farmers and artisans.[60] In some places the farmers providing seedcorn and equipment were paid in kind with the crops they had sown. This meant that if profit margins were low, the smallholders who had hired the larger farmers' plough-teams might not have anything left after they had paid them![61] In this curious situation, it was the poor who bore the risk, not the owner of capital. Village officials watched the entire process carefully, especially to determine when the harvest should

---

harvest times could still have found a bottleneck in supply, accounting for the famous reluctance of parents to allow their children to attend school in the summer. Von Hippel, 'Bevölkerung und Wirtschaft'; Landwehr, *Policey im Alltag*, pp. 220–1.

[58] A quotation of the agronomist Abraham von Thumbshirn, in his *Oeconomia*, p. 83. It should also be noted that in early twentieth-century Württemberg, 37 per cent of days from March to late October on average saw rain, snow or lying snow. Precipitation was probably higher at times in the late sixteenth and seventeenth centuries. Thus quite large parts of the agricultural year would have been unsuitable for many kinds of work. Peasants would at least have had a strong preference for avoiding work on those days. Kleinschmidt, 'Klima und Witterung', p. 77.

[59] See chapter 2 on the possession of agricultural equipment.

[60] Grees, *Ländliche Unterschichten*, p. 45.   [61] Ibid., p. 44.

begin and how it should proceed. Of course the dates could not be laid down beforehand; it was merely stipulated in Gebersheim in 1594 that the gateways or openings in fencing were to be open at the appropriate times for sowing or harvest.[62]

Ploughing presented one of the more prominent 'co-ordination' problems for early modern landowners. In the Strohgäu it was predominately done with horse-teams during the sixteenth and seventeenth centuries.[63] It is unlikely that a plough-team could cover more than half a hectare in a day; this was the girdle put around the rural world, the stolid pace of a civilisation. A survey from 1708 provides us with numbers of horses and oxen (the alternative draught power) held by each settlement in the *Amt* Leonberg.[64] Only three places are heavily or entirely reliant on oxen. Given that a third of the arable (preparing the field for the winter or spring sowing) was ploughed at any one time, we can calculate how long it would take to complete each ploughing given the draught power available, although this assumes healthy, fit animals being used to their optimum. It is likely in practice that plough-teams were not of equal size, as heavier soils required more power. However, assuming three horses to a plough-team, as did the tax instructions of 1738, we can see the task taking between three and fourteen days depending on the settlement.[65] Most places probably ploughed three times during the year.[66] Three ploughings would take on average twenty-seven days among those places entirely reliant upon horses. This does not take into account tired animals, nor breaks enforced by

---

[62] HStAS A584 Bü 832.

[63] Horses were considered more flexible and much faster workers. Given the constraints on labour it is not surprising that a faster draught beast was prized. They could also perform a wider variety of tasks, and older horses could be bought for a relatively cheap price by poorer peasants, because the horse had little value after death. See Abel, *Geschichte der deutschen Landwirtschaft*, p. 224; Langdon, 'Animal power'.

[64] HStAS A368L Bü 136.

[65] The by-laws of Leonberg speak of teams of either two horses or three to four horses in 1582. This may imply different weights of plough, as the larger teams were permitted to go over a furrow only once, presumably to prevent a 'redistribution' of drainage patterns in the strips, although deeper ploughing would protect from soil erosion. HStAS A572 Bü 41; Reyscher, *SWG*, Bd.XVII., p. 502; Blaikie and Brookfield, *Land degradation*, p. 135.

[66] Although by the eighteenth century, Kornwestheim ploughed four times. Löchgau, just north of Bietigheim, had five ploughings 1659/60, but this is probably the upper limit; villagers near Eberbach and Mosbach north of Heilbronn tended to plough three times, once in the summerfield (before St George's day) and the fallow twice or three times before sowing winter corn, although some areas turned the summerfield in autumn so frost could break up clods of soil over the winter. Bentzien, *Bauernarbeit im Feudalismus*, pp. 105–6; Kollnig, *Weistümer*, pp. 171–2, 196, 397.

the weather. We can see how important effective reciprocal arrangements could be to get the work done in a timely fashion.[67]

Arable farming was thus locked into a series of collectively regulated and reciprocal arrangements to try and ensure labour and draught power availability at important junctures during the year. But did this collective effort ensure a sustainable output? Data on yield comes from a number of sources. Petitions and government reports from the second half of the sixteenth century and early seventeenth century report the level of spelt yields in the east of the region at five to six *Scheffel* per *morgen*, with a petition from 1655 claiming a level just half that in Mönßheim in the north-east.[68] Of course harvests varied from year to year and between settlements. The plough did not turn the soil to any great depth, making the crops prone both to drying-out, or swift waterlogging depending on the weather.[69] Tithe data from a few settlements in the *Amt* Leonberg in 1605–6 and 1629–30 (when the same fields would have been under the same crop according to the three-course rotation) give a range from 4.4 to 8.5 *Scheffel* per *morgen* for spelt, and 2.2 to 7 *Scheffel* per *morgen* for oats.[70] As is presented in figure 1.1, in the late sixteenth century the hospital of Markgröningen's demesne fields often achieved yields of over eight *Scheffel* per *morgen* for spelt, although in bad years it could be only a little over two. The post-war period, when the land was mostly sharecropped, saw lower yields.

Oat yields show a similar downward trend, displayed in figure 1.2. The seeding rate was around 0.75–1 *Scheffel* per *morgen* with spelt, so these seed to yield ratios varied between about 1:4 up to an impressive 1:8 or 9.[71] Perhaps less reliable figures recorded in the accounts of the

---

[67] This ranges from nine (Leonberg) to forty-two (Gebersheim) days.
[68] HStAS A34 Bü 21; A230 Bü 97; A261 Bü 1226; See also Boelcke's work on Kornwestheim, in Boelcke, 'Die Grundbesitzverhältnisse', p. 8.
[69] Achilles, *Landwirtschaft*, p. 22.   [70] HStAS A302 Bd.7046, 7050.
[71] StAM Spitalrechnungen H19–35, 49–73, 75, 77–8, 97–8, 102–3, 107–8, 117–8. The demesne farm was worked by hospital employees and waged labour until the Thirty Years' War, then sharecropped from the early 1640s with a brief interlude of demesne farming. The lands were given over to fixed rents in the 1670s, and consequently no more yield data is available. The extent of the land cropped with particular cereals varied somewhat, explaining short-term but not long-term variation in the yield. The harvest of the very cold year of 1573 saw surprisingly good yields for spelt, for example, but this may have been due to a low acreage of spelt being sown that year and a larger than usual proportion of rye as the winter crop being sown. However, the downward trend in yields is not explained by sowing rates that showed relatively little variation. Inputs of labour and manure may provide an explanation, although the trend also follows the long-term shift in temperatures that declined over the seventeenth century.

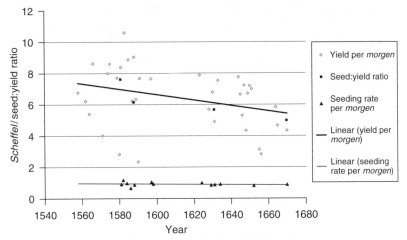

Source: StAM Spitalrechnungen H19–35, 49–73, 75, 77–8,
97–8, 102–3, 107–8, 117–8.

Figure 1.1 Spelt yields of the hospital of Markgröningen

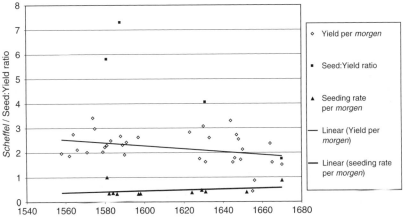

Source: StAM Spitalrechnungen H19–35, 49–73, 75, 77–8,
97–8, 102–3, 107–8, 117–8.

Figure 1.2 Oat yields of the hospital of Markgröningen

University of Tübingen's titheholdings in the region from the early seventeenth century suggest spelt yields of 4–6 *Scheffel* per *morgen*.[72]

These figures can be compared with taxation returns from 1718–23 that supposedly assessed land according to its productivity over a

[72] Ernst, *Wirtschaftliche Ausstattung*, pp. 33 & 71; see also the figures cited in Fertig, *Lokales Leben*, p. 307.

number of years. If we calculate from the 'thirtieth' of the gross yield over six years recorded by tax assessors, we find that on average yields were probably little different from the levels around 1600. The mean across the settlements was as little as 3.8 *Scheffel* per *morgen*.[73] The tax instructions issued by central government reckoned on yields from 3 *Scheffel* per *morgen* on the poorest ground to 8 *Scheffel* on the best across the whole of the Duchy, and thus the estimates presented here for the district of Leonberg seem broadly in line with the expectations of the authorities, if a little on the low side.[74] Yields in the east of the region closer to the Neckar were undoubtedly higher, with a return of around 1:5 or 1:6 to seed sown, although seeding rates varied considerably according to the ground. Spelt crops gave perhaps 11 hectolitres per hectare (10–13 English bushels) after threshing, and so the region compared relatively favourably with yields in eastern France, England and the inland districts of the Low Countries around 1600. By the eighteenth century, these yields are falling behind more dynamic regions in England and Lorraine.[75] If anything, however, these are underestimates. Whilst local communities pleaded that the method of calculation exaggerated the fertility of their ground, it seems rather unlikely that they consistently gave overassessments of their harvest to tax officials. The 1710s and 1720s yields, however, were being obtained from a cultivated area that was for the most part larger than in the early seventeenth century.

In these circumstances, was even stability something of a success? There are signs that the arable expansion was pushing the limits of the possible.[76] Firstly, as we have seen, it seems that some of the taxable ground was not actually being sown. Villagers put this down to land that had been abandoned, in practice, ever since the Thirty Years' War, or that suffered from being on the edge of woodland and exposed to wild boar and deer. At the end of the 1720s, excessive rainfall washed away the topsoil in places and damaged fertility. Some land that had been reclaimed 'now gives no [crop] or almost nothing more, but for the most part has been left fully waste, and is no longer to be cultivated'. In Hirschlanden this was blamed on insufficient livestock, meaning

---

[73] HStAS A261 Bü 1134.   [74] Reyscher, *SWG*, Bd.XVIII, p. 359.
[75] For comparison, see the chapters in Bavel and Thoen, *Land productivity*.
[76] Georg Fertig also notes a rapid expansion of the arable land in the early eighteenth century in Göbrichen, just over the border in neighbouring Baden. He does not consider there to be any kind of 'limit' in this society or ecology, however, although this judgement is predicated upon the incidence of mortality crises and migration. He also considers only mean estimates of harvest size *per capita*, rather than looking at the more pressing problem of *variability*. Fertig, *Lokales Leben*, pp. 291, 310–12.

that 'the arable fields cannot be improved'.[77] Hirschlanden did indeed
have a rather low ratio of livestock to arable land, and had to stall-feed
its beasts, a situation seen as a grave disadvantage in a world where
fodder crops were not grown.[78] Expansion may indeed have dragged
down the average yields somewhat after an initial 'store' of soil nutrients in the newly ploughed land was exhausted. The relatively
depressed prices of the 1720s may also have proved a disincentive to
farm marginal land.

In 1622, the ducal government took surveys to assess the extent of
'reserves' available to feed the population during the crisis years of
inflation at the beginning of the Thirty Years' War. These contain estimates taken locally of the amount available for sale in each settlement in
the *Ämte* Leonberg and Canstatt, and indeed, give the size of the harvest
itself in Zuffenhausen (where the yield appears to have been about 4
Scheffel per *morgen*). It is apparent from this that few places had surplus
spelt that could be 'exported', and most places were running a deficit
between what wealthy farming households considered surplus and the
requirements of those who had no land on which to grow their own
food.[79] This picture (in a middling harvest year) may be misleading,
however, as the 'non-surplus' including household requirements
included both wages in kind that went to labourers, and dues and
rents owed to landlords. Only the dearth years of the early 1570s, that
saw extremely high prices and famine across much of northern and
central Europe, seem to have brought about very large shortfalls.[80]
Generally the region could feed itself and villages of the 'grain basket'
of the east could export.

To ensure the work was done in a timely fashion, payments in kind
were built into a system of reciprocal relations, regulated by the officials
of the village commune both to minimise disputes over access to the
scattered strips, and ensure effective labour allocation. Co-operation

---

[77] HStAS A261 Bü 1134. Soil erosion has not generally been considered a widespread
problem in the early eighteenth century. Bork's extensive studies of central Europe attri-
bute erosion events, where they occurred, to severe inundations, especially on exposed
slopes. However, exposure through cultivation can have deleterious effects and the 1710s
and 1720s were wet decades. Land that was often fallowed or temporarily cultivated was in
fact more vulnerable than cropped land, as the storms that triggered erosion were most
frequent in the summer when crops were ripening in the fields and thus protected topsoil
from erosion. See Bork et al., *Landschaftsentwicklung*, pp. 225, 251; Blaikie and Brookfield,
Land degradation, pp. 122–42.
[78] HStAS A368L Bü 136.   [79] HStAS A237a Bü 580, 586.
[80] Settlements in the region were forced to take on large amounts of debt to import grain.
The Estates also used their position to obtain large amounts of credit secured by taxation
and imported grain. StAL Armenconsignation 1574; Reyscher, *SWG*, Bd.XII,
pp. 416–19; Ginschopff, *Chronica*, pp. 93–5; Abel, *Massenarmut*, pp. 84–98.

that to some degree was enforced via social norms and expectations provided a mechanism to ensure that all of the village land was effectively used, though 'optimally' would be overstating the case. It ensured that the work got done. This supervised system undoubtedly was a brake on certain forms of innovation. One had to abide by the rules of the spring and winter sowing, though it was quite possible, if seed could be obtained, to vary which crops were sown on one's strips within this system. Enclosure and sowing of the fallow was strongly discouraged. However, a considerable incentive to keep things this way was to simplify the systematic folding of sheep on the arable land to replenish soil nutrients through their urine and dung. 'Sheep-corn' systems, where the sheep primarily pastured upon grass, did not easily lend themselves to a transition to stall-feeding using fodder crops and collecting manure from the stalls, as could be done with cows. This again serves to remind us of the degree to which livestock were essential to arable agriculture, and the degree to which corn was dependent on the 'recycling technology' of animal husbandry.

Livestock

Unlike the plant world, animals imposed an immediate daily routine upon the world. Early in the morning, whether the hour was still dark in the winter or cool and clear with the promise of heat in the summer, hay boxes might be cleaned, stalls cleared out, and brews made of all the offcuts of human consumption, straw or hay were given to the beasts. Animals had to be washed once every few days. The inhabitants of Renningen could water their livestock beside the mill on the Maisgraben from vespers on Saturday night until the church service on the Sunday.[81] After initial feeding and thirst quenching, most of the beasts, from oxen and horses down to geese, would be handed over to the responsibility of the herders (often with the aid of children or youths) and driven out in the communal herd in all but the most adverse of weather. As soon as spring came to Renningen, the animals, maybe gaunt with the bones showing through their hide after a hard winter as Johann Steeb noted in the Swabian Alps in the 1790s, were out from half ten in the morning until lunch, and out again after two o'clock until the evening. Grazing overnight with the communal herd was barred in Leonberg without the *Bürgermeister*'s permission, although some places had special

---

[81] HStAS 572 Bü 69; see also Grosser, *Anleitung zu der Landwirtschaft*, p. 39.

Auchtwiesen (usually for the larger beasts that had been used for farm work during the day) for this purpose.[82]

The main sites for grazing, the open pasture and woodland, meadows, fallow and stubble, were utilised to different extents over the year. In Renningen, where more detailed records of practice remain in the *Fleckenbuch* ('village-book' of ordinances and field orders), sheep had priority on the stubble for the first two weeks, then the other animals. The meadows were of course a vital source of hay, a winter fodder, and had to be given time free of grazing to allow the grass to grow. Sheep were banned from them after St George's day in Hemmingen, to exploit the period of maximum grass growth in May. Usually there were two or three cuts of hay, and the communal authorities could be determined enough to make sure sufficient fodder was put by that meadow owners were fined if they had not harvested, after which the meadows passed under communal control. The hay harvests from late June needed dry weather, to prevent mould or rotting in storage.[83]

As discussed above, settlements set limits to the number of livestock that could be held, a 'village stint'. This was recorded for many villages in 1552 after instructions in the 'state ordinance' of that year and again after the promulgation of the ducal 'butcher's ordinance' in 1554. Although the latter explicitly mentioned that this number could be adjusted according to how many could be held 'in stalls or brought out in the communal grazing,' the stinting of 1552 gave some the impression that these levels were to be permanent.[84] The final level was to be decided by the village court, district officials and the ducal '*Zahlmeister*' who oversaw sheep flocks in the Duchy, and fines were levied per beast for transgressions. In Leonberg the town jurors then allotted the permitted total among the inhabitants according to their wealth.[85] It appears that the levels set largely survived right up until the eighteenth century. However, the 1552 measures were clearly a response to disputes arising from the transhumant sheep flocks held at ducal sheep stations taking grazing from local

---

[82] HStAS A572 Bü 69; A572 Bü 41; Steeb, *Verbesserung der Kultur*, p. 32.

[83] The meadows began to grow again after winter when the temperature reached 8 °C, with a peak around 13°–14 °C, during the daytime in May, trailing off to half this maximum by high summer. Two harvests took advantage of the fact that the taller the grass grew, the less became its nutritional value per weight. Damp or sprouting (from high heat encouraging development) hay loses its texture and aroma, factors encouraging the cattle to consume it. HStAS A572 Bü 69; A583 Bü 262; Pfister, *Bevölkerung*, pp. 39–42.

[84] HStAS A348 Bü 5; Ernst, 'Geschichte', p. 366; Reyscher, *SWG*, Bd.XII., pp. 259–64, 827–8.

[85] HStAS A572 Bü 41.

communities, and thus should not be seen as a response to a general 'overgrazing' problem. The ducal government backed the 'discrete' ethos of village ordinances and barred sheep with owners from outside the *Markung* running with the village herd, and also banned people from having sheep folded on land they owned in a *Markung* other than the one in which they resided.[86] Various scholars have hypothesised that such stinting in the early modern period reflected a 'carrying capacity', the establishment of a sustainable relationship between the number of livestock and the fodder available for them within the *Markung*. Whether this really can be the case when population levels, and the area under cultivation, could fluctuate so much over the succeeding 150 years must be open to doubt. It seems more likely that the levels set reflect an ossification of the grazing rights enjoyed in the middle of the sixteenth century. However, this did not necessarily present a problem, as livestock numbers were often, it seems, below the limits set in the 1550s. They were in any case adaptable and a survey of May 1700 shows an expansion in animal numbers in a few places.[87]

Although details of livestock numbers survive from some settlements from the late sixteenth century, 1622–3 and 1700, there is unfortunately little geographical overlap of these figures. Those from 1622–3 cover a broad swathe of the west and south-east of the *Forstamt*.[88] The information contained in these surveys is a stern warning against glibly conflating 'eco-types' and farming systems, because there is very little indication of geographical or ecological patterns. Only a few parameters stand out clearly. Goats, for example, are comparatively rare, and there is no sign that goats substituted for cow-keeping as was the case in some parts of Germany. The cattle herds are almost exclusively for dairying, pointing to a reliance on calves or imports for meat supplies.

We can examine this data in a number of ways. It should be remembered that these are figures aggregated at the level of the settlement, so whilst we can determine the mean number of beasts per household, this does not tell us the stocking rates of *actual* households. Firstly, we can simply look at the proportions of each type of animal within the livestock as a whole. In 1622 this does not show a strong geographical pattern, but

---

[86] Reyscher, *SWG*, Bd.XII., pp. 827–32.
[87] HStAS A368L Bü 91. See also variations from later and earlier 'stints' in Bietigheim in the 1680s, and given by Weitprecht for Leonberg in 1623. STABB Bh A1678; Weitprecht, 'Schreckentage', p. 2.
[88] HStAS A237a Bü 580, 601, 604.

Table 1.4 *Proportion of livestock types by settlement, 1622*

Place	Cows[a]	Calves	Sheep	Pigs	Goats	Oxen
Kornwestheim	27	N/A	55	17	0	0
Zuffenhausen	56	N/A	0	44	1	0
Münster	33	N/A	47	19	0	0
South-East	**39**	**–**	**34**	**27**	**0**	**0**
Merklingen	21	10	49	20	0	0
Gechingen	23	N/A	58	15	4	0
Hengstett	23	8	60	0	8	0
Simmozheim	21	5	53	19	2	0
Hausen	42	N/A	36	22	0	0
South-West	**31**	**–**	**51**	**15**	**3**	**0**
Dürrmenz	34	N/A	35	31	0	0
Wurmburg	17	1	68	14	0	0
Wiernsheim	26	4	49	10	11	0
Glattbach	20	8	48	20	3	0
Weissach	18	7	68	4	3	0
Flacht	15	8	67	9	1	0
Wimsheim	42	13	11	34	0	0
North-West	**30**	**–**	**49**	**17**	**3**	**0**

Note: [a] Where figures for calves are not given, the figure for cows incorporates them. It is not clear whether a calf is defined as up to a year old, or includes heifers, with a 'cow' defined after the first calving, usually after three years. Cattle appear to have been very few in number, if present at all. The mean figures for the proportion of cows by region are totals of cows and calves, or the number of cows where calves are not recorded.
Sources: HStAS A237a Bü 580, 601, 604.

shows that cows and calves typically made up a third of the village's herds, sheep between a third and two-thirds, and pigs the remainder.

The 1700 survey, shown in table 1.5, concentrated on the *Amt* Leonberg in the centre and south of the region, shows a rather higher bias towards sheep, with cows typically taking up between 13 and 36 per cent of the herd, but generally less than a quarter. As these figures exclude pigs, the true proportion is even lower. However, as these herds were little altered from the late sixteenth century, as can be seen comparing tables 1.5 and 1.6, the differences from the settlements examined in 1622 seem to arise from geographical variation rather than a change in herd structure over time. Although not a pronounced feature, there seems to be a rule of thumb in both surveys that the further west one goes, the less significant dairying relative to sheep-holding becomes. While a classic sheep–corn system predominated in the east of the

Table 1.5 *Sheep and cows in the* Amt *Leonberg, 1700*

Place	Cows[a]	Sheep[b]	Total	% Cattle	% Sheep
Leonberg	200	500	700	29	71
Eltingen	250	700	950	26	74
Warmbronn	80	200	280	29	71
Renningen	300	800	1100	27	73
Gerlingen	250	450	700	36	64
Ditzingen[c]	0	550	550	0	100
Weilimdorf	180	450	630	29	71
Gebersheim	40	250	290	14	86
Rutesheim	120	500	620	19	81
Mönßheim	80	500	580	14	86
Heimsheim	250	650	900	28	72
Münklingen	30	150	180	17	83
Höfingen	140	400	540	26	74
Hirschlanden	60	400	460	13	87
Schöckingen	60	350	410	15	85
Hemmingen	120	700	820	15	85
Heimerdingen	160	450	610	26	74
Total	**2320**	**8000**	**10320**	**22**	**78**
1622 Survey[d]				37	63

Notes:
[a] 'Cows' probably includes calves.
[b] As made explicit in Leonberger by-laws in 1582, it is likely that none of these figures included lambs.
[c] The cow numbers for Ditzingen are missing, and so the proportions are meaningless.
[d] The 1622 survey refers to the data in table 1.4, for a different set of settlements.
Sources: HStAS A368L Bü 91; A572 Bü 41.

Forstamt, there was more open pasture available in the west, allowing even larger flock numbers.

However, the picture provided simply by aggregating the number of beasts per settlement is potentially misleading. To assess the real import-ance of livestock holdings for the local economy, we must assess their size relative to the human population. If we examine the (notional) mean number of beasts per household, there is no clear geographical pattern either in the early seventeenth or eighteenth century. There seem to be villages that have relatively high stocking rates of all animals relative to population, and those with low rates. In other words, a concentration on cow-keeping or on sheep-farming do not seem to have been mutually exclusive alternatives. Cow-keeping was the most prevalent form of

Table 1.6 *Sheep and cows in the* Forstamt *Leonberg*

Place	Date	Cows	Sheep	% Cows	% Sheep
Bietigheim	1558	290	800	27	73
Groß Ingersheim	1558	320	850	27	73
Tamm	c.1540	N/A	450	N/A	N/A
Leonberg	1582	225	550	29	71
Leonberg and Eltingen	1552[a]	450	1200	27	73
Renningen	1552[a]	150	N/A	N/A	N/A
Renningen	1594[a]	300	800	16	84
Höfingen	1552[a]	120	400	23	77
Heimerdingen	1552[a]	160	450	26	74
Rutesheim	1552[a]	160	600	21	79
Warmbronn	1552[a]	80	0	100	0
Hirschlanden	1552[a]	40	400	9	91
Hemmingen	1552[a]	100	700	13	88
Heimsheim	1552[a]	150	500	23	77
Münklingen	1552[a]	25	300	8	92
Ditzingen	1552[a]	150	550	21	79
Weilimdorf	1552[a]	180	450	29	71
Gebersheim	1552[a]	40	250	14	86
Mönßheim	1552[a]	140	400	26	74
Gerlingen	1552[a]	255	455	36	64

Note: [a] The 1552 data is in fact an estimate. However, when they can be compared against other sources, the numbers appear to belong to the middle of the sixteenth century. 1552 was the date that the ducal government instructed all communities to record maximum livestock numbers permitted. The source for these figures is an undated 'pasture book' of the second half of the sixteenth century but it seems reasonable to assume that the data was collected in the 1550s. *Sources:* STABB Bh A1678, HStAS A348 Bü 5; A572 Bü 41; Ernst, 'Geschichte', p. 366.

livestock holding, enjoyed by about 60 per cent of households.[89] There is no sign of cattle numbers having increased over the period for which there is data, from the mid-sixteenth century. Given the expansion of the arable, albeit perhaps only irregularly cultivated, this implies a

---

[89] On the basis of data from this region and the *Amt* Göppingen. HStAS A237a Bü 580, 582, 601. The figures obtained from this household-by-household survey data from the 1620s can be compared with those presented by Andreas Maisch from inventories taken at marriage and death. We would expect the mean number of cows per inventory in Maisch's sample to be somewhat higher than in the 1622 and 1700 surveys, as inventory samples are generally biased towards the wealthier while my estimates are a mean drawn across the whole population. Of course if livestock holding was very concentrated (and the evidence of 1622 surveys taken household by household suggests that it was not), then Maisch's mean based on inventories might be somewhat lower than the figures above if it 'missed' the large stock-holders. As it happens, Maisch's figures from Bondorf and Gruorn tally reasonably well with the stocking rates drawn from the survey.

Table 1.7 *Mean livestock per* Bürger[a]

Place	Date	Cows[b]	Sheep	Pigs
Ditzingen	1700	–	3.6	–
Leonberg	1700	0.8	2.0	–
Mönßheim	1700	0.9	5.3	–
Münklingen	1700	1.0	4.8	–
Rutesheim	1700	1.3	5.3	–
Gerlingen	1700	1.3	2.4	–
Hirschlanden	1700	1.4	9.3	–
Gebersheim	1700	1.6	10.0	–
Höfingen	1700	1.8	5.0	–
Warmbronn	1700	1.8	4.4	–
Eltingen	1700	1.8	5.1	–
Heimerdingen	1700	2.0	5.5	–
Renningen	1700	2.0	5.3	–
Weilimdorf	1700	2.3	5.8	–
Heimsheim	1700	2.8	7.3	–
Hemmingen	1700	3.3	19.4	–
Wimsheim	1622	–	–	1.0
Flacht	1622	–	–	0.7
Weissach	1622	–	–	0.3
Dürrmenz	1622	–	–	1.1
Simmozheim	1622	1.0	2.1	1.3
Merklingen	1622	1.4	2.2	1.3
Kornwestheim	1622	1.5	3.1	1.3
Hengstett	1622	1.7	3.2	0.0
Zuffenhausen	1622	1.8	0.0	1.8
Hausen	1622	2.2	1.9	2.1
Münster	1622	2.4	3.4	1.3

Notes:
[a] Where available, the number of *Bürger* in 1622 is taken from population data from 1629/34.
[b] The column for cows includes calves.
Sources: HStAS A237a Bü 580, 582, 601; A368L Bü 91.

reduction of the stocking-rate per arable acre, helping to explain the stagnation of yields.

Does this imply that there was a 'carrying capacity' in terms of *fodder*, that the stocking densities set down represented the maximum that

However, his figure for Gebersheim is significantly lower. This suggests – but does not prove – that, if anything, the inventoried population (taken at marriage and death) underestimates the real number of livestock held. At marriage, herds had not yet been built up and at death, at least in relative old age, had already declined. Maisch, *Notdürftiger Unterhalt*, pp. 106–8.

could reasonably be maintained by local fodder supplies? This is very difficult to calculate. Although the dry fodder of preference was hay, if in short supply straw could always be used as a substitute. Equally, while we can assess the yield of meadowland through tax surveys of the early eighteenth century, the important grazing on open land and in woodland varied greatly in quality and is almost impossible to quantify. The density of canopy tree cover, for example, will have a very strong influence on the quality of pasture below. However, it appears to have been commonplace to ban the export of fodder from common land and sometimes hay and straw, so supply had to be local. As a 'fodder proxy' I have used both the area of meadowland, and more promisingly, the assessed tax value of meadowlands from a survey of 1713 as a way of determining the amount of *winter fodder* available – with the caveat that straw could always be used in addition.[90] The number of animals that could be held was determined by how many could be fed all the year round. The months without any grass growth when most of their nutrients would have to come from stores of hay and straw were the limiting factor in this regard.[91] Interestingly, the yields of many hay meadows were already as high as the yields obtained in the mid-nineteenth century.[92] There is *no* discernable relation between the availability of good quality fodder, or indeed the general area open to grazing, and the stocking density of livestock. While ecological factors clearly played their part, we cannot, on the basis of this evidence, talk of any discernable 'carrying capacities' of the *Markungen*. This in turn suggests that the reason for the relatively static number of cattle lies in the socio-economic structures and obtaining the wherewithal to purchase and maintain livestock on individual holdings.

The picture drawn is one of relatively static animal numbers between the late sixteenth and early eighteenth centuries, especially of cattle. At times, such as the Thirty Years' War and French invasions, these numbers undoubtedly experienced dramatic fluctuations. The levels do not seem to have been determined by any obvious ecological factors, although there are individual exceptions, such as Hausen, which was clearly orientated towards dairying with its rich meadows in the valley of the Würm. Many sheep flocks were part of a transhumant system that took them to summer pastures high in the Swabian Alps or the

---

[90] HStAS A261 Bü 1128. The tax records also give absolute figures of the range of yields per *morgen* obtained from the meadows of each settlement.

[91] See also Schlögl, *Bauern, Krieg und Staat*, p. 129.

[92] KSB, Stuttgart, Leonberg, Ludwigsburg, Marbach, Besigheim, Vaihingen. Most meadows yielded 20–30 quintals of hay per *morgen*, and approximately half that in math.

Black Forest, to remain there 'until the snow grips them' when they were brought back to winter byres in the Strohgäu. This system was particularly centred in the east of the region, where a shepherds' fair on St Bartholomew's survives in Markgröningen to this day. These flocks thus would not have been so limited, in any case, by local fodder stores and did not consume the product of the meadows.[93] While these results appear perhaps surprising when set against the expansion of cultivated acreages and meadowland, they may help explain why yields also seem to have changed little over this period. There does remain one explanation which this data cannot test: the numbers of livestock may not have increased, but the beasts could have become larger and better fed in the eighteenth century than they had been a century and a half earlier. As meadowland tended to expand between the early seventeenth century and the early eighteenth century, one would assume that the animals were better fed.

The most immediate resource gained from livestock was dairy products such as milk, cheese and, especially, *Schmalz*, a type of curd. The processing into other dairy products allowed the milk, predominantly obtained in the summer months, to be utilized all year round. The supply of milk did not solely depend upon dairy cows. The most numerous beasts were sheep, and after weaning these provided several weeks' worth of milk in the summer. In Hemmingen, two shepherds, one from the *Gemeinde* and one from the local lords, the Nippenburgs, organised the flocks of all of the villagers and the local lord. They could milk the sheep from two weeks before St John's (early June) until St Laurence's, about seven weeks later. The lower yields afterwards went to the owners of the sheep.[94] This provided income for the shepherds, and reflected their peculiar role in a grazing economy embracing common herds, sheepfolding and a degree of transhumance. In a trade-off, sheep owners received the right to have the sheep flock folded on their property for a few nights of the year, an important source of precious fertiliser. Goats, where kept, produced most of their milk from April to June. Cows provided much more (perhaps 5–6 litres a day), but the yield declined significantly after October.[95] The importance of flocks as fertilising agents was certainly one incentive for maintaining the practice of fallowing and communal management,

---

[93] Hornberger, *Die kulturgeographische Bedeutung*, pp. 42–8.
[94] HStAS A583 Bü 262; see also Ernst, 'Geschichte', p. 367.
[95] On milk yields, see Mathieu, *Bauern und Bären*, p. 77; Schlögl, *Bauern, Krieg und Staat*, p. 146; Pfister, *Bevölkerung*, pp. 43–8; Beck, *Unterfinning*, p. 257.

although there appears to have been little if any pressure to alter the system.[96]

The ducal surveys of 1622–3, assessing the reserves in the land, also took note of the other resources to be won from the livestock, such as tallow and meat. The latter was won either from old animals, the very young from large litters (especially of piglets) that would not be kept, or imports. The work of butchery was often done within the household although the authorities attempted, under pressure from lobbying, to ensure the use of butchers.[97] Slaughtered animals also provided hides to local tanners for leatherworking. And sheep, of course, provided wool to local spinners and weavers and more famously, especially in the second half of the seventeenth century, to the worsted industry based around Calw at the south-western edge of the *Forstamt* in the Black Forest.[98] This may explain the relative density of sheep-holding in the west of the region, and its apparent (though by no means certain) tendency to expand during the seventeenth century. Normal reproduction of livestock should have replenished numbers easily, but a cattle plague could be a real tragedy, taking years for recovery. Communal regulation of imported animals was consequently often tight, and from at least 1581 Leonberg had an official, the *Schaumeister*, responsible for disease prevention. This was probably a response to a ducal order of the same year.[99] If it came to it, stock might be slaughtered to prevent the spread of the pestilence.

The wood and the trees

The woodland generally stood towards the boundaries of the *Markung* or on steep slopes of little use for other purposes. This tallies well with theories that land use is dictated by labour intensity, as work in the woodland, though vital, was sporadic or so organised as to minimise costs, such as with the institution of the communal herd. Without the requirement to visit the woodland regularly (the communal herdsmen aside), it was best placed at a distance from settlement. The woodlands

---

[96] See Glaser and Schenk, 'Einflüssgrössen', p. 57. The rights of ducal sheep herds to graze over pasture and in sheepfolds may also have contributed to the ossification of numbers and stints, as any rise in the size of village herds would have reduced the pasture for the ducal sheep. However, the actual folding system and its maintenance appears to have been the responsibility of village authorities. See Bailey, 'Sand into gold'.

[97] Reyscher, *SWG*, Bd.II., p. 187; Bd.XII., pp. 264–5, 342 and 830.

[98] Ogilvie provides various examples of wool being traded from the *Forstamt* to the Calwer Moderation for worsted weaving. Ogilvie, *State corporatism*, pp. 99, 101, 104–5.

[99] HStAS A572 Bü 41; Reyscher, *SWG*, Bd.XII., p. 431.

will be examined in more detail in chapter 4, and only a brief sketch is provided here. The predominant woodland form was a scattering of mature oak trees over much of the *Forstamt*, surrounded by a young 'underwood' of oak, birch, hazel and other species. In a few places concentrations of beech, fir and pine could be found, especially to the south and west of the region. The predominance of oaks, in a region where the natural conditions and prevalence of species at this moment in time would lead one to expect a canopy of beech trees, reflects the varying pressures on the woodland, and indeed competition between users. It was the relatively open character of the woodlands and density of grazing animals that allowed the oak to flourish. Christoph Ernst has separated these forms of exploitation out analytically into what he calls the 'wood-production forest', the 'agricultural forest' and the 'hunting forest', to emphasise how these needs competed over one and the same space.[100] Yet even these can be further differentiated. 'Wood production', for example, was required for timber supplies, but also for fuel, wattle, hurdles and fencing. The condition of the woodland had to be finely balanced between all these different demands if they were all going to be satisfied locally. As will become clear, on many occasions this balancing act did not take place, and may not even have been seen as desirable.

Most woodland was managed in a form called 'coppice with standards' in English, or *Mittelwald* in German, although this term was not used at the time.[101] A standard is a mature tree, suitable when cut for building timber. Its broad canopy could also provide the seed for the forest to reproduce itself – and mast for the wild boar favoured by the nobility for hunting. In fact, these were often not all that old, but 'staddles', taller trees preserved against regular cuts of the 'underwood' in the hope of future maturity. The 'underwood' or 'coppicewood' consisted of poles that often re-grew from tree stocks or stools, being regularly cut back after several years. Some space was allowed between the stools, with frequent glades for grazing. The young poles of trees up to about thirty years' old would be cut back during the winter months to provide fuel, usually for the next year. This was by far the most widespread form of harvesting wood, supplying 70 per cent of that felled in the region as late as the nineteenth century.[102] Depending on the age of wood desired, a regular cycle could develop. The woodland was divided into as many 'coupes' or 'compartments' as the age in

[100] Ernst, *Den Wald entwickeln*, p. 16.
[101] On the development of forest nomenclature, see Bürgi, 'How terms shape forests'.
[102] KSB Leonberg, p. 47.

years at which it was considered desirable to cut the trees or prune back
the poles growing from stools. In this way, if one coupe was cut each
year in an ordered progression, a permanent harvest of the desired
kind of wood was guaranteed. Thus if cutting proceeded on a sixteen-
year cycle, the one most frequently practised by villagers, one would
divide the woodland into sixteen coupes, each one year older than the next.
The wood being cut from the eldest coupe each year would always be
sixteen years old. The younger coupes would be vulnerable to the
attentions of grazing animals and were usually protected by law, and
sometimes by ditches or thorn hedges.

This practice of 'coppicing' was in place in the woodlands of some
German cities in the thirteenth century, and seems also to have been in
place in the *Forstamt* Leonberg by the early sixteenth century, if not
earlier. It is difficult to assess, however, precisely what proportion of the
woodland was managed in this careful way, and what was simply
felled as demand occasioned it, and then left to its own devices to
regrow in a somewhat more rough and ready manner. Certainly communes practised coppicing to provide a set supply of fire- and fencing-
wood each year, distributing it free of charge to their *Bürger*. At the latest
by the 1580s and probably before, ducal forestry officials had a good
idea of when woodland was last cut and when it should next be so.[103]
The systematic 'compartmentalising' of the wood was probably comparatively rare outside of the woodlands owned by village and town communes, but some ducal woods were arranged in a series of 'young coupes
each younger than the other', as was the woodland called the Rotenacker
near Markgröningen in 1583. Extensive ducal woodlands that did not
have to supply an annual local demand were built into a wider 'system'
where forestry officials decided which woodland was best suited for
cutting each year. Over 80 per cent of the recorded woodland in 1583,
whether owned by communes, the duke or groups of private owners, was
allotted a date at which it could next be cut. The rest was either low-value
scrub or stands of mature trees. There was very little woodland where
individual peasants could 'cut as it pleases them'.[104] Usually however
there was no physical barrier around the woodland edge, though it was
sometimes marked by a ditch or fence (to keep game out of the fields,
rather than people out of the woods). The hanging of a sign, such as a
bale of straw, indicated particular coupes were out of bounds for grazing.
The forest was thus often not an open space where movement was

---

[103] See the very extensive records in HStAS A59 Bü 13a.   [104] HStAS A59 Bü 13a.

uninhibited and where records survive we have glimpses of some places where the specific permission of an official such as the *Bürgermeister* was required to harvest areas of wood.[105]

As with all woodcutting, harvesting coppice was generally a winter activity, though the coldest periods were avoided. The forester of Altensteig, a region to the south-west of the *Forstamt* of Leonberg, recommended the cutting of firewood between February and April in a report on woodmanship in 1605, avoiding the time when the wood might be frozen.[106] This comment may have been a specific response to a ducal complaint in November 1603 that coppices were being cut in mid-winter, allowing the stumps to freeze and damaging future yields.[107] I have no record of coppice being cut at this time of year in the *Forstamt* Leonberg, and such cutting may have been an emergency response to the cold and snow-rich winters at the beginning of that century. The responsibility to cut the wood nearly always fell to the person buying or receiving the wood, rather than the owner of the woodland. Village and ducal regulations regulated when this cutting time began and ended, and when grazing was possible. The wood ordinances of Münklingen and Leonberg both set St George's day (23 April) as the end of the cutting time.[108] The 1540 ducal forest ordinance stipulated St Edigius (1 September) to the end of March as felling time, while the far more comprehensive ducal forest ordinance of 1567 ordered its removal by St George's (or before the 'winter freeze' if cut in autumn). There was concern that leaving it lying would hinder regeneration of young shoots.[109] This issue remained a matter of dispute between the forester and the burghers of Leonberg, who found it impossible to remove their wood from the communal woodland in time. The haulage involved depended on factors such as the availability of wagons and carts and draught power to carry the wood, and the condition of the trackways. Very wet weather or the thaw could turn them into impassable, mud-blocked morasses.[110] The view offered by the account books of the forest administration shows a similar temporal division of labour. Some wood was cut in October but more generally the autumn was given over to surveying, measuring out coupes and organising sales and the rafting of wood to consumers downstream with the coming of higher waters. December and January offered the most suitable time for marking wood for specific demands like building

---

[105] HStAS A227 Bü 1143.   [106] HStAS A227 Bü 55.
[107] Reyscher, *SWG*, Bd.XVI., p. 202.   [108] HStAS A572 Bü 41; A368L Bü 85.
[109] Reyscher, *SWG*, Bd.XVI., pp. 10, 38, 251.
[110] Still a problem today! Reinhold Schaal, personal communication. HStAS A227 Bü 1139; A368L Bü 85.

or for cartwrights. The felling, cutting and binding proceeded from February through to April; sales were complete by May and the summer was given over to surveying the woodland, pursuing poachers and drawing up the accounts. The annual report on wood was to reach the authorities in Stuttgart by St Bartholomew's in mid-August.[111] Such a division of labour suited the agricultural economy, but also favoured stronger wood cut before the sap rose in spring.

Of course, there was more to wood resources than fire- and fencing-wood. However, mature timbers, usually used for construction, were felled on a much more occasional basis and there seem to have been very few areas of densely stocked mature timber, or *Hochwald*. There was also extensive exploitation of wood at the other end of the scale. Willows, cultivated along riverbanks and boggy valley-bottoms, were regularly pollarded and the thin rods used for basketweaving and binding material. Similarly, the young shoots and switches of trees were harvested very extensively for the use of binding sheaves during the harvest. Communes went *en masse* to both cut and purchase tens of thousands of these switches each year, a practice that the forest administration considered to be particularly damaging to woodland regeneration, as the wholesale removal of switches prevented any developing into young saplings. Other woody plants like broom had their obvious use, whilst the bast could be utilised for ropemaking, and oak bark was an important source of tannin for tanners. Alder bark was used by dyers. There is little direct evidence of these activities except for prohibitions; bast-making in the woodland, for example, was banned in 1540.[112] It is likely that such goods were otherwise easily obtained in communal or private woodland as required. According to the ducal ordinances trees should be stripped of their bark for tanners when the sap was still rising, so long as the wood was to be felled anyway. Nevertheless the forester complained in 1612 that villagers from Feuerbach took no notice of this, compounding the error of their cutting of mature trees here and there as it suited them rather than maintaining managed stands.[113]

The woodland, however, was more home to herders and shepherds than it was to woodcutters who came in at certain times of the year. When in 1568 Melchior Bosch of Ottenbronn described the woodlands near Hengstett as 'almost a pasture' to ducal officials, he was describing

---

[111] HStAS A368 Bü 40, A572 Bü 41, A227 Bü 55, A227 Bü 1139; A302 Bds.7221, 7222, 7223, 7226; Reyscher, *SWG*, Bd.XVI., p. 10, 38, 202 and 251.
[112] Reyscher, *SWG*, Bd.XVI., p. 11.
[113] HStAS A227 Bü 1154. Reyscher, *SWG*, Bd.XVI., pp. 11 and 274.

a situation common to many 'woodlands' of the region.[114] As we have
seen, it appears that the numbers of animals grazed altered little, on
balance, over time. The herds, largely under the supervision of communal herders, often had broad rights to wander beyond the boundaries of the *Markung*. There were of course protected coupes that varied
from year to year depending on the state of the underwood. Herders
and shepherds were in a curious position; although usually paid communal officials, they were nevertheless often socially poor and marginal in communities, despite their role overseeing a considerable
proportion of the commune's 'variable capital', as an economist
would say.[115] Their presence in the woodland put them under obvious
suspicion of causing unnecessary wastage both through foraging practice and superfluous felling. Equally, to perform their task most effectively, there was always the temptation to take advantage of the best
grazing to be had, which was to be found in the protected coupes. This
dilemma was perhaps recognised in the forest ordinances, which stipulated that it was the commune that was to be fined if the communal
herd 'strayed' into such coupes. The administration also worried about
their propensity to cut wood on the sly or start fires, and barred them
from taking dogs into the woodland that might be useful for rounding
up animals or protection, but also chased the prey reserved for ducal
hunting.[116] Woodland pasture was a summer activity, especially for
cattle that required reasonably good grass growth. Only in late spring
and summer was the growth verdant enough to make it worthwhile;
indeed, the shadier woodland also kept animals cool and preserved
pasture that could otherwise wither in the summer heat. If excess rain
was usually the problem for arable land, it was drought that plagued
the pasture.[117] The Renningen herders were to guide the herd out every
day into the bare fields and woods unless it was snowing or raining.[118]
As was common all over Europe, however, there was sometimes a ban
on the holding of the extremely voracious – and consequently very eco-
nomical – goat, not only in ducal ordinances, but also those of the town of
Leonberg.[119] The shepherd, swineherd or cowherd was thus a woodland

---

[114] HStAS A368 Bü 31.

[115] The cowherd of Warmbronn had to provide a surety of no less than 50 fl. to guard
against neglect of duty. HStAS A572 Bü 56.

[116] HStAS H107/8 Bd.1.

[117] See for example the petitions of Bietigheimers who were excluded from pasture in the
forest during a dispute in the dry summer of 1718. HStAS A557 Bü 91.

[118] HStAS A572 Bü 69.

[119] HStAS A572 Bü 41. Barring goats may also have acted as a disincentive to in-migration
by the poor.

character who appears many times going about his business, as a witness
or transgressor of the forest ordinances. Equally their spatially peripheral
tasks brought them into conflict with neighbouring communes and
officials.[120]

Another widespread activity, somewhat more flexible for most
households than letting animals run with the communal herd, was for
peasants to cut the fodder themselves and use it in more trying times of
the year. Just as with pasturing animals directly, the temptation always
existed to venture into protected coupes to cut the longer grass, and this
appears regularly in lists of transgressors and fines in the forest account
books. In Münchengen, at least, this practice was done collectively,
though not *officially* under the *Gemeinde*, and became more orderly
over time, whilst its importance was asserted in 1629 because of the
'shortage of other fodder'. The local authorities in Münchengen also
stated that for at least a century the young two-to-three-year-old coupes
were opened to grazing animals and for mowing after Whitsun celebrations, but for the last three decades or so this had been discontinued
because of damage to the wood. Instead people could only cut grass with
a sickle on Whitsun and in the presence of the village wood warden, who
fined those who damaged the shoots of young trees. This did not
impress the forester Hans Ulrich Bauder who came across, by his
account, some two hundred people cutting whilst he was riding
through the wood. He considered the warden to be too old (though
probably not one hundred, as he claimed!) to be effective, and pointed
to the impossibility of overseeing every sickle, especially when children
were there who would fail to understand the damage they were causing.
The villagers pointed out that the previous forester, Hans Ulrich's
own father, had permitted this, and said that no one thought it caused
much damage. Hans Ulrich could only hope that his father hadn't
turned a blind eye and continued to admonish the villagers. The forest
ordinances considered such cutting of grass in young coupes as damaging as the cutting of switches to bind the sheaves.[121]

We are much better informed about the practice of 'pannage' or
'mast', that is, allowing pigs to graze on fallen acorns and beechmast,
collecting these by hand, or encouraging the process by knocking them
off the trees with long poles. This was claimed as a prerogative of the
Duke that had to be specifically granted and that was permitted only on

---

[120] In 1536, for example, the herders of Weilimdorf, Feuerbach and Kaltental were seized
and gaoled by Stuttgarters, although the Duke eventually ruled that they were not in the
wrong. HStAS A368 Bü 12.
[121] HStAS A227 Bü 1166.

a payment to the forest administration. Certain places were exempted from this stipulation, several having wrung out a concession during the Poor Conrad rebellion that they could take the acorns without explicit permission.[122] Such a privilege probably dates back to an age when the lordship over the forest was primarily a hunting concern, and the pannage was considered important for the sustenance of the animals hunted by the nobility. Where required, permission did not come automatically in a pannage year; in 1618 the rich harvest around Leonberg was reserved for the wild boar, much to the annoyance of neighbouring communes. Pannage years only occurred intermittently but they were valued by the peasantry not only as a source of fodder, but also because the tannin in acorns staved off diarrhoea in the pigs, and above all improved the quality of the meat. Contrary to a belief widespread among historians, pannage was nowhere near sufficient for the keeping of pigs in its own right. They were largely fed from the waste of the grain economy. Occurrence of a good mast year was a regional phenomenon and appears to have been climatically influenced, with the early part of the year being critical.[123]

The period for the pannage was set down for ducal woods in 1556 from St Michael's day to St Andrew's, although as late as 1707 the *Bürgermeister* of Bietigheim complained that their pannage had always been permitted beyond this date.[124] In Renningen's own communal woods it lasted until Christmas. 1604–5 appears to have been a good pannage year across the *Forstamt*, and sales of pannage for 748 pigs made up 14 per cent of the income of the forestry administration. This was not a regular income, however, as in 1585–6 nothing came in, although it was a useful fiscal boost when present.[125]

An alternative or accompaniment to actually driving the pigs into the woods was for the peasants to collect the acorns and bring them back to the farm sty. Sometimes this simply involved gathering up baskets or sacksful of fallen fruit, but at others active encouragement, either by shaking trees or knocking the acorns off with long poles. This was a task overwhelmingly done by youth, both male and female. Shaking the trees to speed up the process was considered harmful – especially, according to the old forest warden of Groß Ingersheim, to young oaks – and banned by both ducal and some communal ordinances. Such practices, although illegal, were nevertheless widespread. When old Ulrich Bauder

---

[122] HStAS H107/8 Bd.1.
[123] HStAS H107/8 Bd.1; A227 Bü 1159; See Schenk, 'Eichelmastdaten'; Beck, *Unterfinning*, p. 143.
[124] HStAS A557 Bü 91.   [125] HStAS A572 Bü 69; A302 Bd.7221–2.

arrived to survey the Brandholz and Vorstwald between the Ingersheims and Bietigheim towards the end of September 1605, he found much damage to the oaks by an assault that had been done 'almost as a commonality'.[126] Woodland was in any case difficult to police. To prevent widespread flouting of regulations in the woodland around Stuttgart in 1618 the *Vogt* had to resort to instructing gatekeepers to prevent any acorns entering the city! This year too, nineteen households from Botnang were caught, and although only four from Heslach, the herders of nearby Plieningen, who had in fact been awarded the pannage by ducal authorities that year, accused the Heslachers of collecting 'as a commonality' (*'in gemein'*).[127]

At both the level of village authorities and central government, efforts were made to create a 'woodland system' that matched and complemented the regulatory impulses that controlled cultivated space. The mechanisms were relatively similar. A woodland 'space' was created which was to be governed by a particular set of rules and rights. Within that space, however, various interests competed which prevented it from being wholly dedicated to any one form of use, whether the production of types of wood or woodland products, grazing, game, and so forth. The complexities generated by this were to be overseen by the region's ducal forest administration organised into 'forest districts' (*Forstämter*), with a forester, and smaller wards with a forest warden (*Forstknecht*). Communes with communally owned woods had their own locally appointed wardens. These officials oversaw limits set on time (set days for wood-cutting or pannage, the 'hanging' of young coupes, that is, putting up signs barring grazing animals from entry) and the forms of the resource (which trees were to be cut for what uses). How this worked out in practice over time will be the subject of chapters 3 and 4. It is important again to remember that this 'system' did not entail the creation *ex nihilo* of smoothly functioning rules and principles, but rather was an attempt to reconcile competing claims and reduce the complexity and likely disputatiousness arising from everyday activity. Not all such activity was regulated, but only that which seemed to warrant clear guidelines to the regulators. As a result regulation was prone to contestation, but was broadly recognised as a necessity and enforced by all levels of authority. Certainly during the sixteenth and seventeenth centuries it would be wrong to distinguish any governmental and 'peasant' *mentalités* that disagreed sharply over the management of the woodlands.

---

[126] HStAS A227 Bü 1147.   [127] HStAS A227 Bü 1159; A227 Bü 1160.

While we can detect a general simplifying of life brought about by these practices, we can also distinguish particular advantages of this mode of operation. The multiple uses to which wooded space was put could be regulated by assigning it all to the legal category 'woodland' and dividing its use up temporally. This, as with the regulation of the open fields, was a considerable labour saving, especially given that the rentability of woodland was considerably lower than that of any cultivated ground and would not have borne the costs of tighter and hence more expensive controls. Management of underwood in a coppicing system made some progress, though with patchy success, towards ensuring a sustainable supply of wood, primarily for fuel. At the same time, from an economist's perspective, we could argue that the delineation of the woodland and the rules requiring its sustainable maintenance meant that an economic asset could not so easily be whittled away by those who did not bear the costs of depreciation. Indeed, the process of demarcation – which emerges on a grand scale in a woodland survey of 1556 but that in many areas dated back at least until the latter part of the fifteenth century – ensured the relative stability of woodland area itself, as once demarcated the responsible authorities were generally reluctant to hand over the ground to other uses. It was not the area of woodland that varied over time, but the quantity and quality of resources that could be obtained from it.

Viticulture

Viticulture was not a universally important presence in the region, and vineyards were always excluded from the grazing regime. In this regard it stands outside the management of other agrarian spaces and has been left to last, although successful viticulture still depended on the application of manure to the soil and the timely employment of labour. However, although the most prominent force in the economy was arable farming, the growing of grapes and the production of wine was still a major activity. In 1599 the Estates of Württemberg declared that viticulture was 'far and away the most prominent source of income for the subjects of this Duchy'. Already in the fifteenth century, Stuttgart was ranked as the 'third wine city of the Empire'.[128] Viticulture was a vital source of cash income, especially export income. It offered some settlements more options in their economic development or strategies for survival and enrichment, and through commercialisation

---

[128] Schröder, *Weinbau*, pp. 52–3; Kießling, 'Markets and marketing', p. 157.

the potential for earnings that might transcend the 'limited goods' of the arable economy. Viticulture has been held up as one avenue by which an economy with tight margins can squeeze more returns, especially cash, out of otherwise marginal land. However, the investment required was considerable by the standards of the day, because although little equipment was required, vines took several years to properly mature and bring a yield. Vineyards were also relatively expensive to purchase, although they subsequently required less capital input (in the form of ploughs, carting etc.) than arable land.[129]

As a consequence, two tenurial forms seemed to develop to deal with this expense. Either newly cleared vineyards were almost entirely rent free and were held as a type of freehold (we have already seen that they took up a low proportion of ducally owned property), or they were held by sharecroppers, where landlords provided the capital for a share of the crop that ranged from a seventh to as high as a half.[130] This did, however, share the risk of variable grape harvests, and as in this region sharecropping as a form of tenure was for the most part found only in vineyards, it seems likely that this was a response to ecological factors rather than the development of the forms of 'debt peonage' that characterised the social order of parts of southern Europe.[131] However, for the smallest landowners, who in Leonberg at least often held no other property except for vineyards, sharecropping could indeed be a form of debt peonage where the share, though relatively low risk, was an expensive way of obtaining capital. The 'owner' would 'sell' the vineyard to the creditor, who then conveyed it back for an annual share of the yield. The 'seller', in fact the 'owner', always had the right of redemption so this mortgage arrangement was not 'true' sharecropping. Vineyards owned by wealthier landowners were frequently cultivated by professional vinedressers for a fixed annual sum.[132]

These options were more pertinent in the settlements in the east of the *Forstamt* along the Neckar. While they brought income-earning potential, they still demanded export of precious biomass beyond the *Markung*. In the areas around the Glems and westward, much lower quality grapes were produced that were often consumed locally in the form of *Most*, a coarse, sweet juice. By 1700, moreover, apple juice was increasingly taking over from local white wines as the drink of preference.

---

[129] Döbele-Carlesso, *Weinbau*, pp. 48–57.   [130] Bader, *Rechtsformen*, pp. 89–90.
[131] Wallerstein, *The modern world-system*, I, p. 190.
[132] Salzmann, *Weinbau und Weinhandel*, pp. 56–8; Döbele-Carlesso, *Weinbau*, pp. 73–7. On related credit arrangements on arable land, see Boelcke, 'Bäuerlichen Kreditwesens'.

Working an acre of vineyard took about twice as many labour-days per year than the equivalent area of arable – not, as has sometimes been claimed, up to eight times more labour input.[133] After the harvest, which generally took place in October but could be as late as November, the stakes supporting the vines were to be drawn out (the worst paid part of the entire process). The vines were then let to the ground and covered with earth to protect them against the winter. When times seemed to be propitious for growth in February or March, they were uncovered and any early shoots pruned. Not all vines would be so treated; it depended upon the susceptibility of the locality to frosts. General early spring work included clearing out drainage channels, repairing terraces and preparing the stakes again. The vines were bound to these stakes with willow-switches. At the end of May more intense work began, such as manuring, hoeing, and the binding of new shoots with straw to the stakes. This was the most labour-intensive part of the process outside of the harvest and had to be repeated several times until the grapes were ripe at the end of the summer. As with the arable harvest, the grape harvest was regulated by the authorities, allowing it to be done speedily by concentrating labour on the ripened areas, and preventing theft. It also concentrated the reception of the grapes into local winepresses, which were entirely ducally controlled. Treading of the grapes began almost immediately, both with feet and wooden blocks. The liquid squeezed out at this part of the process, rather than by the press itself, was considered the best for winemaking.[134]

As with the cereal crops, tax assessments from the 1720s allow us to estimate the level of annual yields for the *Amt* Leonberg. These seem to have been a respectable 20 hectolitres per hectare, averaged out over six years, but of rather poor quality, which seems to have ranked near the bottom of the tax assessors' quality scale. This is little different from early nineteenth-century levels. The very small area of vineyards in Renningen, it was alleged, gave only a quarter of this for half of the six years. Extra costs were incurred by the fact that in Höfingen the poor ground meant that vineyards had to be completely replanted every

---

[133] Mone, 'Weingeschichte', pp. 33–5; Döbele-Carlesso, *Weinbau*, pp. 66–74, 197; Landsteiner, Personal Communication; Schenk, 'Viticulture', p. 196; Herrmann, 'Deutsche Weinwirtschaft'; Hahn, *Deutschen Weinbaugebiete*, p. 82. The figure of labour inputs to viticulture being eight times higher than those to arable is cited by von Hippel but originates in a 1940 gardening magazine. Von Hippel, 'Bevölkerung und Wirtschaft', p. 426; Schröder, *Weinbau und Siedlung*, p. 77; see Feldbauer, 'Lohnarbeit'.
[134] Salzmann, *Weinbau und Weinhandel*, pp. 58–65, 76–9; Döbele-Carlesso, *Weinbau*, pp. 57–64, 85–118.

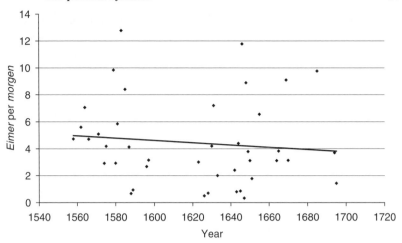

Source: StAM Spitalrechnungen H21–35, 51–2, 54–60, 62, 64–73, 77–8, 97–8, 102–3, 107–8, 117–8.

Figure 1.3 Wine yields from the vineyards of the hospital of Markgröningen

fifteen or sixteen years. However, such yields were extraordinarily variable, as can be seen in data recorded on yields from the small vineyards of the hospital of Markgröningen presented in figure 1.3. These showed a similar downward trend to arable yields from the same demesne farm from the late sixteenth century. However, yields in Markgröningen, and perhaps more generally in the more productive centres of viticulture, appear to have been up to twice as high as those that pertained in early eighteenth-century Leonberg.[135]

The trends over time were partly weather conditioned. The vines could be vulnerable to spring or early autumn frosts, which struck the Stuttgarter vineyards eighty-four times between 1492 and 1667, or nearly every other year, according to the lists compiled by Dornfeld. They were, however, unequally distributed, more frequent in the 1520s, around 1550, from around 1562 to 1581, again from 1586 to 1593, and after 1612 with great frequency right up until the 1640s.[136] Over the

---

[135] HStAS A261 Bü 1134; StAM Spitalrechnungen H21–35, 51–2, 54–60, 62, 64–73, 77–8, 97–8, 102–3, 107–8, 117–18. The Markgröningen hospital vineyards varied in extent from as little as 1.25 *morgen* to over 10 *morgen*, but were generally between 4.5 and 7 *morgen* in extent. The harvests are recorded from each *accounting year*, i.e. 1695 corresponds to the autumnal grape harvest of 1694. The Markgröningen yields approximate to those found in the viticulture areas of Switzerland in the first half of the sixteenth century. Leonberg appears to reflect the more general situation in Württemberg. Pfister, *Bevölkerung*, p. 30; Döbele-Carlesso, *Weinbau*, pp. 161–5.

[136] Dornfeld, *Geschichte des Weinbaus*, pp. 180–9.

seventeenth century, arable yields and wine yields from the land of the hospital of Markgröningen, and the thermal index of temperatures compiled for Switzerland by Christian Pfister all show a similar downward trend (see figures 1.1 to 1.3 for the trend lines).[137] Although a causal link cannot be proven, it is highly suggestive that the coldest period of the 'Little Ice Age' did depress agricultural yields generally in this part of Europe. By the mid- to late 1720s, when we have taxation data, the climate had improved somewhat and thus the yields quoted in tax records probably reflect yields obtained in the sixteenth century before the mid-1580s.[138]

A slow downward trend did not necessarily spell calamity, but other factors such as an unusual excessively wet summer or hailstorms could. Yet even if the harvest was bounteous, as in 1539, one could face the problem that 'the barrels were worth more than the wine', compensated for perhaps by the extraordinary and famous vintage of 1540. In terms of quality, the vintages seem to have been rated as good or middling up until the mid-1520s, becoming rather poor after 1553 until something of a brief recovery after the mid-1570s. The both poor and small vintages of the late 1560s and early 1570s must have made life particularly hard for the vinedressers, and the period 1586–98 also stands out as one of immoderately low yields. By the 1620s the quality, at least, seems to have steadied with interludes of poor years, but soon war would be upon the unfortunate region.[139] As displayed in figure 1.4, in the hinterland of the nearby Imperial city of Esslingen, total income from viticulture had risen from early in the sixteenth century up until the mid-1580s. Thereafter, however, it collapsed and never really recovered.[140]

If we examine the relative prices of spelt and wine, it appears that there was no long-term dramatic shift in favour of one or the other over the period. In other words, there was no clear-cut incentive for peasants to shift from one form of cultivation to the other. For the balance between wine and grain prices I have used the sales of the hospital of Markgröningen, which usually sold both spelt and wine. Trends are displayed in figure 1.5. The costs of production for both consisted

---

[137] See figures above. Pfister, *Bevölkerung*, p. 88; Pfister, *Klimageschichte*, Tabelle 1/29–30.
[138] Glaser and Schenk, 'Einflüssgrössen', p. 50.
[139] Dornfeld, *Geschichte des Weinbaus*, pp. 180–9; Glaser, *Klimageschichte*, p. 108.
[140] Calculated using the data in Salzmann, *Weinbau und Weinhandel*, pp. 90–5. This multiplies the wine price set by the authorities for the purposes of arbitrating credit relationships, by the volume of wine produced. This is a notional figure because in reality prices of particular wines will vary with quality and will be contingent on the length of time for which the wine is laid down, itself in part a function of the wine market in subsequent years. A similar pattern is found in data from Germany and Austria analysed by Landsteiner. Landsteiner, 'Crisis of wine production'; Döbele-Carlesso, *Weinbau*, pp. 155–6, 296–7.

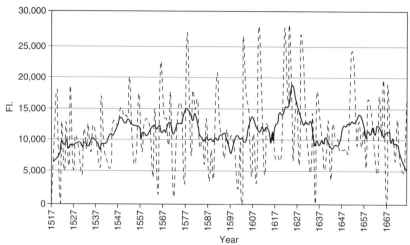

Source: Salzmann, *Weinbau und Weinhandel*, pp. 90–5.

Figure 1.4 Wine income in Esslingen, 1517–1676 (11 yr moving averages)

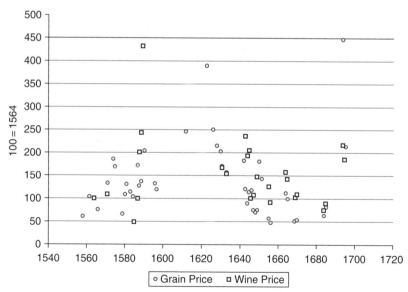

Source: StAM Spitalrechnungen H21–35, 51–2, 54–60, 62, 64–73, 77–8, 97–8, 102–3, 107–8, 117–8.

Figure 1.5 Spelt and wine sale prices, hospital of Markgröningen

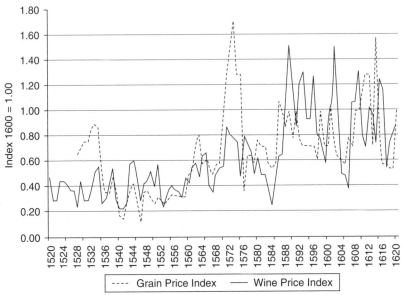

Source: Salzmann, *Weinbau und Weinhandel*, pp. 90–5; Ginschopff, *Chronica*.

Figure 1.6 Relative price of wine and corn in Esslingen and Stuttgart

of labour, fertiliser and farming equipment. Given this basic similarity in cost structure it is perhaps not surprising that prices followed equivalent trends. This pattern also suggests, albeit on limited data, that population fluctuations, the 'conjuncture', did not have much influence on relative prices. From the late sixteenth century to the end of the seventeenth the trendline in wine yields fell about 20 per cent and that for spelt about 25 per cent, so the divergence in incomes in the long term was not significant. Wine yields may have suffered even more than grain yields however at the coldest points in the Little Ice Age.[141]

A similar exercise using annual data from Esslingen and Stuttgart reveals more short-term conjunctures in the period before 1630. It should be mentioned that the prices for wine and spelt in Markgröningen and Leonberg clearly moved in the same range as those in the nearby larger cities. Figure 1.6 shows the relative movement of corn (milled spelt) and wine in the period 1520–1620. The two series are never very far apart, but wine prices are a little more favourable in the middle of the century, grain

---

[141] StAM Spitalrechnungen H21–35, 51–2, 54–60, 62, 64–73, 77–8, 97–8, 102–3, 107–8, 117–8.

prices move ahead for most of the 1580s (aside from the famine of the early 1570s). Wine prices are higher, but with commensurately low yields, until the end of the century.

Wine from the east of the region, on the 'Holland road' of the Neckar, could find its way into the extensive trade networks that brought Württemberger wines especially to Bavaria, with salt being the primary import in exchange.[142] The sourer wines of the west, which were sometimes better sold as sweetened *Most*, had no such pedigree. If they were sold beyond the confines of the village (and some villagers told tax assessors in the 1720s that this would be a stroke of fortune), they went to the neighbouring districts of Herrenberg and Böblingen. In poor years, much might have to be poured away, or by the eighteenth century was not sold 'to a trader but with great effort to local burghers on credit'. Small towns commonly set the price to ensure cheap wine for their traders, but also so that creditors could not exploit indebted vinedressers, who might not even own barrels and would have to sell immediately.[143]

What kind of dynamic?

The previous sections have demonstrated the ability of the peasantry to manage and vary the resources at their disposal without ever breaking the boundaries of a certain level of productivity. Of course, they did not only subsist within an agricultural world. There were artisanal occupations too, and export-orientated worsted-weaving industry in the western fringes of the region. The relative costs of agricultural practice must be balanced against these activities, which will receive greater consideration in chapter 2. Little attention has also been given thus far to gardens. These were often communally owned patches allotted for a year or a period of years to the local citizenry and used for the cultivation of vegetables, above all cabbage and onion. Gardens attached to houses tended to be grassy spaces with fruit or nut trees rather than 'cottage gardens' used for kitchen production.[144] Matthias Mattmüller has held up these spaces as under-investigated reservoirs of agricultural advance and intensification in the eighteenth century, an area where women probably played a prominent role.[145] All the indications from this region, however, hint that while gardens may have been important for individual households, and certainly had a very high

---

[142] Benning, 'Studien zur frühneuzeitlichen Seuchengeschichte Württembergs', p. 82.
[143] HStAS A261 Bü 1134.   [144] Beck, *Unterfinning*, p. 42.
[145] Cited in Troßbach, 'Beharrung und Wandel', p. 133.

value by area in comparison to arable land, their overall importance in the economy remained small.

During the period from around 1600 to 1730 there was a retreat from viticulture in lands west of the Glems, and an expansion, once the calamity of the Thirty Years' War was passed, in the arable area, also primarily to the west of the Glems. To this we can add a more favourable relation of meadowland to arable land. Despite the latter, however, the stocking rate of livestock appears to have been rather steady, with perhaps some increase in sheep numbers.

How can these trends be explained? One model might posit a 'homeostatic' relationship between a region's population and resources. As a result, any changes in the local economy are likely to be endogenous effects of the shifts in one factor (such as population size, or price levels for particular goods) having knock-on effects on the others. We have already identified the most likely vectors for changes in the operation of the agricultural economy to be shifts in biomass transfers (above all, manure) and labour inputs. Can these be identified, at the aggregate level of the village, as being the factors that account for agricultural change within an otherwise fairly stable community? 'Stability' here, of course, indicates only that the post-war reconstruction produced a society that looked much like its pre-war predecessor.

Another model might focus on those shifts that take place 'outside' the system. These are not entirely 'exogenous shocks' in the sense used by historical demographers, such as virulent epidemic disease, because the agrarian system was to some degree built to screen off the worst possible consequences of at least some potential disasters. They were already 'variables', part of the 'environment' of the local system, and taken into account. However, when disturbances were extensive or long lasting, they might force reconfigurations to the agrarian order. Climate change is one such possibility. Another, from the perspective of the village, is the international market for foodstuffs, as, although intimately linked into this system, local farmers were essentially 'price-takers' who exercised little control over the long-term value of their produce. Did these factors operate in a decisive way in the *Forstamt* Leonberg?

Not 'a system for itself'

Firstly, I will take the 'homeostatic' or 'endogenous model'. We have seen that the number of livestock changed little in the long term over this period. Consequently, we might expect vineyards to be disappearing to the benefit of arable land, if manure inputs were held constant.

The manure spared from the former could be used to sustain the expansion of the latter, although if the arable expanded into previously unused grounds, it might take some time before this transfer was necessary. However, there is no discernable general relationship between decline in vineyards and extension of the arable. Where change occurred after the Thirty Years' War, even those areas previously highly dependent on viticulture tended to hold that acreage comparatively steady while greatly expanding the arable, while those areas where viticulture virtually disappeared only had small areas of vineyard in the first place. At least by these measures, there is no *obvious, general link* between the factors of land use and livestock numbers.

Similarly, there does not seem to have been any kind of trade-off in labour terms between the reduction of vineyard acreage and the expanse, even if to unsustainable limits, of arable cultivation. Of twenty-one settlements where such a calculation can reasonably be made, only one, Enzweihingen, shows an obvious trade-off between 1630 and the early eighteenth century of twenty labour-years being saved from viticulture and eighteen more applied to the arable land.[146] These kinds of calculations are inevitably crude, but make the point that the agricultural shifts do not seem to come from a discernable shift in the utilisation of a set pool of available labour. Indeed, this would only really be the case if labour was already allocated rationally and utilised in its entirety. The evidence is quite contrary to this. Many of the tasks required by arable farming or viticulture came at different times of the year. Chapter 2 will show how many households appear to have easily combined the two. A trade-off was by no means a necessity.

Perhaps more tellingly, the evidence suggests that labour in general was under-utilised. It is likely, as discussed earlier, that the availability of equipment and draught animals was a constraint, but rarely the availability of people.[147] Many of the aspects of communal farming, which were indeed labour saving, do not seem to have brought great efficiency gains elsewhere. They may rather have permitted multiple

---

[146] This assumes a blanket rate of 60 per cent higher labour inputs into viticulture by area than arable land.

[147] Wolfgang von Hippel estimated that only some 13 per cent of available labour-days were unused in the early seventeenth-century economy of Württemberg. However, although he probably underestimates the labour required for work in the woodland, he probably overestimates the labour required in viticulture by a factor of two. Before commercial and industrial activity are included, at least a third of available labour was probably free after agricultural needs were met, although of course this time varied over the year. Hippel, 'Bevölkerung und Wirtschaft', p. 430.

occupations over the year, spreading the risk of one income source drying up. Yet in so doing they could also inhibit specialisation and economic growth. The expansion of fields in some districts by the early eighteenth century (even if many were only temporarily cultivated) suggests that quite a lot more labour must have been going into agriculture, *if labour inputs per hectare were being held constant*. Labour input per hectare may in fact have fallen, which might in part explain the stagnating yields, as well as that being the result of expansion onto marginal land (which conversely might require the raising of labour inputs per hectare to work poorer soil, but lower labour productivity). This would hardly surprise, as virtually nowhere was the population in the early eighteenth century higher than it had been around 1630, and in many places it was still between a tenth and a fifth lower. Indeed, if we take as standard the circumstances that developed in a few settlements, of population being a fifth lower and the arable area possibly as much as a fifth higher, a fall of a third in labour inputs per hectare is implied unless labour productivity improved. In truth we do not have the data to decompose this problem further, but a fall of the magnitude of a third in labour inputs per hectare seems unlikely. As yields were roughly the same, the implication is that the general allocation of labour in agriculture became more efficient, unless the proportion of the population active in agriculture rose. The population in 1630 was thus probably not at the margins of productive possibilities, and the local environment was not being ruthlessly and wholly exploited for all it could reasonably produce.

Conjuncture and climate

Some of viticulture's decline undoubtedly was a result of the conjuncture. While prices held up between the 1580s and the middle of the seventeenth century, income levels remained low because of small harvests. After the 1650s prices never really recovered. Higher levels between 1689 and 1717 were conditioned by war and poor climatic conditions. In the 1720s they declined again. In this situation higher quality competitors, especially imports from Alsace, could really gain a foothold, and the previous virtues of local production (relative cheapness in an age of inflation) disappeared. In some places that had an export market, there was scope for maintaining business against better vintages where there was an advantage in transport costs. Generally, however, the poorer vineyards disappeared altogether and local production was retained only for local consumption, with the assistance of some protectionist measures.

The effect of the 'conjuncture' on arable farming is more difficult to discern, especially where we do not know the relative importance of rents, taxes, capital and labour in any detail. The 'long sixteenth century', an age of rising prices and lower relative wage costs, would have led one to expect greater incentives for farmers to produce for the market and possibly to raise labour inputs. Higher sale prices could make the high cost of getting grain to market relatively cheaper, encouraging trade. However, the really high prices of the 1570s, 1590s, mid-1610s and 1620s appeared largely as a result of famine or war. Incentives to produce more, although we have no real concrete evidence of the trend, could as well have come from a desire buffer against dearth, when the creditworthiness of being a successful farmer may have mattered as much as any grain stored in the barn. In the post-war period, cereal prices remained low outside of war years. At the same time, the work of Andreas Maisch on land prices suggests that arable land was persistently cheap right up until the second half of the *eighteenth* century, in real terms well below what it had cost in the pre-Thirty Years' War period. Given the magnitude of this shift, which shows a 'quarter' (*Viertel*) of arable land in the early eighteenth century being worth a mere quarter of the value of the 1580s, it becomes immediately understandable why post-war development seems to have gone in the direction of expanding landholdings rather than more labour-intensive forms of cultivation for more specialist, high-value products such as wine. The *price conjuncture* for grain may have mattered much less than the fact that landholding was a relatively risk-free and cheap investment, and arable land did not require the initial capital outlay of vineyards.[148]

Chistian Pfister postulated that the 'manuring-gap' was one that could not be bridged in the agrarian economy. Lack of manure meant that productivity faced severe limits, and variability in harvests necessitated various 'buffering' strategies designed to deal with disturbance. Crisis had essentially 'exogenous' causes, when strategies to buffer against disturbance could not cope with the scale of the calamity. Agrarian fortunes were thus tied to climate both in the short and long

---

[148] Maisch, *Notdürftiger Unterhalt*, pp. 44–9. This is entirely consistent with a market-based model where the ratio of land price to labour price shifts radically, favouring the expansion of land use with a relatively low labour input. This is consistent, too, with stagnating or falling average yields, although the overall *volume* of production may well have risen, especially in *per capita* terms. However, the shift in the price ratio cannot *a priori* be determined and depends on local social structures. We can point again to the fact that there does not seem to have been a major shift of relative prices between grain and wine, or in the substitution of one form of cultivation for another.

term.[149] There is some support for this thesis. We have already seen how viticulture was adversely affected by colder and wetter years from the 1560s onwards, and especially after the mid-1580s. Similarly, Pfister has argued that the wetter second half of the sixteenth century saw dramatically less protein derived from hay for cows.[150] At the same time, Stefan Militzer has suggested that the end of the 'century of grain' also saw a decline in grain yields, with all these problems arising at the end of a long rise in population.[151] Central Europe appeared well set for a Malthusian crisis, albeit with external prompting. Real problems struck not just, as Pfister suggests, when both winter and summer crops failed, but when the grape harvest failed too, such as in 1570–1. Here the spending power of a swathe of poor already hit by high grain prices disappeared along with any hope of earning from work as vinedressers.[152]

However, while climate shocks brought about stress and some mortality, both Maisch's and Eckhardt's demographic work has suggested mortality crisis was caused by primarily by epidemic disease that had only a very weak relationship with harvests or climate.[153] Actual population decline, aside from the high-pressure regime of crisis and recovery, did not set in until the onset of the Thirty Years' War. I have argued that the region was, at this point, probably not utilising all of its labour effectively and was not at any 'ecological' limit. There is no obvious association between mortality peaks (where they can be measured) and periods when Württemberg had a relatively large population in relation to available resources. Georg Fertig has also argued that dearth was not a sufficient cause for the wave of migration that emerged from southwest Germany after the cold years of the later 1730s and 1740.[154] Indeed, the demographic situation and *per capita* supply of food was probably more favourable in the very cold years around 1700 than a century earlier. Thus while the climate has an obvious effect both on production levels and mortality crises, it is less clear that *climate change* is *the* long-run determining factor, or even necessarily an important trigger, in the development of the agrarian regime and population history.

The beginnings of a case has been advanced here for the existence of a distinctly 'peasant' society in early modern Württemberg, one focused on the constraints of subsistence agriculture, particular

---

[149] Pfister, *Bevölkerung*, pp. 126–9.   [150] Ibid., pp. 90–1.
[151] Militzer, *Getreidebaus*, pp. 122–3.   [152] Pfister, *Bevölkerung*, p. 59.
[153] Eckhardt, *The structure of plagues*; Maisch, *Notdürftiger Unterhalt*, pp. 46–58; Fertig, *Lokales Leben*, p. 298.
[154] Fertig, *Lokales Leben*, p. 358.

ecological limits, flexibility in the face of uncertainty and regulation by various authorities to minimise 'complexity' and the number of decisions with unforeseen and potentially hazardous consequences. This gives a clue as to why the inherent plausibility of homeostatic or 'Malthusian' models remains insufficient to explain the detail of what has been observed in this chapter. Institutions designed to reduce the friction and complexity of managing ecological dilemmas were not necessarily closely responsive to ecological changes themselves, and nor would they be expected to optimise the management of local resources for any particular productive goal. How these institutions operated, and hence the decision-making processes of any peasant, would be influenced by the ability of individuals and groups to exercise power in the context of those institutions. Hence the next chapter will be concerned with the direct and institutionally mediated exercise of power.

Of course, not all could be explained by the operation of local societies. For early modern Württembergers, divine providence or at least supernatural power was the final arbiter in most cases. When a massive hailstorm struck the Stuttgart area on 8 August 1562 and caused colossal damage to crops, trees and, above all, vines, such misfortune was blamed by rumourmongers on a gathering of witches on the Feuerbacher Heath to the north of the city. Despite a tradition of preaching in Württemberg that condemned the attribution of hailstorms to witches, several women were subsequently sent to the stake.[155] This sudden disturbance, however, was more a blip on the radar screen of a population that had also become systematically more vulnerable, if not to disaster, then to indigence. Population was clearly growing faster than food supplies and prices were rising. Because of this, the 'peasant dynamic' required more than local regulation to survive, and increasingly became encapsulated within a broader political economy of market controls, poor relief and moralistic 'disciplining'. The first ordinances on the poor and beggars came in 1531, and from 1562 onwards dearth and its consequences became a regular concern of the central government.[156]

Such measures were not background noise to the local 'agrarian systems'. They were, in fact, integral to them, the primary response mechanism, and should not be seen as further 'exogenous factors'. This was a further case, at a 'state' level, of grappling with 'limited good', and the fulfilment of a certain moral duty, as well as the response of a

[155] Glaser, *Klimageschichte*, pp. 116–17; Midelfort, *Witch hunting*, p. 39.
[156] Reyscher, *SWG*, Bd.XII., pp. 69–73, 319–23.

certain moral panic to the complexities that the simplified decision-making bodies of village life were unable to deal with. The adaptive strategy to approaching 'limits' was transposed into being the concern of another corner of the social realm, the 'state', rather than there being any attempt to reconfigure the local ecological balance. Indeed, the 'limits' that generated difficulty were not necessarily ecological in nature. The kinds of measures that were employed to deal with social stress and tension would be similar at the state and village level and should probably be seen as developing hand in hand. Strategy was based on the kind of trade-offs that were almost a reflex action to early modern society. Regulation reduced both the capacity of the peasantry to 'under-use' resources by determining collectively (or better said, oligarchically) the pattern of the agricultural calendar and the use of space, and in the case of landlords controlling tenants, their resources. At the same time the authorities put extensive barriers in the way of those who might want to reconfigure the agricultural system to their advantage but also bring potential productivity improvements. Of course, the result was that some *were* disadvantaged, especially women and those who took the risk of lowly artisanal work or vinedressing, and the impetus was thus created for the development of a poor-relief system to pick up this slack of poverty. The fact that these collective institutions had redistributory effects, as will be argued in the next chapter, should not blind us to the fact that they still limited the ability of some of the poor as well as the wealthy to become economically more productive. But at no point did this society collectively alter the balance of land use on any scale, reorganise holdings, or move systematically to shift the balance of livestock and cultivated land.

2   Power and property

The key to understanding the particular 'peasant dynamic' of early modern Württemberg is the collective institution that played the greatest role in governing village resources, the commune and its court. While there was little that was 'immobile' about this society, it nevertheless appeared little altered in the early eighteenth century from the world of the sixteenth or early seventeenth century. This was true not only of its levels of productivity and agricultural techniques, but equally, as we will see, the social order. A major contributor to this degree of stability was the continued ambition of certain groups within the village to employ collective measures to regulate village life, measures that generally worked in tandem with those promulgated by central government. This world was generated by institutional effort, and the manner in which village institutions managed the resources available to them. Early modern Württemberg was clearly a very unequal society. Property holding conferred institutional power and thus societal development was shaped by particular interests. Nevertheless, communal institutions themselves allowed far wider access among the populace to resources held as communal property than was the case for the resources that were held as private property, access to which was more inequitably distributed. Even if shares in communal property were also 'inequitably' apportioned, by an overwintering rule, for example, or allotting wood according to the size of one's property, overall this property system still probably worked to the advantage of the poor. The records of material conditions for households are largely based on wealth, and will be used below to present an image of the social structure of the region. Yet the *disposable* income of the poor after subsistence needs were met and dues were paid was probably proportionally even smaller relative to that of the rich than their wealth. Thus even 'unequal' allocations of communal property redistributed resources in their favour relative to what could have been achieved by their spending power alone. Stability in the communal control of property, contributing to the ability of the poorer to avoid penury and the inability of the rich to accumulate all available resources into their hands, must go some way to explaining the long-term stability in the distribution of wealth. Sections of the economy also operated 'in kind', partly as we have seen with the reciprocal provision of labour or equipment, partly via wages in kind, partly through direct access to communal property. This countered local shortages of specie even as it inhibited commercialisation. Peasants preferred taxes in kind because they did not have to try and obtain the coin.[1] Such relations may, of course, have contributed to the inability of the local economy to break the bounds of very limited earning and spending power. The commune limited the possibilities for development, or at least required a broad consensus within the community for radical change. The relatively powerful political communes were able to resist the dissolution of communal property and common rights in many cases long into the nineteenth and even the twentieth centuries.[2]

This situation should be understood as a dynamic, because it was not idly achieved but struggled for and managed by the peasants themselves. It certainly cannot explain all the social and economic developments of the period, far from it. Yet at every moment we may see how the exercise of institutional power profoundly influenced property relations and material conditions, how public life and the material world intersected. At the same time, property holding conferred status and the means to influence those institutions. The first half of this chapter will thus be devoted to examining the distribution of property holding and the fortunes of the economy over the period. The second half will examine the functioning of village institutions, the commune above all else.

Everyone in Württemberg spoke about the rich and the poor. In November 1580, the mayor (*Bürgermeister*) and jurors of Leonberg wrote to the Duke informing him of their practice of allowing 'the poor folk' ('*der arme mann*') to cut a considerable amount of wood in their communal woodland, above and beyond that apportioned out in the free grant of *Gaabholz*.[3] With the peasants subject to the constraints of the agricultural calendar, lack of money and horses at the appropriate moments, compounded by poor spring weather, had prevented much of it being removed from the cutting sites in accordance with the forest ordinances. Did this use of the 'poor folk' mean much the same thing as that of the men of Münklingen who petitioned the Duke over the *Holzgaab* in the same month twenty-six years later? According to these petitioners, wood granted by the commune for the use of the 'poor citizenry' ('*arme burger*') had traditionally been granted equally to each head of household. Recently, the petitioners claimed, those living in

---

[1] HStAS A28 Bü 99.   [2] Warde, 'Common rights'.   [3] HStAS A227 Bü 1139.

shared dwellings had been barred from receiving the full amount, a privilege reserved only for those with their own house (*'aigene Häuser'*). Consequently the wealthier (*'Reiche'* or *'vermögliche Bürger'*) enjoyed a superfluity of free wood when they could afford to purchase it, a luxury denied the poor.[4]

In these exchanges we have two definitions of poverty, of where a dividing line in the social order might lie. In Leonberg in 1580 poverty is defined by a lack of carts and horses, in Münklingen in 1606, by shared residences and tenancies. Poverty, we know, is relative and like beauty lies in the eye of the beholder. However, it should also be clear that people related the use of the term, and social distinctions more generally, to very real material situations of housing, access to equipment and capital ('means of production' is still as good a term as any), and used such terms to identify differing socio-economic constraints ('relations of production'). This combination of a bluntly material understanding of hierarchy, but consequent variation according to the task in hand, enjoins us to bring together as many sources as possible to seek to understand the dynamics of social relations and experiences within the ecological framework outlined in chapter 1.

A feudal world

The majority of the populace of the region were the subjects of the Duke of Württemberg. This was first and foremost because they lived within his principality, in communities under his juridical powers (*Gerichtsherrschaft* in German). This was also true of those living in villages juridically subject to monasteries absorbed into the Württemberger state during the Reformation, such as Hirsau and Maulbronn, with a few exceptional periods such as the Imperial occupation during the Thirty Years War when they reverted to Catholic independence. This judicial subjection should not be confused with the *personal* subjection of serfdom, which was still quite prevalent in the German south-west. Many of the inhabitants were indeed serfs, in some villages a clear majority, although numbers were declining by the early seventeenth century.[5] The burdens of serfdom, however, were increasingly nominal, restricted to an annual payment of a hen and the stipulation that permission was required from the lord to

---

[4] HStAS A227 Bü 1149.
[5] No less than 78 per cent of Renningen households in 1605, for example, though only 62 per cent by 1633. See Trugenberger, 'Malmsheim und Renningen', p. 42; Knapp, *Gesammelte Beiträge*, pp. 113–14; on serfdom, Keitel, *Herrschaft über Land und Leute*.

marry or emigrate. It seems, however, that in practice village communes were far more interested in regulating behaviour than were the dukes.[6]

Although numerous nobles were resident in the region, they had formally cut their ties with the Duchy of Württemberg and become directly subject to the Emperor during the 1510s. Thereafter they ceased to owe any obligations or fealty to the dukes and exercised local influence within the Duchy only where, as was still frequently the case, they chose to work as part of the ducal administration. Within their own lordships they were, however, often the main landlord as well as judicial lord over the populace. For the most part these Knights were rulers over only a handful of settlements or even just one village, often where rights were shared with other lordships (including the dukes), and thus in practice they were heavily dependent on Württemberg's protection and patronage. This meant however that most of the region's population dealt with their overlord, the Duke himself, via the formalised bodies of the state, of which the village court, operating on behalf of its lord, was the lowest tier. There was no intervening 'Estate' of feudal nobility with delegated powers, as could be found in other parts of the Empire.[7]

As well as the lesser nobility, the dukes and religious institutions all played a major role as landlords in addition to any juridical powers. The actual cultivators of the land appear, by and large, to have stood in an immediate relationship with the owners of the land as tenants. There appears to have been very little formal subletting, although temporary land exchanges and forms of sharecropping and farming for wages may have been more prevalent.[8] Landlordship (or *Grundherrschaft*) generally meant the extraction of feudal rents. Tenures themselves were generally secure and heritable, the terms of which had in most cases been laid down in the late medieval period, with payment usually (though by no means always) in kind. By the sixteenth century demesne farming was minimal and limited to a handful of leased-out sheep farms across the region. Most cultivated land owned by the dukes consisted of smaller farms (generally called *Lehen* or *Hube*) that were tenanted, sometimes as a discrete farm unit that survived down the generations in one piece.

---

[6] Keitel has recently argued that restrictions on movement solely applied to 'serfs' (*Leibeigenen*) although the restrictions on emigration are often discussed as if they applied to all Württemberger subjects, a position that some ducal documents appear to adopt. As communal authorities (and thus the Duke) had some control over who might own property in the *Markung*, the potential avenues of restriction on movement and migration were at least double edged and possibly ambiguous at the time. Keitel, *Herrschaft über Land und Leute*, pp. 222–9; Ogilvie, *State corporatism*, p. 41.

[7] Carsten, *Princes and parliaments*, p. 11; Vann, *The making of a state*, p. 48.

[8] On the practice of farming for wages around 1800, see Isermeyer, *Ländliche Gesellschaft*, p. 87; also, Maisch, *Notdürftiger Unterhalt*, pp. 82–3.

In many cases, however, these farms had in practice become subdivided among many tenants who were collectively responsible for rental payments, often with one nominal payee called the *Träger* who oversaw collection and delivery of the dues owed.[9] Partible and equal inheritance among all children was the usual form of property devolution in central Württemberg, but it is clear that there were considerable variations in practice.[10]

A large proportion of arable land and vineyard was however freehold and either owed no, or only minimal, dues. Freeholds were consequently given higher tax assessments and there is some evidence that freehold land was also spatially more fragmented than that burdened with feudal rents, tending to lie in small parcels rather than larger farm units. Not including demesne land (which was in any case limited in most places), the Duke was landlord of around 20 to 80 per cent of the land in various settlements in the *Amt* Leonberg by the early eighteenth century.[11] Local hospitals, monasteries and institutions such as the parish church were also relatively powerful landlords. The precise amount of freehold land is difficult to assess but may have been around a fifth of the total.[12] Meadows seem rarely to have been freehold, probably an indication that this land was apportioned early on in medieval times to tenancies subject to feudal payments.[13] Around a fifth of the area of vineyard owed sharecropping rents rather than a fixed rent, the most common being one fifth of the harvest.[14] All told the average level of rents appears to have been very low, estimated by Wolfgang von Hippel at around a tenth of output on tenanted property, with another tenth being allotted to the tithe. As much land was held in freehold, most settlements in the *Amt* Leonberg appear to have paid rents of under a tenth of their output.[15] Rents paid to the Duke remained virtually unchanged over the entire

[9] See Maisch, *Notdürftiger Unterhalt*, pp. 82–3; Hippel, *Bauernbefreiung*, pp. 105–6, 123; Knapp, *Gesammelte Beiträge*, pp. 397–404.
[10] Hess, *Familien und Erbrecht*; Medick, *Weben und Überleben*, pp. 172–80; Sabean, *Kinship in Neckarhausen*, pp. 21–2.
[11] HStAS A261 Bü 1134.
[12] HStAS A261 Bü 1134; A359 Bü 3; A320 Bü 5. In Bondorf in the district of Herrenberg in 1720, half the land was 'Eigen', that is, not owned directly or indirectly by the Duke. Maisch, *Notdürftiger Unterhalt*, p. 112.
[13] Consequently, as they tended to hold land from the old farm tenancies less frequently, the poor also tended to hold low amounts of meadow relative to holding size. Maisch, *Notdürftiger Unterhalt*, pp. 97–8.
[14] HStAS A359 Bü 3; A320 Bü 5.
[15] According to the tax assessments of 1727, dues (excluding tithes) totalled some 9.6 per cent of the estimated annual arable output of the district. Boelcke, 'Bäuerlicher Wohlstand', pp. 265–8; HStAS A261 Bü 1134; more generally, see Hippel, *Bauernbefreiung*, p. 125.

period, implying steady erosion of value where these had to be paid in cash.[16] Payment in kind however remained the most frequent form of due. Payments in kind helped to maintain ducal income in periods of inflation, as food prices rose ahead of all others.

Communes also owned small amounts of arable land and gave out areas of the common land to villagers for use as allotments, generally for the growing of vegetables. Vegetable plots were tended individually by each household, but the communal fields were cultivated using corvée labour owed to the commune, or by paid workers. At any one time it was also the case that fairly extensive areas of arable land, especially in the east of the *Forstamt*, lay untended. It is unclear whether these were left open to communal grazing, or used privately as grassed leys, but the former seems more likely as there is a lack of evidence of disputes or regulations for dealing with the latter. Sometimes formal rules record that uncultivated arable land reverted temporarily to communal control.[17]

Many people were thus subject to serfdom, and even more, as a consequence of being juridical subjects, might owe corvée labour for carting, woodcutting and military preparations to lords, or to communes for fieldwork and the upkeep of communal property. However, the combination of a freeholding and feudal regime in fact shielded the landholders of the region from the price and rental trends that affected much of Europe in this period. They enjoyed relative freedom to sell (the right of redemption built into property exchange was almost never enforced),[18] security of tenure and inheritance rights, and for the most part minimal disturbance to increasingly low rents, though the predominance of payment in kind to farm labourers did not allow the holders of larger tenancies to reap the benefits of 'sticky' rents and wages during the long sixteenth century.[19] In fact, it was largely communes rather than lords that imposed restrictions on landholding and movement. The right to settle in a community increasingly required proof of having a set amount of wealth and an honourable reputation.[20] Credit was, at least in theory, only to be taken on with the approval of the local lordly official, but this approval, if honoured, was a matter for village bailiffs and town governors rather than

---

[16] I have checked this in the cadastres of various villages: Möttlingen HStAS H101 Bds.344, 373; Renningen and Mönßheim, H101 Bds. 948, 961, 965, 974.
[17] Ernst, 'Geschichte', pp. 288–91. [18] Sabean, *Property*, pp. 352–3.
[19] Wallerstein, *The modern world-system* I, pp. 82–4.
[20] Serfs did however have to make payments at a rough value of 1.4 per cent of their wealth on emigration or transfer of property. See for example in the *Amt* Calw, HStAS H101 Bd.344. See also Ogilvie, *State corporatism*, pp. 41–51; Sauer, 'Not und Armut', p. 145; Sreenivasan, *The peasants of Ottobeuren*, pp. 168–8; Trugenberger, *Zwischen Schloß und Vorstadt*, p. 9; Benning, 'Eine Stadt', p. 10.

a matter that pertained to the role of the duke as landlord.[21] Govind Sreenivasan has recently made a strong case for the lands of Ottobeuren in Upper Swabia that the response to population growth and fears of in-migration was the increased use of *inter vivos* transfer of property, purchase of property by heirs, and impartible inheritance. He argues that this led to the need for more specie, commercialisation, improved productivity, and eventually rises in the age of marriage and increased servant-hood.[22] Württemberg was prey to similar fears, and indeed some similar demographic trends such as rising ages at first marriage, some out-migration and increased levels of celibacy over the seventeenth century. Yet inheritance practices did not change.

Ownership of woodland

Ownership of woodland differed radically from that of cultivated land. Cultivated land, open pasture (which was not recorded in tax surveys) and woodland were nearly all, of course, subsumed into a system of common management that permitted grazing at certain times of the year, and restricted the use to which land could be put. Woodland was however different in two main ways. Firstly, it was subject to forestry legislation that from an early date claimed to apply to land under all forms of ownership and limited the manner in which the wood could be managed. Unlike land only subject to common rights, it was overseen directly by the officials (foresters and wardens) set in place by central government, not just communal authorities. Secondly, the structure of direct owner-ship, meaning ownership by those who had the right to alienate the property, was also very different. The great majority of the woodland was owned directly by communes. Very little was tenanted or freehold land, and only relatively small proportions were owned directly by the duke, the nobility or other institutions.

It is difficult to be precise about the proportions held by each type of owner because of the unreliability of measurement in early, supposedly all-embracing surveys of the woodland taken in 1523, 1556 and 1583.[23] They tended to greatly underestimate the area of large woodlands that were in turn disproportionately owned by communes, thus underestimat-ing their share. However, a survey conducted with much greater care by Andreas Kieser in 1682 gives much smaller margins for error and can be used as a fairly reliable guide. Further comparison of these figures with

[21] Reyscher, *SWG*, Bd.III, pp. 160–4; Bd.XII, p. 216.
[22] Sreenivasan, *The peasants of Ottobeuren*, pp. 157–70, 306–28.
[23] On the manner in which these were conducted, see chapter 4.

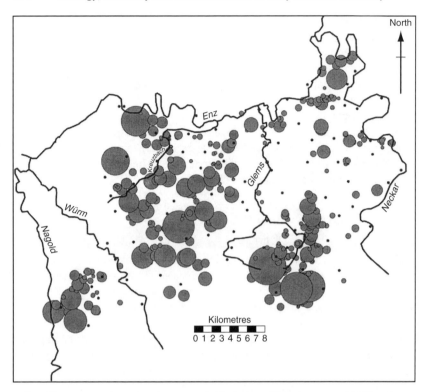

Note: The areas are based on those recorded in Andreas Kieser's survey of 1682 and confirmed at an assembly in Leonberg on 16 April 1683. It has not been possible to identify the location of a handful of the stands, amounting to only a few hectares in total. The position of the woodland has been indicated roughly according to its centre, though some are in fact extremely elongated or uneven in shape. It should be remembered that some of the woodlands exploited by the inhabitants lie outside the actual *Forstamt* in neighbouring districts. The circles are sized according to the square root of the actual measured area, to give a better impression of the extent of woodland cover

Map 2.1. Extent of woodland, 1682

surveys conducted in the later eighteenth century (when, however, some transfer of ownership and redrawing of boundaries had taken place) suggests that if anything the 1682 figures still underestimate the extent of the woodland.[24]

Kieser's survey suggests that 58 per cent of the woodland was owned by communes, 17 per cent was owned directly by the duke, 9 per cent was owned by monasteries, 6 per cent by the nobility, 5 per cent privately (a high proportion of this being land tenanted from the duke), and

[24] HStAS A59 Bü 32 & 13; H101 Bd.107/8 Bd.1 & 5; A8 Bü 41.

2 per cent by other institutions.[25] This most likely reflects the pattern throughout the period. Although transfers of ownership occurred from at least the fifteenth century, they were not sufficient in scale to significantly alter the overall picture. It is, of course, much easier to trace those transactions that involved the duke, and very few of those were with non-nobles. It seems that there was a small drift of woodland into ducal hands over time, in part as foresters consolidated blocks of ducally owned woodland, sometimes in exchange for communes receiving lots nearer to their settlement.[26] During periods of stress such as the Thirty Years War and French invasions some communes sought to sell patches woodland to raise money for tax and contribution payments or to pay off creditors, but again the overall effect of such transfers appears to have been minor.[27] As one would expect, prices for woodland were much lower after the Thirty Years War, but beforehand transactions are too few to draw any firm conclusions from the prices quoted.[28]

Thus communal woodland was the most prevalent form of woodland ownership in the region. We must be clear that these woodlands were owned by the institution of the commune. They were not owned *in common*. We have seen in chapter 1 that such woodland fell under the managerial purview of village authorities and there was no question of it being a 'free good' vulnerable to unconsidered individual over-exploitation. Thus there was in theory no automatic exposure to the 'Tragedy of the Commons', where each user was tempted to take more than a sustainable share of woodland resources on the assumption that other users were likely to do the same.[29] How the commune chose to manage its wood and allocate it among villagers and town-dwellers could have a crucial

---

[25] HStAS H107/8 Bd.5. Proportions are nearly exactly the same in 1769 aside from a transfer of 6 per cent of the woodland from direct ducal ownership to Church (i.e. monastic) property. HStAS A8 Bü 41.

[26] Such exchanges were carried out with Asperg in 1570, part of a series of transactions in the area that year, and Möglingen in 1620. HStAS H107/8 Bd.2.

[27] For example, Malmsheim woodland sold to Renninger *Bürger* and moneylender to pay off debts in the 1630s, Trugenberger, 'Malmsheim und Renningen' p. 124; Felden, *Ortsbuch Hoheneck*, pp. 243–4.

[28] The foresters' cadastres, which had their data updated to at least some degree, and deeds of sale in the Hauptstaatsarchiv Stuttgart record sales between 1540 and 1684, not all of which involve the Duke. Often transactions for which there are deeds still extant were faithfully recorded in the forest cadastre. Some very small patches went for the extra-ordinary price of over 80 fl. per *morgen* in 1570, which possibly reflects a desire to convert the land into more productive uses. Generally prices ranged between 6 and 26 fl. per *morgen* in the late sixteenth and early seventeenth centuries. HStAS A59 Bü 13a; A227 Bü 1126; A348 U16, 17 & 20; A368 Bü 47, U87, 88, 92, 93, 94, 95, 97, 106 and 108; A557 Bü 51, 57, 8; A583 Bü 262; A584 Bü 11; H107/8 Bds.1 and 2.

[29] Hardin, 'Tragedy of the commons'; Ostrom, *Governing the commons*; de Moor, Shaw-Taylor, Warde, *The management of common land*.

impact on their access to this vital resource. Where membership of the commune was easily accessible and cheap, then the communal woodland could provide an important boon to the lowly, cheap access to property and a bulwark against destitution.

Not all communes owned communal woodland, however. In 1583 only forty-four out of around seventy settlements in the *Forstamt* did so, and for some of these the amount owned was of little economic importance. However, this did not necessarily imply a lack of access to communally managed wood. Heimsheim, for example, had less than one hectare of communal woodland, but had extensive rights in the vast Hagenschieß woodland that straddled the border with Baden, as well as ducally owned woods in the vicinity of the town. At the other end of the region, the village of Benningen had rights in the *Hardtgemeinschaft*, a group of seven villages that collectively managed the 880 hectare Hardt woodland on the eastern bank of the Neckar. Most villages subject to the monastery of Maulbronn had rights to firewood and building timber out of monastic woodlands. However, as shown in map 2.2, communal woodland was relatively scarce in the Glems valley and along the west bank of the Neckar, the regions where wood, as we shall see, was also relatively expensive.[30]

These patterns of ownership had their origin in complex jockeying for power and property among local nobles, the house of Württemberg and monasteries, dating back to the High Middle Ages. A rule of thumb in the lower-lying regions of the German south-west is that the closer a woodland lay to the centres of power and management, the more likely it was to fall under noble or state control. Where communes gained ownership in such regions, this was formalised through a grant establishing communal woodland at an early date. In areas less easy for lordly officials to exploit, communes were, in contrast, able to more independently establish property rights.[31] By contrast, in the upland regions such as the Black Forest, relatively under-exploited woodland distant from any settlement often fell under the control of monasteries and lordships that were prepared to claim and document very extensive rights during the Middle Ages.[32] Communal woodland could even be of relatively recent origin, evolving from various property arrangements dependent on the local structures of landholding. In Bissingen, for example, rights in the 'communal' woodland were in fact restricted to the *Höfe* or *Kernhube*, large tenant farms leased by the Duke, of which there were around twenty in the 1520s. As it

---

[30] HStAS A368 Bü 56; Stadt Heimsheim, *Heimsheim*, p. 56; Gemeindeverwaltung Benningen am Neckar, *Benningen am Neckar*, pp. 84–5.
[31] Simon, *Grundherrschaft und Vogtei*, p. 200.   [32] Schaab, 'Waldeigentum'.

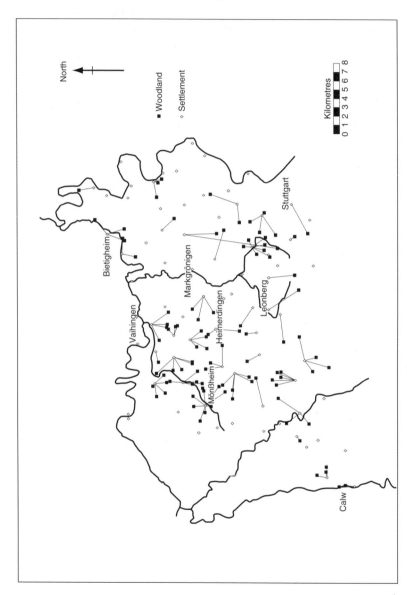

North

■ Woodland

◇ Settlement

Bietigheim

Vaihingen

Markgröningen

Heimerdingen

Mönßheim

Leonberg

Stuttgart

Calw

Kilometres

0 1 2 3 4 5 6 7 8

Map 2.2 Distribution of communal woodland, 1583

was stated in 1583, 'The Bissingers have to purchase much wood. They distribute the *Gaab* to the *Höfe* and not to the *Bürger*.'[33] The fact that *Gaabholz* was nearly always only given to those resident on certain 'ancient' farmsteads, even though these later became much partitioned among different households, suggests that, as in this case, there may more generally have been a manorial origin to much communal woodland, where the manorial tenants had originally been granted access to the local woodland. We should however not automatically assume so.

This brings us to privately owned woodland, which still amounted to over 2,000 hectares in the *Forstamt*. Names of the owners are often recorded in surveys, although incompletely and frequently trailing off into 'and others ...'. Data from 1556 can be compared with tax returns from 1544–5 to give us some idea of the distribution of wealth among the owners of private woodland. However, although while the 1540s taxation data is comprehensive, it may be that the poor are more likely to be lumped among the 'and others' category when woodland owners were recorded in 1556.[34] The fact that many owners of woodland resided outside the *Forstamt*, coupled with high rates of mobility, means that only ninety-six secure linkages can be made between the datasets. By comparing the tax valuations of these ninety-six owners with the valuations of all taxpayers in 1544–5, we can see that the owners of woodland were more likely to come from among the wealthy. This effect is likely to be underestimated because young men in 1544 would have low valuations compared to their real wealth in 1556. In a society where landlessness was rare, it seems that relatively few of the poor owned woodland

---

[33] HStAS A59 Bü 13a; Schulz, *Altwürttembergischer Lagerbücher*, pp. 30–42. This woodland was always recorded as being owned by the commune in 1556, 1583 and 1682. This was also the case in Dürrmenz, which explicitly linked this right to use woodland to the corvée labour to be owed to its landlord. However, in practice these fourteen tenancies to whom the grant was limited in 1556 were divided among many more households by the eighteenth century and probably much earlier. Knöller, *Unser Dürrmenz-Mühlacker*, pp. 41–2.

[34] It may also be the case that the wealthy owned a large proportion of private woodland, though the form of the 1556 records makes this impossible to ascertain. In the 1556 data some 290 names are given alongside some 164 parcels of woodland (including here woodland privately held by Bietigheimers that in fact lay in the *Forstamt* Stromberg). There are a further eighteen entries that talk of 'others'. In 1583 158 parcels were recorded, owned by 193 individuals and thirty-two multiple unknowns. However, it seems that 'corporate' ownership of parcels was not the norm and these have been aggregated for ease of documentation. For example, in Bietigheim in 1556 there were only ten recorded parcels of privately owned woodland covering 113 *morgen* and owned by twenty-two named individuals and nine multiple unknowns. The more rigorous survey of 1583 gives sixty-six parcels comprising 103.5 *morgen* owned by eighty-one individuals, all of whom are named. HStAS A54a Ämte Leonberg, Vaihingen a.d. Enz, Bietigheim, Hoheneck, Canstatt, Stuttgart, Calw, Asperg, Markgröningen; H107/8 Bd.1.

and nearly two-thirds of those identifiable as doing so in 1556 had tax valuations at over 300 fl. in 1544.[35]

Just as with communal woodland, privately owned woodland was not evenly distributed over the region. It was not, however, a substitute for communal woodland and does not appear to have developed as an alternative. Map 2.3 displays the distribution. There was virtually none in the west of the region and very little in the south. Most settlements in the Strohgäu, in an arc from Heimerdingen north to Aurich and east across the Glems to the Neckar had at least some private wood owners. Frequently this did not lie within the *Markung* where the owner resided. Many of the woodlands were on the fringes of ducally owned woodland and may represent a mixture of encroachment, woodland expansion onto fields during the fifteenth century and the remnants of woods long attached to adjacent tenancies. Only a few of the holdings would have been sizeable enough to permit much in the way of wood sales and only one private woodland is mentioned as providing this service in 1583.[36] Some of the woodland seems to have been managed collectively. A fringe of private woodland around the Eglosheimer Holz was divided into nine parcels of oak standards and hazel coppice by its owners in 1583. It was cut on a twelve-year cycle, its few acres quite insufficient to supply the needs of the owners who 'have to buy the majority of their building- and firewood'.[37] A late seventeenth-century reference also refers to the forester's permission being required to sell any timber or remove bark from oaks even in private woodlands.[38]

---

[35] The ninety-six only includes absolutely positive identifications. I have ignored those with problematic occupation-based surnames or simply with common family names. HStAS A54a Ämte Leonberg, Vaihingen a.d. Enz, Bietigheim, Hoheneck, Canstatt, Stuttgart, Calw, Asperg, Markgröningen; H107/8 Bd.1. This should not be taken as meaning that no relatively poor men held private woodland, however, because very small lots were recorded in tax estimates for poor peasants and vinedressers in the east of the region in 1607. For the level of tax valuations, see below p. 122. HStAS A314 Bü 6 (Backnang); A359 Bü 3 (Hoheneck); A320 Bü 5 (Bietigheim).

[36] HStAS A59 Bü 13a.

[37] It also seems that woodland may not have been that cost effective to manage privately, as a number of substantial sales of woodland were made by members of the Siglin, Beutenmueller and Hermann families from the region from Ditzingen east to Zuffenhausen in the late sixteenth century when wood prices were rising. Various men bearing the same surname and almost certainly related appear in forest account books buying wood from the duke from the 1580s onwards. HStAS A59 Bü 13a; A368 U92, Bü 47; H107/8 Bd.2; A302 Bd.7221–7235.

[38] HStAS A59 Bü 35a. The undated fragment is grouped with other documents dating from 1698.

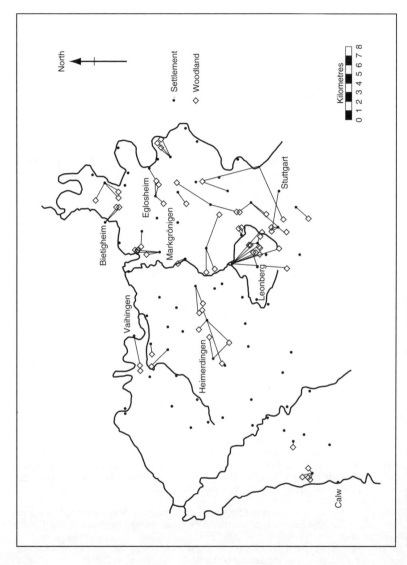

Map 2.3 Distribution of private woodland, 1583

The general course of the economy

The patterns of ownership did not exist in an immobile world, but one subject to the flux of population levels and economic fortunes. Property holding and institutional action thus existed in the context of the broader economic conjuncture, as well as seeking to shape that economic development according to the interests of social actors. One might consider the stability of the relationship outlined above somewhat surprising, because the course of the economy was not a steady one. The fortunes of the European economy over this period are reasonably well known. Rising population growth during the 'long sixteenth century' led to rising prices, exacerbated by an inflow of silver from the New World after 1540, which lasted until the 1620s. Wages remained however relatively 'sticky', lagging behind price increases and leading to a decline in real income for large sections of the population. The expanding demand of this population thus tended to concentrate on the necessities of life; food (especially cereals), drink, fuel and cheap textiles. Nevertheless, a small section of urban merchants and wealthy rural landowners were able to profit from the circumstances of high sales prices and low wages to sustain some demand for luxury goods.[39] After the Thirty Years' war, the situation was reversed. Slowly recovering populations over much of southern, central and eastern Europe left demand sluggish but tended to push up wages. The price depression lasted until the 1740s and squeezed profits over most of the continent, even though for labourers this meant a recovery of real wage levels to those not seen since the beginning of the sixteenth century.[40]

Württemberg's economy was predominately agrarian, with its chief export, as we have seen, wine.[41] It lay in a zone of relatively low prices for western Europe that stretched from the cities of northern Switzerland north-east towards Saxony and the Czech lands.[42] Without any major cities, the trade of Württemberg remained dominated by rich Imperial cities such

---

[39] Wallenstein, *The modern world-system I*, pp. 82–4; Duplessis, *Transitions to capitalism*, pp. 47–140; Abel, *Agricultural fluctuations*, pp. 99–146.

[40] Wallerstein, *The modern world-system II*, pp. 7–28; de Vries, *Economy of Europe*; Duplessis, *Transitions to capitalism*, pp. 141–245; Abel, *Agricultural fluctuations*, pp. 158–93; Slicher van Bath, *Agrarian history*, pp. 206–20.

[41] In Wallenstein's model Württemberg could belong to a classic 'semi-periphery' with an urban mercantile population (although technically independent in the Free Imperial Cities) and relatively buoyant consumer demand. However, there is relatively little evidence, as he suggests, for the prevalence of the sharecropping contract preventing the rise of social polarisation and capitalist farmers. Even with viticulture, sharecropping remained secondary to fixed rents. See Wallenstein, *The modern world-system I*, p. 107.

[42] Braudel and Spooner, 'Prices in Europe', pp. 472–3; also data kindly supplied by Bob Allen.

as Ulm, Strasbourg and Augsburg.[43] These prospered in particular when southern Germany and the Alpine region was the major source of silver in Europe in the late fifteenth and early sixteenth century. This facilitated a north-west to south-east trade axis with its cornerstones in Antwerp, the great entrepôt of the north until the 1550s, and Venice. The south German textile industries boomed, Nürnberg rested as the centre of European metallurgy supported by the iron smelters of the Upper Palatinate, and great financier families, most famously the Fuggers of Augsburg, played a major role in European trade and politics. After the 1540s the advantages of cheap and accessible silver faded as the central European mining industry faltered and New World imports began to flow in. Conventionally the southern German economy is seen as rather stagnant after this point, and those cities such as Strasbourg that maintained stronger contacts with the emerging north-west 'core' of the European economy appear to have weathered better the storm of real wage decline in the second half of the sixteenth century. During this period, Italian merchant firms began to penetrate the German markets.[44] In the long term, right through to the nineteenth century, German industry struggled to compete with England and the Low Countries who enjoyed the cost advantages of readily accessible fossil fuels, extensive water transport, large urban centres as stimuli to production and specialisation, and the benefits of advanced financial and insurance services. Nevertheless, as the collapse of German demand for English broadcloths and Italian manufactures with the onset of the Thirty Years' war is supposed to have prompted major restructuring in their economies, we must assume that domestic demand and possibly production remained relatively buoyant.[45] Württemberg must have suffered however with the decline in wine income prompted by climatic deterioration from the mid-1580s.[46] Ducal toll income, that fluctuated considerably from year to year, can only be taken as a very rough indication of the level of trade (and inter-regional trade, rather than local marketing). After steady growth it appears to have shown a rapid increase after the return of Ulrich in 1534, equally a period of general European price inflation, until the 1550s. Prices of basic foodstuffs remained persistently low in Württemberg until the mid-1560s and it is likely that this rise in toll income really does reflect the economic buoyancy of the German south-west in the middle of the

---

[43] Weidner, *Staatlichen Wirtschaftspolitik*, p. 12; HStAS A28 Bü 99.
[44] Blanchard, 'International capital markets'. Blanchard appears incorrect in his argument that as a result of economic stagnation and monetary factors prices fell in southern Germany from 1575 to 1610, an assertion possibly made on the basis of very high prices in the early 1570s that resulted from climatic problems and years of dearth. See also Braudel, *The Mediterranean*, pp. 152–7.
[45] Wallenstein, *The modern world-system* I, p. 220.
[46] A trend also found in Alsace. See Scott, *Regional identity*, p. 299.

century. The hard famine-scarred 1570s saw particularly low returns. The subsequent period saw some recovery, but given a population that rose until around 1630, and currency devaluation, the stability of nominal toll income suggests relative economic stagnation and possibly falling *per capita* volume of trade in this later period. This is a rather different result from that obtained by Govind Sreenivasan in his study of the lands of Ottobeuren in Upper Swabia. As already noted above, he argues that a trend towards impartible inheritance and increased transfer of property via sale prompted increased provision of credit and a greater monetarisation of the economy, especially after 1580. These developments in turn prompted increased specialisation for sale and rising incomes (at least as measured by inheritances). There is no sign of equivalent developments in Württemberg, possibly because of trouble with the wine trade, but this reminds us to be careful about generalisations. The persistence of partible inheritance may have militated against the consolidation of large, enduring holdings ripe for commercial exploitation. The endurance of this system of property transfer certainly requires explanation. The ability to maintain an income from small patches of land via viticulture is certainly not the answer, as contrary to much historical comment, most settlements in the region only derived a very small amount of their income from vineyards.[47]

[47] Based on the following toll incomes:

Year	Toll income (fl.)
1483	4,732
1506	6,478
1512	6,623
1533	8,699
1535	13,466
1551	20,919
1557	12,317
1568	51,579
1570s (average p.a.)	7,010
1580	35,347
1588	31,000
1600	27,032
1607	42,976
1610	27,000
1615	33,071

These are not deflated to account for changes in the value of silver. Values for 1588 and 1610 are approximate. HStAS A256 Bds. 73 and 96; A79 Bü 6a; Bütterlin, *Württembergische Staatshaushalt*, pp. 167, 169–70; Sreenivasan, *The peasants of Ottobeuren*, pp. 263–79.

The post-war period brought increasing Europe-wide specialisation in textiles and agricultural products such as wine, oil and livestock.[48] This development appears to have favoured Württemberg's linen weavers and producers of woollen worsteds (or 'new draperies') who had already established themselves as significant local industries in the late sixteenth century. In the 1670s and 1680s continual warfare along the Rhine may have kept prices inflated and real wages for labourers and artisans depressed, but the workers of most of central and eastern Europe experienced a relatively favourable period. By the early eighteenth century real wages in central Europe were beginning to decline again while much of the continent saw food prices converge, more a consequence of price falls in previously more expensive regions due to increased productivity and lowered marketing costs than actual price rises that were not apparent elsewhere until mid-century. However, the general volume of trade, perhaps encouraged by relatively low commodity and manufacturing prices, was high once Württemberg recovered from the wars of Louis XIV. The Duchy still managed significant exports of wine and livestock in the early eighteenth century, and toll income suggests a level of regional exchange somewhat higher than a century earlier. This is despite the apparent fall in income from wine illustrated in figure 1.4 of chapter 1.[49]

The ducal government provided its own report on the state of the economy in 1719, intended as an assessment of the ability of the land to support a standing army. Its assessment of the economy appears to be fairly accurate. According to it, 'the most inhabitants live from crops they themselves produced, without having the need to buy this from others with money'. 'Most' is probably an exaggeration, as only a minority could really feed themselves throughout the year. However, the impression of a subsistence-orientated economy is clear. The 'larger part consists of artisans, vinedressers and farmers, through which little money comes into the land'. The report noted that agricultural exports were vulnerable to poor harvest years, and were suffering from low price levels and foreign competition. Although wood, linen and iron had some export potential there was a general shortage of specie. The report noted that the state's monopolisation of the wood trade that year would reduce the income of the subjects.[50]

---

[48] Slicher van Bath, *Agrarian history*, pp. 212–17.
[49] Toll income averaged around 59,600 fl. each year 1714–33. Braudel and Spooner, 'Prices in Europe', p. 395; data on silver prices and wages also kindly provided by Bob Allen of the University of Oxford; Straub, *Das badische Oberland*, p. 44; Wilson, *War, state and society*, pp. 45, 48.
[50] HStAS A28 Bü 99.

Cutting across the phase of population expansion, contraction and renewed growth was the increasing enmeshing of Württemberger economic relations in a guild system, a development supported by both ducal and communal authorities. Sheilagh Ogilvie in particular has drawn attention to the development from the 1550s onward of closed corporate bodies with the full backing of the Württemberger state, 'state corporatism' as she terms it. Most famously this system embraced the worsted weavers of the Black Forest and linen weavers in the south of the Duchy, but nearly all artisans required a guild qualification to practise their trade, whether living in town or country. Württemberger guilds were a statewide or regionally bounded rather than an urban phenomenon.[51] More generally, the fragmented polities of southern and central Germany retained strong guild structures both facilitated by government regulation and the ability of journeymen and master associations to exercise influence both locally and more widely through entry restrictions and boycotts.[52] Even trades like butchery and baking were subject to local restrictions where consumers were in theory at least required to use their local (often sole) guild representative of that particular trade.[53] Rules prevalent across Europe that required the use of public markets and that banned regrating (selling on at a profit) reduced the ability of middlemen and wholesalers to operate. Sumptuary laws discouraged 'superfluous' consumption. Ogilvie argues that the overall effect of such a corporate economy was to reduce innovation, and raise transactions costs and prices.[54] Whether this really was the case is rather difficult to tell, in part because such institutions were so prevalent across Europe that opportunities for comparison with unregulated cases are rare, and in part because we do not have sufficient price series to be able to compare prices between more and less competitive environments. Records of prosecution for transgressing some of these rules can be taken as an indication of effectiveness, but equally as evidence of the widespread flouting of such restrictions.[55] A small test is conducted below to see if the prevalence of artisans and retailers differed in these 'corporate communities' in comparison to comparable, less regulated regions and periods.

---

[51] Ogilvie, *State corporatism*; Ogilvie, *Bitter living*; Stieglitz, *Zünfte in Württemberg*, pp. 42–3.

[52] Stuart, *Defiled trades*, pp. 239–60.   [53] Ogilvie, *State corporatism*, p. 69.

[54] However, in good Lutheran fashion some ordinances permitted local setting of prices, which would presumably be maximum prices and thus tend to depress the overall price level. Thus we can identify countervailing pressures, either depressing consumption, or providing disincentives to produce, and sometimes both at the same time (through production limits, for example). On the theological arguments, see Wright, *Capitalism*, pp. 16–18, 255–6.

[55] Ogilvie, *State corporatism*, pp. 68–70.

Social structures (1): rich and poor in Leonberg

The experience of economic change depends of course on one's place in the social order, and the possibility of changing that place. The social order and the property ranking were of course not the same, not least because one's property holdings would change over a lifetime. But property holding nevertheless provided a clear guide to the prospects for attaining status and wielding institutional power. Tax records from 1575 provide a 'snapshot' of the occupational and social structure of Leonberg, the commercial centre of its own district although distant from the main routes of trade that crossed the *Forstamt*. It provides, perhaps, a test case of a marketing centre predominantly serving its own small hinterland with some trading of local produce to the south. In 1608 it was declared (not entirely truthfully) that 'in the town [there are] no merchants or handicrafts, but for the most part agricultural property'.[56] The results of the 1575 records, which in fact only incorporate those who owned their houses and thus excluded a small number of residents, are shown in figure 2.1.[57] Each column on the *x*-axis shows the proportion of each type of land use within each landholding, measured by the left-hand *y*-axis, while the right-hand *y*-axis gives the size of the landholding. It can be seen firstly that the great majority of households, even in a town with fairly limited agricultural land, were landholders. Secondly, the poorer landholders usually held vineyards, and meadow ownership was concentrated among the rich. Nearly everybody, however, owned or tenanted at least some vineyard. The top thirty or so landholders owning more than 20 *morgen* (around 6–7 hectares), with at least three-quarters of that arable land, were the self-sufficient farmers, though only a handful of men held larger farms of 25–45 hectares. These social divisions are mirrored almost exactly in tax data from the mid-1540s and surveys of the poor and the wealthy dating from the crisis year of 1622. In 1544 and 1575 around 15 per cent of the populace stand out as securely self-sufficient in food supplies, and about 8 per cent in 1622 were able to sell a surplus. In contrast, over half the population (in figure 2.1, those falling around the 110th–120th household) in 1544, 1575 and 1622 fell clearly below the threshold of self-sufficiency and had to purchase food supplies, lacking both the arable land or

---

[56] HStAS A368 Bü 48.

[57] This information has been extracted from data published by Volker Trugeneberger. Trugenberger, *Zwischen Schloß und Vorstadt*, Prosopographie. 1575 returns can also be examined in HStAS A572 Bü 37a. These figures do not include state officials and taxpayers resident outside Leonberg who hold property there.

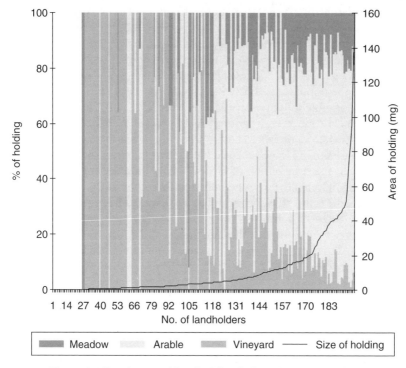

Figure 2.1 Land use and landholding in Leonberg, 1575

sufficient wage payments in kind to tide them over.[58] These poor families were certainly not proletarians in the sense that they had no access to means of production, but they were certainly dependent on the fortunes of the labour market and demand for the products they produced, whether wine, handicrafts or local commercial services.

The social structure of Leonberg seems to have remained relatively stable during a period when many parts of Europe were undergoing social polarisation and the immiseration of the poorest. This stability may well go back as far as the early sixteenth century, as there were nearly as many households in the town in 1528 as 1575, with only an expansion of viticulture as the major agricultural change.[59] Vineyard holding was clearly

---

[58] HStAS A54a Amt Leonberg. This clearly self-sufficient figure for 1544 is based on those with an assessed wealth of over 500 fl., while those who might get into severe difficulty and be largely reliant on purchases fall below 150 fl. in the assessment. See Clasen, *Die Wiedertäufer*, pp. 204–10. The 1622 survey is to be found in HStAS A237 Bü 586.

[59] Trugenberger, 'Der Leonberger Raum', p. 87; Trugenberger, *Zwischen Schloß und Vorstadt*, p. 51.

less inequitably distributed than arable holding so the expansion of viticulture would at the least tend to stave off polarisation. It is true that the late sixteenth and early seventeenth centuries saw the development of a group of households, often seven to eight, who were permanently dependent on municipal bread doles.[60] These represented a small and generally infirm section of the population. The widespread holding of land, abetted by the system of partible inheritance, remained prevalent in Württemberg right up until the late nineteenth century. As late as 1857, 92 per cent of households in Württemberg owned land.[61] As landed wealth was the main form of taxable wealth, widespread landholding would tend to counter polarisation. In fact, the distribution of taxable wealth became *less* polarised over time, being marginally less unequally distributed by 1629 than during the first half of the sixteenth century and quite significantly more egalitarian by the early eighteenth century.[62]

Widespread landholding did not mean the town was entirely agriculturally dependent however. Occupational data from 1575 shows

---

[60] StAL Armenkastenrechnungen.

[61] Sabean, *Property*, pp. 38–9, 456, 479–80; Medick, *Weben und Überleben*, pp. 184, 201; Maisch, *Notdürftiger Unterhalt*, pp. 215–18.

[62] The measure of inequality is the gini coefficient, a frequently employed statistical tool for this purpose. This compares the 'Lorenz Curve' of a plotted ranked empirical distribution (in this case, with taxpayers on the x axis and the cumulative proportion of total taxable wealth that each holds on the y axis), with the line of perfect equality. The line of perfect equality assumes that each element has the same contribution to the total summation of the values of a variable. The gini coefficient basically measures the space between the Lorenz Curve and the line of perfect equality, which is larger the larger the inequality of distribution. It ranges between 0, where there is no concentration (perfect equality), and 1 where there is total concentration (perfect inequality). Tax data in Leonberg shows the following results:

Year	Gini coefficient
1470	0.687
1489	0.576
1495	0.625
1528	0.619
1544	0.678
1553	0.578
1613	0.588
1629	0.596
1713	0.458

Trugenberger, *Zwischen Schloß und Vorstadt*, p. 288, Lorenzkurve; HStAS A54a Amt Leonberg; StAL Extra Ordinari Contribution; 1713 Steuerbuch.

50 per cent of households in the town following an artisanal or professional trade to some degree.[63] In 1730, tax assessments (which indicate the actual practice of a trade) show 48 per cent of households to have named occupations. This again indicates continuity, although there has been some compositional change reflecting shifted terms of trade. Coopers have declined from nine to five, and professional traders in wine and vinedressers disappeared from the occupational listing. There was a rise in tanners from zero (though Leonberg did have a tanner operative at times during the sixteenth century) to five, and shoemakers from seven to twelve. Evidence is fragmentary, but there appears to be a relatively high degree of continuity in Leonberg's property holding and occupational structure across the period.[64]

Social structures (2): glimpses from the wider region

Similar taxation and survey data allow us to examine social structures across the region from the mid-sixteenth until the early eighteenth centuries. We begin with the 'Turk tax' (*Türkensteuer*) of 1544–5 levied on behalf of the Emperor to encounter the feared Ottoman threat to the Austrian frontier. This was a standardised wealth tax, unlike most other taxes of this time where shares were allotted to communes as a whole by district authorities, and only later apportioned among each household. The 'normal' practice meant that amounts paid per unit of assessment by each inhabitant were generally not consistent from settlement to settlement. In contrast, the 'Turk tax' levied a sum of one half of one per cent on assessed wealth, with exemptions for the very poorest. The returns from the area of the *Forstamt* Leonberg cover over 4,000 households. Of these, some 6 per cent were assessed at under 20 fl. wealth, or were virtually penniless and presumably lived as the hired hands or on the charity of others. Some 36 per cent were assessed as having between 20 and 100 fl. wealth, and thus lived in relative penury with only a smattering of property. Some 44 per cent were estimated to own between 100 and 499 fl. wealth, a wide range of middling artisans or

---

[63] This includes one person recorded as a vinedresser, and two merchants. Though as this figure includes only houseowners, the real figure is probably a little lower than this. While there is a general problem that some Württemberger records indicating 'occupation' in fact record a guild qualification rather than the actual practice of the trade, this was not an issue at this point when many guilds had not yet been established.

[64] Linen weavers also rose from one to nine, 1575–1730, though the fact that eight were recorded in a listing of 1568, but only one in 1575, must make us cautious about assuming any real change. Trugenberger, *Zwischen Schloß und Vorstadt*, Prosopographie; HStAS A261 Bü 1134. Weitprecht also talks of many linen weavers and clothworkers in 1618. Weitprecht, 'Schreckenstage', p. 3.

smallholders. Some 12 per cent were substantial farmers or traders, holding between 500 and 1,000 fl., and 3 per cent, or about 150 households, belonged to the rich in this agrarian world, with over 1,000 fl. in wealth. This indicates a wealth profile slightly more egalitarian than that of the town of Leonberg itself. There was of course much variation, the scale of which is indicated in table 2.1, where the 'gini coefficient' is a rough measure of the degree of inequality, wealth being more unequally distributed the higher the coefficient is.[65] Markgröningen had a notably high proportion of relatively and very wealthy citizens (33 per cent over 500 fl.). The eastern region of the *Forstamt* was the wealthiest, also taking advantage of the major trading route from Canstatt through Markgröningen to Vaihingen an der Enz and on towards Speyer to provide carting and trading services, as well as supplying the Stuttgart grain market. At the other end of the scale, a few (but not all) of the villages very dependent on viticulture had high numbers of the almost indigent – Riet, Münster, Aurich, Enzweihingen. What we can ascertain is that in the 1540s the land-poor made up nearly half the population.[66] This remained the case eighty years later in 1622. In the villages around Leonberg, just under half of the population had to buy most of their bread, while just under a sixth had enough spelt to be able to sell a surplus.[67] The wealthiest do appear to have profited from the sixteenth-century conjuncture, even if trends did not lead to rapid polarisation. Comparing the average assessed wealth of the five wealthiest households in 1544 and 1607 in eleven settlements in the district of Leonberg shows an increase in wealth, averaged across the settlement, of a factor of 3.5. Over this period grain prices increased by a factor of three and the prices of other goods less so.[68]

[65] See note 62.

[66] HStAS A54a Ämte Leonberg, Vaihingen a.d. Enz, Bietigheim, Hoheneck, Canstatt, Stuttgart, Calw, Asperg, Markgröningen. The total sample is 4,152 taxpayers, excluding those living in service and institutional payers. See also Bull, 'Die durchschnittlichen Vermögen'.

[67] HStAS A237a Bü 586. The proportion of purchasers comes from a sample of 927 households. The numbers of potential sellers of spelt are recorded in all of the villages in the *Ämte* Leonberg. Numbers ranged from a third in the small grain-growing village of Hirschlanden, a quarter or more of households in Ditzingen, Kornwestheim and Zuffenhausen to 3–6 per cent in the more upland or wine-dependent villages of Gebersheim, Heimerdingen and Gerlingen.

[68] This may underestimate the increase because the 1607 assessments did not include most moveable property. Wealthy households would tend to have a higher proportion of moveable goods than poorer ones in their overall wealth, and would be better able to accumulate these in an inflationary period. HStAS A54a Ämte Leonberg; A368 Bü 48.

Table 2.1 *Distribution of taxable wealth, 1544-5*

Place	Total (fl.)	No. taxpayers	Mean (fl.)	<20 fl.	%	20–99 fl.	%	00–499 fl.	%	00–999 fl.	%	1000+ fl.	%	Gini coeff.
Leonberg	47375.33	134	257	14	7.6	81	44.0	61	33.2	21	11.4	7	3.8	0.678
Münster	5703.5	51	112	14	27.5	19	37.3	15	29.4	3	5.9	0	0.0	0.657
Enzweihingen	48282.33	227	213	24	10.6	87	38.3	90	39.6	19	8.4	7	3.1	0.655
Heimertingen	13660	86	159	2	2.3	45	52.3	31	36.0	5	5.8	3	3.5	0.617
Gebersheim	4122.33	34	121	8	23.5	10	29.4	15	44.1	1	2.9	0	0.0	0.616
Eltingen	18580	141	132	14	9.9	69	48.9	54	38.3	3	2.1	1	0.7	0.614
Weilimdorf	17221.5	92	187	6	6.5	41	44.6	35	38.0	9	9.8	1	1.1	0.612
Renningen	29187.67	134	218	7	5.2	53	39.6	60	44.8	7	5.2	7	5.2	0.610
Ditzingen	34368.33	154	223	18	11.7	53	34.4	61	39.6	15	9.7	7	4.5	0.605
Mönßheim	14778.33	103	143	3	2.9	56	54.4	38	36.9	5	4.9	1	1.0	0.596
Eberdingen	5382	25	215	1	4.0	11	44.0	7	28.0	6	24.0	0	0.0	0.583
Bietigheim	72206.67	251	288	9	3.6	73	29.1	121	48.2	37	14.7	11	4.4	0.575
Asperg	13580	84	162	1	1.2	43	51.2	31	36.9	8	9.5	1	1.2	0.575
Heimsheim	15765	97	163	1	1.0	51	52.6	34	35.1	11	11.3	0	0.0	0.574
Gerlingen	27435	194	141	18	9.3	83	42.8	83	42.8	8	4.1	2	1.0	0.571
Aurich	13258.5	63	210	9	14.3	15	23.8	32	50.8	6	9.5	1	1.6	0.569
Markgröningen	161345	351	460	15	4.3	85	24.2	136	38.7	71	20.2	44	12.5	0.559
Schwieberdingen	15611.67	64	244	1	1.6	30	46.9	22	34.4	10	15.6	1	1.6	0.555
Hoefingen	17416	85	205	5	5.9	32	37.6	42	49.4	2	2.4	4	4.7	0.555
Rutesheim	16568	93	178	7	7.5	33	35.5	44	47.3	8	8.6	1	1.1	0.554
Riet	5045	29	174	5	17.2	9	31.0	13	44.8	2	6.9	0	0.0	0.542
Münchingen	42136.67	159	265	4	2.5	64	40.3	62	39.0	24	15.1	5	3.1	0.540
Kornwestheim	32488.33	89	365	5	5.6	13	14.6	46	51.7	17	19.1	8	9.0	0.532
Hemmingen	3880	27	144	0	0.0	15	55.6	10	37.0	2	7.4	0	0.0	0.530
Möglingen	24838.33	93	267	1	1.1	34	36.6	43	46.2	10	10.8	5	5.4	0.525
Groß Ingersheim	30020	161	186	3	1.9	65	40.4	76	47.2	15	9.3	2	1.2	0.519

Table 2.1 (cont.)

Place	Total (fl.)	No. taxpayers	Mean (fl.)	<20 fl.	%	20–99 fl.	%	00–499 fl.	%	00–999 fl.	%	1000 + fl.	%	Gini coeff.
Zuffenhausen	29186.67	118	247	5	4.2	38	32.2	55	46.6	17	14.4	3	2.5	0.516
Feuerbach	51151.67	159	322	6	3.8	32	20.1	84	52.8	31	19.5	6	3.8	0.503
Botnang	3753.33	28	134	1	3.6	11	39.3	14	50.0	2	7.1	0	0.0	0.499
Münklingen	2725	17	160	1	5.9	7	41.2	7	41.2	2	11.8	0	0.0	0.496
Eglosheim	16188.33	50	324	0	0.0	15	30.0	25	50.0	8	16.0	2	4.0	0.495
Oßweil	23771.67	59	403	2	3.4	13	22.0	26	44.1	13	22.0	5	8.5	0.494
Nussdorf	17925	85	211	7	8.2	22	25.9	49	57.6	6	7.1	1	1.2	0.491
Klein Ingersheim	5310	37	144	0	0.0	18	48.6	17	45.9	2	5.4	0	0.0	0.472
Hirschlanden	2540	10	254	0	0.0	4	40.0	4	40.0	2	20.0	0	0.0	0.470
Bissingen	23676.67	74	320	1	1.4	20	27.0	39	52.7	11	14.9	3	4.1	0.461
Möttlingen	3660	14	261	0	0.0	3	21.4	8	57.1	2	14.3	1	7.1	0.451
Ottenbronn	1923.33	24	80	1	4.2	16	66.7	7	29.2	0	0.0	0	0.0	0.437
Friolzheim	6360	51	123	1	2.0	24	47.1	24	47.1	2	3.9	0	0.0	0.436
Tamm	29770	96	310	0	0.0	23	24.0	52	54.2	20	20.8	1	1.0	0.419
Hoheneck	23691.67	79	300	1	1.3	12	15.2	53	67.1	13	16.5	0	0.0	0.395
Pflugfeld	7025	11	639	0	0.0	1	9.1	4	36.4	4	36.4	2	18.2	0.371
Erlach Hof	600	2	300	0	0.0	0	0.0	2	100.0	0	0.0	0	0.0	
Fuchshof	2070	3	690	0	0.0	1	33.3	1	33.3	0	0.0	1	33.3	
Schaffhof	400	2	200	0	0.0	0	0.0	2	100.0	0	0.0	0	0.0	
Totals	**981983.8**	**3990**	**10854**	**221**	**5.5**	**1430**	**35.8**	**1735**	**43.5**	**460**	**11.5**	**144**	**3.6**	

Source: HStAS A45a Ämte Leonberg, Vaihingen a.d. Enz, Bietigheim, Hoheneck, Canstatt, Stuttgart, Calw, Asperg, Markgröningen.

Wealth, which does not necessarily translate directly into income, is one way to measure well-being and social relations. Another is to assess actual material assets. The owner of a plough-team, for example, had an advantage in choosing when to work his land and could hire it out to others who needed their arable turned over. The number of plough-teams, or the number of ploughs, available to villages before the Thirty Years' war seems to have represented between a tenth and a fifth of households, the higher figure being found in districts more strongly orientated towards grain growing. Poor villages however like Botnang had none at all. Botnang had to obtain ploughing from neighbouring Feuerbach, whose farmers had also bought up much of Botnang's land.[69] By the late seventeenth and early eighteenth centuries there was at the very most a plough-team for every five households in the *Amt* Leonberg.[70] Ownership of wagons was, if anything, even more infrequent. As over half of households held arable land, and the gear was also needed for other activities, one can well understand the problems of co-ordinating the harvest, complaints about lack of traction and carts for moving crops or wood, and the need for reciprocal arrangements. At both ends of the seventeenth century, however, it seems that between a tenth and a fifth of the populace had access to the means of cultivating grain themselves, while the others must have been more orientated towards viticulture, artisanal work and labouring. At the very least arable smallholders would need to work for larger farmers or earn the money to buy in a plough-team.

These rough indications are, of course, only part of the story. Livestock ownership, even of horses, was more widespread than that of farm

---

[69] Some villages have records of plough-teams available (though not their distribution among households). From others we can calculate a rough maximum from the number of horses, though not all of these would have been suitable for plough work. A plough could be pulled by two horses though more may have been preferable on heavy and stony soils, and tax instructions assume three. Villages such as Eglosheim, Oßweil and Tamm had just under a plough-team for every five households in 1634, while Kornwestheim may have had twice as many. Renningen had seventy-three horses in 1590 and about eighty a few years later, or a plough-team for every four households at most. Maisch's data from Gebersheim (poor, but grain-growing) and Bondorf (wealthier grain-growing), utilising inventory evidence and hence probably skewed in favour of the wealthy, shows 25 per cent (1550–1619) and 60 per cent (1620–54) of households with a plough respectively. HStAS A206 Bü 751, 1002; Reyscher, *SWG*, Bd.XVII., p. 502; Burckhardt, *Eglosheim*. p. 150; Felden, *Ortsbuch Hoheneck*, p. 246; Gestrich, '*Aufwiegler, Rebellen, saubere Buben*', p. 41; Gaisberg-Schöckingen, *Schöckingen*, p. 215; Maisch, *Notdürftiger Unterhalt*, p. 105.

[70] This would optimistically assume two horses or two oxen per team, based on a 1708 survey recording 1,570 households, 536 horses and forty-five pairs of oxen. HStAS A368L Bü 136. Maisch's data shows a slightly lower prevalence of ploughs in households ca 1700 than before 1650. Maisch, *Notdürftiger Unterhalt*, p. 105.

equipment. At least half of households probably held cows, at least a third pigs, and a quarter sheep. As it was very rare to hold any other animal if one did not have a cow, this left possibly two-fifths of households without any livestock at all.[71] Animal stocking rates altered little over time. By 1708, one third of the household heads in the *Amt* Leonberg were described as 'peasants' (*Bauer*), meaning in the context of the report that they would be expected to provide draught animal power for corvée labour. A tenth were widows and over two-fifths *Handfrohner*, those who only worked with tools or their hands.[72] Another group is marked out by the way in which wood was allotted in the early seventeenth century, where around a third of rural households, where we have evidence, lived in subdivided houses. Often these households received a smaller share of firewood from the communal woodland than owners of whole houses. This group could also, rather imprecisely it seems, be described as being comprised of vinedressers and day-labourers. The form of one's labour or the quality of one's housing appear to have been important rhetorical forms of social differentiation, although doubtless the overlap of such factors was quite complex in reality.[73]

Agricultural instruments, land and capital were not the only means of making a living. Artisanal work of one kind of another, public office, moneylending and trade could all bring their rewards. At the top of the pyramid were major traders like the Dreher family of Leonberg, dealing in wine, wool and credit. In the early 1590s Leonberg could muster several big lenders in the shape of senior officials (the *Vogt* and Church administrator) and the merchant Bastian Besserer. His relative Hans Hemminger was the dominant creditor (and butcher) in Ditzingen, while in Renningen it fell to the dynasty of the *Schultheißen*, the Schnauffers, though in the early seventeenth century the Ergenzingers took over some of their business contracted as far afield as Ingersheim in the north-east of the *Forstamt*. By no means every village had such men, and nobody seems to have stretched their tentacles beyond the immediate economy of central Württemberg. Loans went to the government, to Stuttgart, Esslingen, Sindelfingen, and their rural hinterlands. Centres of the wine trade such as Bietigheim, Enzweihingen, Leonberg and Markgröningen could generate these real capitalists, although often their debtors were institutions of one kind or another,

---

[71] See chapter 1. HStAS A237a Bü 582, 601.

[72] The numbers suggest an improbably thin spread of horse ownership even among peasants, so some of those recorded as 'peasants' may not really have owned the horses, or in practice shared them with kin. HStAS A368L Bü 136.

[73] See Warde, 'Law'.

not least the ducal government. Some of them appear to have operated only on a large scale, pale imitations of metropolitan financiers, as they did not lend to their less worthy neighbours but appear to have built up credit and annuities with the government or urban centres. The number of these families was very small, but their local influence was strong.[74]

Unfortunately, there are no reliable figures on numbers of artisans for nearly all settlements before the eighteenth century. Even when occupational designations are available, it is often difficult to discern precisely what implications such a title had for household income, partly because an occupational title might designate a guild qualification rather than the primary economic activity, and also because most artisans owned land.[75] This is, again, a lasting feature of the Württemberger economy. We can bend an ear to the comments on the region of nineteenth century political economist Gustav Rümelin. 'The mixing is so varied and represented in all proportions, that in many cases leaves [it] even in an entirely rational book-keeping doubtful, whether someone is to be entered in the list as an industrial worker, who is a farmer on the side, or as a farmer, who as a by-employment pursues a handicraft or trade.'[76] The situation is not so different from that described for the village of Bondorf by tax commissioner Johann Bernhard Ettlinger in 1720. Artisans could not live solely from their trade but also cultivated land, and those that had no land also had to work as wage labourers.[77] In early eighteenth-century Leonberg, barbers, saddlers and bakers traded wine while a ropemaker retailed curds, tallow and oil.[78] Trades were frequently combined with keeping an inn of some kind. We can find fairly wealthy artisans who supplemented their trade from farming and commerce, while others must have made the largest share of their income from their agricultural work. On the better-off side of things, a typical example was the *Schultheiß* of Heimerdingen in 1736, Hans Jerg Schmid. A trained butcher, he really

---

[74] Undoubtedly much of this was connected with trade as well as advances for investment or emergencies. However, several Bietigheimers who appear only as fairly small creditors in 1590 and who did not lend significant sums to the ducal government were owed thousands of *gulden* in credit in 1606, such as Georg Bühl (probably the heir to the fortunes of the Bühels of Enzweihingen) and the heirs of Samuel Unfrid. These cases may be elderly who had sold off all their property and bought annuities, or they may have been wards, whose guardians leant out money that they were not legally permitted to re-invest elsewhere. HStAS A320 Bü 5; A572 Bü 45; Boelcke, 'Bäuerlicher Wohlstand'; Bütterlin, *Die Württembergische Staatshaushalt*, pp. 171–225.

[75] Maisch, *Notdürftiger Unterhalt*, pp. 72–3; Isermeyer, *Ländliche Gesellschaft*, p. 63.

[76] Cited in Medick, *Weben und Überleben*, p. 161.

[77] Maisch, *Notdürftiger Unterhalt*, p. 151.

[78] Hofacker, 'Die Epoche von 1648 bis 1800', p. 151.

however won his '*nahrung*' from his 'fields and vineyard', accounting for his designation as 'wealthy' (*wohl*).[79]

Nevertheless, artisanal activity was clearly more concentrated in the towns, where perhaps two-fifths to half of household heads were artisans or professionals.[80] In the 1730s most villages had only about a fifth to a third of their populace engaged in handicrafts. Given the very mixed nature of activity it is not surprising that the distribution of artisans shows no strong pattern. Activities like working in viticulture and artisanal work were not usually substitutes for each other and thus communities where viticulture was prominent were no different from others in the numbers of resident artisans. Most occupations serviced the agrarian economy, as bakers, weavers of linen cloth, blacksmiths, shoemakers and such like.[81] Artisans in Leonberg generally received more income from their trade than did artisans in surrounding villages. Unsurprisingly millers, merchants and tanners made up the wealthiest trade groups while linen and woollen weavers were the poorest. The assessor in Leonberg noted that the tax assessment was not that relevant for most artisans because for the most part there were too many of them and that 'many had for the whole year nothing to do and to earn'. This comment is perhaps, like so many of its kind in this era, overdrawn. Probably a small majority of artisans could, in fact, have earned a full-time, if meagre, living from their trade. Linen weavers were the largest artisanal group (some 16 per cent of all artisans) and the most dependent on other sources of income, followed by shoemakers (14 per cent) and bakers (9 per cent). In all, forty trades were represented.[82]

---

[79] HStAS A261 Bü 1134; A572 Bü 68.

[80] In the 1730s, 41 per cent of recorded Bietigheim households (about 85 per cent of the total were recorded) and 48 per cent of Leonberger contained artisans or merchants. STABB Bh A1952; HStAS A261 Bü 1134; nearly half of households in the town of Brackenheim in 1745 were artisans. Döbele-Carlesso, *Weinbau*, p. 208.

[81] Drawn from data in HStAS A261 Bü 1134, 1004, 1635; STABB Bh A 1952.

[82] These figures are based on an analysis of 517 artisans, merchants and millers recorded in 1731 in the *Amt* Leonberg. The assessments appear to relate to estimated annual income minus costs. If, as in agriculture, two-thirds of income had been deducted as costs and the figure given was a notional capital value based on the assumption of income being a 5 per cent return, the final figures would suggest an annual turnover, on average, of under 18 fl. (seventy-five days' labouring wages) and a much lower modal income. However, this 'capital' equation makes little sense for artisanal work (see below) and the figures quoted look more like figures for income after deductions for raw materials, equipment and transactions costs. Tax instructions for 1713 order that commerce should be assessed as a proportion of the capital value bound up in the business (half is suggested) but that artisanal work should simply be an appropriate sum, taking into the account the form of the business, assessed by sworn estimators. If the average assessment in this sample was an average income, at 118 fl. *per annum* it made the 'mean' artisan reasonably prosperous,

Broadly speaking, the larger the population, the more artisans were present. While this may seem obvious, it also suggests that guild restrictions were not in any way inhibiting the development of a 'normal' hierarchy of trades. The tax returns suggest a fairly wide range of income being present among the practitioners of particular trades, even if collectively some trades tended to be somewhat richer or poorer than others. For 'traditional' crafts, there does not seem to have been a set income level that artisans aimed for. Indeed, given the availability of other sources of income, there was not the strong incentive to be seen among artisans in large cities to restrict entry to a trade and maintain their only source of income. Densities in the district, such as one butcher for every fifty-four households, and a tailor for every forty-six, do not compare unfavourably with a late seventeenth-century English example.[83] High density and low turnover can of course be a sign of relative economic backwardness, although Württemberg had a higher density of artisanal trades than the communities of Landsberg in Bavaria around the same time studied by Rainer Beck.[84] Neither do official comments that there were too many artisans, alongside the figures presented, suggest the heavy hand of major restrictions on trade. Nevertheless, there was still at least occasional prosecution for illegal trading on the side by those without guild qualifications. This was especially the case in Württemberg in those regions of protected proto-industry such as the worsted weavers of the Black Forest.[85]

For 1736 we can summarise the social structure of five settlements, two major wine producers (the Ingersheim villages), two villages in the centre of the region (Heimerdingen and Hemmingen), and the town of Bietigheim. This data is displayed in table 2.2 and rests upon occupational designations, when of course the household economy was usually 'mixed' in the sense of male labour being divided between some kind of labouring, farming, vinedressing and artisanal work. In Hemmingen and Heimerdingen, for example, of seventy households pursuing some kind of a non-agricultural trade, only fourteen of those did so to the exclusion of other work, mostly small-scale viticulture and farming. The fourteen

though the modal figure was well below this. This includes two merchants who are probably being assessed on half of their 'capital'. Ogilvie similarly treats similar, earlier tax assessments as being of income. HStAS A261 Bü 1128, 1134; Ogilvie, *State corporatism*, p. 150; Reyscher, *SWG*, Bd.XVII, p. 362.

[83] Compare with Muldrew's study of King's Lynn, an urban centre with a population as large as the whole district of Leonberg, where there were at least thirty-eight households to every butcher and forty-nine to every tailor. Muldrew, *The economy of obligation*, p. 56.

[84] In this region, even in the towns, there was about one butcher to roughly every forty households, but in the countryside one for roughly every 200 or more; and a tailor for every forty in the towns, and roughly the same proportion in the country. Beck, *Unterfinning*, p. 309.

[85] Ogilvie, *State corporatism*, pp. 127–80.

Table 2.2 *Household income sources as a proportion of all recorded households,*
1736

Place	Heimerdingen	Hemmingen	K. Ingersheim	G. Ingersheim	Bietigheim
Peasant farmer	42	24	34	26	17
Day-labourer	17	3	0	18	0
Vinedresser	1	22	43	32	19
Artisan	22	27	15	19	48
Other	5	8	4	1	15
Poor	13	15	4	4	0

Sources: HStAS A572 Bü 68; STABB Bh A 1952.

includes the pastors, schoolmasters, a couple of widows and an unmarried blind woman who span and sewed.[86]

Those who were purely peasant farmers were everywhere in a minority, while those who were recorded as engaging in day-labour ranged from a fifth of the male adult household heads and widows to zero. Those pursuing some kind of artisanal trade ranged from around a seventh to over a quarter of recorded households in the countryside, and nearly half in the town. The poor made up 13–15 per cent of Heimerdingen and Hemmingen's inhabitants, and we must suspect that the figure appears lower elsewhere because of under-recording. Men and widows with a little property or a trade who did not really earn a living any more still received their old occupational designations. Yet this was still a society of landholders. Given that the ducal government viewed the economy as consisting largely of subsistence farmers, this indicates how little other occupations earned, as those engaged only in peasant farming were in a clear minority.[87]

In times of stress the poor-relief system could be important, and many households came into contact with it over a lifetime. Relief could include

---

[86] HStAS A572 Bü 68.

[87] 'Peasants' are those who engage *solely* in farming, or for whom it is recorded that they win their income from farming despite having a guild qualification. Day-labourers include any who do day-labour, irrespective of whether they also own any land. This gives an indication of who was dependent to at least some degree on wage-work. Figures from Heimerdingen and Hemmingen include widows, but the others only partially do so, which explains in part their smaller numbers categorised as 'poor'. Again, it must be stressed that many households had multiple income sources, and even those on poor relief or dependent on charity, such as widows, often won additional income from an activity such as spinning. The occupational designations are incomplete (when compared against the total number of households) and it is likely that the poor and widows are under-represented in the Ingersheims and Bietigheim. HStAS A572 Bü 68; STABB Bh A 1952.

Table 2.3 *Social ranking in Hemmingen, 1736*

Designation	%
Women living from charity and spinning	12
Poor or miserable	3
Bad (*schlecht*)	33
Middling (*mittelmässig*)	20
Well (*wohl, schon, recht, recht schon*)	27
N/A	6

Source: HStAS A572 Bü 68.

direct doles and alms, short-term loans, emergency famine relief, and especially the loans (frequently never repaid) from communal granaries that were prevalent from the late sixteenth century, even in the country-side. The villagers of the 1730s appear to have been more dependent on neighbourly charity than formal relief when they fell into infirmity, but communes and parish funds were still frequently creditors in times of need. In the crisis year of 1614–15, no less than 40 per cent of the households in Leonberg borrowed from the town granary, while in the late sixteenth century, probably at least a fifth of the town's population were supported by the poor chest or charitable endowments at some point.[88]

A final word comes from Hemmingen in 1736, where assessors classed all of the male-headed households into rough groups according to their fortunes, displayed in table 2.3. All female-headed households were widows, no less than 12 per cent of all households.

Every one of these female-headed households lived 'from good-hearted people and from spinning'. Just under 10 per cent of households were female headed in the region in 1544, and it may well be, with a few exceptions, that this 'substratum' of female poverty was an enduring feature. A further three of male-headed households were thought to be 'poor' and 'miserable'. A third of the populace had it 'bad', mostly vinedressers, day-labourers and linen weavers, or a combination of the three. A fifth had a designation implying a 'middling', acceptable living, and about the same number had it good, though the assessors distinguished between the 'wealthy', 'respectable' (*wohl*) and 'handsome' (*schon*) livings. Many of these final two groups were artisans of some kind, with arable land and vineyards. It is notable that the age range of all

[88] Warde, 'Sources of welfare support'.

of these groups is much the same (suggesting that the divisions are not a product of the life cycle, though this does not exclude some life-cycle mobility), but that the wealthy tended to have fewer children living at home. We cannot draw many demographic conclusions from this, but might suggest that for some, the presence of larger numbers of mouths to feed drew them down from having a more 'respectable' or even just 'so-so' existence to one that could even be labelled as 'bad'.[89] We must also remember that these households often contained servants, and much of the population between the ages of fifteen and twenty-five was in service. Maid numbers especially were much higher in the eighteenth than the sixteenth century, as the age at first marriage and celibacy rates rose.[90]

The structure of the economy from taxation records

Individuals and households were thus subject to, or could exercise power according to their access to means of production, their institutional leverage (more of which below), and their assets more generally. Taxation records also allow a more wide-ranging appraisal of what assets and income flows were available to society as whole, and consequently, in what activities much of the power lay. Or more precisely, what income streams existed to be manipulated by the powerful. Of course, because of the general interest of the populace in avoiding the payment of tax, most taxation records are to some degree unreliable. Taxation in Württemberg, which was collected by the Estates rather than the ducal government, received some standardisation from 1538 onwards, having previously been allotted almost entirely on variable, local premises.[91] These gradual steps towards a more systematic approach do not for the most part really yield reliable data for comparison across time and space until the eighteenth century, and then must still be treated with caution. However, the previously mentioned 'Turk tax' of 1544–5 is an exception. This does not overcome the problem of the subjective variability in wealth assessment on the part of local assessors, not least because landed property was not assessed at *current market* value, but according to *purchase*

---

[89] The groups designated as '*schon*', '*wohl*', '*mittelmässig*' and '*schlecht*' had average numbers of children to support (this does not include the 15–25 age group) of 0.8, 1.3, 1.9 and 2.3 respectively. Their mean age range all lay between 44 and 49, with a standard deviation of around 11 years for all groups. HStAS A572 Bü 68; HStAS A54a Ämte Leonberg, Vaihingen a.d. Enz, Bietigheim, Hoheneck, Canstatt, Stuttgart, Calw, Asperg, Markgröningen.
[90] Trugenberger, '"Die Magd"', pp. 50–1.   [91] Reyscher, *SWG*, Bd.XVII, pp. 43–7.

price, a method that became increasingly unrealistic in an age of inflation.[92] Equally, *movable property* is generally considered to have been undervalued, it generally being inherently less easy to assess than *immovable* goods. Consequently all types of property were under-assessed to an unknown degree! This does not entirely undermine the uses of such assessments, however. They do allow us to provide a rough picture of social structure, as has been done above, and in many other studies. We can also, whilst accepting some margin of error, use the 1544–5 returns to *rank settlements* and see what kind of area was performing relatively well or badly in terms of average household wealth.

In turn, these results can be compared with the economy as it stood nearly two centuries later. By the eighteenth century the government attempted to assess taxpayers more rigorously, in response to complaints and with the desire to produce a more equitable and reliable yield of tax.[93] These returns, especially from 1713 onwards, were used to estimate what the authorities called the *capital value* of each householder's estate and tax it accordingly. However, this was actually done via a formula that assessed the *income* generated by economic activity and attempted to turn that into an expression of capital value assuming a 5 per cent return on capital, for the most part, once costs had been deducted.[94] Hence instead of a taxation system based on the rather unreliable estimates of wealth, primarily derived from land values, the new system was really based on income flows, then converted into a notional capital value. However, to modern eyes, its form was confused because costs of running the household and the cost of *production* were not kept distinct.[95] Feudal rents, and basic subsistence

---

[92] By 1629, tax assessments should have been based on the saleable value of a property. Reyscher, *SWG*, Bd.XVII, p. 130.

[93] To produce a 'best possible *egalité*' as a tax instruction of 1738 put it. David Sabean has interpreted these trends as a greater interest on the part of the government in productivity, but much of the pressure in fact seems to come from taxpayers who felt that they were not being equitably assessed. Reyscher, *SWG*, Bd.XVII, p. 401; Sabean, *Property*, p. 26.

[94] Property was to be assessed 'not by its general value, as done in previous times, but more by the yield, commodity, earnings and use'. For the 3rd Tax Instruction of 1713, see Reyscher, *SWG*, Bd.XVII, pp. 350–67. While historians often stress under-assessment of wealth and income, it is worth noting that this formula could well have been too optimistic, a report of 1719 noted that a 5 per cent return 'happened very rarely'. HStAS A28 Bü 99. However, the tax revision from 1713 on, and especially between the late 1720s and late 1730s, which provide a huge amount of detailed information on local economies, was never generally completed. Thereafter efforts fell into abeyance and massive under-assessment was rife. However, it does not seem to be the case, as Wilson argues, that locally only property registers from 1629/55 were retained, as there is abundant evidence of new ones being drawn up at various subsequent points. The need for revision is commented on, for example, in HStAS A261 Bü 1127. Wilson, *War, state and society*, p. 138.

[95] One could argue, of course, that doing so only tends to undervalue domestic work.

and running costs were removed from the final assessment. In the case of agriculture the taxable remainder left after these deductions was presumably made up of some of what we would normally class as wages (to the farmer), some as returns to capital, and for the most part, the rent of the soil. Overall agricultural income also ignored the livestock sector and the value added in the production of meat and dairy products, because only the income directly from *land* (and thus fodder inputs such as hay and straw into the livestock sector) was included.

The real meaning of assessed taxable values for trade and artisanal work is more difficult to assess. Authorities instructed assessors to make a fair estimate based on the same principles as for cultivated land. But there was, of course, no 'rent' to speak of involved in being a weaver or a coppersmith (buildings were assessed separately). The income from a handicraft could not be converted into a capital value like the rent of a piece of land, because nearly all the costs came from labour and raw materials. In the tax returns, we find that while the income from agricultural land was subject to a complex set of arithmetical procedures to produce the final 'capital' value, in 1713 those from 'commerce, industry and handicrafts' were simply given a straight figure of returns 'above costs'. It seems likely that in household-based artisanal workshops the category 'costs' refers to raw materials and transactions costs, because otherwise the figures recorded are implausibly high.[96]

This data allows us, with some caution, to estimate the relative importance of some *sectors* of the economy in 1713, and as with the 1544–5 tax, rank settlements in order to establish which were doing relatively well or badly. However, the fact that estimated costs of production were deducted means that the real level of income is not at all clear from the *final* returns. Labourers were not taxed on their income from labouring, for example, and as their labour input into agricultural production on their employers' farmers was deducted from the taxable value of those farms' output, a large section of income was actually missed out. This helps explain the constant fall in taxable 'capital' per person in Württemberg over the eighteenth century, because the system effectively ignored wages.[97]

---

[96] The average return of 118 fl. for 517 artisans with a wage *already deducted* would have been a handsome return indeed, as this already amounts to 357 days of journeymen's wages. This apparently high mean figure is the result of a few wealthy traders and millers being part of the sample. More typical was a return of 60 fl. or less, or 180 days of journeymen's wages. These figures also argue against the idea that the returns might be notional 'capital' figures on the 5 per cent return principle, as, were this the case, average artisanal turnover figures would be absurdly low, only maybe the value of four to six weeks' work at the very most.

[97] This was the amount deductable from farm incomes for costs of production. Reyscher, *SWG*, Bd. XVII, pp. 359–60.

Were wages not generally so low, one would even be tempted to say that the system encouraged consumption by the poor! Undoubtedly the eighteenth century returns are also under-assessments.

In 1544, wealth in the district of Leonberg, as recorded by the assessors, clustered around the town. This was in fact a measure of wealth of the residents of each settlement, irrespective of whether that property actually lay within the settlement's *Markung* or not. The results are displayed in table 2.1.[98] Leonberg had the highest aggregate wealth, followed by the large agricultural villages of Ditzingen and Renningen and the viticulture centre of Gerlingen. The ranking of average household wealth was similar. Although Mönßheim and Heimsheim actually stood more directly on trade routes, the basic agricultural core closer to Stuttgart was where the wealth lay. This agriculturally based prosperity was even more true, of course, of the zone to the north-east around Markgröningen and Münchingen, and the regional 'bread basket' of Kornwestheim and Oßweil. These centres of cereal production and grain export, as well as the towns that serviced them, all enjoyed the highest levels of wealth per household.

With a major restructuring of taxation assessment from 1713, the value of properties was calculated from the average income derived from plots of land over a period of years, minus costs of production and liabilities such as feudal dues.[99] The resulting figure was then, as explained above, converted into a notional 'capital' value. As displayed in table 2.4, the assessments covered arable land, meadows, open pastures, gardens and plots of land for hemp and flax, vineyards, woodland, income from annuities and interest, the returns from trade and industry, and buildings.[100] Assessments were made by locals under the supervision of a ducal tax commissioner, who was admonished in 1728 not to overly trust the local notary, and neither, of course, should we.[101] In contrast to 1544, in the case of agricultural land this was an assessment of income generated *within* the *Markung*. The 1713 figures allow the first datable, and reasonably reliable, picture of the relative weight of sectors of the economy. The table shows the assessment of taxable returns that the assessors actually

[98] See p. 122.

[99] The period was six years for arable land and ten years for vineyards, the costs of production initially treated as two-thirds of output in each case, although this was later considerably refined. In the case of gardens and the cultivation of flax, hemp and vegetables, and in the maintenance of meadows, costs were considered to be only one third of income from the land. Reyscher, *SWG*, Bd.XVII, pp. 359–62; HStAS A261 Bü 1134.

[100] The table is based on data found in HStAS A261 Bü 1128.

[101] Reyscher, *SWG*, Bd.XVII, p. 397.

Table 2.4 *Taxable income in the* Amt Leonberg, *1713 (in fl.)*

Place	Arable land	Meadowland	Vineyard	Flax/veg plots	Gardens	Woodland	Loans and annuities	Commerce	Total
Renningen	11,529	2,456	166	0	209	467	105	3,672	18,604
Ditzingen	11,491	1,286	1,228	0	380	193	77	3,894	18,549
Eltingen	10,173	3,668	818	0	260	357	15	1,120	16,411
Leonberg	2,719	388	769	0	521	233	1,650	9,197	15,477
Gerlingen	6,620	1,054	3,862	29	184	591	280	1,885	14,476
Weilimdorf	8,275	956	843	61	220	334	0	2,645	13,302
Heimsheim	7,153	530	11	0	83	241	8	2,732	10,819
Rutesheim	6,586	424	128	0	225	847	189	1,868	10,267
Heimerdingen	6,623	224	478	0	216	260	0	1,510	9,311
Hofingen	4,784	369	554	34	61	155	6	1,448	7,411
Hemmingen	4,520	216	737	0	76	122	5	918	6,594
Monsheim	2,532	489	428	35	117	306	38	2,306	6,251
Hirschlanden	4,047	80	640	0	36	0	0	510	5,313
Gebersheim	1,519	71	129	3	13	79	0	240	2,054
Munklingen	1,320	219	63	0	74	8	0	334	2,018
Total	**89,891**	**12,430**	**10,854**	**162**	**2,675**	**4,193**	**2,373**	**34,279**	**156,857**
%Total	**57**	**8**	**7**	**0**	**2**	**3**	**2**	**22**	

Source: A261 Bü 1128.

compiled *before any deductions*. It is thus an estimate of income, although the final figure on which tax was paid was not. The exception, unfortunately, is any commercial and artisanal activity, for which only income 'above costs' was recorded. The size of this sector must be considerably underestimated, a problem that must have been more marked in areas such as commerce and retailing where wage costs made up only a small proportion of total outlay.[102]

By 1713, if any credence is given to these records, agriculture was by far the largest sector bringing in three-quarters of total income. Within this, arable farming dominated, and given the integrated mixed farming regime of grain crops, sheep farming and dairying we should really see this as one sector that brought in 65 per cent of income. Viticulture, for all its local fame, was a poor second. Artisanal work and commerce brought in at the very least 22 per cent of income, certainly an underestimate. The tax returns of 1731, based on a range of observations over the 1720s, give similar figures but suggest that commercial and artisanal activity was considerably underestimated in 1713. While overall income was up a little between these two dates, the assessment for incomes from taverns, artisanal and general trade (not including livestock, wine or salt) was up to 37 per cent of income.[103] As there is no evidence of a rise in artisanal activity between the two dates, inaccurate assessment with the new system in 1713 is probably to blame. Given the ambiguities in this data, and the missing livestock sector that assumed considerable proportions in many European economies, these figures can only be generally indicative. On the basis of late seventeenth-century livestock taxes we could estimate that the sector was worth at the very least 50,000 fl., or 31 per cent of the assessed income of 1713, or 28 per cent of that of 1736.[104] If this estimate

---

[102] This is probably reflected in the breakdown of 'commercial' activity, which apportions 73 per cent to artisanal work, 14 per cent to tavern-keeping, 6 per cent to general trade, 4 per cent to the livestock trade and only 1 per cent to the wine trade and 1 per cent to the salt trade! HStAS A261 Bü 1128.

[103] Of course, these figures are net of costs and so considerably underestimate income in that regard. Equally, however, we do not know the local 'balance of payments' and how much was spent on imports, although some estimates are provided in chapter 5. HStAS A261 Bü 1128.

[104] A cow could produce, on the estimates of Rainer Beck and Christian Pfister, dairy products (mostly curds) worth around 12.5 fl. in 1720 with a fairly low milk yield of 625 litres each year. This would mean that the 2,320 cows in the district of Leonberg produced some 30,000 fl. income, if consumed as curds, each year. An extraordinary livestock tax in the year 1693 levied during the French invasion appears to have taxed cows at about 3–4 per cent of their annual product (and horses at about 3–4 per cent of their value). If the same principle were applied to the district's 8,000 sheep, the tax valuation of a sheep would suggest that each produced 3.125 fl. *per annum*, adding around 20,000 fl. more to income. Of course, one should really deduct some of the value of meadows that went directly to livestock to avoid double counting. As the income

is included, then the district's income (with non-agricultural activity certainly underestimated) in 1731 would have shown a breakdown of 70 per cent from agriculture, and 30 per cent from industry, services and commerce. The latter should probably be considered an absolute minimum. This would compare with estimates for England in 1688 of 37 per cent to agriculture, 36 per cent to industry and commerce, 20 per cent to rent and services, and 7 per cent to government. In the 1700s, Italy had an agricultural sector that brought in around 54 per cent of national income. Of course these figures are not comparing like with like, not least because the tiny district of Leonberg contains no large urban sector.[105] Even so, the non-agricultural economy is already prominent. It is quite possible, given steady rates of urbanisation over time and little evidence of rapid shifts in the number of rural artisans outside of particular regions of proto-industry, that the proportion changed little between the early fifteenth and late eighteenth centuries.[106]

The highest earning settlements of the early eighteenth century still clustered in the south-east of the district. Tax records from 1629, 1687 and 1704 have similar rankings though they greatly underestimate the importance of non-agricultural income, being largely determined by landholdings and buildings.[107] The tax records are equivocal and frustrating to work with, but the picture they portray over two centuries is remarkably consistent. The same settlements and qualities come to the fore. The weight of the evidence is against major social structural change. The course of the local economy, despite great conjunctural shifts and demographic catastrophe, was set with a steady and unyielding tiller.

Per capita income in the eighteenth century

A high degree of continuity in sources of income and social structure equally implies a high degree of continuity in the income levels of the population. This was indeed the case. But what kind of spending power

produced by horses and oxen is unclear, and was largely directed towards arable production, this has also not been included. Of course animals could generate additional value in the leather industry but this, judging by the scale of tanning and shoemaking, must have been fairly small. Beck, *Unterfinning*, pp. 172–3, 520, 532, 628; Pfister, *Bevölkerung*, pp. 89–95; Warde, 'Common rights', p. 214.

[105] In the Württemberg case, rents would have largely come out of agricultural incomes. HStAS A261 Bü 1134; Crafts, *British economic growth*, p. 13; Malanima, 'Measuring the Italian economy'.

[106] Urbanisation rates have typically been used to assess the size of the non-agricultural sector in European economies. Wrigley, 'Urban growth and agricultural change'; Zanden, 'Early modern economic growth'; Malanima, 'Measuring the Italian economy'; Allen, 'Progress and poverty'.

[107] HStAS A261 Bü 1126; A368L Bü 56.

did this bring to the populace, particularly in comparison to other regions of Europe, that might equally be competing to purchase scarce resources? National levels of *per capita* income have increasingly been the object of research by economic historians in recent years. This indicator of general individual welfare is as good a measure of the success of an economy as any other one. Indeed, whatever their technological or political achievements, economies must also be measured 'in terms of their ability to create well-being for all individuals who live within them', and *per capita* income is a reasonable measure of the fortunes of the great mass of the population in pre-industrial economies.[108] It is a truism that pre-industrial incomes cannot have fluctuated as much as modern ones. Given that much of the European population lived at near subsistence level in 1800, scope for levels having previously been very much lower was obviously limited. Paolo Malanima, for example, sets a limit of 50 per cent growth between 1000 and 1800 in Italy.[109]

One way to calculate *per capita* income is to use a series of prices and wages to calculate the changing nominal and real income of specific occupations. Building workers in particular have been the focus of these efforts as details of their employment are often the best preserved. This has the advantage of using 'real', and fairly reliable, records of actual payments. However, the results are limited to particular occupations that were paid wages or salaries, in a world where much work was unpaid, done on subsistence holdings, or even more than today, took place in the 'informal' sector of the economy. They are also only records of wages, and not the returns to capital or rents. Malanima estimates that for medieval and early modern Italy some 40 per cent of income went to the state and the wealthiest tenth of society.[110] We also do not know how many people each wage earner, on average, supported.

In the 1720s and 1730s, labourers in large southern German cities earned about four grams of silver per day. Silver, which nearly everywhere was the underpinning to the money of account, serves as a useful international comparison, though the price of silver varied from place to place like that of any other commodity.[111] Labourers in Amsterdam could expect to get the equivalent of nine grams per day and Londoners as much as ten. Northern Italians lagged behind southern German cities but Neapolitans earned slightly more in terms of silver. The labourers

---

[108] Ogilvie, *A bitter living*, p. 15.
[109] Malanima, 'Il prodotto'; see also Zanden, 'Early modern economic growth', pp. 79–80.
[110] Malanima, 'Measuring the Italian economy', pp. 267–8.
[111] Braudel and Spooner, 'Prices in Europe'.

of Istanbul were slightly poorer. Outside of the Low Countries and England these levels were much the same in 1600.[112] Bob Allen has calculated that supporting one person at subsistence level in a southern German city in the first half of the eighteenth century cost about a gram of silver per day. Thus a labourer supporting a family of four would have been right on the breadline. Low silver prices in the cities of the Low Countries and England meant that labourers there were far better off in 'real' terms, not just in the silver value of their wages. Higher prices in France meant living standards would have been a little lower than in Augsburg or Leipzig.[113] At this time the Württemberger unit of account, the *gulden*, contained about 22 grams of silver.[114] A labourer earning 0.25 fl. per day thus would have received 5.7 grams of silver per day, or more than in the great cities of southern Germany! However, the *kreuzer* of the period contained much less silver than the *gulden* relative to its nominal value, or the equivalent of about 15 grams of silver for 60 *kreuzer*, which nominally equalled one *gulden*. This is much more in line with other regional centres such as Speyer where the accounting *gulden* was worth 12 grams of silver. It seems better, then, to calculate silver wages in terms of this smaller and more frequently used denomination.[115]

Württemberg's supposed currency stability from 1559 onwards, aside from the early seventeenth century, based on the silver content of the *gulden*, disappears when set against the coins actually in circulation. This nominal overvaluation of larger denomination coinage may also explain why Württemberger officials constantly complained about the lack of coin. Presumably coins from neighbouring cities and principalities were also frequently employed. Using the *kreuzer* conversion rate to silver, a Württemberger labourer earned at most 3.75 grams of silver a day, which still looks quite good in comparison to urban wages. Of course prices were commensurately lower too. About fifty days' work would

---

[112] See Allen, 'Progress and poverty'; Allen, 'The great divergence'; Özmucur and Pamuk, 'Real wages and standards of living', p. 301. Data also kindly supplied by Bob Allen.
[113] Data supplied by Bob Allen.
[114] *Gulden* were not in fact regularly minted but from 1559 their value was fixed against that of the *Reichstaler* of 68 x. In practice people used a bewildering variety of coins that shifted over time, so the precise 'silver wages' can only be treated as indicative of experience. Klein and Raff, *Württembergischen Münzen von 1374–1693*, pp. 12, 252–5; Klein and Raff, *Württembergischen Münzen von 1693–1707*, pp. 220–1; Schüttenhelm, *Der Geldumlauf*, pp. 532–45.
[115] Klein and Raff, *Württembergischen Münzen von 1374–1693*, pp. 253–4; Klein and Raff, *Württembergischen Münzen von 1693–1707*, pp. 220–1; Metz, *Geld, Währung und Preisentwicklung*.

provide bread grain for a person for a year.[116] Nevertheless, it was a meagre living. A family of four's basic carbohydrates would take up 200 days' labour when the labouring year fell between 200 to 280 days.[117] The bread grains themselves would need to be processed, which needed fuel to cook gruel, or payments to a baker.

Urban craftsmen were considerably better off than their labouring peers, as much as by 50 per cent in early eighteenth-century Augsburg. The 'skill premium' was larger here and in much of southern Europe than in the north-west of the continent, though the master craftsmen of the southern cities still earned less in silver than the labourers of London, Antwerp and Amsterdam.[118] In turn, a Württemberger journeyman, who according to wage ordinances could hope for as much as 4.9 grams of silver a day, earned somewhat more than his Augsburger equivalent. The 'skill premium' appears to have been very high.[119] All these calculations are, however, for *working days*. In the late seventeenth century, averaged out over the entire year a Württemberger weaver earned 2.3 grams of silver per day and a rough spinner half that. In 1761 a survey of the poor reckoned their absolute minimal needs to be covered by 30 fl. in the countryside, or about 0.9 grams of silver per day.[120] Malanima has calculated the 'social minimum' income in 1740s Italy to be 1.8 grams of silver,[121] not so far short of what a journeyman received in Württemberg averaged out over the year. In other words, by these reckonings, those who lived by their labour only or squeezed out a living on the lowest rung of the artisanal ladder were, by western European standards, desperately short of spending power, even if they could obtain goods in kind locally quite cheaply. This suggests that guild restrictions made Württemberg *inter-regionally* or *internationally* uncompetitive by making day-rates for work high, and depressing the amount of work available. The attractions of subsistence agriculture – though beyond the reach of most – are clear. In contrast an English labouring family could expect to earn as much as the equivalent of 4.9 grams of silver

[116] This estimates a need of 2.8 *Scheffel* per person at approximately 2.5 fl. per *Scheffel* of spelt. Figure based on HStAS A237a Bü 582 and 586. Maisch, *Notdürftiger Unterhalt*, pp. 51, 123 n.165; von Hippel, 'Bevölkerung', p. 422; Fertig, *Lokales Leben*, p. 311; Roeck, *Bäcker*, p. 75; Göttmann, *Getreidemarkt*, p. 231; Abel, *Geschichte*, p. 104; Troeltsch, *Die Calwer Zeughandlungskompagnie*, p. 242; for the consumption levels of different age groups, see Wall, 'Implications'.
[117] Troeltsch, *Die Calwer Zeughandlungskompagnie*, pp. 225–6.
[118] Data provided by Bob Allen.
[119] If they earned, as guild ordinances stipulated, 37 x per day.
[120] Troeltsch, *Die Calwer Zeughandlungskompagnie*, pp. 221–2, 234–5.
[121] Malanima, based on a Florentine lira of 3.9 grams and a 'social minimum' of 148 lira. Malanima, 'Il Prodotto'; information kindly supplied by Paolo Malanima.

averaged out over every day of the year in the late 1680s, as much as a Württemberger journeyman on a working day![122]

However, these data provide only indicators of a few sectors of the economy. The average artisan in the district of Leonberg (if we include wealthy traders and millers) earned 4.9 grams of silver per day averaged over a year, not a great amount but not quite penurious by continental standards. The modal artisan earned something more like 4.2 grams and the median in the district of Leonberg just 2.9 grams from his or her trade. This is somewhat more than Vauban reckoned a French weaver as earning in 1707: 120 *livres* per year, or 2.2 grams of silver per day.[123] How well the economy as a whole, however, performed depended on how overall income was distributed. Lacking detailed social structural and sufficiently fine-grained earnings data, historians have instead resorted to calculating *national income* from other sources, which can be divided by the population to produce a *per capita* sum. In some cases these estimates rest simply upon very high-level observations of the extent of trade and returns to taxation.[124] Others, in the case of England using the often surprisingly accurate estimates of Gregory King in 1688, have sought to establish national income from a series of estimates of income at the sectoral level. On the basis of the last, each family in England received about 12 grams of silver per day, every day. This was a bit better than a craftsman's daily wage in London. The *per capita* income was about 3.7 grams of silver.[125] By Malanima's calculation *per capita* income in Italy was about 3.6 grams of silver per day in the 1740s (by which time England had improved a little).[126] Wages might be relatively low by western European standards in much of Italy but income to rents, to commerce and to government was still evidently high. Calculations using Vauban's estimates of 1707 yield a French *per capita* income of 2.25 grams of silver per day.[127]

In the district of Leonberg, people were far poorer. The income recorded in the tax returns of 1731 gives a *per capita* daily income of a miserly 0.8 grams of silver (rising to 1 gram if we include my estimate of

---

[122] This is based on Gregory King's estimate, as used by Lindert and Williamson, of 284,997 labouring families earning £4.27 million in 1688. See Crafts, *British economic growth*, p. 13.

[123] Based on the *livre tournois* being 7.3956 grams of silver. Cited in Braudel, *The perspective of the world*, pp. 302–3.

[124] Ibid., pp. 229–315.

[125] Calculated from the table in Crafts, *British economic growth*, p. 13. The English population stood at some 4.85 million in 1688.

[126] This follows his estimate of 90 per cent of the population earning the 'social minimum' income and 10 per cent of the population and the state earning a sum equal to the income of the previous 90 per cent put together. Malanima, 'Il prodotto'.

[127] Braudel, *The perspective of the world*, p. 303.

income from livestock) and a household income of around 4 grams.[128] Of course the tax figures ignore income from livestock; they do not record waged labour; they do not record government or municipal expenditure. Together these areas would add a fifth or perhaps more to total income. Neither is female labour included, especially as spinners, though very badly remunerated; and also house rents, a very small proportion of total expenditure.[129] Yet even allowing for a large under-valuation of income (which could only have come in the industrial and service sectors, because the calculation of income from agriculture is based on quite realistic yield levels), it is hard to imagine that *per capita* income was very much higher than 1.5 grams of silver per day, or 36 fl. *per annum*. Trade might have expanded according to toll records, but any expansion in the economy can have brought barely any rewards to the expanding population save from staving off complete destitution. This evidence backs up the suggestion of wage data that Württembergers were little better off in the eighteenth than in the late sixteenth century, in part simply because they can hardly have been poorer. Indeed, a day's labour in 1560s Bietigheim was worth about 3 grams of silver, or about the same as many labourers received in the first half of the eighteenth century.[130] In a largely agrarian economy with minimal rents and depressed consumer demand, there was little opportunity for an accumulating class to develop. The similarity between income calculated from taxation records and that calculated from wage rates demonstrates that relatively little surplus was being extracted by the State, the Church and landlords. We would expect Germans more generally to be somewhat better off on average than Württembergers, as Württemberg's *per capita* income will be depressed by its lack of wealthy nobility or large urban centres and mercantile class.

These estimates are supported by earlier data produced for the purposes of tax assessment. An attempt to reconfigure taxation assessments in 1607 led to the ducal government requesting details on individual households from across the region, and some of these survive. Of course, they do not really tell us about 'households'. They are records of taxation units, and as such, record buildings, arable land, vineyard, meadow, garden, woodland, ponds and fishing rights, crops and wine surplus to need and available for sale, credits and cash, debts, tax payments, and

---

[128] Based on a notional income of 177,801 fl. in 1731 divided among an estimated population of 9331. HStAS A261 Bü 1134.

[129] Troeltsch, *Die Calwer Zeughandlungskompagnie*, p. 235.

[130] Based on a daily wage of 0.13 fl., when the *gulden* was worth 23 grams of silver and the gap between the value of the *gulden* and the *kreuzer* had not yet opened.

assessed wealth. This last is an assessment of property value according to local usage, as we have seen, and not a record of either real market value or capital stock. Neither is there any detail on artisanal work.

The households chosen for study come from the tiny town of Hoheneck and the village of Neckarweihingen, close by each other on the river in the east of the *Forstamt*.[131] In each settlement, assessors took 'five of the wealthiest and five of the middling (*mittelmässigen*)'.[132] All had arable land, so we are far from dealing with the poorest. The poor without arable land were of little interest to tax assessors, however, because having little immoveable property the calculation of their small tax payments was not a matter of difficulty or dispute. The two settlements had extensive vineyards and were very much orientated towards viticulture. The twenty households ranged from Jeremias Rueß and his two houses and yards and barn, assessed at 3,915 fl., to Jerg Bertsch and his more modest 861 fl. One can not draw too many conclusions from a sample of only twenty households for whom we do not have demographic data. The picture that can be drawn from the records, however, is relatively clear. Between 35 per cent and 64 per cent of crop income came from grain crops.[133] Even in an area where viticulture was very prominent, output remained rather mixed.[134] However, hardly any of the spelt crop was 'retailed' and the oat crop, as was usual in this region, almost undoubtedly went to horses. This is despite the fact that most of the farms clearly could have produced much more spelt than would have been consumed *in situ*. This was because peasants generally paid labourers in kind. Repeatedly we are told that there is no surplus grain above the 'cost of cultivation' and the 'household'. Or as it is recorded in the case of Jerg Großschedel the Younger, 'Farmer, after he provides for his manservant, maid, smith and cartwright, also others, his household needs and the cultivation of the fields, he has in crops in his store – nothing.' Three out of the twenty in this sample could have retailed grain, worth in two cases perhaps 75 fl., and in the other, 38 fl. If anything was sold, it was usually wine. Thirteen

---

[131] HStAS A359 Bü 3.

[132] This should not be confused with the English phrase 'the middling sort', which has quite a different sense.

[133] This assumes average yields of approximately 20 hl per hectare for wine, which appears to be an underestimate in some of the cases, around 5 *Scheffel* per *morgen* of spelt, and half that of oats, in a traditional three-course rotation. In 1607 spelt fetched about 2.5 fl. per *Scheffel* in Leonberg, and an *Eimer* of wine 8.3 fl. in the local transhipment centre of Esslingen. StAL Armenkastenrechnungen; Salzmann, *Weinbau und Weinhandel*, p. 93.

[134] On the basis of these calculations, median income in this data set would have been 161 fl. Such a household probably possessed a couple of cows whose dairy products would be worth, together, perhaps another 20 fl. or more. Overall livestock probably added another 20 per cent to the total income.

of the twenty had wine for sale, from 50 up to 250 fl. worth. This was not the case, however, for most of the 'middling' vinedressers. Although wine was a more important part of their output than for their wealthier neighbours, it was immediately exchanged for the food they required to survive, without being exchanged on the open market for cash. A modicum, of course, was drunk by themselves.

As contemporaries repeatedly argued, then, the 'public economy' of retail, trade, merchandise and above all cash in this region of the Neckar valley clearly revolved around wine. It would be a mistake, however, even at this high point of vineyard cultivation, to confuse this with the economy's *real output* being dominated by wine. That said, spelt stores were treated as part of taxable wealth at this point while wine was not, which may have created an incentive for grain farmers to exchange grain for wine, storing the latter. Direct taxation, however, remained very low. It comprised no more than about 2 to 3 per cent of agricultural output for most of these households, or in those with wine for sale, about 3 to 7 per cent of the value of that wine. In other words, it is hard to see taxation having much influence, given that its level was based on a *wealth* assessment to which spelt stores made very little difference, and when annual taxation was a mere two or three thousandths of the very likely underassessed value!

The *gross* income from crops tended to fall in the range of two to three thousand grams of silver *per annum* for the 'middling' households, or about 6 grams per day. The wealthy households in these villages would have earned about twice that figure. The low earning potential of this economy, and its stability, is again underlined. Industrial prices advanced more slowly than agricultural prices during the sixteenth century, however, which would have brought some advantage to the terms of trade of this largely agricultural region. Relatively high income from wine, combined with low costs of grain, may explain the healthy volume of trade in the middle of the sixteenth century as much as the general buoyancy of the southern German economy. Evidence presented in chapter 1 from Esslingen suggests that regional wine income in fact fell sharply after the mid-1580s and never recovered, also falling in the late seventeenth century. In other words, periods of relatively high wine prices in fact indicate the times when income to viticulture as a whole was declining.

By the early eighteenth century, incomes were probably much the same. The price trends, if yield figures were held constant for holdings exactly equivalent in size to our 1607 sample, would suggest incomes from crops about 10 per cent higher than the late sixteenth and early seventeenth century. Price trends alone would indicate a growth in the value of the gross crop expressed in silver from the 1540s to around 1600, followed by decline. Wartime values were of course high, but cultivation only intermittent. The nadir of income after the mid-sixteenth century would have lain between about 1660 and 1690. However, fluctuations in prices probably reflect to a large extent fluctuation in harvest size and thus it is not clear that the notional value of the crop altered much over time. For our 'exemplary' holdings, it would have been as Emmanuel le Roy Ladurie described it. 'For all the apparent movement, things had really stayed much the same.'[135] And two things certainly changed; death and taxes. Mortality rates were lower after the wars, but so were fertility rates. And tax rates had continued their inexorable rise.

Taxation

Württembergers paid a range of direct and indirect taxes to a number of different bodies. The mainstay of the system was, however, an annual tax that came to be called the *ordinari* and that was paid to the Estates. This was organised and collected on a communal basis by *Schultheißen* who in this instance operated as officers of the Estates rather than ducal bailiffs. The Estates granted or loaned money to the Duke, usually raising it on urban money markets, and proceeded to pay the principal and interest off by levying taxes on the populace. Annual payments amounted to only about 24,000 fl. *per annum* in the Duchy in the late 1510s, but were over 140,000 fl. by the century's end, a six-fold increase that obviously ran far ahead of incomes and prices.[136] On top of this Württembergers paid a direct tax to the ducal government on a district (*Amt*) level. The level of part of this tax was determined in the late medieval period and amounted to no more than 250 lb for all of the district of Leonberg, a value set in the fourteenth century that remained unchanged until 1836! However, further amounts could be levied from year to year.[137] On top of this, household heads also paid an annual poll tax to their communes that amounted to 2 fl. in Leonberg but in most places was 0.75 fl. by the early eighteenth century. Widows paid half rate. In the 1710s, and presumably the early seventeenth century, this brought in around 1,662 fl. in the district of Leonberg. Tax rates were probably somewhat below this in the late sixteenth century.[138] The town of Leonberg itself levied a further local tax on its own *Bürger*, receiving 573 fl. in 1582. This varied greatly over time but

---

[135] Cited in Grantham, 'Contra Ricardo', p. 202.
[136] Carsten, *Princes and parliaments*, pp. 14–16, 41.
[137] Regnath, 'Die Stadt auf dem Lande', p. 34. In 1603 the district of Leonberg paid a total of 3,257 fl. to the Estates and the district.
[138] HStAS A261 Bü 1128.

was generally about 716 fl. in the early seventeenth century.[139] The most important indirect tax was the *Umgeld*, a consumption tax on wine, which brought in about 3,000 fl. in the district of Leonberg by the early seventeenth century.

In the early seventeenth century, tax on the townspeople tallied to about 0.5 fl. per head from the tax paid to the Estates and the district, up to 0.2 fl. per head from the *Bürgergeld*, up to 0.5 fl. per head from local direct taxes and 0.33 fl. from indirect taxes. Leonbergers thus each paid on average up to 1.5 fl. tax *per annum* each at the start of the seventeenth century, the largest share of which was paid to local administrators. The burden in the countryside was a little lower. The assessed twenty households of Neckarweihingen and Hoheneck paid on average 4.8 fl. in 1606, probably less than 1 fl. per person. Markgröningers were taxed at about the same level in 1581.[140] In the district of Leonberg, assessed wealth was taxed at roughly a rate of 0.4–0.6 per cent in 1607. Leonbergers paid up to the equivalent of 0.06 grams of silver *per capita* per day, when *per capita* income may have been about a gram of silver per day.[141]

The inflationary years of the 1610s and 1620s might have been initially been a blessing for debtors, but soon the populace was pummelled pitilessly for decades by disease, war and the associated fiscal demands. By the 1630s the costs of the war were colossal, at times demanding from the population in a month or less as much as had been extracted in a year in the previous decade.[142] As well as the taxes demanded from the Estates by rulers and occupying armies, local systems of payment and requisitioning were set up by armies that were regularly quartered in the region. This was all aside from simple plunder and destruction. Although much debt must have been wiped out by the high mortality of the era, total indebtedness in the district of Leonberg amounted to 158,033 fl. according to a report of 1656, eight years after the end of the war, the vast majority of this to creditors from outside of the district.[143] This amounted to a figure

---

[139] HStAS A572 Bü 45; A368 Bü 48; Trugenberger, *Zwischen Schloß und Vorstadt*, pp. 35–7.

[140] HStAS A348 Bü 6.

[141] HStAS A368 Bü 48. Although it is often thought that the towns paid higher taxes, the most heavily taxed households surveyed in 1607 were actually in the village of Heimerdingen, though this may reflect a high proportion of wealth being held in the most easily taxed forms of moveable property. However the fact that taxes appear to have been around 5–6 per cent of *per capita* income but were as much as 0.5 per cent of assessed wealth, suggesting that income was a tenth of wealth in any given year, implies the wealth assessments were far too low. Eighteenth-century tax instructions and rules on credit considered 5 per cent a standard return on capital.

[142] See Carsten, *Princes and parliaments*, pp. 57–70.   [143] HStAS A572 Bü 45.

of around 35 fl. for every man, woman and child left in the district – about 535 grams of silver each at the then going rate, probably well over annual *per capita* income.

The 'iron century' of high tax demands and the accretion of arrears and indebtedness continued with the wars of Louis XIV. The combination of the quartering of supposedly defensive armies, invading troops, plunder, extortion on a massive scale by French armies who at times invaded, burned and pillaged even as their 'protection money' was being collected, and the fiscal pressures of the ducal government itself, gave little respite. In 1675, for example, Eglosheim faced a tax burden of 1,566 fl., perhaps 10 fl. *per person* in that year.[144] In a single day of that year, 16 January, German (supposedly friendly!) troops allegedly did some 2,091 fl. worth of damage to neighbouring Hoheneck.[145] The list could go on and on. Höfingen's tax burden was about 3 fl. per person in 1697, after years of dearth.[146] The following year the debts of the Estates, never mind the subjects who owed them money for tax arrears, amounted to 5.4 million fl. or roughly 18 fl. for every inhabitant of the Duchy.[147] By August 1705 average household debt in Gebersheim was 190 fl., a third of this taxation arrears. This figure was the equivalent of 2,907 grams of silver, undoubtedly more than the annual gross value of crops and income in most households.[148]

This period of turmoil, lasting for a full century from the onset of the Thirty Years' war in 1618 to the Treaty of Utrecht in 1714, provided a massive impetus to the expansion of fiscal demands by German princes. Between 1691 and 1724 cultivators were subject to the *Tricesimation*, a tax of one-thirtieth of grain and wine produced. After its replacement by a monetary tax, for most of the first half of the eighteenth century, direct taxes brought in 540,000 fl. or 1.35 fl. per head (as taxes remained steady and the population increased, the *per capita* burden began to decline).[149] However, taxes were many and mostly local. The tax book of Leonberg in 1713–14 recorded thirteen different kinds of payments, and itself was not comprehensive. The taxes to be levied amounted to 5,023 fl.[150] The mean household tax payment was 16.5 fl. and the median payment 12.2 fl.. Around 55 per cent of tax went to the estates, and the rest to communal or district authorities.[151] In Leonberg, on average, the *per capita*

---

[144] Burckhardt, *Eglosheim*, p. 152.   [145] Stein and Felden, 'Die Plünderungen', p. 120.
[146] StAL Höfingen Bürgermeisterrechnungen 1697.
[147] Carsten, *Princes and parliaments*, p. 103.
[148] HStAS A572 Bü 45.   [149] Wilson, *War, state and society*, p. 51.
[150] HStAS A302 Bd. 7048. This figure may seem very high compared to the assessment of Leonberg's taxable income in table 2.3, but this is because the bulk of Leonbergers' landed property lay outside of the *Markung*.
[151] StAL Steuerbuch 1713–14.

burden of taxation may have risen to as much as 4 fl. *per capita* early in the eighteenth century. Rising population and static levies began to lower this figure, retreating to around 2 to 2.5 fl. each year per person, or 0.08 to 0.1 grams of silver per day. But local taxation had clearly also risen over the seventeenth century and remained, in the town, more significant than the sums levied by the Estates. The silver value of taxation was probably at least 50 per cent higher than it had been in the early seventeenth century, and possibly double in some places. The burdens of rents in kind, along with tolls, were little altered. Fiscal demands had risen, but in the long term not perhaps astronomically. And we should be aware of another strategy for dealing with the burden: non-payment. At the beginning of 1713–14, more than one year's worth of tax lay in arrears, and nearly as much remained unpaid by the end of the year.[152]

Assuming static holding size, the 'exemplary' households of Hoheneck and Neckarweihingen would thus have been in much the same situation in the 1720s as they had been in 1607, although they would be less vulnerable to epidemic disease and thus perhaps better placed to accumulate wealth. However, just as in the sixteenth century, as the population grew again in the early eighteenth century and neither productivity rose nor wages fell proportionately (although in real terms wages would fall, especially from around 1740), the share of the economy taken up by returns to labour must have expanded. Yet agriculture remained a best option. In the 1720s even the most modest of the 'middling' examples would have reaped an income from agriculture equivalent in silver values to that of a fairly high artisanal income. A frequent response was to 'mix' activities, with those doing best from agriculture often also being the wealthiest artisans. Although one model of economic development posits specialisation as a response to high transport and transactions costs of the kind faced by Württemberg, there is little sign of this here.[153] The opposite argument that specialisation only accompanies low transactions costs seems more applicable. The wave of conversion of land to vineyard or pasture in the late seventeenth- and early eighteenth-century Europe is attributed to the general conjuncture of low grain prices and a higher relative value for products such as oil, meat and wine. Yet this can only be part of the story. Only areas with very strong comparative cost advantages, high-quality products and exceptional goods that bore the cost of long-distance transport (such as Hohenlohe's cattle-breeding and later

---

[152] In this year some two-thirds of households succeeded in clearing at least some of their arrears, but a third added to them. In Württemberg the rate of enduring tax increase was in fact fastest during the sixteenth century.

[153] Robisheaux, *Rural society*, p. 249.

Württemberg's production of fruit) could really thrive. The Neckar valley's early specialisation in wine production set its economy on a definite path, and helped the sustenance of high population densities, not least facilitating, as we will see in chapter 5, the import of wood, iron and salt. But it did not trigger consistent growth and further specialisation, and it could be questioned whether it reaped any advantages in *per capita* income at all. Swiss industrialisation encouraged some agricultural export and wine continued to flow to territories adjacent to Württemberg with less favourable climates, such as Bavaria. But the shape of domestic aggregate demand showed no development, and with equally immobile rents, returns to labour and capital, and government income, scope for significant change was minimal.

Institutions and social structure: the commune

Households did not stand alone as economic agents. They were bound into the corporate body of the commune, which provided services, regulated their activity, levied a significant proportion of taxation, and as we have seen, was a major property owner. As well as some cultivated land and extensive areas of woodland, most communes also owned and leased out buildings for the bathhouse, smithy and bakehouses. Simple residence in a settlement did not confer membership of the commune. Becoming a member (*Bürger*) required the payment of an annual tax (the *Bürgergeld*), and from the late sixteenth century the small towns set minimum wealth requirements to prevent the in-migration of paupers.[154] Marriage and, for incomers, bearing a certificate indicating honourable reputation were also required. Being the male child of a *Bürger*, however, usually conferred membership. This system, as was overwhelmingly the case in early modern Europe, was massively discriminatory against women, as recently meticulously detailed by Sheilagh Ogilvie.[155] Women only formally enjoyed some rights as widows and lost them on remarriage. The only major public function that they enjoyed was to elect the district midwives. The number of male residents over the age of twenty-five excluded membership was, however, very small.[156] These so-called *Beisitzer* were often made up of those pursuing 'dishonourable' occupations such as the skinner and executioner, who was also a Catholic in Leonberg. Members of almost

---

[154] Trugenberger, *Zwischen Schloß und Vorstadt*, pp. 8–9; Benning, 'Eine Stadt', p. 10; see also Sreenivasan, *The peasants of Ottobeuren*, pp. 164–6.

[155] Ogilvie, *Bitter living*.

[156] 4 per cent of households were headed by *Beisitzer* in the district of Leonberg in 1708. HStAS A368L Bü 136. See also Oglivie, *State corporatism*, p. 54.

'professional' bodies such as shepherds, who often showed a high degree of mobility in a lifetime, were also not taken into the commune.[157]

Interpretations of the commune have usually taken on two diametrically opposed forms. A positive gloss highlights their role as providers of welfare support, as fostering co-operation and allowing the more efficient management of low-yielding property such as the commons, and defending the interests of the peasantry against lordship and government.[158] Less enthusiastic authors have seen their regulations as putting brakes on innovation, entrepreneurship and consumption with their economic regulation, and operating exclusionary and discriminatory politics against women and subaltern groups.[159] They had a tendency, without rigorous outside supervision, to degenerate into oligarchies, fostering in turn corruption, aggrandisement of communal resources by the wealthy, and mismanagement. Leonberg was struck by scandal in the 1740s and 1750s when investigations revealed mismanagement and fiddling of communal account books by an oligarchy of often interrelated officials.[160] Government regulation in fact forbade men with a reasonably distant degree of consanguinity from sitting together on the governing bodies of communes to prevent precisely this sort of thing. Though this must have been difficult in such small communities, late sixteenth-century Leonberg, in contrast to later events, appears to have carefully applied the letter of the law.[161]

As is often the case, there is more than a degree of truth in all of these assessments at different places and different times. Much depended on the background, energy, honesty and scrutiny of senior officials. Lead among these was the ducal bailiff (*Schultheiß*). Formally a ducal appointee in the late medieval period, he increasingly became a man elected by his fellow *Bürger*, although early in the period in practice ducal appointments may simply have been confirmation of local selections.[162] Certainly the shift made no discernable difference to the type of person chosen. The *Schultheiß* was chosen for life (or until infirmity set in), and was responsible for the collection of feudal dues owed to the duke, the collection of taxes owed to the duke, or to the Estates, and stood as head of the village court. *Schultheißen* were almost invariably the wealthiest men in the settlement, sometimes real 'cocks of the village' with no near rivals in status. They, as well as the jurors of the village court, were

---

[157] Trugenberger, *Zwischen Schloß und Vorstadt*, p. 146.
[158] Blickle, *Deutsche Untertanen*.
[159] Ogilvie, *State corporatism*, pp. 45–70; Ogilvie, *Bitter living*; Warde, 'Common rights'.
[160] Landwehr, 'Finanzen, Rechte und Faktionen'.
[161] Trugenberger, *Zwischen Schloß und Vorstadt*, pp. 104–5.
[162] StAR Nr. B349; Warde, 'Law', p. 186; Gestrich, '*Aufwiegler, Rebellen, saubere Buben*', pp. 28–9.

supposed to be literate after a ruling of 1610, but this took time to become universal.[163] Their behaviour was not always edifying for such an obvious village leader. According to the pastor of Botnang, *Schultheiß* Sebastian Wieland, to name but one example, had to be taken home in a cart after drinking sessions in Stuttgart.[164] The *Schultheiß* sometimes received a small stipend, or in the case of Münklingen, was let off tax on the first 100 fl. of wealth. Some villages, though not all, allowed the *Schultheiß* first choice of wood lots to cut from the communal woodland, or a share larger than the usual. In that same village it was dryly noted that, 'otherwise from his office he has nothing except much futile effort and work, and envy and hatred from subjects, the same goes for all the other [*Schultheißen*]'.[165] One reason why the wealthiest ended up in such a position was that few had the time, inclination or status to do it.

The day-to-day management of village property and finances was the task of the mayor, a figure often chosen annually by the other *Bürger* although men frequently sat for longer terms, and he could be co-opted in some cases by the village court. Whilst often a wealthy man, mayors were not universally so. Named *Heimbürger* in medieval times, he was generally called the *Bürgermeister* by the end of the sixteenth century. He usually retained responsibility for the enforcement of by-laws and field orders, management of common land, buildings and resources, the keeping of village or town accounts (mandatory after 1582), and general agricultural management. Some larger settlements had two or more.[166]

The judicial power in the village was vested in a village court (*Dorfgericht*) peopled by men either elected by the *Bürger*, or co-opted, usually for a life term. Decisions could be made if need be by majority vote. These jurors (*Richter*) often formed a kind of village oligarchy of the more prosperous and elder citizenry, although we should not always assume that this was so. However, if we take the jurors of Hemmingen in 1735, all but two of them were either 'well-off' (*wohl*) or doing 'handsomely' (*schon*). Wealth counted for more than age. Indeed, the *Schultheiß* of the village was only thirty-one, a village Napoleon.[167] The court dealt with civil cases under a certain value, and misdemeanours such as the breaking of field orders, and slander. In theory the *Vogt* dealt

[163] Gestrich, '*Aufwiegler, Rebellen, saubere Buben*', p. 29; on *Schultheiß* dynasties, see Landwehr, *Policey im Alltag*, p. 44; Trugenberger, 'Von wegen des Unbaws', p. 11.
[164] Gestrich, '*Aufwiegler, Rebellen, saubere Buben*', p. 33.
[165] HStAS A368 Bü 46.
[166] StAL Höfingen Fleckenlagerbuch 1593; HStAS A572 Bü 69; Ernst, 'Geschichte', p. 301; Dehlinger, *Württembergs Staatswesen*, p. 95; see also Döbele-Carlesso, *Weinbau*, p. 33.
[167] HStAS A572 Bü 68; Benning, 'Eine Stadt', pp. 32–3; Warde, 'Law', p. 187.

with criminal matters, though in consultation with locally selected jurors. He held a court called the *Vogtgericht* in the village once or twice a year. The village court also decided on the regulatory framework of village life and promulgated ordinances, though these last seem to have required at least the approval of the *Vogt*. The village court met either to resolve particular disputes or annually on a prescribed day, usually associated with a particular date in the agricultural calendar and the allocation of communal resources, as the name of *Birengericht* ('berry-court') hints for Gebersheim, Eltingen, Flacht, Malmsheim and Renningen. Non-attendance was punishable with a fine and men were expected to carry a symbol of their honour such as a stick or weapon.[168]

In some places a smaller advisory group was established among the *Richter*, the *Rat* (council, usually of four) or a body to represent the commune simply called the *Gemeinde*, or, where this reflected the number of participants, the 'twenty-four'. These do not seem to have had any formal powers but demanded that they be consulted and widened participation in village decision-making.[169]

Despite the overweaning power of the wealthy within this institution, it did not necessarily operate detrimentally to the poorer inhabitants. Indeed, as we have seen, it maintained a high degree of social cohesion, for good or ill, as Württemberg was buffeted by numerous disturbances. Clearly, there was scope for corruption, such as in the case of *Schultheiß* Berer of Botnang who gave his friends a more favourable tax assessment than others. When complaints emerged about this he simply pulled rank and decried his opponents as 'to be called nothing else but stirrers, rebels, greenhorns, ruined good-for-nothings and beggars' dogs' – quite a list.[170] In this case and others we only know of malpractice when complaints were raised and there always remains a 'dark figure' of possibly widespread favouritism. David Sabean has argued that complaints of an oligarchy of 'cousins' developed more prominently during the eighteenth century, with increasing financial responsibilities of the commune, and increasing rates of marital endogamy both within villages, and within social groups, thus establishing more clearly a local ruling group.[171] In small communities the supposedly illegal interrelation of village power-brokers was nearly impossible to avoid. Certainly matters such as the auctioning off of the ducal tithe to local farmers who undertook to collect

---

[168] Landwehr, *Policey im Alltag*, pp. 144–55; Warde, 'Law', pp. 187–8; Landwehr, 'Die Rhetorik', p. 271.
[169] Benning, 'Eine Stadt', pp.32–3; Trugenberger, 'Der Leonberger Raum', p. 97; Landwehr, *Policey im Alltag*, p. 51.
[170] Gestrich, *'Aufwiegler, Rebellen, saubere Buben'*, p. 33.
[171] Sabean, *Kinship in Neckarhausen*, pp. 37–8, 41, 50.

and deliver it to district officials was stitched up within villages so that bids were kept artificially low, allowing the farmer to cream off all of the tithe collected in excess of that amount promised to the duke in the auction. The 'victory' in the auction was cycled around all interested parties in on the game from year to year.[172] However, this mutual back-scratching is rather different from the systematic exclusion from resources of poorer, less empowered inhabitants of the commune.

It is clear that extensive communal property holding was beneficial to poorer members of the community. There were trade-offs, of course, whether conscious or not. The prescriptive *Flurzwang* that enforced communal management of the fields and prevented people from planting crops as they desired was perhaps offset for some by the cheap access to communally owned gardens, often carved out of the village common land. The large extent of communal woodland, which clearly dominated the regional wood economy, delivered this essential resource to the inhabitants of settlements where a communal wood existed, at a cost far lower than if they had to purchase it from elsewhere. The precise level of this benefit is outlined in chapter 5. Even those who were not members of the commune were permitted discretionary grants or cheap firewood, partly through institutions such as the parish fund or poor chest that were essentially run by the same people who were responsible for govern-ing the commune.[173] Once one could afford to overwinter a cow, the communal herd allowed, again, cheap access to property and the labour-saving service of communal herdsmen to police the animals and direct them towards rich sources of fodder. Of course, such herdsmen had to be paid for, but at the price of a loaf per pig (less if one could pasture many) or 0.15 fl. per year for a cow in sixteenth-century Leonberg (i.e. a day's wage), this was surely a good deal.[174]

Some of the apparent 'corruption' of early modern village officials derived from the discretion and apparent arbitrariness that could be built into such personalised, everyday governance. 'Discretion' was a boon until someone else appeared to be benefitting significantly more. This can be illustrated by an example from Renningen in 1566–7, when a dispute arose con-cerning the allocation of cuttings from juniper bushes to the village barber for heating water in the bathhouse. It is the very banality of this example that best illustrates how village resource allocation could operate.[175]

---

[172] Sabean, *Property*, p. 46.
[173] See for example, StAL Bürgermeisterrechnungen, *passim*, Armenkastenrechnungen, *passim*.
[174] HStAS A572 Bü 41.
[175] The following discussion is based on a case to be found in HStAS A227 Bü 1122.

In October 1566 the barber, whose prime function was to run and maintain the village bathhouse, petitioned the duke over his wood allowance. The dispute was not over *Gaabholz*, but whether he could, as the barber claimed, cut or collect *Afterschlag* (the small leftovers from the cutting of timber) free of charge. The village account books for the 1560s show us that he clearly had previously been paying. This petition led to the intervention of the *Vogt* and *Untervogt* of Leonberg, who questioned an extensive list of witnesses on 19 December of the next year, and perused sworn statements that had been taken as far afield as Canstatt. In all, twenty-one statements were taken. Only one of these mentions *Gerechtigkeit*, that is, a specifically legal claim to the practice. The others simply commented, sometimes from direct personal experience, on what the barber had been permitted to cut or if he had to pay for it.

The story runs back to the 1510s, from the teenage memories of most of the elderly men in the village.[176] Hans Bader ran the bathhouse and had cut his wood in the Wasserbach and Meisenberg, two ducally owned woods to the north of the village, for which he paid. He may also have bought some wood from the commune.[177] Some time before the Peasants' war of 1525, Hans lost the use of his right hand and began to cut from juniper bushes that thrived on the commonland, being unpalatable to grazing animals. However the village officials at the time soon barred him from this, despite it being 'often customary' (*'offter mals herkommen*') and having no other means of obtaining fuel he sold up and moved out, first to Stuttgart, but eventually to the regional metropolis, Strasbourg. His (perhaps not immediate) successor seems to have been a man from Tübingen named Martin. For a couple of years the young Hans Kienlin, who still resided in Renningen in his sixties, had served in the bathhouse, learning the trade. He was sent out into the communal woods to gather deadwood, and even cut it. Far from being refused, the *Schütz* (warden) had even assisted him in loading the larger pieces. His master did not last long in Renningen, but his successor, another Hans, took a cart out into the woods to cut wood on Thursdays or Fridays before the bath on Saturday. This Hans was probably Hans Miller who appears in the tax lists of 1544 and in old age was living in

---

[176] As is usual in such cases, some of the testimonies are irreconcilable in their chronologies and the names of the barbers, so the sequence of barbers and practices must remain speculative; some heuristic assistance is given by comparison with other sources. HStAS A227 Bü 1122.

[177] Hans Malmsheimer, the brother-in-law of Hans Bader, cited the figure paid out of 1 fl. – at that time a fairly significant sum – whilst Joß Müller stated 5ß, less than a fifth of a *Gulden*.

the hospital in Canstatt. He testified that wood not good for anything else was given to him *gratis*, but that he had to pay for better material. Certainly various *Bürgermeister* stated that they had charged for wood in the years before Veit Hümel, the plaintiff, took over early in the 1550s. But what was to be counted as chargeable, and what was to be given for free? When wood for carpentry was cut, the generous mayor Thomas Pepplin permitted the barber to remove two to three wagonloads from the leftovers, as he also allowed the *Bürger* to cut old stumps and rotting timber in the woodland. However when another Hans, briefly the barber around 1550, had his manservant cut several fathoms, the wood was confiscated by communal officials. Jörg Renningener never got round to charging the barber during his two terms as *Heimbürger* and distributed extensive amounts of windfalls to the populace for no more than the cost of cutting the wood up.

What does this rather confusing tale have to tell us? Two notes from either end of the period provide clues. Ludwig Kirnstein, a nephew of Hans Bader, commented rather caustically that everyone who knew the account books knew that the barber had to pay for wood. Hans Bader had only been given wood *gratis* 'out of mercy' (*erbermd*), not right (*Gerechtigkeit*) because he and many of his ancestors had been *Schultheißen* or village jurors.[178] On the other hand, under interrogation by the *Vogt* early in 1567, the *Schultheiß* and *Gericht*, who originally insisted that the barber purchased wood, admitted that they had actually given it out 'when it suited them' ('*wann inen geliebte*'). There is a certain irony in Veit Hümel appealing for the return of the old ways, evoking what he saw as established custom, when what was clearly established was the practice of discretion. Generous officials like Thomas Pepplin and Jörg Renningener looked for no payment and gave two or three wagonloads instead of one, but a barber like the Hans who had his wood confiscated, seen to interpret his rights rather generously himself, was reprimanded (and indeed died a month later, one hopes from unconnected causes).

The commune as it operated in the sixteenth century, then, was a form of local governance that, like 'central government', rested on the personalities of its chief officers. Many of the decisions required of village officials, such as the date of harvesting, could hardly be prescriptively determined in any case. The peasant recommendation passed on by agronomist Martin Grosser, that spring grain sowing should begin when one hears the frogs' chorus, is indicative of the kind of

---

[178] It is not entirely clear to whom Ludwig Kirnstein is referring, but there are no other native barbers in the period to which he refers, and after at the latest 1530 the *Schultheiß* came from the Auberman family.

knowledge that underlay these choices.[179] Communal property could be very extensive, and thus at times these officials could afford to be generous. But in the end, decisions largely rested in the hands of a distinct and to some degree self-replicating group. However, stasis of one kind could lead to conflict when other variables altered. The robustness of the regime of property and power depended on how it could weather conflict.

Social conflict, social identities and dispute resolution

Many conflicts were doubtless played out in extra-curial forms and leave no record. Indeed, much of the imputed crime that emerges in village records actually comes from slander cases where the plaintiff complained about a slur on their reputation.[180] By and large, courts dealt with complaints brought by private individuals rather than cases initiated by officials. For minor civil matters and misdemeanours they could be convened rapidly, but matters worth over 2 fl. or requiring gaol terms were held over until theoretically quarterly, but in practice more infrequent, court sessions.[181] In all of these cases the poor were unlikely to be judged by their peers, although they were very likely (except for more serious offences), to be judged by those who knew them. Matters of regulation, including the setting of ordinances, were left to the jurors of the settlement's court.

However, there were extra-village avenues of redress should people not be happy with these regulations and outcomes. After 1555, the town court formally became the court of appeal for villagers, where matters could be set before the *Vogt* and jurors of the *Amtsstadt*.[182] Beyond this lay the possibility of an appeal to the high court (*Hofgericht*), though this was an expensive enterprise. Some kind of ducal high court had existed from the late fourteenth century, but by the late fifteenth century the tradition was established of appealing decisions to the town courts of Stuttgart and Tübingen. Already by this date appeal cases had to be worth 20 lb hlr, a sum that rose to 50 fl. by 1610. The *Hofgericht* was established as the final appeal court for the Duchy in 1495.[183] Matters pertaining to government and ducal property (so any kind of village regulation, in practice) could also be appealed to the supreme council in Stuttgart (*Oberrat*).[184] All of these avenues of redress tended to generate more business than the government really wanted, especially for hard-pressed councillors who

---

[179] Grosser, *Anleitung*, p. 24. [180] For example, see the *Urteilsbuch* of the StAR.
[181] Landwehr, *Policey im Alltag*, pp. 144–5, 154.
[182] Reyscher, *SWG*, Bd.IV., pp. 218, 260; Landwehr, *Policey im Alltag*, p. 50.
[183] Frey, *Das württembergische Hofgericht*. [184] Warde, 'Law', pp. 187–8.

had administrative tasks as well as sitting as judges. The increasing level of encounter with trained jurists led in turn to calls from the wider populace for less use of obfuscating Latin and more consistency in court judgements. In 1565 the Estates requested that law be written 'as far as possible in good German words', which the duke agreed, so long as 'no barbarisms come into it as a result'. This process of give-and-take, of responding to the demand for legal redress, led to increased systemisation and use of Roman law to iron out variations in local practice. The duke encouraged the use of proceedings that were swift and avoided lengthy transcription, in 1573 also banning the use of advocates in cases worth under 50 fl.[185]

However, there was also an 'extra-curial' form of appeal, the *Supplication*, based on the medieval right of a subject to appeal to his lord. This could be submitted directly to the supreme council. As in practice councillors usually referred it back to the *Vogt*, the formal first port of appeal, but were prepared to take decisions themselves on his advice, this operated effectively as part of the legal system in a way that could attract the attention of central authorities more swiftly. Poorer groups within the village thus had a cheaper avenue to air grievances, and, as we shall see, it was one that they used. This was especially so in cases where courts lower down had operated as they saw it fully in accordance with the law, providing no grounds for appeal as usually understood. A set of cases where disputes over wood were handled in such a manner will be dealt with in more detail in chapter 5.[186]

It is a well-worn adage of social history that social identities were and are contingent. This was certainly true of the Württemberger peasantry. Contingent, however, is not the same as infinitely flexible. Definitions of 'the poor' could alter according to one's perspective, but the manner in which the 'lower end' of circumstance or fortune was defined usually ebbed over the same people. They rarely held any kind of official position of power, although they sometimes took up the least prestigious and onerous official duties of the commune, such as tending the plague-ridden and running errands for the infirm. Classically in medieval documents they were those who provided services with their hands (i.e. without owning horses or oxen), '*Handfrohner*', or where linked to a small tenancy with lesser corvée requirements, *Söldner*. Gradually, however, *Söldner* simply became a synonym for smallholder, while those who frequently laboured for wages were defined as wage-labourers. The lack of draught animals and labouring for others thus embraced a first, wide-ranging tier of subaltern status. As the sixteenth century wore on and the

[185] Frey, *Das württembergische Hofgericht*, pp. 48–50.
[186] Warde, 'Law', passim.

population grew, people increasingly subdivided farmsteads or farm-houses in the nucleated settlements. Thus not owning a house became a further, slightly more restricted definition of the poor, and one as we shall see later that was prominent in disputes over the allocation of wood. It may well be that the ability to identify the 'spatially disadvantaged', as those sharing houses, or cotters, was a major motor of the conceptual identification of social polarisation within a community that in terms of the *distribution* of wealth was not obviously becoming more polarised. In other words, distinctions had a very clear material basis.[187]

Yet village life, the organisation of labour and payment for labour, was still organised in a personalised, 'face-to-face' and reciprocal economy. Of course the wealthier, the employers, held more of the cards in this relationship. Yet the wealthy still invested energies into a system of the communal organisation of welfare and property holding that brought many benefits to their poorer neighbours. These village elites held the reins firmly in their hands, of course, and frequently used them to favour their peer group. However, while there is abundant evidence from all over early modern Europe of this self-interest and local 'corruption', these avenues of exercising power through the village court, the appeal system, and communal property holding also provided potential forms of scrutiny for which there were no obvious contemporary alternatives. And the commune could benefit the poor in a direct material fashion through cheap access to property.

As we have seen, controls were not only exercised over property (whether permanently communal, or subject to common rights), but the manner in which labour was employed. Guilds were supported by, and worked closely with, communal authorities. Owners of farm equip-ment were expected to make it available to others. In 1652, authorities complained about the practice of some vineyard owners with more acre-age than they could cultivate themselves bidding up wages during spells of good weather to attract other vinedressers to do their labour instead of employing servants. This was drawing the vinedressers away from vine-yards that they contractually cultivated on longer-term or sharecropping arrangements, so the work there was not being done in a timely fashion. Vinedressers were banned from doing extra day-labour until the work on the vineyards that they contractually cultivated was complete. This sti-pulation of course benefitted some landowners over others, and depressed wages. But it also reflected a prevalent attitude that, while an open labour market was acceptable in certain circumstances, this only

[187] Ibid., pp. 204–5.

held after longer-term arrangements on a reciprocal basis to ensure the timely performance of labour had been fulfilled.[188]

Thus communal property holding and discretionary decision-making could prove very advantageous to the poor. Equally, it provided a forum where the allocation of a large amount of resources was subject to public scrutiny and could thus be manipulated by different social groups in their favour. Precisely for these reasons the poor contested the right of village elites to control this allocation, which can give the impression that an institution of which they generally appear to have approved was acting against them and only in the interests of narrow oligarchies. The real situation was more complex. It was only the ability of property holders to dominate communal life, but at the same time the existence of communal property to alleviate the inequitable distribution of property more generally that made the commune an institution that all social groups were prepared to invest in over the centuries of its existence. Hence a 'moral community' was defined that was vested with responsibility for overseeing the local economic and social order.

At the same time, the commune was a unit of state power, and subject to the interests and expectations of the state in regard to the management of resources. State bodies provided the avenues of appeal that provided a degree of scrutiny of the performance of communal officials. How the drive for state regulation and the realities of communal life interacted is the subject of the next chapter.

[188] Trugenberger, 'Die Magd', pp. 56–7.

3   The regulative drive

The sixteenth and seventeenth centuries have long been seen as a key era in the development of the modern state in central Europe. After 1500, the consolidation of patrimonies and the promulgation of territorial laws, especially under the influence of Roman law, provided the legal grounds for 'state' action. A developing bureaucracy and the information technology of improving literacy skills and printing expanded the ability of officials to oversee the populace and divorced the exercise of authority from direct personalised relations of lordship. The increasingly expensive wars of the seventeenth century provided the greatest impetus towards the creation of a 'tax state' that moved beyond princely rulers' earlier reliance on more limited personal finance. Taken together these breakthroughs provided the underpinnings of the self-consciously interventionist and modernising state of the eighteenth century, whether in its 'absolutist' or 'enlightened' guises. These processes have been encapsulated in the term 'state building', describing the conscious centralisation of power.[1] However, equally important for this process was the gradual accumulation of local loyalty across the entire period, integration of village powerbrokers into the machinery of government, and the 'social disciplining' of personnel to conform to centrally determined norms. These processes were far less directed and were subject to the approval of relatively lowly subjects. They were, however, essential for a state that bound the ambitions of 'the centre' and those of the 'locality' (or at least those who wielded influence locally) into a coherent unit that

---

[1] The literature on these subjects is of course enormous. For studies dealing with Württemberg, see Wilson, *War, state and society*, pp. 17, 36; Strauss, *Law, resistance, and the state*, pp. 61–5, 85; Landwehr, *Policey im Alltag*; Marcus, *The politics of power*; on state building, see Schilling, *Konfessionskonflikt und Staatsbildung*. More generally, Blickle, *Resistance, representation and community*; Ertman, *Birth of the Leviathan*; Tilly, *Coercion, capital and European states*, pp. 67–9; Wilson, *Absolutism*.

expected both to act to resolve problems, and was expected by its subjects to provide solutions to problems.[2] It is this second, wider set of processes that is understood by the term 'state formation'.

Certainly many aspects of this story hold true for Württemberg and south-west Germany more generally. The regulation of wood obtained a paragraph in Württemberg's first 'state' or 'territorial' ordinance of 11 November 1495.[3] At the end of the fifteenth century, and progressively through the sixteenth, an increasingly burdened but differentiated bureaucracy appeared to deal with myriad forms of government business.[4] The woodland itself had been regulated in many parts of central Europe since at least the eleventh century,[5] but it is only in the early modern period that central government began to attempt to rigorously enforce norms of behaviour and standardised practices across all of the territories under its control. Indeed, one might say to create a 'centre' rather than an amalgamation of discrete units, although this was a process that had many phases, setbacks and chronologies in different parts of Europe.

The activity of the forester, his agents, and the ordinances they attempted to enforce did not then simply reflect the pressures and interests within the *Forstamt* Leonberg. It has frequently been argued in 'forest history' that the explosion in the promulgation of forest laws across Germany, but most notably in the south between 1470 and 1550, reflected increasing problems of wood shortage as a growing population encountered resource scarcity.[6] The veracity of such suppositions of scarcity, which generally have been inferred from the laws' self-justificatory preambles, will be examined in the next chapter. What is certainly true, however, is that the experience of the localities was at least in part shaped by 'central' responses to perceived problems, and the interests of the waxing Württemberger state. Of course states attempted to regulate many more things than woodland at the beginning of the sixteenth century. Simply taking the agrarian economy, the state ordinance of 1495 devoted paragraphs to credit and debt, corn

---

[2] Hindle, *The state and social change*, pp. 15–34; Braddick, *State formation*; Landwehr, *Policey im Alltag*; Oestreich, *Geist und Gestalt*; Raeff, *The well-ordered police state*, pp. 146–66; Rublack, 'Frühneuzeitliche Staatlichkeit', pp. 358, 375–6; Münch, 'The growth of the modern state'; Hohkamp, *Herrschaft in der Herrschaft*; Rublack, 'State formation', pp. 210–4.

[3] Reyscher, *SWG*, Bd.XII, p. 9.

[4] Bernhardt, *Die Zentralbehörden*; Marcus, *The politics of power*; Dehlinger, *Württembergs Staatswesen*, pp. 94–103.

[5] Epperlein, *Waldnutzung*.

[6] Mantel, *Forstgeschichte*, p. 298; Scott, *Society and economy*, p. 61.

markets, ensuring fair and transparent sales of property and produce, buildings, inheritance, and urban granaries.[7] This makes us suspect that it was the general ambition of government to regulate resources, rather than the condition of particular aspects of the agrarian world, that was the prime mover behind legislation in this instance. But government had decided that resource management, and woodland in particular, fell under its purview. This in itself is hardly a surprise. We have already seen that most resources were fairly tightly managed and that the peasantry expected this to be so. But it is a key point, almost too simple to be worthy of attention. Just as with the managers of open fields, of communal herds, of farms and vineyards and marketplaces, 'government', understood as government from the centre, had set itself a problem. This did not, however, bring obvious answers as to how the problem should be resolved, and government would take decades, nay centuries, pondering this very issue.

The interconnection between state regulation and village life has been subject to detailed and rewarding scrutiny in the case of Württemberg by David Sabean. Cadastres recorded ducal property rights, and in some cases juridical rights, in villages from the fourteenth century. Equally, district authorities, communes under the authority of the ducally appointed *Schultheiß*, and taxation, were features of fourteenth-century life in the region. However, especially from the second half of the sixteenth century, the quantity and quality of documentation began to grow. Communal accounts had to be kept and were subject to official scrutiny, and communities were to keep records of births, marriages and deaths, compile inventories on the occasion of marriage and death, record all property transactions, mortgages and loans, and oversee the implementation of regularised inheritance laws.[8] State officials could also regulate land use and in one form or another collected around a fifth of most agricultural output as tithe or rents. Taxation may have taken 6 per cent of *per capita* income around 1600 and possibly 10 per cent in the early eighteenth century, falling most heavily on the owners or tenants of land.[9] This clearly gave the state considerable

---

[7] Reyscher, *SWG*, Bd.XII, pp. 7–15.

[8] Sabean, *Property*, pp. 26–7; Sabean, *Power in the blood*, pp. 201–2. Cadastres existed much earlier than the late fifteenth century as Sabean claims. Policies of 'peasant protection', keeping large farms through impartible inheritance as fiscal units, are well known in some regions after the Thirty Years' War, and in a few cases already in the late sixteenth century. Robisheaux, *Rural society*, pp. 81–3; Holenstein, *Bauern zwischen Bauernkrieg und Dreissigjährigem Krieg*, pp. 38–9; Brakensiek, *Ländliche Gesellschaft*, pp. 277–80; Friedeburg, *Ländliche Gesellschaft*, p. 59; Sreenivasan, *The peasants of Ottobeuren*, pp. 158–69, 181–3.

[9] See previous chapter.

scope to influence socio-economic conditions, and it has already been conjectured that this was achieved, in part, by keeping rents stable. Sabean argues that in the period covered by this book, 'the state's intervention ... proceeded from fiscal concerns', but he is equally sensitive to the fact that, 'from the point of view of villagers, many arrangements and procedures became internalised and were regarded as essential services to be expected from the state'.[10]

The nature of state intervention in village life will be examined in this chapter with regard to the forestry administration. However, there are good reasons more generally for suspecting that much of the *demand* for record-keeping and regulation actually came from the peasantry themselves, and in turn from a state that disliked bearing the costs of resolving their disputes over property, inheritance and tax assessments. It is not clear at all that many of the state ordinances would have actually brought any fiscal return to the government. Property regulation and documentation applied to ducally owned property and freehold alike, although the state could expect no rents from the latter, and it is not clear that volumes of property holdings and transactions were consulted in collecting the tithe. In turn, the tax assessments of individual households made by communes were very rarely recorded, and the principle of tax assessment was not always clear to those being assessed.[11] There was no system to 'ascribe clear tax liabilities'[12] to individual plots of land, at least not for centuries after the system of recording property was brought into being. Neither do I know of evidence that in the period under consideration these books were ever used for fiscal purposes. The collector of central taxes was not the government at all, but the Estates. It is true of course that any measure concerned with economic well-being can be reduced to a fiscal interest. And it is certainly true that some state activity was dominated by fiscal expedients. But is this sufficient to make it the primary cause of actions? A test of the role of the state in the locality is, in the end, the practices and attitudes of those state officials charged with implementing the rules on the ground, in this case the forest wardens. These represented the front-line troops of the only major branch of the administration (outside of the Church) that was not mediated via communal officials and village court jurors. After rising to the dizzying heights of chancelries and treasuries for much of the chapter, we will return to the experience of local governance at the end.

---

[10] Sabean, *Property*, pp. 15, 27.   [11] Landwehr, 'Finanzen, Rechte und Faktionen', p. 98.
[12] Sabean, *Property*, p. 27.

Formulation and implementation

How could one inculcate good practice in the forests when the reading of the ordinances was so boring that people drifted off and fell asleep during the procedure? How could one reconcile legislative innovation with the carefully crafted customary practice of innumerable communes? What kind of information was required to guarantee the smooth functioning of the administration? How could one deal with the problem that 'smooth functioning' often seemed to require oiling the palms of supposedly disinterested officials? Like so much government, early modern rule was less a grandiose plan (though these were of course attempted, so often conceived, as Braudel notes, beside the cosy winter fire, when 'Nothing seemed too difficult or too dangerous'[13]), more an *ad hoc* question and answer session. At the core of these kinds of questions, asked repeatedly by administrators, were two issues.

One was to establish what the state did or should do, as it both responded to the demands of its subjects, and invented a proper role for itself. This has been broadly defined as a question of how to establish 'order', and the lines between proper orderly behaviour and behaviour that threatened the right order of things.[14] The state emerged in a moralised universe and from the very beginning (and well before the Reformation) spoke of the social order in moralised terms. Hence a familiar litany of measures to tackle drinking, swearing, gaming, superfluity of dress, and extravagance at weddings, are there at the very beginning of state legislation, part of a more general disciplinary trend that Peter Burke has christened the 'triumph of Lent'.[15] The state was not clearly distinguished from other religious or communal institutions, but tended to stand alongside them as a body that sought order at the scale of the territorial unit. However, governments also soon found that admonishing subjects to love their fellow man and desist from sin had rather little practical effect in generating 'order', though that did not prevent them from continuing to make such admonishments. Particular sins tended to become subsumed into a larger concept of what contributed or was inimical to good housekeeping, eventually encapsulated in the verb '*hausen*', 'to carry on in a household or live together in a household', examined by David Sabean.

---

[13] Braudel, *The Mediterranean*, p. 189.   [14] Robisheaux, *Rural Society*.
[15] Reyscher, *SWG*, Bd.II, pp. 18–20, 23–4, 26, 29–30; Burke, *Popular culture*, pp. 207–43; Raeff, *The well-ordered police state*, pp. 70–92; Hindle, *The state and social change*, pp. 176–203.

This expression only became regularly used, however, in the nineteenth century.[16]

The state did not give up on morality. On the contrary, it tended to become more strident on the matter during the sixteenth century. What it did discover, however, was that simple admonishment of moral failings as the cause for all woe was a bad formulation of the 'problem' to be addressed. Government was, in the end, interested in a solution – not least the solution to the problem of what it should be.[17] It only took a few decades to work out that the immorality of humankind was not something that the state was equipped to overcome. Indeed, within a Lutheran framework states were more inclined to take the fallen state of man as a given. This did not remove the necessity of moral action, but lead to the problem of identifying *effective* measures to improve well-being, backed up by the moral claim that they were implemented by the state for the common good. This has been conceptualised by some as a shift from holding a medieval notion of the 'discovery' of laws, which simply reflected moral certainties, to the idea that the government should actively innovate and legislate to achieve a desired result. This claim increasingly delineated any action inimical to these measures as immoral, treasonous, and unjustifiable by this very fact, whatever the utility or intention of such actions might be for others. Thus the state did not appeal to common morality, but came to define morality as adherence to its injunctions. By taking this road the state could claim that its actions were moral simply by the fact of them being carried out by the state.[18]

Thus the business of government was first and foremost to formulate or 'construct problems', or a set of problems to which the eventual solution would be the existence of the state itself as the only body

---

[16] Sabean, *Property*, pp. 101–16. There are certainly some incidents of its use in Leonberg in the 1750s. Landwehr, 'Finanzen, Rechte und Faktionen'.

[17] 'The problem always has the solution it deserves, in terms of the way in which it is stated (i.e. the conditions under which it is determined as a problem).' Deleuze, *Bergsonism*, p. 16.

[18] By using the *Urfehden* or binding-over via an oath of allegiance to deal with crime, for example, the state turned all future transgressions against the law an issue of perjury and contempt for one's sworn oath to the Duke. Scribner, 'Police and the territorial state', p. 109; Wright, *Capitalism*, p. 15. In some ways the state laid claim to a sacral sense of community that was exemplified for Bernd Moeller in an admittedly idealised view of the city commune. See Brady, *Communities, politics and Reformation*, pp. 3–4; the use of the oath also had religious connotations. Obedience to state authority was a key aspect of the arguments of influential Lutheran reformers in Württemberg such as Brenz, who provided a godly ideology of obedience to state law. Sabean, *Power in the blood*, pp. 42–6; Landwehr, 'Die Rhetorik', p. 252.

competent to deal with such matters.[19] In this sense 'order' is neither
primary nor secondary as a motivation for government action, but only
code for a continual process of problem setting and solving. This
perhaps also explains the vehemence with which political theorists
lamented the idiocy and the irrationality of rebels and rioters, even
though the same people seemed perfectly capable of sensible action for
most of the rest of the time. In the language of early modern government, the 'rabble' or the 'mob' was not a problem to be dealt with
reasonably. Rather, these were the names for those who in the elite's
eyes refused to conform to any kind of problem-and-solution framework as they understood it, the key to all order, and one that the elite
felt that they alone should define. Put another way, one thing among
others that characterised the state was that it was a 'discourse' spoken
among particular social actors, and the inclusion of outsiders or the
undermining of its terms threatened the whole institution. Of course,
rebels had their own problems and their own solutions, but it was that
very fact that set them outside the discourse of state power, even when
they were appealing for more effective state action. Only when the governmental response proved particularly inadequate to the real problems
of exercising political power did the 'centre' suddenly find itself explicitly
forced to reconstruct the problems it was supposed to be addressing in
terms provided by those who it had previously relegated to a more sub-
ordinate role. A prime example of this in early modern Europe was the
'Poor Conrad' rebellion of 1514 in Württemberg, which will be discussed
below. A tension always existed in particular between the claims to
provide 'order' and justice more generally and the idea that the state
was at the disposal of a ruler as their personal patrimony. Rhetoric
aside, in reality, of course the agenda and construction of the centralised
state was always faced with the adequacy of its dealings to the society it
attempted to rule.[20]

Following this logic, it could also be argued that it was almost
inevitable that the 'wood shortage' debate emerged as soon as governments began to consider it their role to deal with woodland, because
without a problem, there could be no government. The spectre of wood
shortage was no more than the recognition that resources could be
scarce, which was why all parties involved, and the state as the most
powerful among them, were prepared to enter into a rhetorical alliance
to exorcise this spectre. This is far from saying, of course, that they

---

[19] See also Landwehr, 'Die Rhetorik', p. 280.
[20] On the 'Poor Conrad' more generally, see the excellent survey by Schmauder,
Württemberg im Aufstand.

agreed on the means by which this should be brought about, or that the intensity of the debate would not vary over time. Concerns about shortage were clearly expressed more categorically in the later sixteenth and eighteenth centuries than the period between.[21] From the late fifteenth century central government set out to construct, and in doing so offer remedies, for a problem that is still encapsulated today in the debate about 'wood shortage'.

The second 'big' problem that emerges from the questions and considerations contained in government documents is that of implementation. Implementation is of course a part of the solution to any problem set and hence not independent itself of the way in which the problem was formulated. Nevertheless, institutions have a life independent of, if always bound up with, the aims that they have and the actions that they perform. We know things need to be done – but how can they be done? Historians have increasingly recognised 'implementation' as a serious problem for government, and hence the need to get out into local archives to understand the experience of governmental agents on the ground as they grappled with the reality of enforcement, laggardy and simple ignorance.[22] However, in escaping the restricted viewpoint of lawgivers and legal proclamation, they have often stepped sideways into the literature of complaint, whether of petitions or countervailing views among the elite. One is confronted with repetitive and adversarial comment, both in the sources and among the commentators. These sources are important, but often do not show us what the agents of the state actually did in the field, and how this might relate to the long lists of instructions and demands drawn up by bureaucrats, princes and aggrieved subjects. Here that source base will be widened in an attempt to bring a wider set of perspectives to the problem.

This chapter will be concerned, then, with early modern state formation, and in particular how it related to the problem of managing the fundamental resource of wood. As soon as it set itself this task, of course, the quality of wood supply and the form of the woodlands became in themselves a measure of the legitimacy of the state. The approach to 'state formation' will be, therefore, very much from the very top right down to the bottom, or from the periphery to the core, or

---

[21] Schäfer, 'Ein Gespenst geht um'; Mantel, Forstgeschichte; Sieferle, The subterranean forest, pp. 67–77; Schmidt, Der Wald in Deutschland; Radkau, 'Das Rätsel'; Radkau, 'Zur angeblichen Energiekrise'; Allmann, Der Wald; Ernst, Den Wald entwicklen.

[22] Hindle, The state and social change, pp. 1–36; Landwehr, Policey im Alltag, pp. 29–38; Harris, The politics of the excluded.

the centre to the locality. It does not really matter how it is framed, because such things were only a matter of perspective. Further sections of chapter 5 will also deal with the rhetoric of disputation that officials and peasants employed when arguing about the allocation of wood resources in local communities. These arguments were an important part of 'state formation', but less concerned with the development of the forest administration itself, which will be my main concern in this chapter. I hope to shed some light on the persistence of historiographical debates such as whether shortages are the key to institutional innovation, or about the relative weight of hunting and wood production in woodland management strategies. The formulation of the problem, and the implementation of the putative solution, haunt all these more specific questions.

One room, one view – the chancelry

In 1482, in the time of the Count and later Duke Eberhard im Bart ('the Bearded'), the Württemberger chancelry settled in Stuttgart. It would have four departments for most of the early modern period: the supreme council (*Oberrat*), the treasury (*Rentkammer*), church council (*Kirchenrat*) and privy council (*geheimen Rat*). From the 1540s onward it worked from the impressive building still standing across from the ducal residence now called the Altes Schloß, then on the southern edge of the city. The supreme council, which acquired this name first in 1549, was the most elevated of these bodies, and dealt with all those matters that touched the duke in person – legislation, officialdom, ducal prerogatives and so forth. This body oversaw local administration, legal matters, and acted as a court of appeal for certain categories of criminal and civil cases. The actual management of ducal finances, the receiver of monies from the forestry administration, and the auditor of accounts, was the treasury. This body in theory oversaw all of the granting out of wood from ducal woodlands and received annual reports on the matter, and scrutinised the accounts of the forestry administration.[23] The church council performed all these functions for those woodlands that fell under the properties of those monasteries that came under the protection of the Dukes of Württemberg and were absorbed as an autonomous unit of the administration at the time of the Reformation.

---

[23] Bernhardt, *Die Zentralbehörden*, pp. 1, 16–17, 27; Strauss, *Law, resistance, and the state*, p. 82; Vann, *The making of a state*, pp. 63–5.

By later standards, the central bureaucracy was small.[24] In this period, the treasury dealt with wood-related business every Thursday. This however was only the end point of a system where all forest wardens throughout the duchy were supposed to record all transactions in which they were involved and bring in the money to the forester who recorded receipts in his own account book. These books do seem to show actual receipts being brought in by the wardens, although in itself this is no indicator of the overall reliability of the system. The forester usually brought down in person to Stuttgart that money that had not been spent locally, often requiring more than one journey in April, before the end of the financial year on St George's day. His handiwork was audited over a few days around New Year, when other business was slack. It is important to remember when analysing the accounts maintained in the treasury that they only refer to the money actually brought in to be accounted centrally, not the actual receipts of the forestry administration, much of which was spent by the forester in the district where he resided.[25]

The supreme council met, appropriately, in the top storey of the chancelry building in Stuttgart. It was both an executive and a judicial body, producing legislation and running the administration. From 1552 a separate office was established to deal with 'forest matters' (*Forstsachen*), mining, and game, staffed by two permanent members who were supposed, at least, to work seven hour days. Although this reorganisation certainly was part of the increased administrative vigour brought in by the accession of Duke Christoph, and 1552 saw the promulgation of an extensive forest ordinance, there is little evidence that this represented a proactive approach to the forests, rather than a generally increased volume of business. Thanks to the work of Walter Bernhardt we have a good idea of the career paths of many of the men who staffed the council. A high proportion of councillors were legally trained, and most of them worked across a range of governmental activities and would have been familiar with most issues that came before the authorities. Nevertheless, some clearly developed particular expertise, and forest matters were no different from others in this respect. Georg Gadner, son of a Bavarian building master, dealt with forest matters from the 1550s until his death in 1605, including the production of a series of maps of all *Forstämter* in the 1590s. Johann Kielmann von Kiellmannsegg took up his mantle from 1602 until 1628. Noé Meurer went from service as

---

[24] Bernhardt, *Die Zentralbehörden*, p. 49; Marcus, *The politics of power*, pp. 2–3, 19.
[25] The forestry account books are in HStAS Bestand A302.

a Württemberger councillor between 1553 and 1557 to produce the first printed work on woodland management in the German language, and had a hand in drafting the influential forest ordinances for the Palatinate, drawing on Württemberger antecedents. These men show a high degree of continuity and familiarity with forest issues, can be presumed to have dealt with many of the complaints and petitions coming up from the peasantry and other ducal officials, and were well travelled within and without the Duchy. The heart of the forestry administration was familiar with the forests that it dealt with.[26]

These proto-bureaucrats were still, of course, very much at the mercy of their employers, and some of them had fortunes that rose, fell, and in some cases fell very abruptly, along with the regimes with which they were associated. The Habsburg regency of 1520–34 gave a powerful boost to efforts to record and exploit ducal property across the Duchy. Similarly, the careers of individual dukes, most notably Christoph (1550–68) and Friedrich (1593–1608) exerted a strong influence on the administration. A large range of matters from inheritance custom to butchery and the building trade found their first systematic, stand-alone sets of regulations in Christoph's reign. He equally appears to have at least tripled the cost of the bureaucracy in his first ten years of rule. Friedrich's concerted efforts to raise revenue, often to the chagrin of his subjects, showed very clear effects in income from the forestry administration during his reign, as well as a rise in the promulgation of instructions for officials. He promoted mining, iron production, linen weaving and silk production, with mixed results. The rulers of the Duchy could influence activity at a more prosaic level as well. They were well accustomed to riding through forest districts while hunting, and had plenty of opportunity to assess the state of their realm. Moves to improve the quality of the woodlands between Stuttgart and Böblingen, and record local woodland ordinances, seem to have stemmed from critical comments made by Duke Christoph during a hunting trip in the area in 1564.[27]

---

[26] Bernhardt, *Die Zentralbehörden*, pp. 304–8, 312–13, 349–53, 428, 494–5, 638–9; Bull-Reichenmiller, 'Beritten, beschriben und gerissen', pp. 11–23; Mantel, *Forstgeschichte*, pp. 51–6.

[27] HStAS A59 Bü 6a; Soll, *Die staatliche Wirtschaftspolitik*, pp. 15–21; Bernhardt, *Die Zentralbehörden*, pp. 11–13; Marcus, *The politics of power*, pp. 47–8; Hauff, *Zur Geschichte der Forstgesetzgebung*, pp. 43, 49, 54–5; Dehlinger, *Württembergs Staatwesen*, p. 38; Vann, *The making of a state*, pp. 54–6.

A multiplicity of views – the *Landtag*

Württemberg enjoys a degree of renown for what was considered its peculiar constitutional status during the early modern period. Although 'absolutist' rule is no longer viewed in the same kind of tyrannical, overbearing light as it once was, the extent of formal procedures of consultation with ducal subjects makes Württemberg unusual among central European states. Representatives of the towns, nobility, and clerical estate began to meet occasionally in the territorial diet, the *Landtag*, from 1457 onwards, the first of these meetings being held in Leonberg.[28] After 1515 the nobility effectively seceded from ducal rule, though many continued to work in the ducal government. After the Reformation this left the diet as an effectively secularised body staffed entirely by 'representatives' of the local districts and monastic administrations. They were not representative by modern standards, of course, but provided an important forum for the population to present grievances to their ruler.[29]

This situation gained a more formal grounding in the Tübingen Contract of 1514. Its leading historians have interpreted this event not as an agreement among the duke and assembled Estates, but essentially as a settlement between two independent powers (the Estates, and the Duke), with its guarantors being the Holy Roman Emperor and Electors. In theory, at least, this meant that one side's non-compliance could permit a withdrawal of obedience on the part of the other. The Tübingen Contract therefore placed a publicly recognised obligation on the part of the duke to respond to the grievances of his subjects whenever the diet met. This was not an arrangement to which the dukes always happily acquiesced. Friedrich in particular attempted to by-pass the obligation to deal with complaints, but this trend was ended by his death in 1608. The nature of the obligation was also disputed, as to whether it consisted of a requirement to respond generally to any grievances or to each and every complaint in its particulars.[30]

This Württemberger constitutional arrangement went further than the usual late medieval expectation of reciprocity between tax-paying subjects and their law-giving rulers. From 1514 onwards the diet took on the burden of ducal debts, and most of its meetings were called for the purpose of this burden being expanded or rescheduled. However, as the formal bearer of the debt, the Estates managed the collection of revenue

---

[28] Carsten, *Princes and parliaments*; Grube, *Der Stuttgarter Landtag*, pp. 14–15, passim.
[29] Carsten, *Princes and parliaments*, p. 11, passim; Vann, *The making of a state*, pp. 46–8.
[30] Carsten, *Princes and parliaments*; Fuhrmann, 'Amtsbeschwerden', pp. 76–7, 83–4, 93.

for this purpose by itself, keeping the accounting of their revenues and ducal revenues entirely separate. Certainly by the eighteenth century the Estates' income was considerably larger than that of the Duke. This amounted to the creation of a parallel administration, if much more narrow in focus than the ducal government. Officials such as village *Schultheißen* were answerable to the diet as much as to the Duke on certain matters. After the Thirty Years' War the district assembly developed into a form of election of local representatives by the acclaim of all the district's *Schultheißen*, forming, in contrast to the dominant absolutist trend in Germany, a limited form of democracy.[31] Indeed, in the early eighteenth century dukes attempted to by-pass the diet by appealing directly to the possibly more easily intimidated district assemblies on several issues. A further precedent had been set by the transfer of the management of ducal property to the Estates during the Austrian lordship of 1520–34. Often particular issues of interest to both Estates and Duke were dealt with by setting up *ad hoc* committees, but as business transacted increased during the 1550s, a semi-permanent 'small committee' of the Estates was set up that allowed it to take a degree of legislative initiative. This co-opted members and continued to act even during long periods, such as the reigns of Eberhard Ludwig and Karl Alexander between 1699 and 1737, when the diet did not sit.[32]

These formal arrangements, in the shape of the territorial diet and its standing committees, were also supplemented by a steady flow of petitions directly to the supreme council. Taken together, they had a considerable impact. Rosi Fuhrmann has argued that the forest ordinance of 1552 was a direct, and rather hurried, response to the number of complaints on woodland issues that came before the assembly of 1551, as the populace sensed a chance to roll back some of the provisions of the ordinance of 1540.[33] This ordinance of 1552 was criticised in turn at the diet of 1565, for much the same reasons that also appeared in petitions at a local level in the *Forstamt* Leonberg, such as requirements to clear felled timber from the woodland, set staddles and disputes over game. That these came before the assembly of 1565 and not that of 1554 suggests a pattern that seems generally applicable from other sources – a slow, but not negligible, process of implementation of the centrally promulgated ordinances. In 1565 a committee was set up to examine

---

[31] Grube, 'Dorfgemeinde und Amtsversammlung'; Wilson, *War, state and society*, pp. 46, 52, 59; Fulbrook, *Piety and politics*, pp. 66–75.

[32] Grube, 'Dorfgemeinde und Amtsversammlung', p. 210; Carsten, *Princes and parliaments*, pp. 101, 120–1; Vann, *The making of a state*; Fuhrmann, 'Amtsbeschwerden', p. 80.

[33] Fuhrmann, 'Amtsbeschwerden', p. 114.

the issues, dovetailing neatly with the simultaneous complaints from Christoph himself about the forests, and leading to the ordinance of 1567. All of this was a repeat of an earlier and more dramatic series of events, when some of the grievances expressed during the 'Poor Conrad' rebellion concerned 'forest matters'.[34]

The lesson here is that even central government, if we limit that to the offices of the supreme council and the treasury, was part of a wider process of information sharing, complaint, initiative and communication. These embraced various formal procedures, some with a strong 'constitutional' influence, such as the assembly, and others, such as petitions, that might be dealt with in a more discretionary fashion. The latter will be dealt with at greater length in chapter 5. There was plenty of influence from 'below', although we must not exaggerate the breadth of social standing in 'representative' institutions that for the most part reflected the views of small town elites. The evidence of the 'Poor Conrad' also points to considerable competition between the towns as well as within them for influence on government.[35] There was plenty of scope for officials to gauge the opinion of the wider polity, and develop a sense of the consequences of their initiatives. Legislation was by no means solely a top–down process, though consultation could have unanticipated results. The great 'state law' of 1554, for example, engaged on a vast, and fortunately preserved, consultation exercise on local inheritance practices, only to sweep them away with the ruthless application of a one-size-fits-all principle rooted in Roman law. The law itself, however, was very much developed at the behest of local communities frustrated with the complexities of inheritance and property laws that varied over very short distances.[36] This pattern was replicated over a wide swathe of government legislative activity.

The regulative drive

From at least the eleventh century, local ordinances and orders survive that show a limited regulation of woodlands, either from lords, town governments, or their subjects.[37] Much of this regulation appears to have been practised by, and acceptable to, the peasantry, with the affirmation

---

[34] HStAS A34 Bü 1c; A227 Bü 1139; Schmauder, *Württemberg im Aufstand*, pp. 154–60; Hauff, *Zur Geschichte der Forstgesetzgebung*, p. 51.

[35] Schmauder, *Württemberg im Aufstand*, pp. 194–200.

[36] Reyscher, *SWG*, Bd.IV, pp. 95, 333–420; Strauss, *Law, resistance, and the state*, pp. 86–7; Hess, *Familien- und Erbrecht*, pp. 16–17, passim.

[37] Epperlein, *Waldnutzung*; On Germany more generally, see Günther, *Der Arnsberger Wald*; Grimm, *Weisthümer*; Timm, *Die Waldnutzung*.

of such practices in the lord's court by no means necessarily meaning that the initiative flowed from above, or that the lord was the sole recipient of benefits from it. By the end of the fifteenth century some form of ducal forestry administration was clearly in place, but equally, small towns at the very least were also regulating their own woodlands.[38]

The state's claim to be able to regulate all woodlands, however, as opposed to imposing order on those that were the property of certain individuals or institutions, was a particular and unusual one. The origin of 'forest' rights all over Europe has been a source of endless debate, but in the sixteenth century found its justification in hunting rights rather than woodland *per se*. So much is clear in the opening passages of Meurer's *Vom Forstlicher Oberherrligkeit* of 1560, although we should remember that this was simply a description of already long-established practices. In his view *Forst* derived from the Latin *fera*, a wild beast,[39] and originally designated a hunting area, but had been expanded 'to a particular law, with more rights appended besides the hunting'. As such it did not pertain to real property but was established by customary practice, although because of the nature of hunting, this could be discontinuous and thus had the lengthiest legally permissible duration to establish custom available, that of being practised within human memory. The trees themselves should remain the property of the landlord, but anything that impugned the rights of the possessor of the forest as a legal entity, such as the mast where required to feed game, could, if necessary, be regulated by her or him. Such fine distinctions, Meurer noted, were not always grasped by forest wardens, who might think, 'I have the forest, therefore, I have the mast.'[40]

The first inclusion of a passage on wood in state regulation came in the 'state ordinance' (*Landesordnung*) of 11 November 1495. Already, this section entitled 'Fire- and building-wood', complains of 'the great shortage of wood for fuel and building'. Local officials are ordered to make ordinances for their woods in consultation with foresters.[41] The problem was not, in fact, seen as one that required central regulation, aside from an admonishment to utilise coppiced coupes and fines more systematically. The ordinance of 1495 simply asserts the ducal interest in maintaining wood supplies and does so as an offshoot of the Duke's

---

[38] Kieß, *Die Rolle der Forsten*, passim.

[39] It is now generally argued that it in fact derives from the Latin 'foris', meaning 'outside', presumably applied to land outside the cultivated areas or established property rights.

[40] Meurer, *Vom Forstlicher Oberherrligkeit*, pp. 9–10; Mantel, *Forstgeschichte*, pp. 71, 92–4; On 'forest' see Kieß, *Die Rolle der Forsten*, pp. 4–9; Günther, *Der Arnsberger Wald*, pp. 15–19.

[41] Reyscher, *SWG*, Bd.XII, p. 9.

role as ruler of Württemberg's subjects, rather than possessor of forest rights. The problem is thus envisaged as one of general welfare rather than the assertion of rights to control woodland. Around the same time, however, jurisdictional disputes, especially over the Schönbuch woodland to the north of Tübingen, resulted in local agreements over the management of woodland that may well have fed into the measures envisaged in the state ordinance. Certainly the 'learned councillor' Dr Johannes Vergenhans worked on both documents. The early sixteenth century saw a number of such local agreements, including one that pertained to the Hagenschieß lying just to the west of the *Forstamt* Leonberg.[42]

The ambiguity of this situation almost certainly led in part to the flood of complaints that accompanied the 'Poor Conrad' rebellion of 1514, leading in turn to the promise in the Tübingen Contract for a new ordinance for 'the forest, the wardens of the same, and the common man'. There is no evidence that this ordinance was ever made, and it seems likely that it was not.[43] The events of 1514 will be dealt with in more detail below, but those sections of formal petition presented by the peasants during the uprising that dealt with woodland numbered no less than twelve out of fifty-four in total. These almost entirely imposed limitations upon the powers of the ducal foresters. The petitions that had led to the Contract complained of interference in communal woodland, especially limits on pannage and felling certain types of tree, charges for pasture in ducal woodland and corruption or venality by officials. The charges against foresters varied across localities and derived, one must suspect, from the localism of the injunctions of 1495. In turn, the state was being drawn to define more closely the boundaries of its competence in areas where the subjects felt that guidelines were insufficient. Local communes sought to assert that foresters were supposed to assist their officials, not overrule them. For the most part, petitioners in the run up to the Tübingen Contract during the tense summer months of 1514 appealed to '*alte Herkommen*' ('ancient custom') that ducal officials, not least foresters, had transgressed. Although in many senses a defeat for a central administration, the demand to regulate the regulators, to 'discipline' the officials, would in fact become a staple of early modern governmental measures, often at the behest of subjects and not just to iron out financial irregularities.[44]

---

[42] HStAS A368 Bü 46; Hauff, *Zur Geschichte der Forstgesetzgebung*, pp. 10–14.

[43] See Hauff, *Zur Geschichte der Forstgesetzgebung*, pp. 16–17; Reyscher, *SWG*, Bd.II, p. 48.

[44] HStAS A34 Bü 1; Schmauder, *Württemberg im Aufstand*, pp. 194–200; Hauff, *Zur Geschichte der Forstgesetzgebung*, p. 8.

The regulative drive really began under the Habsburg administration, which saw a fairly extensive survey of forest rights and even
the surveying of the woodlands themselves in 1523. In 1520 foresters
were formally included in the *Regimentsordnung* ('staff ordinance') that
governed the conduct of officials. In 1526 an 'advisory' order was
drawn up instructing foresters to sell wood for 'as high as possible',
though the reason given is that this would prevent subjects buying
cheap, selling the wood elsewhere, and using the profits to buy 'unnecessary things'. Wood regulation was set firmly, then, in an economy
of morality. These instructions, which also ordered the maintaining
of coupes and set cutting and clearing times for wood, were finally
published in October 1532. This led to an immediate flurry of complaints from communes and foresters alike, a recurrent theme of which
was that these centrally drafted ordinances were inappropriate for
different climes and local economies. Furthermore, in some regions at
least it appears that a desire to generally regulate woodland, including
that owned by communes, was an unwelcome innovation and considered an unjust extension of forest rights. In response, councillors
suggested that local discretion should apply.[45]

The return of Duke Ulrich in 1534 put this process temporarily in
abeyance. Developments since 1495, however, had expanded the scope
of foresters' activities, established a principle by which central government had a legitimate interest in regulating wood supplies, and lastly,
conceded the notion that locals may well know what was best for their
district. All these things would be acted on swiftly under the new
regime. The new state ordinance of June 1536 again incorporated regulation of wood use, bewailing the 'marked wastage' of wood which
it attributed to a growing population, disorderly felling and damage
from grazing. This time, a promised 'wood ordinance' would actually
appear, in 1540, the first major attempt to regulate the woodland across a
range of issues. In the meantime, a committee set up in November 1536,
including most officials of any standing in the Black Forest, was convened
to draw up a specific ordinance for this region. The report remained,
however, subject to being 'changed or improved' by the mercurial Ulrich
when finally drawn up.[46]

The fact of consultation, of course, did not guarantee that many
subjects got what they wanted. Pressure for new legislation in 1551, on
the accession of Duke Christoph, seems to have again come from

---

[45] HStAS A59 Bü 32; A237 Nr.19; Hauff, *Zur Geschichte der Forstgesetzgebung*, pp. 26–33.
[46] Reyscher, *SWG*, Bd.XII, p. 111; Bd.XVI, pp. 4–21; Hauff, *Zur Geschichte der Forstgesetzgebung*, pp. 34–7.

'below'. The handing over of rule usually required the re-affirmation of old laws by the new incumbent, even if most governing personnel remained in place, and was frequently an occasion to press new demands. In April the district governors (*Vögte*) were ordered to consult with all officials over the forest ordinance, the results being delivered to an inquisition moving through the towns. Foresters, wardens and ducal hunters were to be consulted, but also other officials and village mayors. The territorial assembly brought a range of complaints that resulted in a new, more extensive ordinance on 2 January 1552, the day that a new territorial diet convened.[47] As a new department within the supreme council to manage forest matters was set up, correspondence and hence consultation appears to have become more continuous. However, the frequency of communication, and perhaps the frequency of complaint, may have been higher in the period immediately prior to further forest ordinances promulgated in 1567 and 1614. The latter remained in place until the nineteenth century, but the former was the greater leap in ambition. From four sections in the ordinance of 1540, their number grew to thirty-nine in 1552, sixty-seven in 1567 and seventy-one by 1614, although some of this alteration was caused by the sub-division and editing of pre-existing passages.[48] Foresters were extensively consulted in 1563, 1569–70, 1581, 1605 and spring 1614. The latter consultation very explicitly sought recommendations on the forthcoming revision of the forest ordinance, although if this seems to describe a smoothly functioning bureaucracy, it should be noted that the supreme council was concerned that nearly all the old copies of the forest ordinance from 1567 had been lost. However, the interaction between the 'centre' and local authorities was clearly extensive. The regulation became significantly more extensive too, but while a report of 1563 from the forester of Leonberg, Jacob Koch, shows that the regulation (of 1552) equally applied to communally owned as well as ducally owned woodlands, the forester was only permitted to enforce it should communal officials fail to do so.[49]

Once the principle of intervention had been established, more a product of paternalism than the assertion of forest rights, there are few obvious breaks in the chronology of regulation before the Thirty Years' War. The ambitions of the men regulating the forests generally

---

[47] Hauff, *Zur Geschichte der Forstgesetzgebung*, p. 39; This drawn-out process suggests that the ordinance was not quite so rapid a reaction to the approaching diet as Fuhrmann protests, Fuhrmann, 'Amtsbeschwerden', p. 114.

[48] Reyscher, *SWG*, Bd.XVI, pp. 4–21, 30–71, 229–97.

[49] HStAS A59 Bü 5, 8, 12, 17, 32; A227 Bü 55; Hauff, *Zur Geschichte der Forstgesetzgebung*, p. 56.

marched in step with a bureaucracy that sought to regulate a great range of other activities. As the same personnel were often engaged in a wide range of regulatory activities this should hardly surprise us. Across the sixteenth and early seventeenth centuries, however, ordinances relating to the forest also responded to the exogenous pressures of war and the personal predilections of rulers. Prior to the 1590s more frequent instructions (*General-Reskripten*) issued by the supreme council were for the most part devoted to ensuring that game was slaughtered for the entertainment of the duke rather than the gratification of his subjects. The topic of wood only first received a missive in its own right in 1565. This does not necessarily reflect administrative priorities, as hunting brought the duke into the forests every year to be confronted with a superfluity or a lack of targets. Documents reiterating prohibitions on poaching are hardly to be compared with extensive forest ordinances. But a trend in the interests of the supreme council can be discerned. Hunting, relatively speaking, was more of a priority in the earlier decades. Although already to be observed under Ludwig (1568–93), who personally showed no special interest in the forests, Friedrich's (1593–1608) reign saw a concerted effort to regulate wood use, which, as we shall see, had commensurate effects on fiscal returns from the forest. During the Thirty Years' War we can discern themes, such as the supply of saltpeterers for gunpowder making, and the need to deal with wolves, coming to the fore. A high rate of activity in the 1640s reflects strenuous efforts in that decade to keep the administration functioning and to begin to put the government back on its feet in the closing years of the conflict. While not an exact match, the pre-war general magnitude of activity in 'forest matters' follows fairly closely the general propensity to issue regulatory ordinances plotted by Achim Landwehr.[50]

Unsurprisingly, the administration took some time to get going again after the war. The 1650s saw little new by way of regulation, with efforts up until 1665 primarily aimed at putting the practices of princely hunting back in order.[51] The post-war period saw a wide-ranging extension of 'policing' ordinances (*Polizeiordnungen*) governing many aspects of moral and economic life. These ranged from the flowering of 'state corporatism', embracing the use of monopoly patents and guild controls, to the setting up of a systematic centralised authority for religious and moral regulation under the auspices of Lutheran reformers such as Johann Valentin Andreae, as well as the attempt to

---

[50] HStAS A237 Nr.19; Landwehr, *Policey im Alltag*, p. 352.
[51] Reyscher, *SWG*, Bd.XVI, pp. 387, 390–2, 409–10, 419–20, 461–7, 473–7, 479–80.

introduce universal primary education from 1649.[52] The decades up
until 1674 and the accession of Wilhelm Ludwig saw this occurring in
close consultation with the territorial diet.[53] Thereafter ducally sponsored entrepreneurial projects, export bans and largely fiscally moti-
vated excise taxes became increasingly important policies. Such dirigiste
economic trends marked not so much a break with previous policy
as a more determined flexing of governmental muscle and its expansion into most areas of trade, especially new (and morally suspect!)
products such as tobacco.[54] No such trend affected the regulation of
wood use or woodland, which clearly diverged from mainstream
activity and barely won a mention for decades. As woodland was still
for the most part owned by either a branch of the government or ducal
house, or communes, its management remained within this regulatory
context. However, direct regulation of woodland was not even mentioned until 1712, and a renewed concern with the supply of wood and
regeneration of woodland does not reappear until the 1720s.[55] Thus
woodland management and wood supply were not matters widely
deemed worthy of any more centrally determined regulation until the
third decade of the eighteenth century. In this, woodland broke away
from being part of a general trend towards increasing regulation over
the early modern period. However, it is difficult to interpret this trend
solely on the basis of legislation. It may have been the result of government satisfaction with the forest administration; or perhaps a lordly
obsession with the chase to the detriment of other interests; or alternatively a superfluity of wood relative to demand making regulation
redundant. Certainly legislation about hunting was driven to some
degree by an active and powerful diet using the opportunity to bring
forward perennial complaints about the damage that game did to the
fields. But none of these hypotheses can be tested by simply examining
the legislation itself.

Early modern woodmanship – lessons from the laws

What, then, did the laws aim to achieve? And did their priorities and
ambition alter over time? The 1495 state ordinance contained no great
details on woodmanship, save that, significantly, woodland should be

---

[52] Ogilvie, *State corporatism*; Fulbrook, *Piety and politics*, p. 26; Landwehr, *Policey im Alltag*,
p. 352.
[53] Vann, *The making of a state*, pp. 97–121.
[54] Soll, *Die staatliche Wirtschaftspolitik*, pp. 53–79.
[55] Reyscher, *SWG*, Bd.XVI, pp. 545, 564, 569, 584–5.

managed in coupes. Other evidence suggests coupes were widespread, though far from universal.[56] The forest ordinance of 1540 of course reiterated complaints about the condition of forests. It provided its own justification, protecting 'not only Ourself, as Prince, but also all our subjects and for the welfare and good of the common weal', 'from future loss and shortage of wood, that certainly and therefore plainly lies before the eye'. This would come to be the classic way of formulating the problem; things are obviously deteriorating, but without this intervention they will get much worse, 'where if not met with good order, in a short time, our people will suffer and endure no small shortage of wood'. Yet this could still be 'anticipated and rejected'.[57]

Coupes were to be coppiced for firewood, and cut right back to the ground, rather than leaving a projecting stump. These had to be protected from grazing animals, and indeed grazing was only permitted again with the approval of the forester, though with the length of protection or coppicing cycling determined as appropriate to each locality. Woodcutting should not begin before St Edigius' day (1 September), to prevent damage to the tree during the growth period, and felled wood should be cleared out of the coupes by the end of March. For each 'coupe' (which seems here to imply a *morgen*), sixteen staddles were to be left untouched after cutting, preferably of oak, then birch, then aspen. The ordinance as a whole was divided into four sections, 'How each forester should behave in the management of his forest', 'in regard to oak wood', 'of pine wood', and 'of beech wood', the latter incorporating other deciduous trees. This structure suggests that the ordinance may have been cobbled together from earlier, more specific drafts of instructions, and indeed the stipulation on staddles which appears in the first section is repeated to a degree in the final one. No set number of staddles per coupe is given in the latter section, but the cutting of coupes should ensure the preservation of oaks and 'fruit-bearing trees'. Legal theorists of the time, and many forest historians, have interpreted this as the desire to provide fodder for game, but here it explicitly states that it is for 'building timber, or other needs'. Thinning of stands of pine trees and birch trees is encouraged to prevent the choking of trees and allow the selection of the most promising saplings.[58]

However, instructions on woodmanship go no further. Far more extensive are orders for forestry officials to oversee woodland tasks. These include stipulations that allocation and sale of building timber or

---

[56] See chapter 4. Reyscher, *SWG*, Bd.XII, p. 9.   [57] Reyscher, *SWG*, Bd.XVI, pp. 4–5.
[58] Ibid., pp. 4–21.

clearances can only take place with the permission of ducal councillors; that carpentry should not be done in the forest but where the shavings and waste will be productively taken up and used; restricting the uses to which particular trees could be put (no birchwood for fuel, but rather for barrel-hoops, for example); banning fire-setting in the forest; banning bast making and bark stripping. In other words, the ordinance of 1540 was far more interested in limiting waste or perceived superfluity in the carrying out of traditional woodmanship, rather than altering it in any way. It spoke the language of good and prudent husbandry rather than improvement.[59]

The 1552 ordinance's innovations largely concerned the conduct of officials and restrictions on use rather than any development of woodmanship. All official perquisites, unless formally included in the ordinance, were to be abandoned. Officials were to ensure the full implementation of the ordinances, and marking of wood and its alloca-tion for sale was to be done by a number of men on set days of the year to ensure there was no corruption. Virtually every form of cutting and sale required the permission of forest officials, even in privately owned woodlands. Although these rules appear to have been framed with the Black Forest in mind, they were universally applicable. No wood better suited for another purpose was to be used in preference to decrepit or no longer mast-giving trees, windfall, or lop and top. In theory, the regime was ferociously restrictive. Barely a twig could be despatched in any direction unless it was for a proven need and with official approval. Woodmanship measures were not simply repeated from the last ordi-nance, however. Most sections were edited or expanded in some way, without fundamentally altering the foresters' tasks. The government clearly encouraged the opening up of inaccessible areas, and by impli-cation the rafting trade, to overcome shortages in the lowlands. However, it was to be done entirely under the scrutiny of the forest administration.[60]

The ordinances of 1567 and 1614 continued in the same vein, tight-ening up rules on hunting and poaching, but adding little else. The ordinances teach us that the government largely expected the populace to know what was good woodmanship, but did not trust their sub-jects nor their officials to act in the common good. Indeed, proposals

---

[59] Ibid. In this regard, the ordinances fit into the general pattern of woodland regulation in Europe in the fifteenth and sixteenth centuries, and were perhaps a little more proactive than most laws that tended to emphasise the prohibition side. Appuhn, 'Inventing nature', p. 871; Corvol, 'Les communautés d'habitants'; James, *A history of English forestry*, pp. 119–27.

[60] Reyscher, *SWG*, Bd.XVI, pp. 30–71.

encountered some resistance from both subjects and officials who felt that the measures were too schematic. The committee charged with examining these themes before the ordinance of 1567 judged forestalling of wood and profiteering from sales to be unimportant, but such opinions did not impress the Duke. The forest ordinances thus reflected a general distrust of superfluity and middlemen, preferring to blame shortage on bad practice and immoral undertakings. This did not preclude the development of a tightly regulated rafting trade, but it did so firmly under the auspices of the moral community of the Württemberger state, discouraging, for example, export of wood beyond its borders.[61] Similar measures forbidding regrating and forestalling were frequently applied to livestock, meat and grain in dearth years.[62] Overall, the development of, and tinkering with, legislation, and the process by which it came about, suggests a genuine intent to implement the laws and achieve results. Governmental ordinances were not designed to give the appearance or illusion of state authority, but get results on the ground.[63]

Realities on the ground (1) – the growth of the forestry administration

To establish the real effect of the legislative effort we must go back to the little world of the *Forstamt* Leonberg. The lynchpin of this effort was the forester. Just as there was no Duchy without a Duke, so there were no forest districts without a forester. The survey of 1556 was the first time that the boundary of the district was clearly laid down in writing, and where not following a river or stream, the boundary's precise course was somewhat vague. Markstones were only laid out in the contested territories along the border with Baden and the Lords of Gemmingen. The boundary internal to Württemberg could run miles and miles without any features being recorded.[64]

A 'forest book' dated by Rudolf Kieß to the first half of the fifteenth century has no mention of a forester, though there were forest wardens in Gerlingen and Botnang who probably oversaw the extensive possessions of the then Counts of Württemberg in the region. By the middle of the century there was a forester in the Leonberg area, a little after foresters begin to appear in other parts of Württemberg.[65] A first sure

---

[61] Hauff, *Zur Geschichte der Forstgesetzgebung*, pp. 47–9, 51.

[62] Soll, *Die staatliche Wirtschaftspolitik*, pp. 41–2.

[63] This opposes the suggestion, at least in this case, of Jürgen Schlumbohm that ordinances primarily aimed only to give the appearance of legitimate rule. Schlumbohm, 'Gesetze'.

[64] HStAS H107/8 Bd.1.   [65] Ibid. Kieß, *Der Rolle der Forsten*, p. 11, passim.

mention comes with a Hans von Eltingen who oversaw an exchange of woodland near Leonberg in the late 1450s. At this point his duties were probably to manage ducal property and prerogatives, such as collecting money for pannage. Another forester by the name of Auberlin was present in 1461. Later disputes and orders suggest that the forester already possessed certain perquisites, such as to faggots from the woodlands around Asperg noted in 1489.[66] After 1495, as we have seen, the responsibility of the forester to regulate was extended, but in such a way that local conflicts rapidly ensued. The conflicts of the 'Poor Conrad' of 1514 associated with wood mainly emerged in settlements a little more distant from Leonberg, but still within its own administrative district (*Amt*). This fact suggests that in the first part of Ulrich's reign, the forester, Menrat Jagesyn, was active over a wider area than previously, but most of the later extent of the forest district (*Forstamt*) remained relatively untouched.[67] In 1532 forester Bartlin Frieß divided the district into the 'Gerlinger area', 'Area across the Glems', and the 'Area across the Würm', suggesting that the focus of management still lay to the south and west of the *Forstamt* at this time.[68]

The first foresters are simply names that appear here and there in the record. From 1527 onwards, from Bartlin Frieß, we encounter them in their own hand. Gall von Sachsenheim, forester from 1551 to 1560, was minor nobility. Von Sachsenheim had amassed the considerable fortune of 9,685 fl. by his death, admittedly long after his period of office.[69] From the fourth decade of the sixteenth century however, while men of standing and independent means, most were essentially professional foresters. They often had prior experience and held their offices for considerable periods of time. Hans Hagen, for example, was in place from 1534 to 1551, and remained available for consultation thereafter. Ulrich Bauder was transferred from the forest of Wildbad in 1589, and was succeeded by his son who lasted as forester until the end of the Thirty Years' War.[70] These men moved in the leading social circles of Leonberg. Gall von Sachsenheim and his successor Jacob Koch married

---

[66] HStAS A572 Bü 17; A557 Bü 87; Kieß, *Der Rolle der Forsten*, p. 71.
[67] Renningen complained about new charges on pannage and grazing in the ducal woods, but most prominent among the local complainers were more distant Mönßheim, and Heimsheim. However, in Heimsheim the locals claimed 'by custom and in the memory of man' they had freely given a portion of lop and top to the forester. HStAS A368 Bü 17; A557 Bü 127; A572 Bü 69; H101 Bd.948; Schmauder, *Württemberg im Aufstand*, p. 164.
[68] HStAS A59 Bü 3.
[69] HStAS A368 Bü 5; Trugenberger, 'Malmsheim und Renningen', p. 145; Trugenberger, *Zwischen Schloß und Vorstadt*, Prosopographie.
[70] HStAS A256 Bds.1–183.

daughters of the district governor. Few of the men were originally local, but they put down roots. Over time the Bauders built up a network of marriage relations to various local dignitaries. Eight years after his arrival in 1589, Ulrich Bauder was made a *Bürger* of Leonberg, by which time he was a local creditor to the tune of 2,500 fl. About half of these debts were from the vicinity of Leonberg (the others were presumably carried forward from his time as a forester in Wildbad), but their geographical range did not go that far beyond the town.[71] Even by the end of the sixteenth century, as we shall see, the forester's activity remained focused around his town of residence. Professional men continued to act through the seventeenth century, until the noble Friedrich Jacob von Reischach handed over to Ernst Friedrich von Gaisberg, ex-forester of Reichenberg, in 1687. Ernst Friedrich was succeeded by his son Friedrich Albrecht in 1695, a cavalry officer who appears to have been less interested in the everyday humdrum of forest administration.[72] As a footnote to the character of these men, we might also add the library of forester Jacob Harnisch, containing a number of Lutheran and classical texts, but also a '*Kreutterbuch*' of Petris de Crescentis when he died in 1575. This was probably a version of Pier de' Cresenzi's early fourteenth century *Liber cultis ruris*, which included a section on trees and among other things propagated the theory that trees should be planted according to the phases of the moon to the early modern world.[73]

The cash pay of foresters was not especially good, as was usually the case with early modern bureaucrats. They were clearly expected to have independent sources of income commensurate with their status. The bulk of pay came in payments in kind, of grain, two sets of clothing, hay, wine, straw, free use of a house, and until 1605, a large amount of wood. The payments in kind were far beyond what any one household would need, and hence could form the basis for trade and credit relationships. A cash payment was made that was a little above a labourer's annual wage. This was only occasionally altered and thus tended to fall behind the general advance of prices in the sixteenth century. Certainly these payments would have made foresters relatively wealthy men, but would not, on their own, have propelled them into the more esteemed ranks of the highest local dignitaries.[74]

---

[71] HStAS A572 Bü 37b; Trugenberger, *Zwischen Schloß und Vorstadt*, pp. 84–5.
[72] HStAS 256 Bds.160–83; HStAS A368L Bü 2.
[73] Trugenberger, *Zwischen Schloß und Vorstadt*, Prosopographie; Ambrosoli, *The wild and the sown*, pp. 41–3.
[74] HStAS A2 Bü 17; A368L Bü 2; A302 Bds.7221–35.

From a rather different social milieu, but the immediate point of contact for most people with the forest administration, were the forest wardens (*Forstknechten*). According to the forest ordinance of 1540, wardens were to be nominated by the forester but approved by the councillors in Stuttgart, but it seems likely that candidates emerged on a much more local basis than this in reality.[75] Each warden was assigned a ward (*Hut*). These areas were established according to the distribution of ducal woodland, but this was scattered enough to give them a good coverage of the entire district. Each woodland was assigned to a ward, but the wards themselves had no delineated boundaries, and woods could be transferred from ward to ward as the occasion demanded. A ducal wood warden was present in Eltingen as early as 1350. The two wards of the 1440s had risen to eight by 1523, with wardens already within a day's walk of all of the district, rising to ten in 1556, eleven by 1583 and thirteen in 1585. The base of wardens did not always remain the same, and was probably determined by where suitable candidates lived.[76]

Wardens usually held the post for a significant amount of time, often a decade or longer. There were also father-to-son handovers. A Hans Leucht was warden of Münklingen around 1490, and it was probably his son Jacob who held the same post from the 1520s until around 1547. Similarly the Jung family and the Stahel family held the posts in Eltinger See and Malmstal respectively in the second half of the six-teenth century. Such families were not only made up of woodland characters, but almost became woodland dynasties, allowing the opportunity both to develop good practice, and practices somewhat shadier. An inquiry swooped on the wardens of Enzweihingen, Malmstal, Eltinger See and Ruteslheim in 1559–60.[77] Whilst these men were caught, proximity to superiors was obviously no bar to corrup-tion, as the last three in the list were the wards closest to the seat of the forester in Leonberg. Corruption, of course, could range across the social scale. 'Whoever loans money [to an official], is soon a forest warden', commented a witness from Schorndorf in 1478.[78] Equally, exploiting the rather loosely formulated early ordinances regarding

---

[75] Reyscher, *SWG*, Bd.XVI, p. 7.
[76] HStAS A59 Bü 13a, 32; H107/8 Bd.1; H107/19 Bd.1; A302 Bd.7221; Ernst, 'Geschichte', pp. 336–7.
[77] The careers of these individual wardens can be found in HStAS A302 Bds.7221–6; A557 Bü 127, 210, 212; A227 Bü 1119, 1120, 1124, 1125, 1126, 1130, 1132, 1143, 1147, 1152, 1154, 1170, 1171, 1428; A59 Bü 13a; A368 Bü 5, 12, 29, 31, 37, 46; A4 Bü 4; A44 U5231, 5235, 5236, 5237; H107/8 Bd.1 and 2.
[78] Hauff, *Zur Geschichte der Forstgesetzgebung*, p. 82.

the forests, the wardens seem to have on occasion stretched the interpretation of their rights more than was considered fair. In Mönßheim
before the 'Poor Conrad', for example, the warden seems to have
allotted pannage to his own pigs for free, but charged others. The
appointment of honest men to the office of forest warden, and the
responsibility of the forester to look out for corruption among his
underlings, was a major theme of ordinances from 1540 onwards. The
government clearly viewed the lowest tier of its own administration
with some suspicion. Yet despite the initial imprisonment of the warden
Eberhard Stahel for 'unfaithful service and bad behaviour' in 1560, he
was still in the job twenty years later and was succeeded by his son. None
of the men arrested that year were short of friends to put up hefty
guarantees of good behaviour.[79]

The temptation to 'cheat' was not simply because one could profitably
get away with it. Forest warden pay was not terribly good. It was generally
recorded as a cash payment, with perhaps the odd perquisite in kind, a
share of fines (a third) and possibly free housing and sometimes clothing.
Payment to wardens actually varied quite considerably from place to
place, in 1585 from 5 fl. in Simmozheim and Enzweihingen, to 20 fl. in
Mönßheim and Rutesheim. These variations certainly did not reflect the
size of the area they had to oversee and may be related to the intensity of
management. When grants of wood and clothing in kind were converted
into cash payment in the early seventeenth century it is clear that only the
two wardens of Mönßheim and Rutesheim earned what could be construed
as a meagre living wage. Forest wardens were thus usually poor, though
they must have owned other property or worked outside of their duties.
Among the handful that can be identified in the tax returns for 1544–5,
no-one has an assessment over 160 fl. and some are very poor. These men,
who in theory at least had to devote the greater share of their time to
overseeing the woodlands, were in fact the most numerous and familiar
of all of the officialdom of the central administration of Württemberg.[80]

Realities on the ground (2) – what did the officials actually do?

Having officials in place was one thing. Getting them to do anything
was another. Wardens had acted as managers and overseers of ducal
woods since the early fifteenth century, and presumably understood

---

[79] HStAS A44 U5235; A302 Bd.7221–3; A557 Bü 127; Reyscher, *SWG*, Bd.XVI, passim.
[80] HStAS A302 Bds.7221–3; A59 Bü 5; A54a Ämter Leonberg, Vaihingen a.d. Enz,
Bietigheim, Hoheneck, Canstatt, Stuttgart, Calw, Asperg, Markgröningen.

their duties. From 1540 the ordinances laid out these duties in more detail. The forester was to reside at a set place in the district, be accessible to all subjects, and make careful records of income and expenditure. He was to recommend candidates for wardens to the treasury. One of the first things to be codified were the regulations that ensured the officials themselves acted in the interests of the state. After the initial call to go out and regulate in 1495, it rapidly became clear that one needed to regulate the regulators. This tradition continued in 1551, when the beginning of Christoph's reign saw an inquisition set up to hear complaints of village jurors and mayors against forest officials before a new forest ordinance was drawn up.[81] The precise form of tasks was increasingly closely specified in each new ordinance. Above all foresters had to oversee the choosing, cutting and removal of wood in the forest. In practice many of these tasks were undertaken by the forest wardens, and after much wrangling, the idea that close oversight applied to communal as well as ducal woodland was dropped in 1608.[82] It seems doubtful, however, that close supervision of cutting was ever widely applied outside of the ducal woods. Foresters and forest wardens also fined transgressors and presented them before courts. They were gamekeepers of the duke's game, managers of the woodland and guardians of order in the woodland.

At least that was the theory. Protocols, court cases and correspondence provide plenty of details on the activity of these officials and their enforcement of the ordinances, but the nature of these records tends to stress discord. A more general, though in itself incomplete, picture comes from the account books of the forestry administration. When away from Leonberg, the forester filed expense claims such as for food and lodgings for both himself and others active on behalf of the administration, such as wardens, surveyors, servants and messengers. In the years that account books survive, these provide considerable information on his movements, although limited to the times when he was away for the night or bought lunch or fodder for his mount on the road. Often such claims are accompanied by an explanation of the trip's purpose. In the accounting year 1585–6, forester Philip Roßach filed no less than 186 claims. This is a considerable amount of time on the road, especially as one must factor in those days spent in and around Leonberg in his itinerary. He was certainly making up for the fact that as a greenhorn arriving in 1583 he felt himself insufficiently acquainted with his district for the survey of that year. His trips

---

[81] Reyscher, *SWG*, Bd.XVI, passim; Hauff, *Zur Geschichte der Forstgesetzgebung*, p. 39.
[82] Hauff, *Zur Geschichte der Forstgesetzgebung*, p. 65.

took him at the very least to most of the villages of the district that year, save those on the eastern fringe along the Neckar. In 1604–5 Ulrich Bauder was somewhat less enthusiastic, making 113 claims. This was back up to 129 by 1609–10 when his son, Hans Ulrich Bauder, was probably deputising for him. The forester was far from being an aloof bureaucrat. The Bauders spent rather less time in the poorly wooded centre and east of the district than Roßach. The post-war foresters appear to have been rather less assiduous, though expenditure varied considerably from year to year and this may have reflected greater devolution of responsibility to forest wardens. However, apart from the cavalry officer Friedrich Albrecht von Gaisberg at the end of the century, foresters still seem to have made a point of riding over most of the district in June or July.[83]

Something under a third of the forester's time was spent actually dealing directly with 'wood' in 1585–6. Roßach was rather keen on surveying, and was hence active in the summer months, while the Bauders gave a high proportion of their time to overseeing cutting, hence in the autumn, winter and spring. However, a considerable amount of time, perhaps slightly more than that devoted to wood, went to the hunt. As time devoted to the forest matters dropped after the Thirty Years' War, this proportion appears to have loomed larger. Foresters sought out stags with fine antlers suitable for the ducal chase, supervised the transfer of hunting dogs to the right points for hunts, or spent uncomfortable nights out chasing reports of distant gunfire from poachers with little apparent success, although poaching gangs were tracked down by some means and appear paying hefty fines in the account books. The forester was also an administrator, and spent three to four weeks a year either in Stuttgart or dealing with visiting officials, primarily wardens who were either bringing in earnings, looking for instructions or receiving their own pay. On top of this came the supervision of grazing, especially in the woodlands near Leonberg, going to court hearings, and of course the management of the forester's house and his own estate. On occasion he would ride the bounds of the whole forest, presumably important in the sections that abutted alien lordships where the boundary stones had to be kept in good order.[84] The diligent forester certainly had something like a full-time occupation and might know his woodlands well, although the evidence remains too scattered to determine how often this really was the case. Peasants

---

[83] A further example of the forester riding the bounds of the district in February 1604 is recorded in HStAS A59 Bü 29; the accounts are in A302 Bds.7221–35.

[84] HStAS A59 Bü 29.

testifying in court could frequently name foresters from decades past, so they must have been a fairly recognisable presence. Rienhart Pfahlburger, for example, resident in an Esslingen hospital in the 1570s, could accurately recall the forester Bartlin Moutzen (also known as Frieß) visiting Feuerbach in the early 1520s. Witnesses to a dispute over woodlands in the far south-west of the district spoke of the relatively frequent appearance of the forester and forest wardens in the first decades of the sixteenth century.[85]

In spring 1613, the supreme council, in anticipation of the forthcoming forest ordinance, wrote to all foresters inquiring as to what might be altered in the new laws. Hans Ulrich Bauder provided a remarkably open reply on what did or did not work out of his allotted tasks. He admitted that in parts of the district, notably the villages along the Neckar, there were people who knew nothing of the forest ordinances. He blamed this on the failure to read them out as they should have been at the *Vogtgericht* (in a later missive of 1614 he explains this by the fact that there are too many villages to get to for this task to be universally completed). It was not necessarily the case that hearing the ordinances would have made much difference to the listeners, however. An earlier communication of May 1612 finds Bauder complaining that peasants in villages near Leonberg ignore the laws despite having had them read out.[86] Bauder also reports that other tasks were never in fact carried out. Surveying the condition of all buildings was simply 'unnecessary', and it seems unlikely that any forester ever embarked on such a task. He thought that only allowing wood to be cut in the presence of the local mayor, *Schultheiß*, and jurors was an unnecessary expense, and that a general section on poachers was just a duplication of other laws. Enforcing the ordinances in privately owned or communal woods was 'not to every man's liking'. In his report, Bauder shows a critical assessment of what the laws really needed to do, as well as a disinclination to fulfil duties that seemed to him unnecessarily onerous. One might add that the large numbers of people supposed to be present at all woodcutting was to ensure no corruption and a fair allocation, a result of complaints from the peasantry. The forester of Leonberg presumably did not expect censure for not performing a task that he thought 'unnecessary', but he was criticised by the supreme council for not ensuring the reading of the ordinances at the annual *Vogtgericht* of each village. This dialogue seems to show officialdom in both 'centre' and 'locality' recognising the limits of implementation, and being

---

[85] HStAS A368 Bü 31; A227 Bü 1130.   [86] HStAS A59 Bü 17; A227 Bü 1154.

prepared in principle to reformulate measures that had not worked. Such flexibility, as we shall see, did have its limits.[87]

The activity of wardens was more sporadically documented, either in disputes, or in the forest account books when they brought in receipts of sales or appear making expense claims. Tasks were spread over the year in much the same way as the forester's, responding to the demands of the agrarian calendar. All wood sales in their wards had to be recorded and the bills (and the money!) delivered to the forester in Leonberg. In June each had to report the number of stags on their ward, and, in October, do the same for wild boar. The transfer of dogs, checks on fox numbers, and seeking stags with fine antlers were year round preoccupations. Hunting poachers was obviously a task more suited to the wardens than one forester, and they appear to have organised themselves into groups for this purpose. In theory they were to go into the woodland every day, and their purview extended to overseeing non-ducally owned woods when local officials and wood-wards were negligent.[88]

Wardens however were 'embedded' in local communities in a way that foresters were not. They were more likely to catch miscreants, but also had to live with them afterwards. Indeed, in some instances the position was handed down the generations. The temptation was clearly present to live a little familiarly with those who stretched the rules. As recipients of free wood and perquisites as part of their pay, they could exploit poorer neighbours in the sale of these resources as well as more directly corrupt means. Hans Ulrich Bauder pondered these problems in a letter to the Duke of December 1619. To set a local warden over the village of Botnang, a village rightly notorious for the large and universal practice of wood theft, would be like setting a fox over hens. However, there was the equal danger that to avoid appearing a 'tyrant', the warden would turn a blind eye to transgressions. No one of any wealth or standing would want the job anyway, a thankless task that could extend, as in the case of a warden from Gerlingen who confronted armed men from Botnang in the woodlands, to receiving 'a hole in the head' for his efforts.[89]

Nevertheless, for all these pains, by the second half of the sixteenth century there was a working forestry administration in place, and at times it seems to have worked. Corruption, favouritism and lethargy doubtless all played their part, but some of the time the forestry administration functioned. It was staffed by men who held their posts for long

---

[87] HStAS A59 Bü 17.   [88] HStAS A302 Bds.7221–35.   [89] HStAS A227 Bü 1428.

periods and who brought a degree of 'professional' expertise to their work. They were one of the very few, and perhaps the most numerous group, who acted on behalf of the state in village life in a direct fashion unmediated by other institutional claims. By the time this administration was clearly in place, complaints against corruption or their activity more generally also appear to have been on the decline. In some matters at least either the 'disciplining of staff', or a cosy accommodation with the locals, had taken effect.

Communal and monastic authorities

Village communes owned over half of the woodland in the district. Alongside the developing regulation of the central state, the communes provided their own woodland regulations and regulators, independently of central authority. We should, of course, be wary of opposing the 'state' and the communes. Communal courts were headed by the *Schultheiß* who was a ducal appointee. Most serious crimes were dealt with at a court headed by the district governor, the *Vogt*, and in theory at least communes did not even have the right to call a communal assembly without the permission of ducal officials.[90] Unlike central government legislation, however, the presence of widespread local regulation has rarely been taken as an indicator of the local condition of the woodland. This is perhaps in part because while sometimes appearing as a discrete 'wood ordinance' or 'woodland ordinance', communal regulation of wood more often appears in general lists of by-laws and field orders. They were entered into the 'village-book' or 'custom-book' kept by many communes, where particular decisions of the village court were also noted. It is thus not always clear when precisely wood ordinances were made, or whether (as certainly was sometimes the case) they appeared as only a small part of a much wider set of regulations for the conduct of village life. Equally, wood ordinances may only be the written record of practices long established, as communes certainly maintained coupes, regulated cutting and had procedures for allocating wood in the fifteenth century before written records were made.[91] The government in Stuttgart was very much in favour of written codification as it speeded up court business. Occasionally ordinances appear to have been made as the direct result of central intervention in a local dispute, as occurred in Heimerdingen

---

[90] Reyscher, *SWG*, Bd.XII, p. 14; Warde, 'Law', pp. 186–7, 201–5.
[91] There were, for example, limits on woodcutting and collecting in Bietigheim from before 1462. STABB Bh Bd.2. Annalbuch c.1540.

in 1619, or even, as with Magstadt in the mid-1560s, when the Duke himself expressed displeasure at the local condition of the woodlands in a hunting trip. Like the by-laws of Gebersheim approved in March 1595, they may have required the approval of the district governor at the *Vogtgericht* or *Rüggericht*. The early 1590s may have represented a period of systematic encouragement of the recording of village by-laws in the district of Leonberg, as alterations or renewals occurred in Höfingen, Gebersheim and Renningen. Senior officials were not however obviously involved in the determination of content. As with ducal forest ordinances, communal regulation could also embrace privately owned woodland that may have been subject to a communal grazing regime.[92]

By-laws promulgated relating to wood appeared most frequently between around 1550 and 1625.[93] This roughly reflects both the period of most energetic state regulation of the forests, and the supposed period of declining communal autonomy. There is no evidence, however, that this was a result of pressure from above, or that it was following the example set by state forest ordinances. Certainly there is no repetition of measures from the forest ordinances, and given the patchy record of implementation, this is unlikely to have been from a need to avoid duplication. Occasionally, village ordinances did include a stipulation to obey the state forest ordinances.[94] But there is a striking discrepancy between the general woodmanship concerns of ducal officials and the extremely *ad hoc* form of most communal ordinances. These often read more like a list of immediate worries and it is likely that most practices were regulated by custom or discretion. When Hemmingen for example banned 'weapons' (i.e. cutting implements) from the woodlands in the early eighteenth century, and ordered a limit of one 'wood-day' each week when woodcutting was allowed, it was also noted that this day was traditionally Thursday. How long any of these measures had really been in place can only be guessed at.[95]

The 'problems constructed' in communal regulation give an insight into the concerns of local jurors both in regard to wood, and the form of communal politics they envisaged. As will be examined in chapter 5, the interests of the commune at large and the jurors of the court were by

---

[92] HStAS A584 Bd.832; A227 Bü 483, 1427; A572 Bü 69; StAL Höfingen Fleckenlagerbuch 1593; STABB Bh A1678; Warde, 'Law'.
[93] This is based on a sample of 349 by-law type documents from south-western Germany. The chronology also reflects the observations of other scholars. Warde, 'Recording regulation'; Rheinheimer, *Die Dorfordnungen*, pp. 273–4.
[94] For example, StAL Höfingen Fleckenlagerbuch 1593.
[95] HStAS A583 Bü 262; Warde, 'Recording regulation'.

no means necessarily the same. A recurring issue was the allocation of the *Gaabholz*, the annual wood allowance to *Bürger* from the communal woodland. Both the extent of the allocation and who was to receive it were regulated. Provision of building wood was restricted by requiring the permission of particular officials to fell timber, or by setting numerical limits to timbers that could be cut. Dwindling stocks appear to have been a matter for concern for some communal authorities as well as central government. Bieitgheim was unusual in requiring ten staddles per *morgen* for building timber to be left in all woodlands, including privately owned ones.[96] Limits to the sale of goods obtained from common land were established (or reiterated), and the communally owned woodlands demarcated and fines for transgressions recorded. The boundary dispute, often between communes as well as within them, is a classic form of conflict in the medieval and early modern worlds. Communes showed, however, little concern for providing accurate measurements of their woodlands until the 1680s, then simply noting down the results of Andreas Kieser's survey. By this time woodland was becoming a more important resource for the payment of taxation. The practice of limiting rights to building wood, and that of barring newcomers' access to it that is occasionally seen, matches a more general, indeed Europe-wide, trend of the narrowing access to communal resources by groups of more privileged commoners during the early modern period. The refusal of wood to newcomers appears in Gebersheim in 1608 (though it was first discussed in 1592).[97] This symbolic link between communal rights and woodland management was reinforced after the 1650s with the practice of each *Bürger* planting two trees annually as an expression of their corporate rights. Much later in the nineteenth century, villagers would fell two trees in night raids as an expression of their grievances with communal authorities.[98]

Communal regulations appear therefore to be a result of the problematics of managing the commune rather than a sign of the interpenetration of 'central' and 'local' authorities. They are a parallel development to the forest ordinances, and all of this regulation flowed from older traditions encapsulated in *Weistümer* ('manifests' or agreements between lords and peasants over local regulations and rights), city ordinances and the regulations of corporate groups of commoners

[96] STABB Bh B546. This was in an undated, probably mid-sixteenth-century wood ordinance.

[97] HStAS A584 Bd.832; for examples of permission being required to fell trees, and limits being set on building, see A572 Bü 42, 69; StAL Höfingen Fleckenlagerbuch 1593, Holzordnung 1538; StAR Nr B252, B349.

[98] Kaschuba, 'Kommunalismus', p. 87; Kaschuba and Lipp, *Dörfliches Überleben*, p. 82.

(*Markgenossenschaften*). Parallel too were the regulations of other lordships such as monasteries, and the collective agreements that resulted
from large areas of 'inter-commons', usually woodlands that were subject
to the claims of various lordships. The Hagenschieß to the north-west of
the *Forstamt* Leonberg saw an agreement in 1513 to regulate the claims
of villagers subject to either the von Gemmingen family or the monastery
of Hirsau. This partly arose from a dispute as to whether local wood
supplies should be for the use of the villagers or lords within the jurisdiction of the entitled villages. Hirsau had wanted to use timbers for a barn in
distant Ditzingen. This problem is similar to that in village by-laws which
limited the 'export' of materials and suggests again that these rules came
at least as much from a concern with maintaining assets as any ecological
sensibilities. The agreement allowed this if the wood was paid for. The
use of timbers for 'large or notable' constructions required the approval of
both lordships, and any potential building timbers were not to be used for
firewood or other purposes. Regulation of a woodland as large as the
Hagenschieß at such an early date suggests again that these measures
reflect a desire to profit from access to timber rather than a genuine
shortage.[99] Here, even more than in the communal regulation, the
emphasis was on regulating the allocation of wood rather than the management of the woodland itself.

Communal or other regulation, just as government ordinances,
required implementation. Wood sales from the Hagenschieß funded a
forest warden who, however, could not prevent the gradual running
down of wood supplies and an abandonment of the agreement with a
partition of the woodland in 1576. The woodlands of the monasteries
fell under the purview of their bailiffs, such as the *Amtmann* of
Merklingen who ran Herrenalb's possessions in the region. He
appointed a forest warden in turn to manage their woodlands locally
at some point in the fifteenth century. Somewhat confusingly, this
warden also seems to have acted as the forest warden under the forester
of Leonberg. In practice, the local villagers who enjoyed common
rights over Herrenalb's woodlands seem to have provided the real management. Indeed, Marx Fuhlen the Elder, *Schultheiß* of Gechingen, was
so assiduous in this matter that his ghost was reputed to continue to ride
through the Schledorn wood between Hengstett and Ottenbronn, a fact
thought worth testifying to in a dispute over the ownership of the
wood. Witnesses were often rather hazy over the question of who
actually owned woodlands, rather than use rights. In the case of the

[99] HStAS A368 Bü 46.

Schledorn an inquiry to the forester at Leonberg confirmed that the woods did in fact belong to Herrenalb. This fact had been obscured because the use rights were enjoyed independently by villagers and the forest warden appeared to act as an officer of the forester rather than the monastery. It appears that the forester generally left the woodlands of the monasteries to their own devices. In turn Hirsau had a forest administrator and Maulbronn a woodland-master who administered their possessions through village officials.[100]

Communal woodlands, as with the rest of the commons (*Allmenden*), fell under the control of the *Schultheiß* and court. However, more direct management and the keeping of accounts was the responsibility of the mayor (*Bürgermeister*). This latter official had a considerable amount of day-to-day discretion in his hands. In Leonberg for example, one required the mayor's permission to remove tree stumps, remove lying or dead wood from either coupes that were banned from graziers or the 'high-wood' (a woodland, presumably at some point of mature trees, some miles from the town), to cut rods, and to drive pigs into the woods for pannage.[101] Village mayors were assisted by wardens who were responsible for protecting the commons, fields, vineyards and woodlands. Renningen had two wardens who alternated weekly between overseeing the village and its environs, and the woodland. The woods required special protection on feast days and Sundays, presumably when the populace could not be engaged in other agricultural labour. Some places had a designated wood warden. At Leonberg the wood warden was duty bound to be at work as soon as the town gates opened in the morning, heading out along the trackways to the wooded hills above the town. There had been a wood warden since at least the 1460s. One of his responsibilities was the upkeep of the track. He was to measure out fathoms of felled wood, prevent any woodcutting that did not have mayoral sanction and report any transgressions to the mayor. Just as with the forest wardens, who had essentially the same job, he was admonished not to exploit his office by cutting fodder for his own use.[102]

The temptation must have been there because Leonberg did not pay its warden well. He received plenty of loaves over the year, but only about forty days' labouring wages in cash, and some ticking cloth. This wage was raised in 1589 on condition that he did not avail himself of free wood. In the late sixteenth century the post seems to have been

---

[100] HStAS A368 Bü 56; A557 Bü 212; A303 Bd.9475–9484; A303 Maulbronn Klosterverwalters Jahrrechnungen Georgi 1610–11.
[101] HStAS A348 Bü 6; A572 Bü 45; A572 Bü 41; StAL Holzordnung 1538.
[102] HStAS A572 Bü 69; A572 Bü 41; A557 Bü 41.

handed from Hans Örtlin to his son of the same name. They owned a small vineyard and were clearly at the poorer end of the economic spectrum.[103]

Leonberg also involved more prestigious individuals in the management of its woods. These were the so-called 'ordained in the wood' (*Verordnete im Wald*), who supervised the movement of livestock, marked trees to be protected as standards, and oversaw felling of timber. This was intermittent work and judging by the wages rarely lasted more than a few hours. These men usually held the post for some time (the average is eight years), with two to three in place at any one time. Virtually all of them held other municipal offices and some had several terms as mayor. Rather than shying away from a clash of interests, the town seems to have encouraged families with some expertise in the use of wood. The Beltzners (tilemakers), Bilfingers (wealthy coopers) and Schuhmachers (saddlers) all used wood in their work and provided at least two generations to this post. Not all the appointed men actually performed their duties and sometimes they provided substitutes who often, it appears, had more expertise. The appointment of a third 'ordained in the wood' in 1577 saw the leading men of the town directly involved in managing the woodland. The new man was Bastian Besserer, the largest landowner and wealthiest man in town. Another post was taken by the wealthy clothier Christoph Dreher. Besserer had led seventy youths in a perambulation of woodland boundaries in September 1576. Leonberg already had a wood ordinance as early as 1538.[104]

Clearly communally owned woodland was a major source, if not the major source, of firewood, rods for fencing, wattle etc., and timber for the communes. Much was given *gratis*. However, communes also sold additional wood to both locals and outsiders. A series of account books shows Leonberg receiving, on average, around 5–6 per cent of its income from wood sales in the 1580s and 1590s, although this would later decline. Wood sales were unimportant to the incomes of the relatively wood-poor east of the district, but were rather more important to others. In the early 1580s, Gebersheim's commune received no less than 45 per cent of its income from wood sales. Heimerdingen received 12 per cent of its income from wood, Hemmingen 8 per cent, Rutesheim nearly 23 per cent and Eltingen no less than 50 per cent,

---

[103] HStAS A572 Bü 41; StAL Bürgermeisterrechnungen; Trugenberger, *Zwischen Schloß und Vorstadt*, Prosopographie.
[104] HStAS A572 Bü 41; StAL Holzordnung 1538; Trugenberger, *Zwischen Schloß und Vorstadt*, Prosopographie.

though this is gross income, not net of outgoings for woodcutting and carting. Harsh times could even see the alienation of woodland to buyers or creditors.[105]

Nearly all of these sales were to locals, however, rather than outsiders. Only the heavily wooded Rutesheim had an 'export industry' of any note that benefited the commune. This was still the case in the mid-seventeenth century and early eighteenth century, when Rutesheim sold wood to outsiders and by this means paid all of its local taxation. Renningen also paid their local dues by this method, but only by selling from their woodland to their own *Bürger*, which may have had a slightly progressive effect for the poor who consumed less wood than the rich in their homes.[106]

Communal woodland was thus of some importance to many places, and the institutional wherewithal existed to regulate it as they wished, independently of the forestry administration. There is no sign that the form, extent, or enforcement of this regulation was influenced by the central state to any great degree, though foresters, of course, had the theoretical power to ensure that the forest ordinances were enforced in communal woodlands. The presence of a forester or even more so the Duke could apply pressure on communes to do something more than they habitually did, but the same could be said of the ability of the Duke's subjects to influence central government. This relationship will now take our full attention.

Of consensus and conflict

Crudely expressed, the story of 'state formation' in north-western Europe has two primary narratives. They can appear in opposition to each other, or in any number of intertwined forms. The first narrative tells of the rolling back of communal autonomy, though not without ebbs and flows in the relationship between village communes and territorial state. Ultimately, however, village institutions cannot resist the attention of the 'well-ordered police state' that tends to reduce the commune to a cipher of central interests.[107] The second narrative is

---

[105] Small settlements such as Münklingen, Warmbronn and Hirschlanden still used wooden tallies rather than keeping accounts in the 1580s. Wood sales made up 15 per cent of Gebersheim's income in 1629–30, and between 20 per cent and 37 per cent over the rest of the 1630s. HStAS A572 Bü 45; StAL Bürgermeisterrechnungen; HStAS A584 Bds.1–11.

[106] HStAS A368L Bü 136; A261 Bü 1126; A572 Bü 45.

[107] Raeff, *The well-ordered police state*; Scott, *Society and economy*, p. 259; Imsen & Vogler, 'Communal autonomy', pp. 17–18.

more inclined to see a double co-option. In this story the state established itself via the integration of village elites into its functions, who subsequently aspired to maintain its vision of order and gradually felt less and less the need to emerge in open resistance to higher authority. In turn, however, those aspects of central legislation that held less interest for village notables tended not to be implemented. The high point of both trends is generally situated after 1550, as social polarisation all over Europe appears to have distanced wealthier villagers from their neighbours and acted as a solvent on earlier ideas of solidarity and communal economic organisation.[108]

This section will examine the course of the relationship between commune and central government in the more general context of confrontation and, occasionally, violence in the period. The most spectacular of these events did indeed fall before 1550, in the age of great late medieval rebellions.[109] In Württemberg, we see the 'Poor Conrad' uprising of 1514 and the Peasants' War of 1525. But disputes also arose within communes, between communes, between communal institutions and the forestry administration, and between individuals and all of the other groups. Some of the manners in which these relationships were conceptualised and expressed will be dealt with in chapter 5. Here, the focus will be on the right to regulate, the distribution of jurisdictional and institutional power among what, we must remember, were all parts of the Duke's patrimony. Crime will be examined elsewhere. The issue here is not behaviour that was more generally recognised as being against the letter of the law (however one might feel it was justified), but who had the right to lay a particular law down.[110]

The very few records from the fifteenth century show the foresters becoming embroiled in disputes between others over boundaries and rights, rather than being protagonists themselves. This appears to have altered after the flexible, but loosely conceived ordinance of 1495. It is clear that a considerable amount of resentment built up in the period prior to the 'Poor Conrad' rebellion of spring and summer 1514. The volume of petitions dealing with forest matters, and their prominence

---

[108] Hindle, *The state and social change*; Schmauder, *Württemberg im Aufstand*, pp. 176–7.
[109] For a recent summary of extensive literature, see Scott, *Society and economy*, pp. 225–48.
[110] The material becomes much richer from the 1550s, when the establishment of a dedicated secretariat within the supreme council allowed the preservation of an archived body of material relating to disputes over woodland and 'forest matters' (*Forstsachen*) in the *Forstamt* Leonberg. There is no real trend in this documentation, small in extent (never more than a dozen cases per decade), and covering petitions, court cases, jurisdictional disputes and government investigations.

in the Tübingen Contract, has suggested to many historians that peasant unrest in Württemberg and other south-western lordships was crucially influenced by resentment against an expansion of lordly exploitation of the forest. Not only, as Rudolf Kieß has argued, was the extension of forest rights a tool for the development of the territorial state; the forest was a key first battleground for the process of 'territorialisation' within it, the establishment of polity-wide, centrally determined rules and norms.[111]

This argument is rather less convincing when we look in detail at the course of events. The 'Poor Conrad' began on 2 May 1514 when in reaction to a new tax on meat a butcher in the village of Beutelsbach threw the weights distributed in order to make the tax assessment into the river Rems. Swiftly, as Andreas Schmauder has recently shown, a network of secret sworn associations developed right across Württemberg in the name of 'Poor Conrad' with the express aim of overturning the contemporary socio-economic order. Leading proponents included the pastor and preacher in Markgröningen, Dr Reinhard Gaisslin. He railed that 'the rich stash away their corn behind themselves, also other corn, and do not share it with the poor in times of need, until it is half ruined and no more use is to be had of it.' A minority of the leaders of the 'Poor Conrad' were relatively wealthy figures, though not belonging to the ruling and often university-educated groups, but most were poorer men. Rather than being a 'communal revolt' it is clear that many sworn members of the 'Poor Conrad' had very little trust in their local authorities. Once Duke Ulrich reacted by calling a *Landtag* so that submissions could be heard, groups of peasants and townsmen describing themselves as the 'commune' often set themselves up in opposition to established communal authorities and asserted their opinions in petitions and insisted on some kind of representation at the assembly.[112]

Schmauder identifies among the rebels a 'primary' wish for the 'removal of the territorial forest right (*Forsthoheit*)', and furthermore that resistance was being expressed to 'the increasing intervention of the developing territorial state in part of the hitherto autonomous village (and municipal) economy and in communal self-government'. Nevertheless, this rarely took the form of a rebellion in the name of the whole village as a focus of solidarity. Certainly we can see a new range

---

[111] Kieß, *Der Rolle der Forsten*, passim; Schmauder, *Württemberg im Aufstand*, pp. 89, 288; Blickle, 'Wem gehörte der Wald?'; Ulbrich, 'Agrarverfassung'; Below and Breit, *Wald – von der Gottesgabe zum Privateigentum*, p. 51.

[112] Schmauder, *Württemberg im Aufstand*, pp. 51–7, 70–1, 100–1, 106–8, 136, 150–1, 162–3.

of activity from foresters subsequent to 1495, limiting rights to cut certain trees (especially building timbers), introducing cutting by coupes and restricting cutting rights. Complaints about these specific practices come only from a few communities however. There was no widespread alteration in claims by the Duke over the forest and especially to woodcutting. These new measures were rather haphazard, as one might expect given that there was no set of normative, state-wide regulations. Equally, they mirrored exactly the kind of restrictions that appeared in other lordly and indeed village ordinances in the late medieval period, and do not display anything particularly avaricious on the part of Württemberger foresters.[113] As we shall see, if foresters were concerned at dwindling stocks of building timber, they were probably right to be.

One of the areas of concerted resistance was the district of Urach bordering on the Swabian Alps, where a pattern of limited lawlessness was already established. No less than 118 men swore recognizances here as a result of poaching in the period 1493 to 1513, including forty-two in 1494 alone! Although Schmauder in part attributes this to attempting to overcome harvest shortfalls, this seems a rather inefficient way to go about obtaining nutrition. It seems more likely that another reason he and other historians have raised is more crucial. Poaching was both a sign of resistance against lordly authority (given that game was reserved to the lords), but also an expression of rage against the depredations of game on the villager's crops, that may have been particularly severe in that region.[114] This level of recognizance-giving for poaching is far and away above anything found in the *Forstamt* Leonberg. Around Leonberg a very prevalent cause of dispute was pannage. The ducal authorities clearly felt this pertained to their forest rights because pannage provided mast for the game that they hunted. In the early years of Ulrich's reign, foresters attempted to enforce this right (and hence only allow it on payment of money, or more usually oats) across their jurisdictions. This outraged communal authorities, and many of them obtained written concessions from the Duke allowing them to exercise the right freely in their own woodlands as a result of the rebellion.[115]

Clearly, more active foresters and a more determined assertion of 'forest rights' riled many involved in the rebellion. Yet the locally very

[113] Ibid., pp. 89, 154–61, 174.

[114] There is no reason to think that 1494 was a year of dearth. Ibid., p. 45; Glaser, *Klimageschichte*, pp. 71, 82, 87, 92.

[115] HStAS A557 Bü 127; H107/8 Bd.1; Schmauder, *Württemberg im Aufstand*, p. 156.

variable effect of this activity, and the tensions that focused especially around matters to do with hunting rights, should warn us away from glib arguments that see these events as an intensified struggle over the increasingly valuable and ever-scarcer resource of wood. Pannage rights were probably not in themselves terribly valuable, but would have been more so to richer members of the village who, as a century later, probably owned most of the pigs. Certainly communes protected what they felt to be their rights against innovations, although the legal situation could well have favoured the Duke. Similarly, in the town of Heimsheim, that had been gradually coming under Württemberger sovereignty since 1442, the forester asserted ducal ownership of the woods that had previously been technically owned by local lords who sold up to Württemberg in the late fifteenth century. An attempt to regulate apparently uninhibited communal use-rights over the woods was resisted in a case taken by the commune of Heimsheim that went to the *Hofgericht* in 1505. The forester lost, and the Heimsheimers were permitted to manage the woods, which were subsequently recorded as communal property into the eighteenth century. The ordinance of 1495 seems to have prompted increased vigour among foresters, but how this was expressed depended very much on how they locally could inveigle themselves into jurisdictional loopholes, or even assert fairly clear-cut rights, if previously rarely exercised.[116]

Much the same kind of debates have been engaged with regarding the great Peasants' War of 1525. The region contributed its fair share of troops to a peasant army that was eventually heavily defeated in the vicinity of Böblingen.[117] The fifth of the famous Twelve Articles, a widely adopted peasant manifesto composed from a great number of peasant complaints and demands in the vicinity of Memmingen, stormed against lordly usurpations of woodland, especially where peasants were then charged for, or limited, in their extraction of wood. David Sabean and Govind Sreenivasan have both interpreted the agents of peasant unrest to be primarily the wealthier end of village society who as much sought to protect themselves against the increasing claims of the poorer end of village society as resist feudal or state oppression. They have viewed disputes over pasture rights and control of wood in the context of demographic expansion and increasing social stratification, as well as enhanced opportunities for lords to make money out of claiming the commons. Certainly, the kinds of divisions exposed in the 'Poor Conrad' rebellion conform to these arguments.

---

[116] Stadt Heimsheim, *Heimsheim*, p. 56; HStAS A368 Bü 17.   [117] *HABW*, VI. II.

Again, however, the disputes during the Peasants' War related more to pasture and very particular types of trees (building timber, or 'fruit-bearing trees' claimed by lords as providers of their pannage right) rather than wood in general. In practice, while the war saw elements of an ideological conflict between communally orientated peasants and feudal lordship, the particulars of local disputes related to particular jurisdictional rights, not a struggle over the right to regulate resources in general.[118] Wood does not emerge as a theme at all in Württemberg, although a group of men from Eglosheim were caught out at the time-honoured practice of poaching in June 1525 and left their recognizances to posterity.[119]

From the issuing of instructions for the forest in October 1532 onwards, Leonbergers and their neighbours played their part in challenging ducal instructions and petitioning for change in anticipation of new ordinances.[120] As well as the formalised procedures of the *Landtag*, Württembergers had a right to petition higher authorities over a wide range of issues, especially where complaints were brought forward against local officials or touched upon their interests. The right to petition developed out of medieval antecedents but had a formal place in the territorial ordinance of 1495 and was developed in 1515 after the 'Poor Conrad'. It could be, as Rosi Fuhrmann argued, a useful channel of information for the central government in the regulating of its own officialdom. The availability of such channels however could also cause confusion with conflicting judgements and the expense of cases that the chancelry would have preferred to see dealt with in the lower courts. As Fuhrmann notes, however, the right to petition in the legislation pertained to complaints against the person, officials or appeals. As such they corralled a more general right to complain about the conduct of the lord and his neglect of obligations to the welfare of his subjects inherited from medieval times, to a more specific right to complain about the way in which laws were implemented. Communes and subjects could appeal about the conduct of the government and even the equity of the outcome of its actions, but not the

---

[118] The situation of course varied from lordship to lordship. We are thus better looking at abstract, ideological reasons that gave unity of purpose to the war as a whole, as does Blickle, rather than simply seeing it as the coincidence of innumerable local struggles that continued after the war. Undoubtedly different groups used the context of the war to try and achieve particular aims. Scott and Scribner, *The German Peasants' War*, p. 255; Sabean, 'The social background', pp. 6, 64–5, 76–7; Sreenivasan, 'The social origins'; Blickle, *From the communal Reformation*, p. 174.

[119] HStAS A44 Bü 4, 5, 6.   [120] Hauff, *Zur Geschichte der Forstgesetzgebung*, pp. 28–34.

fundamental right of the government to determine the common good as it saw fit.[121]

Petitioners across the Duchy found fault with the ordinances of 1540 and 1552, and also the local ordinances promulgated, for example, in the Stromberg forest in 1552. Forest officials complained that universal application of coupes did not let the wood regenerate properly, even where staddles were present. Applying a coupe system for cutting universally also meant that artisans could not select the wood most appropriate for their needs, which may in part explain why they later appear in account books purchasing apparently singularly inappropriate trees for particular jobs. Complaints did not only come from below. Emperor Charles V considered a ducal instruction to sow bare patches in monastic woodlands with trees in 1551 too wide a claim. It appeared to expand the forest itself in territory where the duke was the 'patron' (*Schirmherr*), rather than the direct lord, over the monastery. In the 1560s the division of labour remained that the forester and wardens looked after ducal woodlands, and the communes their own, though the forester could intervene when the forest ordinance was not enforced by communes.[122]

In the mid-1560s the observations of the duke himself, and subsequent reports by councillors, found the woodlands between Gerlingen, Leonberg, Eltingen and Magstadt to be wanting in this regard. The Leonbergers protested their innocence, or at least provided excuses, pointing out that they had their own ordinance, but that the wood was distant and inaccessible from the town. The villagers in contrast simply said they had never been managed differently. Everyone evaded a fine on the promise of enforcing the ordinances in future and because it was a dearth year.[123] Compliance was not, however, forthcoming, as is clear from the extensive woodland survey of 1583, and continued problems with the Gerlingers and neighbouring villages on into the seventeenth century.[124] The regime of forester Hans Mentzingen was unpopular in several places in the mid-1560s. In Feuerbach he levied hefty fines for non-compliance to the ordinances, and the subjects, 'especially the night shepherds', complained of the officials' 'mischief and violence', that they were 'evilly sworn at and cursed'. Villagers both here and elsewhere did not maintain staddles, removed berries and switches from the woodland without permission, and (as we shall see below) were particularly aggrieved by restrictions on keeping dogs. Mentzingen

---

[121] Fuhrmann, Kümin and Würgler, 'Supplizierende Gemeinden', pp. 288–9, 292–4, 300, 303. See also Holenstein, 'Bittgesuche', p. 357.
[122] HStAS A59 Bü 5; Hauff, *Zur Geschichte der Forstgesetzgebung*, pp. 39–49.
[123] HStAS A59 Bü 6a.   [124] HStAS A59 Bü 13a; A227 Bü 1154, 1430.

answered charges that he was overbearing by claiming that he was
in fact 'not suffered' in his work, especially when he tried to apply
the forest ordinances 'seriously'. He was aggrieved by allegations
obviously born of a deep antagonism, not least that he had caused the
death of a boy arrested for collecting berries, who according to
Mentzingen died of disease, as his father did soon after. Hans Ulrich
Bauder spoke of much the same situation in 1613. Attempting to
supervise private and communal woodlands was 'not to every man's
pleasure and satisfaction'. Gerlingen is singled out for malpractice, and
berries and dogs were again bones of contention.[125]

Overall, the 'long sixteenth century' of ordinances saw very little
actual questioning of the right to legislate. Communes simply ignored
the application of the laws in most of their own woodlands, as will be
made clear in chapter 4. In particular they disregarded matters that did
not in their mind have much to do with the forest, or touched upon the
perennially fractious issue of hunting rights and protecting their fields
from game. In 1577, for example, the district was blessed with a
bumper crop of berries. The forest warden of Rutesheim reported
that people everywhere were shaking trees to bring them down, contra-
vening the forest ordinance. He himself had caught four men and
youths in the act, but had received the retort that 'they have such
power, and have always used it so'. Forester Jacob Harnisch fined the
commune of Eltingen for the same, but they simply ignored both the
right to appeal and the fine. The forest officials were dutifully going
about their business, but were forced to write to the supreme council
for further instructions. The council investigated and found that this
practice of shaking trees was long established (*'ultra memoriam hominum'*) and had not been prevented by prior foresters. As the forest
gained nothing by applying the law (it had minimal effect upon income
at least), the rule was to be left in abeyance. The fines imposed were
dropped.[126] Was this 'success' or 'failure' of the forest administration?
It is perhaps not so important to decide on such terms. The administration was present on the ground. It learned, at times, from experience.
It had the greatest effect in the management of ducal woodlands, and
while its impact on other woodlands was not negligible, it had relatively
little power in the face of determined communal consensus. This perhaps sits best with the 'double co-option' argument, as it is clear that
the forest ordinances were only consistently effective where local authorities wished this to be so. However, we must remember that local elites

---

[125] HStAS A59 Bü 17, 32.   [126] HStAS A227 Bü 1132.

in fact benefitted rather little from the forest ordinances themselves, because there was a parallel development in communal regulation. Approval of the forest administration rested more on the fact that local officials and the forest administration were recognisably in the same business. Where they were not, antagonism could be more entrenched, and this was especially the case with hunting.[127]

The debate about hunting

Parts of the *Forstamt* Leonberg belonged to the favourite hunting districts of the Dukes of Württemberg. The woodlands around the fortress of Asperg had been a focus of hunting since their acquisition in the fourteenth century. However the key regions stretched westward from Stuttgart to Böblingen and Leonberg, and further to the north-west over the contiguous woodland area from Rutesheim and Hemmingen to Mönßheim and the Badener border. In 1763 part of the Gerlinger woodlands was turned into the palatial hunting lodge at Solitude, with a grand avenue approaching from the new ducal capital of Ludwigsburg to the north-east.[128] Huge numbers of game could be assembled for special hunting events, but these were unusual occasions and do not reflect the usual stocking rate. Nevertheless, levels of game and the damage they could cause both to woodlands and surrounding crops and vineyards were a source of considerable grievance to the peasantry. But if hunting rights had provided a fictional springboard to govern the forest, they soon became an autonomous sphere of antagonism divorced from responses to other regulations. They bred contempt for an otherwise widely accepted forestry administration, and were an enduring symbol of the tensions between lord and subject. It may be the case that the tendency of rulers to have their hunting and their woodlands regulated by the same sets of officials has resulted in historians falsely transposing genuine hostility to the game laws into a more general attitude of rejection towards regulation of the woodlands.

From late medieval times the dukes asserted a general right to hunt all game, and that subjects or feudal dependants could only enjoy such rights under specific concessions, a right confirmed by Imperial grant in 1484. Indeed, jurists such as Noé Meurer considered, rightly or wrongly, forest rights essentially to be derived from lordly hunting rights.[129] The dukes generally reserved the right to hunt boar and deer of all

---

[127] See Landwehr, *Policey im Alltag*, pp. 4–6, 38.
[128] Stadt Gerlingen, *Gerlingen*, pp. 157–8.
[129] Meurer, *Vom Forstlicher Oberherrligkeit*, p. 9; Eckardt, *Herrschaftliche Jagd*, p. 39.

kinds to themselves. In most woods, however, the rights to smaller game such as hares and foxes was granted to the lesser nobility who from 1515 were independent of feudal ties but who had hunting rights over Württemberger ground.[130] It is clear that forestry officials, both the forester and wardens, also arrogated to themselves hunting 'rights' which legally can only be considered a form of self-sanctioned poaching. For such groups, the letter of the law was rather variably enforced, which is not to say that it was not enforced at all. One can find the holders of the castle of Nippenburg above the Glems being chastised by the forester for illegal hunting in precisely the same spots in the early seventeenth century as in the early nineteenth century.[131] A servant of the Truchseßen of Höfingen reported in January 1598 that when sharing a repast and some drinks with the forester and the forest warden of Rutesheim whilst on business in Leonberg, the forest officials had commented that a couple of hares wouldn't be missed. They may not have been too scrupulous about the 'petty hunting' that concerned only hares, foxes and wildfowl.[132]

A strand of writing on forest history has long considered hunting to be a central interest in the establishment of forest administrations and management of the woodland, often to the detriment of wood yields.[133] However, measures that encouraged game, such as leaving staddles to provide beechmast and acorns, were equally beneficial to the rejuvenation of forest stands, and it seems that the Württemberger forest ordinances were primarily conceptualised as measures to conserve wood supplies. Indeed, the ordinance of 1540 barely mentions hunting at all.[134] Certainly, as Rudolf Kieß has demonstrated, claims to forest (hunting) rights could operate as a tool of territorial expansion. For example, the monastery of Hirsau had negotiated an alteration in the area of their hunting rights in an exchange with the ducal government in the fifteenth century. In 1630, when Catholic authorities were installed after the Edict of Restitution, they quickly came into conflict with the Duke who claimed that such rights were entirely his gift, rather than a treaty agreed between autonomous powers, and that the necessary confirmation of their rights required from a new ruler had not in fact been forthcoming. The Duke had thus established himself as an overlord in all of the areas handled in the treaty. Significant as it might have been on some borders, however, territorial expansion through the

---

[130] HStAS A59 Bü 3; H107/8 Bd.1; Reyscher, *SWG*, Bd.XVI, p. 50.
[131] HStAS A557 Bü 197.   [132] HStAS A557 Bü 210.
[133] Ernst, *Den Wald entwicklen*, pp. 11, 67–8, 87, 175, 183.
[134] Reyscher, *SWG*, Bd.XVI, pp. 4–21.

forest was always secondary to purchase or concessions on the part of other lordships.[135]

During the sixteenth century central government frequently issued instructions concerning hunting rights, and jurisdictional cases came before the supreme council. Foresters, and forest wardens, as we have seen, prepared hunting grounds, were present for hunts themselves and provided the logistics both to maintain numbers of game through providing fodder, and in setting up the shooting galleries and providing salt for the preservation of meat.[136] They were also obliged to provide annual reports on the numbers of stags, deer and wild sows and boar available for the hunt. It is difficult to gauge the reliability of the reports, which are intermittently extant from 1649 onwards. Numbers were clearly low during the Thirty Years' War and rose steadily from the end of the war until 1675. It is likely that the inability to prevent widespread killing of game during the war, along with the depredations of wolves, brought about this nadir in stocking rates of game. Thus the continually rising numbers in the subsequent decades are probably indicators of the increased post-war effectiveness of the administration.[137]

In contrast, a petition with very different interests that came from Leonberg and Rutesheim in 1578 bewailed the fact that numbers of game were greatly up on thirty years ago, and that forty or fifty animals were grazing on their crops each day! This very high number is probably, to be generous, related to the fact that field wardens were not able to recognise an individual boar if it wandered back for another bite to eat. The survival of reports by forestry officials from 1569, 1578, 1583, 1589 and 1590 suggest however that these complaints had some substance. The construction of scenic lakes on the upper reaches of the Glems in 1566 and 1618 were intended to make the region an even more attractive courtly hunting environment.[138] The numbers of game present in this period were not reached again until perhaps the late 1670s,

---

[135] Kieß, *Der Rolle der Forsten*, passim; HStAS A557 Bü 212.

[136] HStAS A302 Bds.7221–35.

[137] HStAS A248 Bü 1790. The stag-report was partly by forest ward, partly by woodland, and classified animals as huntable or not worth hunting, and included sightings of boar. Sometimes fairly large areas of woodland have only one stag, which seems a little unlikely. The whole area in 1649 only reported eighteen huntable stags, nine not worth hunting and forty-six boar. In 1651 these numbers were twenty-two, thirteen and sixty-eight respectively; and by 1654 up to forty-one, twenty-three and 118 before a slight fall as a result of ducal hunting and wolves in 1655. Lists compiled for the entirety of the Duchy, though often missing returns from individual districts, survive from 1639 to 1641 and 1649 to 1675.

[138] HStAS A227 Bü 1128; A59 Bü 14; Gestrich, *'Aufwiegler, Rebellen, saubere Buben'*, p. 25. At the earlier date there were no less than eighty-seven huntable stags recorded and 107 not worth hunting. In 1589 there were 138 huntable, ninety not worth hunting, and 451

if then, and probably thereafter only at the highpoints of the courtly hunt in the eighteenth century. Some time after 1723 Leonberg reported that its woodland was 'almost ruined by the game and nothing more will grow of young trees'.[139] But Leonberg was the only area that complained. It is likely, in fact, that the concentration of game in a few places caused some damage at these periods of peak stocking.[140] Yet their numbers were far behind those of domesticated livestock who spent a considerable amount of time grazing in the woodland.

The anger of the peasantry, however, spans the entire period. There were four elements to their complaints: firstly, the damage that game did to their crops, particularly when they were not permitted to defend their property against foraging or trampling; secondly, bans on dogs that the government suspected would be used to poach but that the peasants saw as important guardians of their property; thirdly, the obligation, on top of the previous restriction, to raise and maintain dogs for ducal use; finally, the obligation of all subjects to provide labour services to the ducal hunt, including the delivery of dogs over long distances.

As a result of the 'Poor Conrad' rebellion the Duke's subjects were permitted to scare off or shoot animals that strayed within fenced property, although this defence was little use against the damage that birds could do in vineyards. That the rebels were prepared to continue to defy the Duke, in part over this issue, even after the negotiation of the Tübingen Contract, is an indication of the seriousness with which they viewed the damage caused by game. Some communities in the German south-west even claimed that up to half their crops were damaged by game each year. The dead animal itself was still the property of the duke. The pre-emptive action of setting traps remained barred.[141]

---

boar. If the trends in Leonberg were similar to those across the Duchy, then the number of game recorded locally in the 1650s would imply a total figure around three times higher by the mid-1670s, still well below the total recorded in 1589. Numbers of game in the Duchy probably peaked in the mid-1730s. HStAS A248 Bü 1793; Eckardt, *Herrschaftliche Jagd*, p. 90.

[139] HStAS A368L Bü 136.

[140] If these figures are remotely accurate, at the end of the sixteenth century, in the 1670s, and again by the 1720s, there was probably one stag for every sixty hectares of woodland, one wild boar for every thirty hectares, and an unknown number of deer. Eckardt provides figures for the forest of Tübingen that fluctuate from a low of one deer for every 60 hectares in 1569 to one for every 8 hectares in 1714; and one boar for every 200 hectares in 1586 and one for every 44 hectares in 1714. On the effects of stocking densities, which are still a matter of controversy, see Vera, *Metaforen voor de Wildernis*, pp. 127–8; Leibendgut, *Der Wald in der Kulturlandschaft*, pp. 136–7; Eckardt, *Herrschaftliche Jagd*, p. 78.

[141] Reyscher, *SWG*, Bd.II, p. 50; Schmauder, *Württemberg im Aufstand*, pp. 223–4, 239, 272; Blickle, 'Wem gehörte der Wald?', p. 173.

The number of recorded complaints appears to have swelled in a series of petitions and reports compiled in anticipation of the *Landtag* of 1565. Villagers wished to drive off game from their fields with dogs and distinguished between those dogs that were potentially 'damaging' to game and those that were not. Indeed, the forest ordinances permitted the holding of even large dogs that wore a heavy wooden weight around their neck to prevent them catching boar. Villagers also kept dogs for guard duty (and to scare off beggars), and no doubt for prestige, as did some of those who were forced to keep the hunting dogs for the Duke.[142] The foresters seem only to have intermittently actually fined villagers for breaches of these rules. Forest wardens, however, frequently acted to bar dogs from woodlands, and in 1565 the warden of Eglosheim went so far as to have all the dogs in several nearby villages killed. This was, he claimed, in anticipation of a hare hunt, presumably to prevent the dogs from removing potential prey.[143]

In 1565 nearly every village reported great costs from having to protect the fields and vineyards from attack, including employing no less than twenty-six men to stand watch during the grape harvest in Feuerbach and Botnang. Rutesheim claimed over 30 hectares had to be abandoned because of the problem. The forester submitted a report claiming that these costs are greatly exaggerated and gave a detailed refutation. The problem of thieves, he claimed, loomed larger than that of damage by game, and the villagers of Friolzheim, who provided no protection for their land at all, said it had never done them any harm (according to the warden).[144] Such problems were by no means resolved by the ordinance of 1614, and rumbled on into the seventeenth century.[145] A report before the *Landtag* of 1583 claimed that over the Duchy as a whole, nearly 1,800 hectares could not be cultivated because the depredations of game, making for a loss of revenue of 45,000 fl. The cost of keeping watch allegedly came to nearly 12,000 fl. Such costs were indeed formidable, because that year the treasury only received about 18,000 fl. from the exploitation of the forests. In

---

[142] Some young men of the village of Weissach, for example, got themselves into trouble for parading around with their lord's dogs in the early 1560s. HStAS A59 Bü 32.

[143] Ibid.

[144] The claims of the villages, if true, would represent a burden on some communal finances, and reports on communal accounts in the early 1580s present an even bleaker figure for Leonberg and Eltingen. However, the forester's account, which certainly appears to be more scrupulously compiled, gives very much lower figures. It may be because the latter only allowed for costs exclusively for the protection of crops from game while the villagers recorded all of the cost for having field wardens, who did of course perform other tasks. Ibid.

[145] HStAS A59 Bü 17; A34 Bü 21.

1673–5 it was estimated that keeping watch for game cost 18,153 fl., and by Eckardt's calculations, damage to crops came to 83,000 *Scheffel* of grain and 2,094 *Eimer* of wine. These figures imply annual costs of over 100,000 fl., or in other words, that boar and deer between them consumed or destroyed crops worth more than the game themselves were worth every single year. Indeed, Eckardt supposes that a boar destroyed about a ton and a half of grain per year, a huge multiple of its own probable body weight.[146] Eckardt is right to say that 'for the subjects, damage by game meant a "hunting-tax" additional to other dues, collected not by the lordly officials but by the lordly game'.[147] If the destruction was really as high as claimed, however, then the animals were industrious indeed.

The foresters consistently attempted to enforce those rules concerning dogs, although one commented that one would have to watch people all night long to prevent them being broken. In turn, villagers appeared to be willing to break them, even though the damage caused to crops was probably much exaggerated. These issues may, in the end, have turned on issues of honour. People felt that they had a right to keep dogs and defend their property. Poaching, as we shall see, was considered a 'victimless crime' that had popular sympathy. In turn, the great efforts put into tracking down poachers or defending game seem completely out of proportion with any value the duke could reasonably extract from them. This conflict, which continued until local communes were accorded the right to govern hunting in 1848,[148] had little if anything to do with 'state formation'.

There was, in fact, an answer to many of these problems: the erection of fences between the woods and the fields. Petitions for these to be erected were concentrated in the latter part of the sixteenth century, an unfortunate time, because foresters then fretted that they used up too much wood. They were usually miles long, at heights of four to eight feet. In 1599 Rutesheim won the agreement of the duke to a thorn hedge to protect nearly 50 hectares they had found unusable because of damage from wild animals, probably the same land that they complained about in 1565.[149] The process was slow. Renningen did not start on its fence until 1711, though Kieser's maps show that much of the region had barriers by the 1680s. The forestry officials also attempted to prevent communes building traps into the fences, or sharpening the stakes so that animals would impale themselves whilst

---

[146] HStAS A34 Bü 21; A256 Bd.68; Eckardt, *Herrschaftliche Jagd*, pp. 101 and 105.
[147] Eckardt, *Herrschaftliche Jagd*, p. 106.   [148] Pfister, *Der Leonberger Stadtwald*, p. 27.
[149] HStAS A227 Bü 1133; A227 Bü 1146.

attempting to leap over them; this was the reason given why forester Jacob Harnsich threw down the fencing protecting the fields of Weilimdorf in 1573.[150]

These measures did not protect the woodlands. According to a Leonberger report to the *Landtag* in 1593, damage to shoots in winter meant that coppices previously cut every fifteen to twenty years now had to wait thirty or forty. As a result wood shortages threatened, and the Duke among others would receive less money from sales (the fact that the price might go up to compensate for lower quantities seems not to have occurred to the authors on this occasion). Shortages would cause problems for nearly everyone: blacksmiths who needed charcoal, hospitals who heated rooms for inmates, poor chests that might pay for fuel, and so on. Damage from game was again a major theme in explaining low yields of wood and crops in the early eighteenth century, either as an argument as to why taxes should remain low, or an explanation of why communal finances (of which wood sales could be a major component, as we have seen) were rather unhealthy. The data suggests that in truth damage was probably localised to the favoured hunting grounds of the district at the peak periods of stocking.[151] However, as the peasantry derived no benefit from the game, one can understand their anger at any damage incurred.

The labour services owed by villagers bore much more heavily on those in the proximity of places frequently exposed to hunting. These were the only consistently applied labour services owed by the ducal subjects in Württemberg and were commensurately resented. The real rate of these ranged in some places to a couple of days per household per year, to others where the services 'have not been much used', and others still where lifetimes passed without anyone being asked to provide them.[152] Theoretical ducal demands vastly outweighed the real burden, although this burden probably rose after the Thirty Years' War. In the surviving account books from before the war, expenditure on hunting by the local forest administration was a tiny proportion of total expenditure. By 1660 the proportion was 24 per cent and in 1670 it was 23 per cent. These figures are probably underestimates as they only include the costs formally recorded as being for ducal hunting, but not all activity that may have been hunting related. The burden

---

[150] HStAS A227 Bü 1125; H101 Bd.107/8 Bd.5; StAR Urthel- und Vertragsbuch; Kieser, *Alt-Württemberg in Ortsansichten*. Eckardt incorrectly states that such fences played no role in Württemberg, though he notes an order for their removal in 1720, because of damage the entrapped game were doing to the woodland. Eckardt, *Herrschaftliche Jagd*, pp. 101 and 104.

[151] HStAS A34 Bü 21; A261 Bü 1134; A572 Bü 45.   [152] HStAS H107/8 Bd.1.

probably turned on the predilections of individual rulers. By the 1730s the local inhabitants had to pay a tax to *avoid* being called up for corvée labour for the hunt. Over 5,000 men were prepared to pay 0.33 fl., just under three days' labouring wages.[153] This payment was clearly felt to be worthwhile, and was a bonus to the government that would probably never have contemplated requiring the labour of so many people. It probably reflected the real burdens on those who were called up to work, which appear to have been around two to three days each year in the 1660s, sometimes staying nights away from home. Peasants employed the usual evasive tactics of sending the young or elderly (and so minimising the loss of labour to households), or simply hiding.[154]

Before the Thirty Years' War, however, the burden appears overstated in peasant complaints, just as, it seems, the expense of protecting fields and the damage wrought by game was constantly exaggerated in the petitions of villagers and dignitaries to the *Landtag*. The presence of the hunt was in any case double edged. Communities petitioned for more hunting to rid their land of an excess of game, but resented the corvée labour associated with the hunt. This does not mean that such claims were entirely false, and the troubles negligible. Yet as befitted a practice associated with martial display and masculine assertion,[155] all these arguments were beset with bombast and hyperbole. In this they also looked back to a feudal past more than to the regulatory world of the emerging state. Rather then being a part of the growth of the modern state, hunting disputes were a holdover of medieval rights and tensions. The tax to avoid corvée labour was of course part of the paraphernalia of the absolutist drive to squeeze taxation revenue from all corners of life, but the documentary record suggests much more continuity than change both in the practice of hunting and the antagonisms that it generated over all of the early modern period.

Forest incomes – a crucial test

Explanations of revolt, unrest, and developing bureaucracies have often turned around the expanding fiscal ambition of early modern rulers. The

---

[153] HStAS A302 Bd.7221–35, 7241. There were central costs incurred for the maintenance of the ducal hunt running to several thousand *gulden* in the early eighteenth centuries. Eckardt's estimates of a cost of 100,000 fl. are produced however by lumping the entire cost of the forestry administration in as costs for hunting, vastly inflating the real cost. Eckardt, *Herrschaftliche Jagd*, p. 70.

[154] Reyscher, *SWG*, Bd.XVI, pp. 466–7, 473–6.

[155] Eckardt, *Herrschaftliche Jagd*, pp. 46–51.

period has been characterised by some as one where fiscally ambitious states came to appropriate an ever-larger share of peasants' production, at the cost of peasant consumption and rents.[156] There is certainly no doubt that the fiscal history of Württemberg from the late fifteenth century onwards is one of mounting debt and an increasing reliance on new forms of income as traditional means of extracting wealth from the populace failed to match growing expenditure.[157] It is equally true that more careful monitoring of the revenue and expenditure of the administration was an early concern of legislators, though possibly as much from a desire to combat corruption as to raise awareness of sources of wealth and fiscal efficiency. At least a minimal test of the motivation behind legislation and its implementation is whether the government made any money out of the process. It has been argued above that increased expectations of the role of government on the part of both officials and some of the populace, along with a trial-and-error learning process, were far more important for 'the regulative drive' than a simple desire to make more money from an important resource. Any fiscal interest was for the most part indirect, because it was recognised that the need to buy overly expensive wood could harm the spending power of the populace more generally. The money earned by government from the exploitation of the woodlands, and the form it took, will now be examined more carefully to underline these points.[158]

Ducal income from the forests rose very rapidly from the Habsburg period until the 1560s, around eightfold. As illustrated in figure 3.1, although there are some signs of advance beforehand, the 1540 forest ordinance at the very least consolidated this trend and may have significantly contributed to it. Incomes seem to rise in the short term after the ordinances of 1552 and 1567 without marking significant shifts in the long-term trend. This remained upwards, at a greatly reduced rate, until some brief few years of heavy supervision of cutting under Friedrich (1593–1608) produced a marked shift upwards that lasted until the end

---

[156] Wilson, *Absolutism*, p. 92; Blickle, *From the communal Reformation*, p. 10; Schlögl, *Bauern, Krieg und Staat*; Ogilvie, 'Germany and the seventeenth-century crisis', pp. 60, 66–72, 76.

[157] Carsten, *Princes and parliaments*, passim; Bütterlin, *Württembergische Staatshaushalt*.

[158] As Winfried Schenk has pointed out, the resulting account books are numerous in German archives, and are vastly under-utilised mines of information. The foresters' account books from Leonberg survive rather intermittently (only around one per decade) from 1586 onwards. A far more complete record of income can be found in the receipts of the ducal treasury. The earliest record here dates back to 1482, but apart from gaps in the Thirty Years' War, the record is fairly complete from 1534 onwards. HStAS A302 Bd.7221–35; A256 Bds.1–183; Schenk, 'Möglichkeiten und Begrenzungen'.

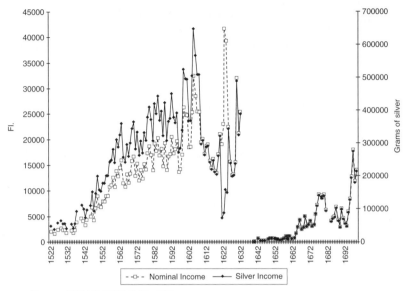

Source: HStAS A256 Bd.1–183.

Figure 3.1 Ducal income from forests, 1522–1699

of his reign, when income from the forests was nearly 50 per cent higher than at the beginning. Friedrich's measures were unpopular, and income fell back thereafter. During this period the Duke sought to investigate the possibility of more extensive sales from the Black Forest, as well as enforce the more rigorous oversight of sales at higher prices.[159] The real income (accounting for the currency manipulation of the early 1620s) remained at late sixteenth-century levels until wartime pressures raised it again after 1629, almost entirely due to sales of hunting rights to raise money quickly. After the war income remained at a very low level until an upward trend returned in the mid-1660s. By the end of the century the forests brought in roughly the same as they had in the 1560s.[160]

Economic historians are never satisfied with raw figures, and rightly so. They want to use an index that takes into account changes in relative prices, or that gives a 'constant' measure of value, to check that changes in forest income are not being caused by something else such as currency devaluation, as was clearly the case in the early 1620s. The usual method

[159] HStAS A59 Bü 14; L6 Bü 922; Reyscher, *SWG*, Bd.XVI, pp. 186–94.
[160] HStAS A256 Bd.1–183.

is to measure incomes against something like the cost of the staple food-stuff (grain) or the store of value in the currency (silver). No alternative measure is perfectly satisfactory in itself, however. If we use grain prices, apparent changes in the 'real' income from the forest may reflect cycles in the grain market. This might have been important to the administration if they were largely using money to purchase grain, but far less so if they were not. Similarly, we can measure the 'real' price of wood itself by comparing it to changing grain prices, but this may just tell us that grain (as with most subsistence foodstuffs) tends to rise in price more rapidly than wood unless wood is extraordinarily scarce. Wood may still be becoming quite expensive relative to other goods, and be perceived as such by the populace. Aside from the early 1620s, in fact, as shown in figure 3.1, the nominal trend of forest incomes is a fair reflection of its value in silver. Incomes really did go up.

Perhaps the best measure of what this income actually meant to the government was the proportion of total income that came from the forests. This is complicated in Württemberg's case because of the 'double' administration, of the ducal treasury and that of the *Landschaft* that independently administered taxation. If we measure forest incomes against total incomes to the ducal treasury (which is precisely the figure that ducal officials would have seen), we find that in the early 1520s forest incomes accounted for only 1 per cent of the total. This rose to 2 per cent by the 1530s, 5 per cent during the 1550s, remaining relatively steady until making up 8–10 per cent in the later years of Friedrich's reign. These latter were, however, years of relatively low total income. The proportion remained at less than half this figure until the years 1629–31 when it reached a peak of 14 per cent, but these were also years of low total income. After the revival in forest incomes in the 1660s they represented around 2–5 per cent of total income. If we include the tax income paid to the *Landschaft*, forest income represented only around 3–4 per cent of total revenue to the authorities from the 1550s, with a brief peak of 6–7 per cent in the early seventeenth century.[161]

Converted into the purchasing power over corn in Stuttgart, where prices were low in the period from 1536 until 1560, forest incomes rose even more dramatically until the latter year (see figure 3.2). The 1560 income measured in grain was only surpassed in the years 1599 and 1605–6, and otherwise remained much lower. In this forest incomes followed more a general trend whereby the government's total revenue peaked dramatically when measured in its corn purchasing power with

---

[161] HStAS A256 Bds.1–183. Tax payments to the Estates are taken from Carsten, *Princes and parliaments*, passim.

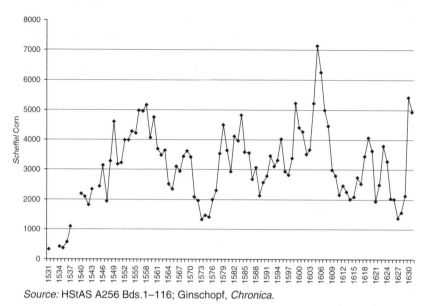

Source: HStAS A256 Bds.1–116; Ginschopf, *Chronica.*

Figure 3.2 Ducal forest income in *Scheffel* corn, 1531–1630

the low-price era of the 1530s and 1540s. Total revenue remained fairly stagnant in the face of inflation after the late 1560s and went into decline in the 1610s.[162] Price trends and their influence on the population will be examined more closely in chapter 5. But three things are clear. Firstly, forest incomes only expanded rapidly in the period of cheap foodstuffs before 1560. Secondly, forest incomes did respond to some degree to legislation, especially early in the period, but the favourable conjuncture may mean that this is as much a demand-side phenomenon, perhaps partly from an income effect of low food prices, as a government squeezing the populace with new charges. Thirdly, while forest income was a by no means negligible part of government income, neither was it a very large one, and its periods of greatest prominence were a combination of increased forest income and decreased total revenue, rather than simply being a function of one of these trends. It is worth noting that where communal woods existed, the income from these was of considerably more importance to communes than the forests were to the state as a whole.

---

[162] HStAS A256 Bds.1–116. Prices of corn are taken from Ginschopf, *Chronica.*

Income remitted to the treasury from the *Forstamt* Leonberg itself is recorded as early as 1483, but more frequently after the early 1520s. Of course, this is no measure of the real revenue of the *Forstamt*, because much of the money was spent locally and never reached Stuttgart, and the year to year variations in the income recorded reflect choices about money allocations made by the foresters. However, in the long run these central accounts reflect the net worth of the *Forstamt* to the treasury. This shows the district behaving very like the forest administration of Württemberg as a whole, displayed in figure 3.2. A very steep rise, around eleven-fold between the mid-1530s until the mid-1550s, was succeeded by slower growth until a reversal in the trend after 1608. Again, 1540 appears to have been an influential year in kick-starting long-term growth. Slow growth resumed in the post-war period from the mid-1660s, but at a much lower level than in the sixteenth century. The snippets of information from before Ulrich's return show very erratic returns from the *Forstamt*. This may reflect genuinely fluctuating income (high values reflecting income from years of good mast for pigs, for example), but may simply be a reflection of the accounting habits of the forester. It is intriguing to note that the years 1512–13, just before the 'Poor Conrad', show high levels of revenue – but so did 1507.[163]

Of course, only a proportion of local revenue went to Stuttgart, as is indicated in figure 3.3. Data is rather sporadic but in 1585 and 1605 it seems that most of the revenue, some 70 per cent, was transferred to the treasury. In 1620 and 1631, however, under half went to the treasury and after the Thirty Years' War the amounts transferred appear to have been under 15 per cent of revenue in the district of Leonberg. The far lower apparent incomes based on treasury receipts after the war, and fall-off in income after 1608, may in fact come from a more expensive local administration eating up funds. Part of this was the effect of converting wages in kind into cash. Hunting costs were also much higher after the Thirty Years' War, though unable to account for most of the difference. On top of this, more wood was supplied to the ducal household and other governmental projects in the post-war period and required hired labour to cut and bind it. Finally, there may have been a deliberate policy of holding more cash in reserve in Leonberg than in the pre-war period.[164]

There can be little doubt that the trend in income moved rapidly upwards between the mid-1530s and mid-1550s, and continued to rise until 1608. It probably did not fall nearly as much as treasury receipts

---

[163] HStAS A256 Bds.1–183.   [164] Ibid.; A302 Bds.7221–35.

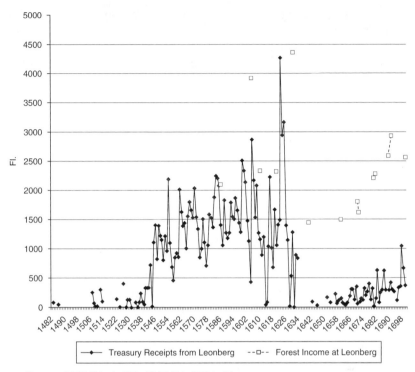

Source: A256 Bds.1–183; A302 Bds.7221–35.

Figure 3.3 Income and treasury receipts of *Forstamt* Leonberg,
1482–1700

from the district fell between 1608 and 1629. These pre-war trends can
only be explained by either a significant rise in the price of wood, or
considerably more wood being sold, because it is clear that outside of
exceptional years wood sales took up at the very least 70 per cent of
revenue.[165] The price trends presented in more detail in chapter 5
suggest that much of the late sixteenth- and early seventeenth-century
growth in income comes from rises in the *price* of wood, not a higher
quantity demanded. As we have seen the population history of the
period remains surprisingly obscure, but it is likely that repeated plague
outbreaks kept population relatively stagnant in the late sixteenth century, so rising wood prices may be an indicator of lower yielding woodlands. The data is unfortunately not robust enough to definitively
examine the crucial period of income growth from the 1540s until the

[165] HStAS A302 Bds.7221–4.

1550s, but it does tally with population expansion. It is likely that population growth fuelled both increasing demand, and, to a lesser degree, some price rises against the prevailing phenomenon of low inflation. Indeed, there may be an income effect of low food prices allowing more expenditure on other things. In the end, the increase in forest incomes can only have come from increased effective demand, and not the 'exactions' of the forestry administration. There were plenty of other places to purchase wood in Württemberg; one did not have to get it from the ducal woodlands. This suggests that 'scarcity', in the narrow sense of a need for a more spatially extensive market to supply fuel, may have got under way in the 1530s and 1540s in this part of Germany. By regulating the woodlands as a whole more systematically, the government may also have brought about more rigorous collection of revenue through an increase in its presence on the ground. But the system does not seem to have been designed to channel money into ducal coffers.

The reality of state formation: Gregori Wannen, Heinz Vohensteinss and Ulrich Ruotthardt

The sixteenth century was the crucial era for the founding of the Württemberger forest administration, though it built on late medieval antecedents. Bureaucrats looked at the woodland and they worried that it was not being managed well enough. Legislation was duly passed, the rather traditionally minded ordinance of 1540 being key. They made money for the Duke thereby, but it was not made in order to make money, and indeed they could not have made money unless the population had been willing to spend it. Widespread debates over the 'spectre' of wood shortage in the eighteenth century have led some to conclude that legislation and regulation were about appropriating a resource for particular interest groups, and that wood shortage was a chimera. Ingrid Schäfer's book on the County of Lippe in northern Germany asserted both that, 'the century of Lippe's wood shortage can be seen neither as an expression of a general energy crisis nor as an ecological crisis, but rather as the crisis of wood-dependent and private wood-consuming industries', and that, 'the mercantilist-absolutist territorial lords decided, who faced wood shortages and to what extent'.[166] Of course political interests bound themselves up with these questions, and Württemberger legislators clearly responded to what they saw with

---

[166] Schäfer, 'Ein Gespenst geht um', pp. 179, 196.

their own eyes, or how they were lobbied. But with no great wood-consuming industries, and two and a half centuries before the later debates, they began to legislate and regulate for fear of shortage. And in some places, for particular kinds of wood, there were shortages. The presence of personnel on the ground, and their right to regulate in general (though disputed on specifics), did not come into question but was swiftly established. The final product of this process, the ordinance of 1614, would be considered a model of good practice.

However, state formation was not just about income, the passing of laws, and the toing and froing of the mighty. It is precisely questions of the implementation of laws, local practice, the response of the affected and the legitimacy of their actions that the concept seeks to highlight. Foresters might be appointed who were serious, professional men who knew their job and obligations – most of the time. But the key to the system and its implementation was the forest warden.

Thus the key to our understanding of the end result of these endeavours and interactions were men such as Gregori Wannen, Heinz Vohensteinss and Ulrich Ruotthardt. They were not remarkable by historians' standards; we know of no peculiar cosmologies, prophecies or achievements. They were the simple forest wardens of Ingersheim, in the Neckar valley in the north-east corner of the district, in the late sixteenth and early seventeenth centuries. Fortunately for us they did not get on very well, and consequently we know something about them. The proximate catalyst for this record was a letter from Heinz Vohensteinss attacking Ulrich, his successor, in the summer of 1605.[167]

Gregori Wannen was forest warden of Ingersheim between 1589 and around 1594. We know little about him, save that he imposed a stiff 20 fl. fine on villagers if they entered the Brandholz to collect fruit and berries, but then collected berries himself, purely for household needs, he claimed. As a result of this he was fined and removed from office. Heinrich Vohensteinss was probably his direct replacement. Heinrich was still listed as the warden in April 1605,[168] but plainly he was not, as his successor was active in autumn 1604. Heinrich appears to have been a fairly conscientious warden, perhaps taking a little more than was permitted him – a bag of cut grass here, acorns that really should have been left for the wild boar, and fruit. He was a figure of authority, at least to the 'poor day-labourer' Eberhardt Landfaut, who would work at his command. According to his successor Heinrich was not averse to the odd pot-shot at game, a claim that Heinrich, interestingly, did not

---

[167] HStAS A227 Bü 1147.   [168] HStAS A302 Bd.7222.

contest. And Heinrich was not a man short of things to say. He lost his office, for reasons unknown, sometime in 1604. Whilst he claimed not to resent this, he 'had nevertheless to eat'. This comment was made in the hearing of several men on 7 August 1605 while having a drink with a friend in Conrad Kurzmaul's inn in Ingersheim. And it was not all he said, railing against the *Vogt* of Bietigheim and his successor Ulrich Ruotthardt. Ruotthardt was no better than a dog, a man entirely unsuited to office who only fined the poor and let the rich go scot-free.

Ulrich Ruotthardt was not only disliked by Heinrich Vohensteinss. According to Michel Rauscher he comported himself in a manner 'puffed-up and swanking about as if he were the Emperor Charles [V]'. Others said he was lazy, getting up late and returning from work early, never going properly into the woods. He stayed up late drinking with 'guests', poached or received the odd hare and duck, and took no action when the 'night warden' of the village warned him that shots were being fired in the woods. He gave out wood illegally, and shook the trees for acorns, a practice that prompted large-scale emulation by many other villagers in the autumn of 1604. He had also cursed Heinrich and others. Thus far we could see an aggrieved, quietly conscientious warden replaced by a lazy and corrupt self-server.

Yet the complaints go on, and not that Ulrich was too lax, but rather too strict. Ulrich wanted to ban dogs without leads, following the forest ordinances. He fined and punished people too harshly, creating enemies in the village, even briefly locking some up. Enderis Beurlin was understandably aggrieved in that he blamed Ulrich for causing the premature birth and death of his twins by fining his wife for wood gathering. The fines he appears to have meted out were, for this part of the *Forstamt*, certainly high and more frequent than was usual. Ulrich did not deny some acts of petty corruption. They were one-offs, he claimed, minor favours, such as allowing Eberhardt Landfaut, still doing odd-jobs for the warden, some deadwood for his pains, or allowing a woman to cut grass in the woods in exchange for some milk. Doubtless he underplayed his misdemeanours, but he clearly took his job seriously some of the time. His regime was not absolutely strict. He couldn't 'fine or see everyone, that's impossible', as he put it.

The forest wardens of Ingersheim had been present since at least the 1520s. They were an accepted part of the local community and people thought it important that they did their job properly. So too did the administration. Ruotthardt was fined for his laxity, and while some wardens had been allowed to continue after corruption trials in the 1560s, Gregori Wannen was given the reason for his removal from office by no less a personage than the ducal councillor von Degenfeld in the mid-1590s. That wardens took a little on the side, considering it a harmless perquisite, is clear. Ruotthardt was paid after all only about half of a labouring wage for his efforts, and he was one of the better-paid wardens. It is also clear that some of the populace did not expect laws on dogs, fruit or deadwood collection to be rigorously enforced, although such attitudes were not held by all. Oversight of the wardens by higher authorities was sporadic, but when they focused their attention on a problem, even apparent trivia could come before the highest reaches of government. One should also exercise caution in interpreting the apparently massive breaking of rules by shaking down acorns and masting pigs in Groß Ingersheim, Klein Ingersheim and other villages in the autumn of 1604. There had not been such a crop of acorns for many years in their woods, and this bounty may have prompted transgressions by the forest warden and populace alike. In the end, the transgressors were fined. More generally, Ulrich Ruotthardt may well have exercised favouritism. He was rich enough to have a maid, though he shared a house, and had his imperial image to keep up. But he remained living in Ingersheim and a warden in 1610 – but now officially, perhaps tactfully, warden of 'Bietigheim' with an extra warden appointed to oversee Ingersheim.[169]

The oversight of the state was everyday, and its subjects expected it to be so. They thought regulations generally a good idea, and indeed petitioned for them, but thought some regulations wrong-headed and expected officials to 'look through their thumb', as the saying went, in their application. As much as they were expected to fulfil obligations, wardens and officials were also expected to have reasonable and delimited spheres of influence, that did not always extend, in the case of *particulars* (such as overseeing woodcutting in communal woods), as far as the central authorities sometimes wanted. But all in all, the state was well embedded in Württemberg society. Whether it was capable, however, of achieving the goals of averting wood shortage and maintaining well-managed woodlands is another question to which the next chapter is devoted.

---

[169] HStAS A302 Bd.7223.

4   From clearance to crisis?

In 1544 the forester Hans Hagen stated that 150 oaks and pines that had been requested for a new barn at a ducal sheep station was beyond the capacity of any of his woodlands to supply.[1] Mature timber was certainly in short supply in the *Forstamt*, but it is hardly likely that the 2,300 hectares of ducally owned forest could not supply a mere 150 pieces of timber. What Hagen presumably meant was that he could not fell so many in one place without jeopardising the staddles and mature trees that provided acorns for natural regeneration and fodder for wild boar and pigs. Scattered across the woodlands, and according to the survey of 1583, rather better maintained in ducal woodlands than elsewhere, these fairly isolated mature trees would most likely have grown up fairly crooked with numerous large lateral branches, and thus often also been far from ideal building material. They would have been able to develop amid the clusters of juniper and thorns left alone by grazing animals. As such the ducal woodlands seem to have had enough trees to supply occasional construction needs, especially for repairs, but nowhere enjoyed the density of stock to supply large amounts of timber for even quite minor projects. Is this evidence of a 'timber famine'? Certainly it shows the relative lack of a very particular kind of tree for a certain use. But it also illustrates that each demand for use, each source of supply, was embedded in a particular ecological and economic context. Demand and supply are not absolutes but consist of particular choices and costs in a world where resources and labour always have alternative uses. One person's 'opportunity cost', or their valuation of a resource given the next best thing that in their mind could be done with it, may not match that of others or of that of the broader community. Hagen's disinclination to provide timber does not necessarily indicate a failure in the management of the woods.

---

[1] HStAS A368 Bü 23.

224

There is no question that early modern people at all social levels claimed to be worried about imminent wood shortages, and the degraded state of the woodlands. As the previous chapter has shown, the rhetoric of 'wood shortage' or 'timber famine' was prominent in extensive legislative efforts from both central and local government to regulate wood use and woodlands. Historians have followed in the wake of this rhetoric, choosing to believe or disbelieve it.[2] Rather more rarely have they embarked on a detailed examination of the state of the woodlands themselves. Such an examination is precisely what will be undertaken here in the first half of this chapter, using all the relevant written sources available from the region. However, the woodland is only one side of the story. We have seen above that the existence of any resource 'scarcity' can only be defined relative to what is demanded of the resource. We have also seen in chapter 1 how the need for grazing and firewood played a dominant role in determining woodland structure. The second half of this chapter will seek to outline in more detail and quantify the changing level of these demand-side pressures. Taken together, a composite picture of demand and supply will allow us to assess the impact of economic change and regulation on the woods. The results might have seemed depressing to those legislators seeking to uphold the 'discrete economy' of locality. Demand for fuel alone had probably outstripped supply in the second half of the sixteenth century, taking, somewhat artificially, the entire *Forstamt* as a single unit. Imports of building timber were required considerably earlier. Thus much of the regulation of woodland did appear at a time when this lowland region of Württemberg was increasingly unable to supply its needs locally, although the very earliest regulations appeared some time before this point had been reached. The quantifiable evidence presented will allow a fuller examination of the dynamics of this situation, the ecology of wood use, the integrity of different systems of management and exploitation, and the impact of disturbance, in the final chapter.

---

[2] See Introduction, pp. 25–32; Mantel, *Forstgeschichte*, pp. 298, 395; Hornstein, *Wald und Mensch*, p. 116; Sieferle, *The subterranean forest*; Gleitsmann, 'Und immer wieder starben die Wälder', pp. 175–204; Radkau, 'Zur angeblichen Energiekrise des 18. Jahrhunderts'; Allmann, *Der Wald in der frühen Neuzeit*; Ernst, *Den Wald entwickeln*; Radkau, 'Das Rätsel der städtischen Brennholzversorgung'; Below and Breit, *Wald – von der Gottesgabe zum Privateigentum*; Weiss, 'Mountain forest policy in Austria'; Schäfer, '*Ein Gespenst geht um*'.

The woodland from the 'supply side'

By the fifteenth century, depopulation and settlement concentration in the wake of the Great Famine and the Black Death had brought about a situation where once cultivated districts of northern Swabia had become woodland. But we do not begin this story with a wild, unmanaged land-scape. The woodlands and commons were incorporated into the juris-dictions of communes or managed as the property of monasteries and the nobility. Indeed, as Hans Jänichen has demonstrated, such areas were sold, bought and exchanged during the fifteenth century.[3] By the 1520s the basic features of the woodland landscape seem well estab-lished. Few boundaries established in this period would have surprised an observer of the 1680s. The sixteenth century undoubtedly saw considerable agricultural expansion in Germany, frequently charac-terised by economic historians as a period of clearance and the expan-sion of fields. Most striking to contemporaries was the expansion of viticulture, often extending up previously wooded slopes in the vicinity of Stuttgart. Nevertheless, these assarts comprised only a small part of the total wooded area. The Thirty Years' war brought massive depopu-lation and some retreat of cultivation. The accounts of the *Amt* of Merklingen reported in 1657 on the easy availability of wood, 'with which the whole stretch of fields is overgrown'. In these circumstances people took wood when and where they wanted and the usual forestry administration broke down.[4] A decade later however, normal service had been resumed. Indeed, arable cultivation may have expanded beyond its 1620s maximum in the subsequent period up until the early eighteenth century. Again, however, this appears to have made only a marginal impact on the extent of woodland. The 1680s wood-land surveys of Andreas Kieser recorded an area of woodland far in excess of that estimated in 1583, but this seems down to large errors in the earlier estimates, rather than any actual change in the land under tree cover. Neither period of agricultural expansion, nor, even in the medium term, the crisis of the war years, appears to have had much lasting impact on the landscape. Despite the comments of observers such as Sebastian Münster or the Zimmern Chronicle that there 'was scarcely a patch, even in the bleakest forest and on the highest hills, which remained uncleared and uncultivated' in the early sixteenth century, the woodland area of the *Forstamt* Leonberg in fact altered little.[5] This was probably true for many other areas of Württemberg

---

[3] Jänichen, *Beiträge zur Wirtschaftsgeschichte*, pp. 202–16.   [4] HStAS A303 Bü 9480.
[5] Sabean, 'The social background', p. 63.

too, government bans on clearing woodland for vineyards notwithstanding. Where the cultivated land expanded, it tended to do so at
the expense of open pasture. In this Württemberg is not unlike most of
the German-speaking lands in the period after 1500.[6]

The availability of wood or the state of the woodlands is not determined
by the extent of the 'wooded' area, however. Far more important is the
structure of that wooded area, the density of stands of trees, the age-
structure of stands, and the variety of species and other flora and fauna.
Very little of the debate about wood scarcity has actually taken the form of
attempting to measure the changing (or unchanging) yields from woodlands under different forms of management, preferring to make do with
often obviously self-interested claims and counter-claims encountered in
court records, petitions and official reports. What work there is on all
these matters has barely addressed the sixteenth and seventeenth centuries at all. This chapter aims to redress some of this imbalance. It will seek
to demonstrate that the condition of different types of wood, primarily
underwood for fuel and mature timber for building, could be rather
different. The *Forstamt* was consistently bad at maintaining any great
number of mature trees from an early date, and the forest ordinances
appear to have had only a limited effect in this regard in ducally owned
woodlands. Despite relatively careful and responsive management across
the board, underwood yields seem to have declined under the pressure of
population growth in the late sixteenth and early eighteenth centuries.
Neither central nor local regulation could arrest this problem, although it
may of course have prevented it from becoming more acute. The answer
to the 'shortage' was to import wood. Whether the need to import really
represented an ecological problem, given that trade is a quite normal
response of societies to local relative scarcity, will be the subject of
chapter 5. However, it appears that it was war that may have been most
detrimental to the condition of the woodlands. In this regard at least, an
almost complete absence of regulation, coupled with immense economic
pressures, had a clearly negative impact.

Chapters 1 and 3 have already examined both the range of uses to
which woodlands were subject, and moves by the ducal authorities to
structure and order the wooded landscape. There was no one measure
of woodland productivity or condition, but rather a variety of interests
and needs that had to be maintained in balance. Even if we limit
ourselves to measuring the success of the regulation of woodland by
examining wood production, simple measures of yield per hectare do

---

[6] For recent estimates, see Bork *et al.*, *Landschaftsentwicklung in Mitteleuropa*, p. 161.

not satisfy, because wood of different species, age and quality was useful for rather different things, and sought by a variety of different consumers. Even were wood an undifferentiated product where users were indifferent to the form in which they obtained it, the age, size and location of tree would have had important cost implications, both for the labour in processing it into a usable product and transportation. Thus in the following discussion, one must always bear these facts in mind. A 'yield' is always a 'yield' for a specific purpose and interest, not 'good' or 'bad' in itself.

As a consequence, it is important that we appreciate precisely what each source available can tell us, and to read the sources against each other. The following sections will begin the chapter by examining the strengths and weaknesses of each source in some detail. Historians have tended to rely upon anecdote and second-guessing legislation for at least the first half of the early modern period; but they need not have done so. The sources employed here can be roughly categorised as general surveys, court and administrative records, tax records and account books.

The story that unfolds will highlight the fact that the story of the *Forstamt*'s woodlands follows neither edicts from on high, nor choices made by locals acting autonomously, but rather their interaction in developing a woodmanship that was broadly understood and accepted by all. Wood shortage and degradation of woodland was real, not mere rhetoric, but it was also situation-specific and contested even while the concepts and the arguments about shortage were universally accepted. The success with which we can investigate this story is thus intimately linked with the multiple perspectives that different sources can give us. Fortunately, the source material for the period is rich.

The surveys

Surveys conducted by the ducal government provide a sweeping, relatively systematic, appraisal of the state of the woods at one point in time. Four significant surveys were made of the area in this period, in 1523, 1556, 1583 and 1682.[7] There are considerable methodological difficulties in dealing with these sources. Measurement inaccuracies aside, the hazard looms large that officials only recorded what they were interested in (and in an inconsistent manner). The sixteenth-century surveys were taken rather rapidly, often without the forester having the opportunity to check with his own eyes the returns that were supplied from each ward or *Markung* by local dignitaries or forest wardens. In 1583, forester

[7] HStAS A59 Bü 32; H107/8 Bds.1–2; A59 Bü 13a; H107/8 Bd.5.

Philip Roßach recorded that he was new to the job and did not have time to ride around all of the district, relying on other reports and testimony.[8] The advantage of a single consistent observer was lost, but neither could one person impose their myopic eye on the whole.

The inspiration behind the 1523 document was the effort of the new Habsburg rulers of Württemberg to establish their administration and assess their newly won resources. This decade saw a huge effort across the Duchy to update all cadastres in a systematic fashion, much of it guided by the energetic hand of Balthasar Moser, the first official to be charged with organising the 'renovation' of cadastres on a wide scale. However, officials were for the most part only interested in accurately recording land that paid rents to the duke, in practice covering only small areas of private woodland (held by tenants of the duke), or some parts of the ducal woodland itself.[9] In the case of the *Forstamt* Leonberg, we know that the information was gathered by the forester Bartlin Moutzen (also known as Frieß) with the aid of forest wardens and 'others', such as local *Schultheißen*. Moutzen was present when some, but not all, of the surveying was done. This survey covered some forty-three areas of woodland owned by the duke, often giving details on the age of the wood, its condition ('hail-damaged', for example) and the use to which it was put. The area of the woodland often appears to be so inaccurate that it seems probable that officials only recorded areas likely to be exploited in the near future, and did not incorporate wider areas of grazing into their calculations. Nevertheless, the age of many stands makes it clear that these woodlands had been in a managed system under the auspices of ducal foresters since at least the late fifteenth century.[10]

The survey of 1556 was part of an altogether larger and more successful Duchy-wide effort to record woodland resources and rights, itself part of a general drive for more vigorous government and demarcation of rights and practices during the 1550s in Württemberg. Village officials (usually the *Schultheiß* and *Bürgermeister*) were charged with appearing before a panel consisting of the forester Gall von Sachsenheim, his predecessor Hans Hagen, and for some of the time, the Master of the Hunt, Melchior Jäger. Hearings began in the town hall of Leonberg on 5 August 1556 and seem to have lasted for three days. Hagen was the more experienced forester and would have had reasonable knowledge of the areas being

---

[8] HStAS A59 Bü 13a.

[9] Richter, *Lagerbücher- oder Urbarlehre*, pp. 42–3, 63; HStAS A17 Bü 42.

[10] HStAS A59 Bü 32. The interest in what was available to cut and the extent of future reserves appears rather earlier than examples given from mining regions that are sometimes considered the earliest examples of such practices in the mid-sixteenth century. See Schäfer, '*Ein Gespenst geht um*', p. 60.

recorded. The resulting material was bound in two copies, one retained (and annotated over succeeding decades) by the forester, the other sent to the supreme council in Stuttgart.[11] Given that this woodland was in the vast majority of cases not taxable, and that the returns were not being produced by private owners in the case of private woodlands, there is no reason to expect a systematic bias in the returns. This did not prevent a very considerable margin of error, most marked in proportionate terms in the area of monastic woodland. Given that these woodlands were not, as we shall see, as closely managed or monitored as others, this is no great surprise.

In 1583, the newly installed forester Philip Roßach followed a similar strategy. For all those areas of the *Forstamt* with which he was not personally familiar, he summoned members of the local *Ehrbarkeit* ('notables'), and forest wardens or woodcutters to give testimony in Leonberg. Where he was able, he rode the woodlands in the company of local wardens. A particular problem with the assessments was getting information on small patches of privately held woodland, often only a fraction of a *morgen* in extent, and consequently these tended to be lumped together in the returns. This perhaps partly explains why the area of private woodland recorded in 1583 was considerably smaller than that of 1556. The whole process stretched from a receipt of an instruction to survey the forest on 6 August to the sending off of the returns on 9 October.[12]

The 1682 enterprise was altogether different, comprising a systematic measurement of the woodland by the surveyor Andreas Kieser, using rods to mark out geometric areas whose extent could then be easily calculated. This technique introduced margins of error that were insignificant for our purposes.[13] The surveying, which over the 1680s embraced nearly the entirety of Württemberg's forests, was of course a slow procedure but one that provides us with the first truly reliable overview of the extent of the woodland. A further *Lagerbuch* recorded woodland boundaries and local rights in 1699–1700, without attempting any assessment of their extent.[14]

As we have seen in chapter 3, anyone relying on the preambles to government legislation would expect the woodlands to be in a rather poor condition throughout the period.[15] 'Marked wastage' was the theme in November 1536, and that 'the woodlots and woodlands daily, the longer, the more, are come into a burdensome and damaging decline',

---

[11] HStAS H107/8 Bds. 1–2.   [12] HStAS A59 Bü 13a.
[13] HStAS H107/8 Bd. 5; Kieser, *Alt-Württemberg*, pp. 34–55.   [14] HStAS H107/8 Bd. 6.
[15] Resycher, *SWG*, Bd. XII, p. 9.

continued to be the clarion call to action in the forest ordinances of 1540, 1552, 1567 and 1614.[16] The story told by the surveys is altogether more complex, demonstrating considerable chronological and geographical variation in the condition of the woodlands and the implementation of governmental initiatives. Some parts of the *Forstamt* were undoubtedly subject to local shortage, with yields dwindling away almost to nothing. Mature timber was in particularly short supply. Nevertheless, officials declared themselves to be satisfied with the condition of the majority of woodlands in 1583, and over time both the forestry administration, and communes, responded to the instructions of central government, although advances were often slow, incremental and partial.

This variation and incremental response to regulation can be illustrated by mapping the returns of the surveys. Today the *Forstamt* can be split in two, divided by a line drawn roughly from the old border with Baden on the Enz to the town of Leonberg, and then east along the northern boundary of the Keuper hills above Stuttgart. To the north and east of this line lies the viticulture region of the lower Neckar and Enz, wooded primarily by deciduous species with a high proportion of oak. Beech is also common, with lesser numbers of elm, ash and lime. To the south and west of this line, oak and beech still predominate, but with a stronger representation of coniferous trees the further west one goes. On the hills above the Nagold, the Black Forest proper, beech and coniferous trees such as the silver fir predominate. Birch and alder are also relatively common.[17]

The woodland survey of 1583 mentions oak, birch, beech, hazel, alder, aspen and 'pines' and 'firs', used to denote the scots pine and silver fir respectively.[18] There is a danger with this kind of source that surveyors record only the species that they are interested in. A clue to those 'key species' are provided by the forest ordinances themselves, which refer explicitly to oak, beech, birch, fir, ash and alder in 1540.[19] It would be surprising if hornbeam or ash were really absent, as they are in the surveys. Hornbeam appears only rarely in the account books of the

[16] Reyscher, *SWG*, Bd. XVI, pp. 4, 30 and 229.
[17] Schlenker and Müller, 'Erläuterungen zur Karte', pp. 10–12, 19–20, 25–26'; *Forstliche Standortskartierung Baden-Württemberg*; Eichlert, 'Die Pflanzen'.
[18] HStAS A59 Bü 13a.
[19] Reyscher, *SWG*, Bd. XVI, pp. 13–16, 43, 48, 61–7. In the subsequent ordinances from 1552 onwards, however, fruit trees such as apple and pear, and the denizens of river- and streambanks, willow and alder, are mentioned. Forest trees include oak, beech, birch, aspen, ash and hornbeam. The fact that an article of 1552 refers to 'beechwood, under which all deciduous wood is understood, birch, ash, hornbeam, alder', raises some concern as to the manner in which species were recorded, although birch and alder appear in the forest surveys.

forestry administration, but was noted as being plentiful in some neighbouring regions, so there is no reason to think this is a product of mis-
recording on the part of forestry officials.[20] Hazel, that does not feature in
the forest ordinances, is mentioned extensively in 1583, but only once in
1682.[21] Elm is a notable absence from all surveys.

The distribution of trees, as indicated in maps 4.1 and 4.2, in 1583
highlights oak as the most ubiquitous species.[22] Coniferous trees are
found nearly exclusively to the west of that line which still traverses the
region today. Beech is also almost exclusively found to the south and west
of this line, also in the region where it is most prevalent today, and was
rare as mature timber. As underwood it is only found in ducally owned
woodland in the south of the region, and only appears at all in communal
woodland in the north-west, near Groß Glattbach and Iptingen. This
suggests that deliberate management strategies are responsible for such a
clear pattern. It is very likely the coppicing of underwood that accounts
for the relative scarcity of beech, as it responds poorly to being cut back
more regularly than every three decades, and has been on the retreat in
the face of increased human intervention in the woodland since early
medieval times. By the 1590s beech was also so scarce in the Schönbuch
forest north of Tübingen that local coopers had to import wood from the
Black Forest.[23] Aside from the Keuper hills above Stuttgart, birch is only
found west of the Glems. Its success there may be explained by its
tendency to out-compete other species on poorer soils. Aspen, which is
far more demanding of well-drained, acidic soils, is found in the extreme
north-east or south-west, although isolated patches exist elsewhere.[24]
Hazel is to be found everywhere aside from the keuper hills of the
south-east.[25] This picture undoubtedly simplifies the real variety and
distribution of species, but it is surely not entirely a product of the
surveyor's myopic eye. The account books of the forest administration
carefully record large numbers of windfalls and old rotten trees that were

---

[20] Hornbeam is vulnerable to grazing and this is probably the best explanation for its
scarcity. Vera, *Metaforen voor de Wildernis*, pp. 278–9.

[21] HStAS A59 Bü 13a; H107/8 Bd. 5.   [22] HStAS A59 Bü 13a.

[23] Despite this, the agronomist Conrad von Heresbach, whose work often depended more
on classical sources than practical experience, recommended cutting it as often as every
six to seven years! Birch, too, coppices relatively poorly, and oak rather better. Hazel will
die off if left for up to forty years and then cut. Küster, *Geschichte der Landschaft in
Mitteleuropa*, p. 233; Vera, *Metaforen voor de Wildernis*, p. 113; von Heresbach, *Foure
bookes of husbandry*, fo. 104v; Evans, 'Coppice forestry', pp. 18 and 25; Hauff, *Zur
Geschichte der Forstgesetzgebung*, p. 67.

[24] Hart, *Practical Forestry*, pp. 114, 116–17.

[25] As hazel starts to be eliminated by shade once trees reach about fifteen years of age, its
prevalence is another indicator of an open canopied woodland. See Rackham, *Trees and
woodland*, p. 72.

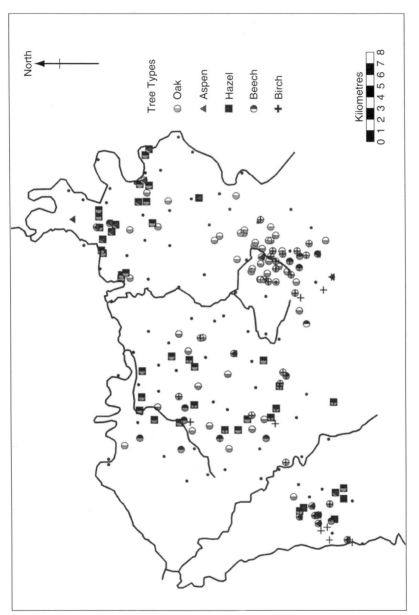

Map 4.1 Distribution of underwood tree types, 1583

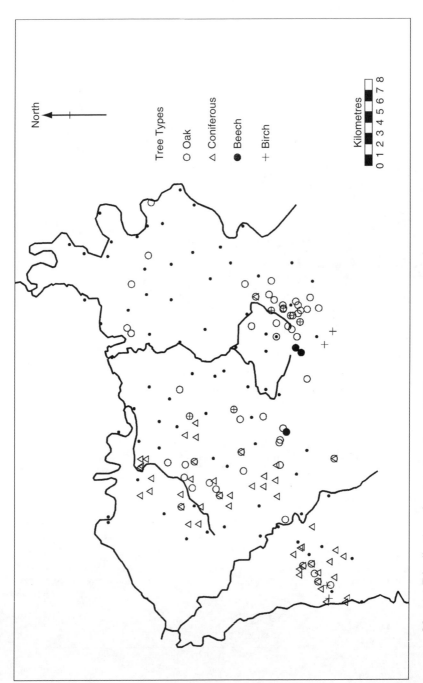

Map 4.2 Distribution of mature tree types, 1583

sold by officials, and the records of these species and their geographical spread tally very well with the distribution of species found in the surveys. Beech, in fact, could be relatively highly valued, both as timber and charcoal, and was certainly extensively exploited where it was present. These species distributions, especially that of oak and beech, tally well with what we know about the agro-forestry regime of the period, combining grazing and the exploitation of underwood.

The survey of 1682, though accurately measured by the standards of the time, provides less comprehensive information on the species of tree in particular woodlands.[26] Nevertheless, its contents suggest both the accuracy, and continuity, of the situation recorded by surveyors in 1583.[27] Hazel does not feature at all, but it seems that the surveyors in this case were not greatly interested in underwood species. As before, coniferous trees are found only in the west of the region. Insofar as this evidence stretches, with species only listed in around 40 per cent of the woodlands, there is no sign of the wartime period and population collapse having any significant impact on the species composition of the woodlands.[28] The distribution of the felling recorded in the foresters' account books also matches the prevalence of mature timber suggested in 1583.

One further way that we utilise the surveys is by trying to assess the age of stands of timber, and thus their likely form. Occasionally there is a record of woods being coppiced systematically on a set cycle length, mostly in the woodlands of village communes. Communes seem generally to have coppiced on sixteen-year cycles across the *Forstamt*. In the survey of 1583, the anticipated cutting date for underwood stands is recorded for no less than 223 areas of woodland, about three-fifths of the total number of stands of underwood. This implies of course that these woodland stands were not cut according to an annual regime, as in the latter case part of the stand would be cut every year.[29] Unsurprisingly, species like hazel, alder and aspen (though always mixed with others) cluster towards the lower end of the range, with only one stand including

---

[26] HStAS H107/8 Bd. 5.

[27] Of the twenty woodlands that contain birch, there is only one outlier from the earlier data, with the species being found in woodland near Oßweil in the east of the region. Data for beech, recorded in nine instances, shows it in exactly the same clusters as before: the Keuper hills between Leonberg and Stuttgart, and in the north-west near Iptingen and Groß Glattbach. Isolated outliers can be found near Bissingen and Besigheim in the north-east. Evidence from account books in the early 1680s that record a handful of mature beech trees being felled give the same picture, although the 1682 survey does not record tree species in those woodlands actually exploited by ducal officials during this short period.

[28] HStAS H107/8 Bd. 5; A302 Bds. 7231–2.   [29] HStAS A59 Bü 13a.

hazel to be cut as much as twenty years in the future. This kind of data does not tell us the structure of the woodland, but does give some idea of where ducal authorities could expect wood resources to be available in any given year.

By western European standards sixteen years or more is rather long, especially for underwood species such as hazel, and is much longer than recommended in both classical sources, and the few contemporary agronomists such as Conrad von Heresbach who wrote on these themes.[30] It suggests that these stands were not being managed according to their maximum potential productivity. Equally, once the cycle lasts longer than a decade, there is a danger with many species of the stool dying off after cutting. This may partly account for what we will see to be comparatively low underwood yields in many parts of the *Forstamt*.[31] Coppicing practices can be further investigated using the 1583 survey, as in forty-six cases the date when *last cut* was recorded, as well as the date when the *next cut* was anticipated. Again, the results do not suggest a very rigorous management.[32] Stands including hazel were to be cut on a cycle as long as twenty-four years! The entire range runs from eight and a half years to forty, with a mean cycle of nearly nineteen years and a median of seventeen. The impression gained from these figures is confirmed across the range of evidence for woodmanship, and the management and consumption of wood. Especially with underwood, in practice people did not discriminate greatly between species in their management and use, whatever their theoretical properties.

Mapping the cycles on which underwood was cut (see map 4.3), at least according to the survey of 1583, also introduces a striking pattern that is replicated in many aspects of woodland management. Cutting cycles appear to have been notably shorter in the north of the *Forstamt*, and especially the north-east. Who owned the woodlands concerned played no discernable role in this geographical phenomenon, as the spatial variation encompassed woodlands owned by the dukes, communes, monasteries and groups of private individuals. In the north-east, woodlands were cut as often as every ten to twelve years, a pattern replicated to some degree in the north-west. In the south, cycles were generally upwards of fifteen years, and in the hills above Stuttgart, rose as high as thirty or in one case forty years. While there is a measurably greater propensity for some regions to support rapid tree growth with the most

---

[30] Heresbach, it should be noted, wrote in the Duchy of Cleves where wood shortages in the lowlands may have led to shorter coppicing cycles. Von Heresbach, *Foure bookes of husbandry*, fos. 102v–104v.
[31] Buis, *Historia forestis*, p. 653.   [32] HStAS A59 Bü 13a.

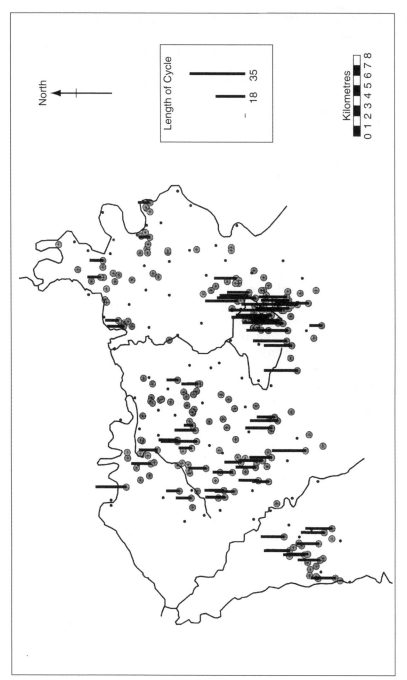

North

Length of Cycle

——— 35

— 18 35

Kilometres

0 1 2 3 4 5 6 7 8

Map 4.3 Underwood and cutting cycles, 1583

favourable conditions in the north-east,[33] it is likely that these practices are to some degree explained as a response to the market for firewood, as we shall see in chapter 5. The woodcutting practices in parts of the north-east and east of the region were thought worthy of comment by officials in 1583, who noted that Bissingers and Bietigheimers 'cut it young' or that they did not allow their wood to become old. As beech stools tend to die off if cut more often than every thirty years, this also explains why beech trees are generally so rare.[34]

Unfortunately, the post-war survey of 1682 was not taken on the same basis, and results are only very loosely comparable.[35] Underwood appears (where specified) under three descriptions, '*Laubholz*', '*Buschholz*', and '*Brennholz*'. The spatial distribution of their usage is displayed in map 4.4. *Laubholz* designated woodland in the south-west cut on rather longer cycles and managed less intensively, in a region of low population density and low prices for firewood.[36] *Brennholz* (which appears in tandem with *Bauholz* in seven out of the ten cases where the latter is mentioned) designated rather more closely managed, and more frequently cut, stands of underwood for regular supplies of firewood. *Buschholz* was far more ubiquitous, covering around a third of all the recorded woodland. The term probably designates less carefully managed, more open underwood with few, if any, mature standards. Where areas of felled wood are designated as *Buschholz* in the account books, this seems to cover fairly low value and probably relatively young stands.[37]

If *Buschholz* covered only a third of the region's woodlands in 1682, however, *Bauholz*, meaning 'Building-wood', or mature stands of timber, covered even less, a mere 14 per cent. *Bauholz* did, however, more frequently occur in tandem with well-managed crops of *Brennholz*. Given that perhaps over a quarter of an area having canopy cover will impede the growth of underwood, however, these woodlands cannot have been that densely stocked with mature trees.[38] The rarity of *Bauholz*

---

[33] Filzer, *Die Flora Württembergs*, pp. 11, 45 and 50.

[34] HStAS A59 Bü 13; Vera, *Metaforen voor de Wildnis*, p. 113.

[35] HStAS H107/8 Bd. 5.

[36] In the ward of Simmozheim, over 11 per cent of woodland was designated as *Laubholz*. *Laubholz* was used seventy-one times in the survey of 1583, and showed no sign then of being a regionally specific expression, which suggests that the surveyors of 1682 had a somewhat more precise sense of what they meant by using it. In 1682 *Laubholz* was used exclusively of the other two terms.

[37] Especially as it tends to stand in contrast to *Stangenholz*, designating somewhat older poles. In the three cases where they can be securely identified, those areas designated as *Buschholz* in the account books running from 1679–81 are also so designated in Kieser's survey of 1682. *Buschholz* is never used where any *Bauholz* is present in 1682.

[38] Vera, *Metaforen voor de Wildnis*, p. 140.

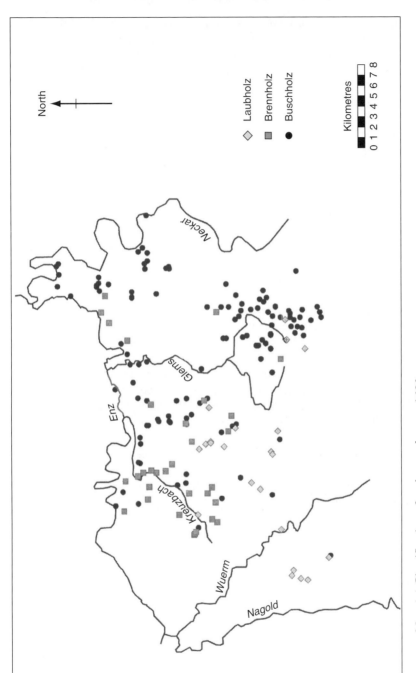

Map 4.4 Classification of underwood types, 1682

reflects a long-enduring pattern, though it is difficult to believe that it was in quite so short supply as the 1682 survey makes out.

If we draw back to the 1583 survey, 236 stands are described as having some kind of larger timber, and 80 of those with wood suitable for building.[39] As a century later, this is an area significantly lower than that covered by underwood, especially as most of these older trees were probably set fairly far apart. Some of the wood noted as suitable for building could only be used for spars for half-timbering, rather than as beams or rafters. Most of the areas with mature timber are identified as containing standards or staddles. Staddles are relatively young trees in their first few decades protected with the promise of providing building timber at maturity, as well as natural regeneration by re-seeding and a crop of mast for pigs and wild boar. They usually stood above coppiced, or alternatively bush-like woodland where underwood predominated. Some of these woodlands are explicitly noted *not* to have any timber suitable for building.

Mapping the distribution of these tree-types is immediately revealing (see map 4.5).[40] Mature trees are rather poorly represented in the north-east of the region, although the survey did not include Bietigheim's extensive *Vorstwald* which contained some mature timber. The picture is clearer still if we disaggregate into staddles and wood that is recorded as having potential for building. The only building wood in the north-east lies in the ducally owned Rotenacker. Virtually all the staddles in this district are also set in ducally owned woodland, and outside of this, maintenance of mature trees appears to be almost non-existent. Building timber was concentrated either in the west of the region, or in the hills above Stuttgart. In the latter area, little building timber is recorded west of the Lindenthal, and that to the east was entirely set within ducally owned woodland. Staddles were also universal in the region between Stuttgart and Leonberg in 1583, but widely scattered, with no close correlation with ownership, over the rest of the *Forstamt*. Unfortunately the survey evidence, as already noted, is far too meagre from 1682 to argue convincingly that these patterns were sustained, although none of the ten areas wherein *Bauholz* is recorded lie in the north-east. If my interpretation of the meaning of *Buschholz* is accurate, it might be noted that the proportion of the woodland in the *Forstamt* in that condition in 1682, a third, is balanced out by the recorded proportion of

---

[39] HStAS A59 Bü 13a. The stands with at least some larger timber covered 62 per cent of the total area recorded in 1583.

[40] It should be noted that there are no recorded staddles outside those areas recorded as underwood, which lends some credence to the records. As the point of staddles was that they were not cut back regularly like the rest of the stand, to exist in isolation of underwood would be nonsensical.

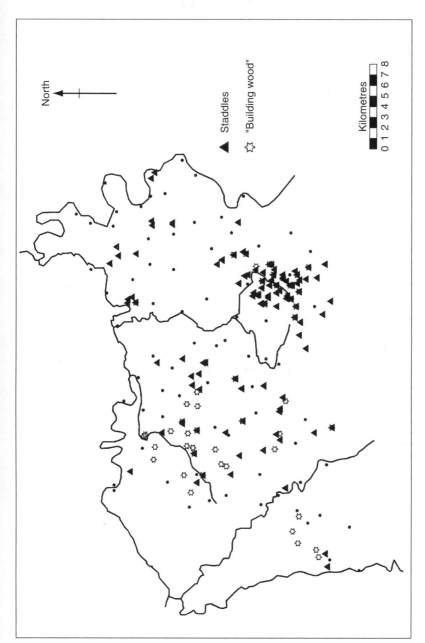

North

Staddles

"Building wood"

Kilometres
0 1 2 3 4 5 6 7 8

Map 4.5 Distribution of mature trees, 1583

the *Forstamt* with older trees present in 1583, just under two-thirds. However, the measurements of 1583 are far too unreliable for this statistic to be anything but suggestive of continuity. As the evidence stands, however, we can see considerable regional variation in both management practices and the structure of the woodland. The most predominant form was underwood with staddles or standards. As far as the surveys go, these sources suggest continuity between the late sixteenth and seventeenth centuries. There is no evidence, certainly, that the years of war and depopulation had any radical long-term influence. Neither were the provisions of the forest ordinances for the setting of staddles widely followed. They were not, however, ignored, and were most successfully implemented in ducal woodlands. A striking observation from the mid-1560s dated the first setting of staddles in woodlands near Hengstett in the south-west of the region to the summer of 1540, in other words, the very date of the first forest ordinance. Even here, however, staddles were only set at the requisite number of sixteen to the *morgen* in the early 1560s.[41]

The 1682 survey also provides one extra crucial piece of evidence as to how the woodlands were managed – which areas were subject to grazing.[42] No less than 74 per cent of the woodland was recorded as being subject to pasture rights, against a mere 7 per cent explicitly being barred from pasture. For around 19 per cent of the woodland, nothing is recorded regarding pasture, and nor can the antiquity of the rights be established. Pasture rights in woodland appear to have been particularly limited in the east of the *Forstamt*, where peasants must have been far more reliant on that pasture to be found on the fallow fields. This is likely to have proved a significant disincentive to alterations in crop rotation systems. It is noticeable that no rights to pasture existed in several woodlands that were important and frequently used sources of underwood for the ducal foresters.[43] The origins of these exclusions may well have come as early as the purchase of a complex of woods in the east of the *Forstamt* in the fourteenth century, which were then subsequently used as ducal hunting grounds.[44]

Court and administrative records

Surveys provide a reasonably consistently generated snapshot. Comments in court records span the entire period, providing a more continuous

---

[41] HStAS A368 Bü 31.   [42] HStAS H107/8 Bd. 5.

[43] Comprising the Birckach near Mönßheim, the Meisenberg near Renningen, the Seeholz and Eglosheimer Holz in the east of the region. This was not a general policy. The Pulverdinger Holz was subject to grazing and used for woodcutting by ducal foresters.

[44] Burckhardt, *Eglosheim*, pp. 160–4.

picture and helping us to pinpoint when various individuals or groups perceived the condition of their woodland to be deteriorating. Sporadic commentary on tree species present and the uses of areas of woodland provide additional insights. The evidence from these sources, and the tax records examined below, can be utilised to test the reliability of the survey data. They tend to confirm over the long term the structure and condition of the woodland hinted by the surveys. However, it is important that the source is taken in context. Claims about the condition of woodlands are meaningless if not set against a background of dispute and resistance to the claims of others. Above all, the evidence of court records must of course be treated with caution. Such testimony contains a literature of complaint, which refers by and large to very specific circumstances. The available evidence consists, in the main, of those matters that came to the attention of the supreme council either via the medium of a *Supplication* expressing some grievance or matters that the forester wished to raise with his superiors. Grievances might arise from intra-communal strife, inter-communal strife or objections to the activities of the forester and his wardens.

Laments about the condition of the woodland appear in documents of the 1480s, and refer even further back in time. According to the testimony of Hans Ülenman, who was the wood warden for Leonberg in the 1450s, 'noticeable damage' was done to the beech woods by extensive cutting at that time. Accusations of damage in this case, ranging around the 1450s and 1460s, were made however in the context of a jurisdictional dispute between Leonberg and Eltingen over the woods where they both claimed woodcutting and pasture rights. 'Damage' here means an infringement of one's proprietary rights, rather than degradation. Allegations resurfaced in 1487 and can be found as late as 1601. Despite the assertion of the Leonberg authorities of a 'high and unavoidable need for wood, [that] appears in such a great shortage', the *Vogt* found in favour of Eltingen that the woodland was not in too bad a way. In fact, the Leonbergers had been failing to maintain proper coupes, and this was blamed, rather than any fundamental deficiency in supply, for any problems.[45]

It is only in the second half of the sixteenth century that concerns were raised with any frequency. By 1561 the forester Jacob Koch spoke of 'severe spoilation' of the woods around Feuerbach, although in the context of disputes over other matters, including the implementation of the forest ordinances in their communal woodland, fining and corvée to be provided to the forester.[46] A similar instance in neighbouring Weilimdorf in 1578 saw the forest warden claiming that the woodlands were 'quite

---

[45] HStAS A572 Bü 42.   [46] HStAS A227 Bü 1120.

cut away' during a dispute over hunting services and pannage. A report of the *Vogt* of Leonberg, in contrast, found that because of the abandonment of ditches dug to protect woodland and demarcate hunting areas, they were overgrown with *Bauholz!*[47] By the 1540s, however, significant amounts of timber for building already had to be acquired from more remote parts of the western *Forstamt*, or more frequently, imported from the Black Forest.[48] No 'building timber' was reported to remain in the Württemberger portion of the Hagenschieß by 1577.[49] Leonberg reported in 1581 that because 'from year to year such decline and short-age' of wood prevailed that the previous generosity of the *Holzgaab* was no longer possible, and no more wood could be sold from their woodland. In 1583 it was similarly reported that there was a 'great shortage of firewood and not much building timber', and that Leonbergers used for fuel wood that could have been for barrel-making. From the 1580s, sales of wood from Leonberg's communal woodlands do appear to have gone into a precipitate decline, as displayed in figure 4.1.[50]

Communal regulation of woodland did not begin in the latter half of the sixteenth century. Leonberg's wood ordinance dates from 1538. But as the century drew to an end, the amount and severity of regula-tion increased, almost certainly reflecting fears of the poor condition of the woodland. Renningen in particular restricted previously rather gen-erous allotments of building wood, which was 'very wasted' and con-tinually becoming more difficult to get in the early 1580s. By 1616 at the latest Renningen had gone over to constructing a stone *Etter* around the village rather than a palisade. This was a possibility recommended by the *Vogt* in a missive of 1593.[51] In January 1592 and March 1608, the village court of Gebersheim took measures to limit the free allow-ance of building wood which in future had in part to be purchased, because 'the woodland will move quite into deficiency'.[52] Renningen had already ceased to grant large timbers from its woodland in 1588, allowing a small remittance from taxation to allow for the costs of purchasing this wood.[53] As early as 1582, building wood in the com-munal woodlands of Leonberg was being 'exhausted day by day', according to the town ordinances, which prescribed that ground stories

[47] HStAS A227 Bü 1130.   [48] HStAS A368 Bü 23; A421 Bü 1.
[49] HStAS A368 Bü 46 and 56.
[50] HStAS A572 Bü 45; HStAS A59 Bü 13a; StAL Bürgermeisterrechnungen, 1588–94.
[51] HStAS A572 Bü 69; A368 Bü 48; StAR Nr B349. Around the same time in 1593 the sheep ranch at Heimerdingen built a durable stone wall instead of a fence around its arable land, in order to save wood. HStAS A368 U46; similarly in Bergheim, 1597 and 1603. HStAS A368 Bü 13.
[52] HStAS A584 Bd. 832.   [53] HStAS A572 Bü 69.

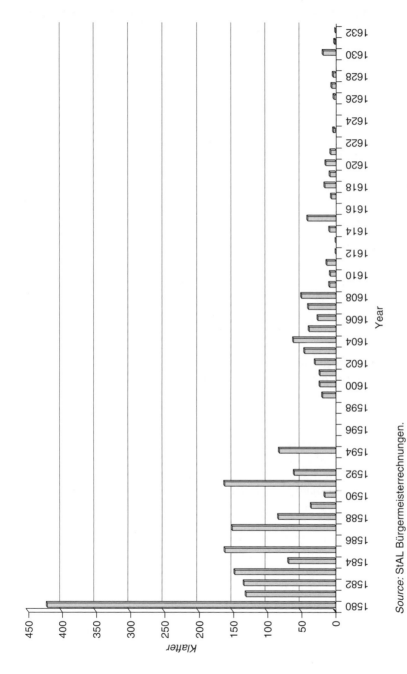

Source: StAL Bürgermeisterrechnungen.

Figure 4.1 Wood sales from Leonberg woodland, 1580–1632

and guttering were henceforth to be of stone, a measure bringing local practice into line with the state building ordinance of 1565.[54] More frequently, villages set limits on the allocation of the freely distributed *Gaabholz* granted out for fuel to members of the commune. Heimerdingen, Eberdingen, Zuffenhausen, Feuerbach and the vicinity of Stuttgart were all noted to have rather poor patches of woodland in the forest survey of 1583. Rutesheim's relative shortage was marked by the fact that the villagers were then able to sell rather little from their extensive woodlands. Iptingers, who had brought in communal income by selling timber in the 1550s, were unable to do so by the early 1580s.[55] Regulation fits with a wider pattern in the German southwest where by-law regulation of wood use was heavily concentrated in the second half of the sixteenth century and the period leading up to the Thirty Years' war.[56]

This late sixteenth-century period of increased social stress, price rises and climatic fluctuation had a particular impact on the woodland in crisis years. On 6 February 1572 the forester found around 100 *morgen* in the Pulverdinger Holz 'wasted' because of woodcutting by Enzweihingers. This was no surprise in the third hard winter and dearth year in a row, with weather so cold that the water froze in the wells. The problems around Enzweihingen continued over the next two winters, at a time when corn prices were the highest of the century, wine incomes collapsed and grain had to be imported from far afield.[57] Years of woe brought evident damage to the woodland again in 1598, when snow lay deep across Württemberg, although government policies at this time managed to hold price rises in check. By April 1604, neither mature stands nor deadwood were left in many areas between Stuttgart and Leonberg, according to petitioners from Ditzingen. This seems to have been the cumulative effect of a run of cold winters and a spectacularly bad wine harvest in the Neckar valley in 1602. Although grain harvests were sustained at a reasonable level, the winter cold was not relieved until a 'year without winter' in 1607.[58]

The truly wretched years, however, came in the 1630s and 1640s. Even before the massive destruction wrought by conquering and quartered armies after the battle of Nördlingen in 1634, forester Ulrich Bauder wrote of a general disregard for the forest laws and the fact that communes were selling off oaks to obtain income. Things were much worse by

---

[54] HStAS A572 Bü 41.   [55] HStAS A59 Bü 13a; A572 Bü 45; Warde, 'Law'.
[56] Warde, 'Recording regulation'.
[57] HStAS A227 Bü 1124; Ginschopf, *Chronica*, pp. 93–5.
[58] HStAS A227 Bü 1152; Ginschopf, *Chronica*, pp. 105–10; Glaser, *Klimageschichte*, p. 134.

1643, when wood sales in all woodlands had left many areas 'markedly exhausted, wasted', although it cost more to cut the wood than it could be sold for. Not an oak was left standing within reach of Markgröningen in January 1644. Villagers throughout the east of the *Forstamt* then responded to an exceptionally hard frost in early May, which froze the vines, by further plundering the woods. Although the forester attempted to fine many, they retorted that woodcutting was the only way in which they could hope to pay their war contributions to the locally quartered army.[59]

Thereafter, complaints and concerns die away until the beginning of the eighteenth century. This was not, as is sometimes argued, because the war itself gave a chance for woodland to rejuvenate. Both the anecdotal evidence presented above, and the yield estimates presented below, argue for the extremely detrimental impact of war on yields that lasted a couple of decades after the cessation of hostilities, and was reignited with the French invasions of the 1690s.[60] Only catastrophic population loss led to some respite for the woodland due to a massive decline in demand.

We cannot take such scattered and anecdotal evidence, so often produced in conflict situations, as a completely reliable source for the whole of the *Forstamt* or indeed even localities within it. Neither can the extensive importation of wood to the region by the late sixteenth century be taken as evidence that the woodlands themselves were in a poor condition, as opposed to simply being unable to fulfil the demands put upon them. However, court and administrative records tend again to confirm the picture gleaned from the surveys. Rather poor yields, and a system under stress, appear to have been the experience in parts of the *Forstamt* by 1600, and the testimony of taxation records from the early eighteenth century, when the population was well on the way to recovering its 1620s levels, reiterates this view.

Tax records

While they have all the usual pitfalls of fiscal records, tax valuations, along with commentary provided by the tax assessors, introduce new perspectives on the condition of the woodland in the early eighteenth century. Before then, measurements of woodlands were too unreliable to provide yield estimates, but by the early eighteenth century, this situation had changed. The taxation of the time, refined in a series of instructions between 1713 and 1741, sought to establish a capital value for land, a

---

[59] HStAS A227 Bü 1170, 1171.   [60] HStAS A302 Bd. 7234.

Table 4.1 *Tax assessments on woodland, 1713 (in fl.)*

Place	Assessment per morgen (fl.)	Estimated yield per hectare (m³ stacked wood)
Mönßheim	0.31	3.3
Gebersheim	0.25	2.7
Hirschlanden	–	–
Münklingen	0.15	1.6
Rutesheim	0.49	5.3
Höfingen	0.30	3.2
Heimerdingen	0.30	3.2
Hemmingen	0.43	4.6
Eltingen	0.27	2.9
Warmbronn	0.25	2.7
Heimsheim	0.34	3.7
Leonberg	0.18	1.9
Renningen	0.37	3.9
Weilimdorf	0.42	4.5
Ditzingen	0.50	5.4
Gerlingen	0.25	2.7

Source: HStAS A261 Bü 1128.

proportion of which was then taxed. By comparing assessed income from these woods with the local price of wood, we can come to a rough estimate of their productivity.[61] We already know that the yield from woodland was overwhelmingly fairly young underwood, and the data here is offered with that in mind.

It appears that the tax assessment of woodlands in the *Amt* Leonberg shows an estimated annual income per *morgen* in 1713 and a capital value in 1727.[62] Given this, the estimated annual income of a *morgen* of woodland in 1713 was low, ranging from 0.15fl. in Münklingen to 0.5fl in the woodlands owned by Ditzingers. The range of values is displayed in table 4.1.

---

[61] Reyscher, *SWG*, Bd.XVII, pp. 361, 406 and 529. Private woodland was considered particularly difficult to assess consistently in 1713, but shows no signs of differing markedly in value from adjacent patches of communally owned woodland.

[62] HStAS A261 Bü 1128, 1134. Tax instructions did not actually provide a blueprint for calculating the capital value of woodland, but assessors appear to have worked on similar principles to those used assessing other land uses. If following the principle of other types of land, the 1713 income estimate would be 5 per cent of the capital value. This interpretation seems to be confirmed by occasional comments in the 1727 returns of earlier capital value estimates that match those of 1713.

The mean price per fathom of wood cut in ducal woodlands in 1700 was just over 1 fl. At these prices, an annual increment of 1.6 to 5.4 m³ per hectare is implied. Some of the value would have been stored in mature trees, of course. This average is somewhat on the low side given the theoretical possibilities, but by no means unusual for the early modern period. The implied capital values, from 3fl. to 10fl., are slightly on the low side of the range suggested in the instructions for tax assessors for 'mixed wood' (which seems to mean underwood with a few standards), also suggesting that this form of woodland was also prevalent in the *Amt*, as large stands of mature timber would have brought a higher tax assessment.[63]

By 1727, the range of annual average increment implied has sunk a little, to 2 to 4 m³ per hectare.[64] While the implied yields in Leonberg and Mönßheim were very slightly better than in 1713, in most cases they fell. Very nearly every woodland's condition is described by the assessors as 'rather bad'. Many contained completely bare patches, or areas that were 'pure *Egarten*.' The woodland was often 'fully cut down', sometimes 'ruined' and in Höfingen and Hemmingen, no fathoms were distributed in the *Gaabholz* because the diameter of the wood was too small. Instead they received 'bushels of thorn faggots'. Blame was laid on the stony or sandy soils, and, again universally, the presence of wild boar eating the young shoots and allowing no more saplings to grow. Only Gerlingen and Rutesheim acknowledged that the grazing of domesticated livestock played a role, and even then the Gerlingers blamed the problems on the Leonbergers! Privately owned woodland was certainly in no better condition than that managed in common. In Hemmingen their values were exactly the same, and in Ditzingen the 121 ha. of privately owned woodland had 'for the most part' given no wood within living memory, and would not do so 'for a long time in the future'.[65] However, this may not always have been the case. Tax records left from 1607 from some holdings in Bietigheim, the Ingersheims and Hoheneck suggest that yields from small plots of private woodland were rather higher at this point, possibly as high as the best recorded yields per hectare in the woodlands of 1700.[66]

The claims as to the miserable condition of the woodlands may also have stemmed from the fact that both locals and assessors judged the 'best' form of woodland to be that with a large amount of mature timber. Certainly this brought the highest tax assessments, and assessors were to distinguish (as they indeed did) oaks and beech trees, areas of 'mixed

---

[63] HStAS A261 Bü 1128; Reyscher, *SWG*, Bd.XVII, p. 361.
[64] HStAS A261 Bü 1134. This implies holding the price of wood constant at 1 fl. per fathom, when it is likely to have risen in some places, which would imply lower yields.
[65] HStAS A261 Bü 1134.   [66] HStAS A320 Bü 5; A359 Bü 3.

woodland and birches', and pines and firs. Most woodland in the *Amt* Leonberg fell into the middle category, with some 'small oaks', and rarely 'a few beech'.[67] Given the lack of canopy cover, the underwood of birch, hazel and aspen must have been relatively favoured, and where the ground was not bare the figures suggest that yields of this small diameter underwood, probably still cut on a sixteen-year cycle, were not too bad. Grazing-resistant plants like thorn probably thrived too, allowing a few mature trees to develop under their protection. But the general experience in the early eighteenth century seems to have been of declining yields. Communally or privately managed woods do not demonstrate balanced, sustainable yields, even if the picture was not perhaps as grim as locals made out. Mature timber was scarce. By 1747, Leonberg stopped giving out wood from their communal woodlands altogether, although the practice lasted until the 1780s in Eltingen.[68] By the 1760s, when ducal exploitation of the woodlands had got somewhat out of hand, a report claimed that two-thirds of all the ducal woodland in the district was 'for the most part cut down'. The forester estimated that only about 2,200 m^3 could be cut in a year from the ducal woodlands, or about 1.2 m^3 per hectare. The north-east of the region could provide no wood at all, and generally there was only the odd tree that could be used for handicrafts or building. By this time wood cost 5–6 fl. per *Klafter*, about five or six times more expensive than it had been in the early 1730s![69] Eighteenth-century pamphleteers who fretted about the 'wood shortage' were not, in many cases, far off the mark.

Further light is shed on the situation by a survey of villages and their economic situation carried out sometime around 1700. At this point the condition of some woodlands seems to have been promising, such as Mönßheim's 'lovely woods', or the woodlands of Renningen (the highest valued in 1727) and Gerlingen that earned income for the commune. Warmbronn, at the southern tip of the district and outside of the *Forstamt*, already had a prevalence of grazer-resistant juniper that the locals sold. However, Leonberg's woodlands were almost 'ruined through the wild boar' that prevented the growth of young trees.[70] The warning signs were already there for communally owned woodlands even at the beginning of the eighteenth century. Renningers commented on population pressure on their woodland in 1716, presaging later problems.[71]

---

[67] HStAS A261 Bü 1134; Reyscher, *SWG*, Bd.XVII, p. 361.

[68] Hofacker, 'Die Epoche von 1648 bis 1800', pp. 132–3. Minimal amounts of faggots were still supplied to some and officials received wood payments in kind as part of their salaries. StAL Wald- und Holz Particularrechnungen.

[69] HStAS A8 Bü 40; HStAS A302 Bd. 7260.   [70] HStAS A368L Bü 136.

[71] StAR Urthel- und Vertragsbuch.

Account books

The final sources we may utilise to provide a broad view of woodland condition are the account books of the ducal forestry administration. Account books have the advantage of providing serial, rather than synchronic, information, even if their series are very incomplete. For the *Forstamt* Leonberg, the first account book survived from the accounting year (St George's to St George's) 1585–6, a plague year but one of bountiful wine harvests before the collapse of viticulture incomes in the subsequent year. Further volumes survive from 1604–5 and 1609–10. Thereafter, account books survive approximately every ten years, with a few extra, through to the eighteenth century.[72] Those for the war period record very little, a reflection of the impossibility of effectively running the administration in that era. It is possible to use these books to provide estimates of yields of wood for underwood, and the level of cutting for large rods, poles and mature timber, that while falling far short of being effective time-series, do allow some appraisal of long-term trends.

The actual volume harvested from a measured area of underwood was unfortunately only recorded in one year, 1603–4, and otherwise we must resort to the expedient of estimation. For the most part, this relies on two sets of figures. Either data on the area of wood felled (but not the volume of wood that this yielded) and its price; or data on the volume of wood felled (but not the extent of the area from which it came) and its price. Thus we have no real figure for the *volume yield by area*, which would tell us the productivity of the woodland over time. However, by simply taking the average price of each *morgen* of felled underwood recorded, and dividing it by the average price per unit of wood sold in volume units (fathoms), we should have an estimate of yield per area. This assumes that similar types of wood were sold by area, and sold by volume. The two would have a roughly similar average price for each unit of volume. Hence we treat the value of wood sold by area as the 'Total Value Product', as economists say. If we divide that by the price per unit (price per unit of volume), we should have the yield expressed in those units (in this case, fathoms).[73] The estimated yield per fathom provides the best general guide to the

---

[72] The following discussion relies on the account books HStAS A302 Bds. 7221–35 and 7302.

[73] It appears that labour costs were not generally included in the price of wood sold as fathoms or faggots. Even when these were obtained from trees felled for other purposes (such as their trunks being used for timber), it appears that the purchaser usually incurred the labour costs, although this certainly cannot be proven in all cases.

level of wood production. Indeed, wood cut and sold in this form provided the primary source of income from ducal woodlands.[74]

However, the price of wood varied significantly across even a relatively small area such as the *Forstamt*. This becomes of methodological importance when we try to assess yields across the entirety of the region, because if cutting is geographically concentrated in any one year, an apparent variation in the aggregate yield might simply be the result of this geographical focus. The results adjusted for geographical bias show a closely related trend to the 'raw' estimates that do not take the spatial distribution of the cutting into account.[75]

Yields from ducal woodland, as displayed in table 4.2, appear to have been very high in the mid-1580s, and were very much lower in 1603–4, after the hard and cold years around 1600. They then show something of a recovery, although somewhat lower in the estimate for 1629–30 than that for 1609–10. By the end of the war, around 1650, yields are very much lower, and reach a nadir in 1659–60, before being sustained at a higher, if fluctuating level until 1691. The yields for 1699–1700, after another decade of war, appear very low again.[76]

However, these 'trends' can be misleading. If we 'correct' for geographical bias, the yields in 1603–4 do not appear to be so low as the raw data would suggest, and the clearest troughs fall in 1649–50 and 1699–1700, those years subsequent to prolonged periods of warfare.[77] The yields from 1585–6 remain noticeably higher. Given that the yields obtained in adjacent years, such as 1603–4 and 1604–5, and 1669–70 and 1670–1, actually differ fairly substantially from each other, we must suppose that the figures represent deliberate cutting strategies on the part of the forest authorities. The average stock of wood per hectare across the ducal woodlands in the *Forstamt* obviously could not fluctuate so rapidly from year to year. Particularly in the year 1603–4, officials seem to have chosen to sell off rather poorly yielding areas of woodland that had perhaps already been plundered in hard winters. But these limited samples suggest that yields were much higher in the 1580s than during the seventeenth century, and were probably especially low after periods of warfare.

---

[74] It should be emphasised again that even where we have actual details of yields per volume per area, the 'fathom' is still a notional unit, as not all the wood was really stacked as fathoms, and the same mass of different diameter wood takes up different amounts of space when stacked. In other words, the volume unit recorded does not correspond to a volume of *solid timber*, and hence we must still estimate this.

[75] This was done by setting 1605 as a benchmark year and in each year for which there was data taking the ward by ward prices and applying them to the volumes of wood felled in each ward in 1605.

[76] HStAS A302 Bds. 7221–35 and 7302.   [77] See note 75.

Table 4.2 *Estimated yields from ducal woodlands in the* Forstamt *Leonberg*

Date	Mean value per morgen [fl. (N)]	Mean price per Fathom [fl. (N)]	Yield per morgen in fathoms	Yield per morgen in fathoms, 1605 cutting patterns[a]
1585–6	13.1 (82)	0.78 (281.5)	16.80	20.64
1603–4	8.1 (86)	1.09 (157.5)	7.47	8.15
1604–5	10.4 (88)	1.05 (176.8)	9.86	9.83
1609–10	12.7 (86)	1.09 (207)	11.63	10.93
1619–20	9.8 (112)	1.09 (169.3)	8.95	8.04
1629–30	11.1 (126)	1.27 (308.5)	8.74	6.86
1649–50	4.3 (23)	0.58 (187)	7.34	6.74
1659–60	5.8 (77)	0.81 (276)	7.13	7.09
1669–70	5.4 (57)	0.70 (195)	7.69	7.81
1670–1	6.2 (64)	0.60 (168)	10.37	14.28
1679–80	8.2 (83)	0.86 (162)	9.59	9.40
1680–1	12.8 (48)	1.06 (788)	12.07	12.21
1689–90	10.1 (135)	1.05 (208)	9.62	8.68
1690–1	10.4 (83)	1.03 (148)	10.10	8.09
1699–1700	7.2 (37)	1.07 (147)	6.67	5.37
1730–1	11.0 (46)	1.05 (181.25)	10.48	–

Note: [a] See note 75.
Source: HStAS A302 Bds.7221–7235, 7241 and 7302. The data does not include all wood felled in these categories, but only that which can be identified as being cut in a specific location.

We can also view the results through another prism. We cannot be sure on what cycle these woodlands were being felled, unfortunately, but by setting maximum, and probable, annual increments of wood growth per hectare we can assess the 'sustainability' of forestry practice. If these woodlands could produce, on average, $5\,m^3$ of stacked wood per hectare per year, then the woodland areas felled each year for which we have surviving accounts would have to have been left on average for periods of fourteen to twenty-six years.[78] This seems within the parameters of what we know about underwood management. However, it is likely that much of the woodland was not really so high yielding, and indeed that in some periods, such as the 1640s and 1690s, was subject to considerable plundering. If we set the mean annual increment of wood per hectare at $3\,m^3$, considerably longer would have been required to grow such a stock of

[78] HStAS A302 Bd. 7235. This estimate of untouched underwood's productivity in central Europe comes from Sieferle, 'The energy system', p. 14. See also figures for yields from twentieth-century coppiced woodlands in south-west Germany in Abetz, *Bäuerliche Waldwirtschaft*, p. 167; Pfister, *Der Leonberger Stadtwald*, p. 22.

timber, from twenty-four years up to forty-three years. It seems from the evidence that we have that most woodlands were in fact cut more frequently than this. If such high yields were being achieved, it can only have been done by clearing areas of standing timber so thoroughly that the prospects of equivalent rates of regrowth were impaired, or by felling areas of woodland that had been left relatively untouched for a considerable length of time. This is even more the case in the mid-1580s, where perhaps forty-five to sixty years would have been required to grow such a stock of wood per hectare. Because demand on wood was slight relative to its total area, this would have been possible in ducally owned woodland.

Complaints, regulations and disputes suggest that mature timber was relatively scarce by the mid-sixteenth century, and, as with underwood, tended to become progressively more so.[79] It, too, suffered in wartime. As most trees, or parts thereof, were sold as a discrete unit rather than a specified volume of wood, it is unfortunately not possible to estimate the size nor age of the tree being purchased from account books. Prices varied geographically and over time, and there is no constant against which variant prices for different species of tree could be compared to gauge the likely form of that tree. There are no surveys of woodlands classed by age, as produced by the forest authorities in Hesse from the very end of the seventeenth century onwards.[80] However, what we can discern from account books is the level of exploitation in ducal and some communal woodlands, and unless the surviving records all come from anomalous years, we can state that the numbers of timber trees felled in ducal forests was in fact very low. In the years 1585–6, 1604–5 and 1609–10, for example, only 107, 163 and 276 trees respectively were sold out of ducally owned woodlands. The post-war sales were considerably lower. In 1604–5 a further 137 oaks and 203 fir trees were supplied

---

[79] 'Mature timber', in distinction to 'underwood', is in truth more of an analytical distinction than a real one. As we have seen, much of the woodland probably did not conform very closely to the ideal of 'coppice with standards', or *Mittelwald* as it is known in German. Much of the wood cut for fuel or fencing was considerably older than coppiced woodland generally is, possibly reaching several decades. Equally, some of the wood described in categories other than 'firewood' or *Morgenholz* in the account books was in fact relatively young. Many of the 'poles', for example, sold off as *Raiffstangen* (technically for the hoops used in barrel-making, but apparently serving a rather wider usage than this), were no more than 18 *Württemberger* feet long. The account books and general parlance tended to define wood according to its use. Nomenclature has already been discussed in relation to underwood. Other types were 'building- or carpentry-wood' (*Bau-* or *Zimmerholz*), 'cartwright's wood' (*Wagnerholz*), 'turner's wood' (*Drehholz*), and then the 'lop and top' (*Afterschlag*) left over from these, or the removals of old, rotten and decayed stumps or windfalls.

[80] Schenk, *Waldnutzung*, p. 128.

by the foresters to various purposes for which the ducal authorities were liable, such as repair of millworks, riverbank strengthening, winepress construction, and so forth. This made for a grand total of 503 trees, many of which were explicitly mentioned as being small. In 1679–80 the total felled was 534 (mostly firs), and the next year 337 (mostly fir again).[81] It can be pointed out again that the Duke owned 2,300 hectares of woodland in the *Forstamt*, and so in 1679–80, one tree was felled per four hectares of woodland. If even the very modest rate of 16 staddles per *morgen* was being enforced across the ducal woodlands, then four hectares should have held over 200 mature trees. One would think that the exploitation of timber was proceeding very far within the limits of natural rejuvenation of this fairly unambitious regime. As we have seen at the head of the chapter, however, this does not mean that the right trees could automatically be found at the right place and time. The great majority of trees that were felled were firs from the woodlands in the hilly south of the district, with a scattering of oaks elsewhere and only very few beech, hornbeam and birch – conforming to the impression created by the forest surveys.

Smaller poles could be removed in quite large numbers from specific locations, especially for projects such as the straightening of the Neckar, or the fencing and stakes used in the park of the ducal residence at Stuttgart. However, none of this demand appears to have amounted to more than the clearing of a handful of hectares in any given year. Similarly, on occasion the ducal forester sold off tens of thousands of young switches that were used to bind sheaves during the harvest. The forest ordinances considered the unsupervised collection of these switches to be particularly damaging to woodland rejuvenation, but yet again, the scale of this activity was rather minor in the overall context of the wooded landscape. In fact, foresters seemed determined, in compliance to the ducal ordinances, to prefer the sale of windfalls, lop and top, and lying deadwood to the felling of living trees. This meant that in the pre-war years these old, dead or surplus timbers brought in more income to the *Forstamt* than any other accounted items save the sale of underwood for fuel and fencing. By the end of the 1660s this pattern had reasserted itself.[82] The practice of clearing areas and not allowing wood to lie prevented rotten wood soiling the forest floor, which would have encouraged pests and prevented rejuvenation, although like much of the forest management this was probably carried out more rigorously in the woodlands between Leonberg and Stuttgart.

---

[81] HStAS A302 Bds. 7221–35.   [82] HStAS A302 Bd. 7302.

Making sense of the sources

We are now in a position to synthesise the evidence of the various sources and tease out the full force of the trends they suggest. The period after the mid-sixteenth century to the Thirty Years' war, and again in the early eighteenth century, seems to show all the indicators of a woodland system under some stress. Regulation was not completely ineffectual, but it was unable to arrest this process. Many communally owned woodlands appear to have been cut on a fairly standard cycle of sixteen years, and there is no sign that coppicing practices were reconfigured over time. However, there are regional patterns that must have been established by the latter part of the sixteenth century if not before, and they do seem to be responses to, among other things, the general availability of wood in a locality. Taken with the relative lack of mature trees for reseeding, and the constant depredation of wild animals and livestock, this lack of flexibility in the observable period meant that local shortages could arise even in areas where the theoretical area of the communal woodland was quite extensive.

These more general trends may be illustrated by the evidence from the village of Renningen, where a series of documents relating to woodland management were copied out for a court case in the mid-1560s. The village maintained twenty-three coupes for the *Holzgaab*, each seventeen *morgen* in extent. Each *morgen* was divided among seven households, each of these receiving three to five fathoms a year – a considerable variation, we might note. This gives a yield of $10–17\,m^3$ per household, or between 70 and $119\,m^3$ per *morgen*, or 222 to $377\,m^3$ per hectare! This would imply that the annual average increment in Renningen's woodlands was between 9 and $16\,m^3$ per hectare, on a twenty-three-year cycle, an extraordinary achievement and colossal in contrast to the early eighteenth century yields.[83] The lower end of the scale matches the most favourable yields of coppiced woodlands in areas of south-west Germany in the early twentieth century, or the intensely managed coppices of Flanders studied by Guido Tack, Martin Hermy and Paul van den Bremt.[84] We might surmise that this lower end relates more to the real situation than the upper end of the range, and where the local official recorded 'about 3, 4 or 5 fathoms' as a *Holzgaab*, the five fathoms were cut by the fortunate few. This testimony seems to back up the impression garnered from ducal accounts twenty years later, that the productivity of some carefully

---

[83] HStAS A227 Bü 1122.
[84] Abetz, *Bäuerliche Waldwirtschaft*, p. 167; Tack, Bremt and Hermy, *Bossen van Vlaanderen*, p. 93.

managed woodland (and Renningen generally seems to have had a reputation for good housekeeping) was very high for much of the later part of
the sixteenth century. Yet Renningen itself illustrates the dramatic deterioration that could set in. Rules on building timber were being tightened
in the years around 1600. The communal authorities were again worried
about the supply of the *Gaabholz* in 1716. By the second half of the
eighteenth century, the once admirable woods produced only eighty-
two fathoms and 1,050 faggots for the *Gaabholz* of 1762, probably
under $40 \, \text{m}^3$ per hectare. Another sixty fathoms could be scraped
together from old or rotten trees. Only a few dozen mature trees
remained. Other stories from the sixteenth century are less optimistic.
The woods of Asperg, according to a complaint of 1570, were producing
around $170 \, \text{m}^3$ per hectare.[85]

The situation in ducal woodland was very different. In 1682, this
covered around 2,300 hectares.[86] In the year of most extensive cutting
'by area' recorded, 1689–90, only some 135 *morgen* or around 0.2 per
cent of the area was actually exploited in this way.[87] Even if cutting
recorded by 'volume' was very extensive and covered areas of relatively
low yield, it is unlikely that more than 1 per cent of the total area of ducal
woodland was ever exploited in any given year. Even if the ducal woodlands had been used wholly systematically, they would always have a
stock at least a century old. In reality, foresters felled some stocks rather
more often, and given the amount of wood that they obtained, it suggests
that the density of growth, and the depredations of the peasantry, livestock and game, left an annual increment that was considerably less that
the 'ideal' $5 \, \text{m}^3$ per hectare. Nevertheless, the stocks were in reasonably
good shape in much of the ducally owned woodlands of the *Forstamt*
throughout the period.

This allowed the ducal officials flexibility in choosing where to cut
wood. Where the mean yields appear to vary from year to year considerably, this is indeed simply a function of a change in the geographical
spread of woodcutting. In fact, wood yields in the same *ward* appear to
vary very little year on year. Particularly high annual average yields could
be achieved when foresters chose to fell just a few *morgen* in the highly
stocked Hirsauer woodland in the south of the *Forstamt*. However, it
could also be the case, as aross the years 1669–71, that forest officials

---

[85] HStAS A368L Bü 90; A557 Bü 87. The Asperg figure is based on the complaint that 12
morgen of woodland, admittedly described as 'bare and light', produced two wagonloads
per household head. A wagonload was at most a fathom, and there were nearly 100
households in the town.
[86] HStAS H107/8 Bd. 5.   [87] HStAS A302 Bd. 7233.

allocated for sale rather differently yielding stands within the same wood-land (in this case, the Pulverdinger Wald). The rather dramatic shift in yields between 1603–4 and 1604–5 is caused to a large extent by the concentration of cutting in 1603–4 in the relatively poorer yielding north-east of the *Forstamt*. Indeed, variations in yield geographically always seem to be more marked than variations in yield over time. Eglosheim ward was always relatively poor yielding, while at the opposite end of the *Forstamt*, Simmozheim was remarkably good. The latter reflected per-haps as much as sixty years' growth, on average, each time an area was felled, unless growth rates were particularly high in which case one might argue that woodmanship was highly effective. The Eglosheimer ward lay in that part of the *Forstamt* where coppicing cycles appear to have been relatively short, and to some degree the apparently lower 'yields' may reflect this rather than poor growth rates per hectare. Evidence presented later, however, will show that these shorter coppicing cycles may have been a response to local wood shortages themselves.

The evidence of widespread plundering of woodlands by desperate communities during times of warfare, along with the suggestively low yields from ducal woodlands during these periods, hint that persistently low yields to be found at the end of the 1640s and 1690s reflect real damage being done. The breakdown of authority did not facilitate the 'recovery' of the woodland, even if some scrub and bush was able to expand over abandoned fields. The lower post-war population levels may have allowed the ageing of some stocks, but those being felled in ducal woodlands in the 1680s were not noticeably different in age (if we infer this from estimated yield) from those being felled before the war. In short, the wars made little difference to forestry practice, but if they had any medium- to long-term effect on productivity, it was negative. This may have been true of mature timber too. Very, very few mature trees from before the Thirty Years War survived in the region around Leonberg according to a forester in the early twentieth century.[88] Equally, the availability of older well-stocked stands – if we can infer from the survey of one year, and anecdotal sources – appears to have been much greater in the mid-1580s than in any subsequent period. It appears to be the case that areas with more extensive upland woodland, such as the districts of Schorndorf and Tübingen, had rather higher yields of

[88] Pfister, *Der Leonberger Stadtwald*, p. 13. Schenk blamed low coppice yields in Hesse in the 1660s on the shade cast by a dense canopy grown up during the war period, but as we have seen this cannot have been the case in the *Forstamt* Leonberg. Schenk, *Waldnutzung*, p. 118.

underwood in ducal woodlands than the more densely populated *Forstamt* Leonberg.[89]

What might account for the decline in yield during wartime? Although foraging wild boar and deer were often blamed for low yields of every kind of crop, all the evidence points to a fall in their numbers, rather than a rise, during the Thirty Years' war. Livestock numbers, as we have seen in chapter 1, were remarkably steady at either end of the period, and were certainly not higher during the wars. This leaves two options: humans, or the coincidental change in climate that was detrimental to the growth rates of the most prevalent tree species. Certainly the years after around 1565 until the 1630s were rather poor weather years from a human perspective, while the last decades of the century present the temperature nadir of the 'Little Ice Age'.[90] This does not necessarily translate into poor growth conditions for trees, however, although growing seasons were almost certainly shorter in some of these years. Hollstein has carefully reconstructed tree-ring variation from a large sample of historic building timbers, including samples from Stuttgart, that show late sixteenth-century lows, poor growth in the Thirty Years' war period and again at the end of the century.[91] However, although this chronology of the growth of *individual trees* matches a suggested chronology of yield by area variation quite well, we should not confuse the two. The rapid growth increment of an individual tree will act to the detriment of neighbouring trees and may in fact depress yields measured by area. Even the wide decadal growth variations demonstrated by Hollstein are unlikely to provide a powerful explanation change in recorded yields measured by area.

There is plenty of evidence that peasants across Europe sought to exploit wood reserves during times of stress, whether for direct use as fuel or for sale. The soldiery too probably made fairly uninhibited use of local resources, and the region suffered especially from quartering of armies, with the Imperial troops under Gallas headquartered at Leonberg 1634–8, followed by Rosen's Swedish army in the mid-1640s, and French armies during the 1690s. In the year 1690–1, for example, a note in the forester's account book records the inhabitants of Markgröningen, Tamm and Oberriexingen cutting wood 'indiscriminately', just as they had in the 1640s, in response to the hard winter and the quartering of troops locally.[92] Many fines were levied, but were simply

---

[89] HStAS A302 Bds. 11576, 11297–8.
[90] Glaser, *Klimageschichte Mitteleuropas*; Glaser, *Klimarekonstruktion*.
[91] Hollstein, *Mitteleuropäische Eichenchronologie*.   [92] HStAS A302 Bd. 7234.

not paid. The hard inflationary years of 1622–4 similarly saw a leap in the number of fines for wood theft in Bietigheim.[93]

Records on mature and building timber are much more extensive in ducal sources because most wood supplied locally for construction was granted *gratis* out of communal woodland as a right to *Bürger* and required no record. It is only possible to estimate the exploitation of the woodlands from the demand, rather than the supply, side. However, communes were generally reluctant, and increasingly so, to dispose of mature timber by sale. Communal and municipal accounts from 1581 show that Rutesheim was the only place that felt able to sell wood beyond its *Markung*.[94] Some time soon after 1723, Malmsheim, Münklingen and Gerlingen were all explicitly noted as places that could make some money out of their wood reserves, Malmsheim in particular by selling pines. Mönßheim's woods had potential for exploitation, but were not so used.[95] People came from quite far afield, such as Markgröningen, to buy wood from the commune of Renningen in the 1560s. But the sums obtained from this woodland seem to be the equivalent of the value of twenty to thirty mature oaks each year between 1563 and 1566. Renningen had about 380 hectares of communal woodland, so sales should have made little impact on stocks.[96] By the end of the sixteenth century, the scale of building meant that the village authorities opened up a stone quarry because the woods were considered much 'exhausted'.[97] We must assume that numbers of mature trees must always have been low. Rutesheim's wood sales of 368 lb *heller* in 1581 may have included a timber component that saw between one and two hundred trees felled, but the 536 hectare communal woodland was probably well able to absorb this rate of felling. Other communes' wood sales were considerably less, although, as we have seen, they could comprise an important component of communal income in some cases.[98]

Of course, periods of pressure on communal finances could alter this pattern, as timber was an asset easily made liquid. Gebersheim provides accounts in the 1630s. In 1630 and 1631, the commune sold eighteen

---

[93] STABB Bh A1678. It is also unlikely that we need to reach to any other economic factors, such as labour availability to maintain coupes, for an explanation of low yields from woodland, that might be the result of the inability to thoroughly cut the area under consideration. The wood yield estimates come from small allotments of the forest bought up for the wood on them by individuals or communes. There would be no incentive to pay over the odds to secure access to a resource that was still relatively plentiful and cheap during these times, or that was not then adequately exploited.

[94] HStAS A572 Bü 45; see also A261 Bü 1126.   [95] HStAS A368L Bü 136.

[96] HStAS A227 Bü 1122.

[97] HStAS A572 Bü 69; Trugenberger, 'Malmsheim und Renningen', p. 141.

[98] See chapter 3. HStAS A572 Bü 45.

trees each year. This leapt to 108 trees in 1632, 45 in 1633, and 115 in 1634. In 1635 it had sunk to 51, followed by 23 in 1636 and 48 in 1637. Most of the trees sold appear to have been oaks. From 1636 the commune sold off much wood from the abandoned houses of dead *Bürger* that had no inheritors. In those places that had not actually been burned in the invasion of 1634, there was a glut of used timber from this source. Gebersheim had about 100 hectares of communal woodland, so the 'wartime' level of exploitation could have seen considerable erosion of the stock of mature trees if it continued over the 1640s. Gebersheim had staddles, but no stocks of building timber in 1583.[99] If they conformed to the government ordinances and had sixteen staddles per *morgen*, felling fifty trees per year would have eradicated all mature timber in a century, assuming of course that none grew to replace it. Such levels of exploitation did have the potential to diminish stocks in the long term if no measures were taken to ensure rejuvenation. Münchingen's woodland still only had forty standards per hectare in 1828, still under the required number of staddles stipulated in the forest ordinance of 1540, and other places were probably conforming no more closely to requirements.[100]

By 1730, tax returns in the *Amt* Leonberg speak of communal woodlands having only a handful of mature trees, usually oak, perhaps supplemented with beech, birch or fir. Nearly half of Renningen's woodland, some 160 hectares, was not even worth valuing, although fifty hectares of the Hardtwald presented a respectable fir wood. Gebersheim's woodland, like that of Höfingen, comprised a few 'small oaks' and a neglected birch and hazel underwood. Heimerdingen's pine wood was 'entirely declined', and apparently had only about twenty oak trees, some twenty-five hectares of birchwood and otherwise hazel and other scrub in an area of 275 hectares![101] The 1583 survey had already established the impression that in the centre and east of the *Forstamt*, mature timber was somewhat scarce and that communal woodlands in these districts were in a worse state than those owned by the Duke.[102] The levels of exploitation to which they were subject suggests that this pattern was only compounded over time, and by 1730 mature trees were extremely scarce in some districts. Only a few woodlands in the west of the *Forstamt* seem to have been readily able to provide large amounts of building timber over time to the local peasantry.

The woodlands were of course managed with a high priority being accorded to pasture, whether for domesticated livestock, or the beasts

---

[99] HStAS A583 Bds. 1–11; A59 Bü 13a.
[100] Gemeinde Münchingen, *Heimatbuch Münchingen*, p. 98.
[101] HStAS A261 Bü 1134.   [102] HStAS A59 Bü 13a.

of the chase. The latter were not creatures that favoured dense stands of woodland and their relative abundance in some areas of the *Forstamt* at particular points in time demonstrates the favourable conditions for their survival and multiplication. Only a small proportion of the woodland, perhaps as little as 7 per cent, was not subject to grazing rights, and those areas not exposed to the teeth of boar and deer were probably even smaller. Given this, it is not surprising that yields remained relatively low, well below, by the eighteenth century, the theoretical annual yields that such woodlands might be expected to produce. Without the widespread systematic sowing, mature trees would only be able to develop where deliberately spared within compartments by woodcutters, or in exposed districts, where the protection of a juniper or thorn bush allowed the sapling to evade the attentions of larger herbivores in the first few years of growth. Mature standards seem to have been a scattered presence in the landscape. There were few densely stocked stands. The evidence suggests that, during the late sixteenth century, and again in the early eighteenth century, yields were declining with increased exploitation. Equally, it seems that periods of economic stress and warfare may have brought about overexploitation (in the sense that previous annual yields of wood could not be sustained).

However, this picture of a 'forest of grazing' should not be overdrawn. If some local situations were especially bad by the early eighteenth century, evidence also points to very high productivity within managed coppicing regimes, especially those glimpses we have from the latter part of the sixteenth century. The ducal woodlands in particular, subject to far less year-in, year-out pressure for wood than the communal woodlands, may have had both relatively higher yields of underwood, and a much greater prevalence of maturer trees, than other districts. In fact, yields were not much if at all worse, and may have been substantially better, than the remaining areas still managed by these traditional regimes in the middle of nineteenth century![103] There is also a geographical pattern, with yields (and older stands of timber) progressively declining, very roughly speaking, as one moves from the south-west to the north-east. Again very roughly speaking, however, this mirrors the length of the coppicing cycle or age of stands that can be discerned from the survey of 1583. The geographical variation in yields from ducal woodlands does seem rather more than could be explained simply by differences in the age

---

[103] The average yield from *Mittelwald* in the *Amt* Leonberg in 1852 was given as 10 *Klafter* or 33.9 m^3 per *morgen*, somewhat less than Renningen's yields in the 1560s, and on a sixteen-year cycle, no better than the early eighteenth-century yields. Königlichen-statistichen-topographischen Bureau, *Beschreibung des Oberamts Leonberg*, p. 47.

of stands being cut in the different wards of the *Forstamt*, but this could well have been a contributory factor to the yield pattern. Evidence from closely managed coppicing cycles suggests that very high yields could in fact be achieved, approaching $10\,m^3$ per hectare *per annum*, up with the very best in northern Europe in both those times and in the twentieth century. We can only make sense of these practices, however, and their relative success in supplying local needs, in reference to demand. Thus far, this chapter has addressed the 'supply side'. We must now turn to an assessment of the needs that this supply was supposed to meet, and how they may have altered over time.

Calculating demand

We have established that wood is a differentiated product, and that its immediate availability from local sources was rather variable. Demand displayed the very same traits. One did not use the same part of or kind of a tree for firewood, construction, barrel-making or vineyard stakes. Demand will be quantified here according to the main kinds of use to which the wood was put, which roughly reflects the form of the wood demanded. Domestic fuel was the most important product. Agriculture required wood for equipment, fencing and, above all, vineyard stakes to support the vines. Artisanal demand was much lower, and again most significant for fuel. Building of course had very particular demands. These areas will be taken one by one so that the nature of local pressures, aggregate demand and chronological change are given their due place for each. With this information in hand, chapter 5 will outline how individuals and communities struggled to keep these demands and supply in balance through local and imported sources.

Calculating levels of demand for any product in the early modern period is a more hazardous exercise than the estimation of production levels, and more prone to wide margins of error. At least for the latter we often have estimates of yields or production figures assembled for the purposes of accounting or taxation. Very few households, however, left accounts of how much they *consumed*, and those few that did are generally extremely unrepresentative of the run of the general population. As a response to this, historians have tried to make rough estimates of consumption *per capita* or per household, and then used population change as a proxy of demand levels. For a fairly autarkic, subsistence-orientated economy, this would seem to make much sense. We have, however, already seen in chapter 2 that most households showed quite a high degree of market integration for many of their activities. Only a minority of households could have been self-supplying even in basic foodstuffs.

We can hardly imagine, given the year-to-year fluctuations in the prices of many basic goods, that demand for particular goods remained completely inelastic, as population-based models of consumption presuppose. However, although some tentative efforts have been made to calculate the price elasticity of demand for certain foodstuffs in early modern Europe, this has not been systematically attempted for any fuel or building material, even for the critical transition between wood and coal as a primary source of heat energy.

However, despite these reservations, the 'population' method of calculating demand is employed here. This can be justified on three grounds. Firstly, unlike with foodstuffs, there is little evidence of 'substitution' taking place between comparable goods when one became relatively more expensive. Coal was never an option as a fuel in Württemberg, and while stone became more prevalent as a foundation or for the ground floor of buildings during the sixteenth century, most construction was still from wood, although the species composition of wood used changed. Secondly, as we have seen, much wood was provided *gratis* or within communally determined limits that meant that the market price may have played a relatively weak role, though not a negligible one, in determining levels of demand. Thirdly, we have also seen in chapter 2 that the social structure of Württemberg, measured both by occupation and wealth distribution, appears to have remained remarkably stable over the period despite rapid shifts in population levels. This means that an estimated *per capita* consumption level of, for example, firewood, is unlikely to have altered greatly over time because of the rise or decline of particular social groups who had a propensity to consume more or less of the product.

Domestic fuel

Domestic fuel undoubtedly provided the greatest source of demand for wood, not only in Württemberg, but the entirety of the Holy Roman Empire, even in many industrialised regions. This remained the case in the 1850s, when firewood made up 70 per cent of the production of wood in the *Amt* Leonberg. Around 1600, it made up nearly 90 per cent of the wood sold from ducal woodlands in the *Forstamt* Leonberg.[104] However, if its primacy is not difficult to establish, the actual levels of demand are

---

[104] HStAS A302 Bds. 7221–2, 7302; compare with the district of Tübingen in the 1680s, A302 Bd.11576; KSB, *Beschreibung des Oberamts Leonberg*, p. 47. Schenk finds that 90 per cent of wood felled in the districts around Fulda in 1604 was used for firewood, and even in already coal-rich seventeenth-century England, Collins estimates that 90 per cent of wood felled was consumed as fuel. Schenk, *Waldnutzung*, pp. 93–4; Collins, 'The wood-fuel economy', p. 1109.

another thing altogether, partly because the great bulk of this wood was, of course, provided in the *Holzgaab* by communes. We know surprisingly little about the detail of its use. Was such fuel to be used for cooking or heating? How efficiently was it used? Cooking and heating are not mutually exclusive activities, of course. The sixteenth-century houses studied by Johannes Gromer show that in buildings with multiple rooms, a kitchen range where the fire was lit usually had a tile stove (or an iron stove in wealthier households by the end of the century) backed onto it in one or more adjacent chambers. These perhaps gave off the 'airless heat' with 'the smell of the red-hot material of which they are made', that gave headaches to contemporaries of Montaigne not used to German ways.[105] How often in a day this was lit or how long it remained burning, even for cooking, must remain however a matter for conjecture. Contemporaries seem to have considered firewood a serious matter in regard to heating rather than cooking. Other fuels may, in fact, have been used as substitutes by a few. Willi Boelcke noted the use of straw as fuel by the poor in Kornwestheim, although this must have been incredibly inefficient and seems more likely to have been used for cooking rather than heating.[106]

However, how much of the year saw heating? Can we transpose the comment of Lord Burghley, who had perhaps less need to be stingy with fuel than many, that 'soldiers in peace are like chimneys in summer'?[107] (Most houses in early modern Germany did not, in fact, have chimneys, but flues that guided smoke up into the attic.) The length of the 'heating season' doubtless varied from year to year depending on the climate, but seems, even in the continental climes of central Europe, to have been quite short. In the exceptionally cold year of 1658, one of the coldest of the century, it was noted that heating was still required in May in Leipzig, and remarkably, in July in Franken! Similarly, in 1671, a cold September that required heating was worthy of comment, while in 1683, the same was true of April. However, other years that were so warm that pasture was available all winter, such as 1530, may have required barely any heating at all.[108] When was heating for reasons of comfort, and when for survival? These topics await their historian.

There is a scattering of references to levels of firewood consumption from across the *Forstamt*. From these, I have come to a reasonable range of wood consumption for firewood of one to three fathoms per household, or $3.4–10\,m^3$ of stacked timber. This is still a large range, but if we took two

---

[105] Gromer, *Bäuerlichen Hausbaus*, pp. 50–1; Montaigne, *Essays*, p. 363.
[106] Boelcke, 'Bäuerlicher Wohlstand', p. 255.
[107] Cited in Hale, *War and society*, p. 99.
[108] Glaser, *Klimageschichte*, pp. 105, 156, 162, 167.

fathoms as an average, and mean household size to be some 4.25, we have a figure of 1.6 m^3 *per capita*. This is only just over 1 m^3 of solid timber, and is perhaps low compared with other regions of the German-speaking lands, where I have estimated slightly higher *per capita* consumption.[109] A variety of sources are agreed on these kind of levels. The *Holzgaab* of Renningen in the 1560s, for example, gave out a generous three to five fathoms. By the end of the century not every inhabitant received such an allowance and even three fathoms (about 10 m^3) appears to be fairly generous.[110] The *Holzgaab* of Leonberg comprised two to four fathoms per household in the 1580s and 1590s, with one fathom being granted to those households either not eligible, or where the usual recipient was unable to cut their own wood. In Friolzheim, in the relatively well-wooded west, the grant amounted to only one fathom and 100 faggots (equivalent, but quicker-burning, to two fathoms at the most). Payments to municipal officials in Leonberg ranged from one to four fathoms, although often such payments were connected to wood used for work purposes.[111] In Stuttgart, there was a limit on wood storage of three fathoms.[112] The most direct evidence comes from the wood given to inmates of Leonberg's hospital between the 1580s and 1620s, although these elderly or infirm individuals are perhaps unusual, and, living in the hospital, did not have the same heating regime as those in houses. All of the hospital records show people receiving one fathom *per annum*, irrespective of whether the recipients were an individual or a couple.[113] The account books of the forestry administration provide similar evidence. Officials, in theory at least, were not to sell any wood that was destined for re-sale, and were to limit the size of transactions to that wood which was of proven need to the household. Once we eliminate wealthy buyers (such as councillors in Stuttgart, or members of the nobility) or those clearly buying for their business (saltpeterers), the 247 identifiable buyers between 1563 and 1691 bought, on average, 3.3 fathoms, with a median purchase of two fathoms and mode of one. Some of these buyers were still probably using the wood for trade purposes, and 'bulk' buyers that have been eliminated from the sample above (such as 'the citizenry of Leonberg') were also buying small amounts relative to the size of the population.[114]

[109] Warde, 'Forests, energy and politics', p. 590.

[110] HStAS A227 Bü 1122; A572 Bü 69.

[111] HStAS A572 Bü 41; StAL Bürgermeisterrechnungen 1588–94; A59 Bü 13a. The Leonberg midwife's allowance of four fathoms in 1582 (which may have been linked to heating water) was cut to two in 1612. More generously, Magstadt gave out eight fathoms per farmstead in 1580, but in practice this could be split between up to three households. HStAS A227 Bü 483.

[112] HStAS A572 Bü 29.   [113] HStAS A572 Bü 25.   [114] HStAS A302 Bds. 7221–35.

These figures can be compared with others gathered from central and western Europe across the early modern period. In 1789, for example, the Württemberger official von Rochow estimated that a poor household needed to spend 5–8.5 fl. *per annum* on heating and lighting. This was somewhat less than the price of a fathom in the towns.[115] A range of estimates from other sources gives a range of *per capita* consumption from as low as $0.4 \, m^3$ (the poor in Prussia ca 1800) to $3.9 \, m^3$ (urban households in the Palatinate in the 1770s).[116] It seems reasonable to suppose a *per capita* consumption explicitly for fuel at the lower end of the range, of about $1.2 \, m^3$ of solid timber. Indeed, such an approach minimises the risk of overestimating the extent of 'wood shortage'.

We have already seen that the population of the *Forstamt* was around 24,000 in the mid-1540s, 27,000 by 1598 and 35,000 by 1634. By the 1650s, the population had probably dipped below 14,000, recovering to around 20,000 by the end of the 1670s, and perhaps 27,000 by the beginning of the eighteenth century, back where it had been a century before.[117] This, assuming that *per capita* fuel consumption remained constant, allows estimates of the level of demand for firewood at these points in time. If consumption was around $1.2 \, m^3$ *per capita per annum*, then we have figures of $28,800 \, m^3$ for the 1540s, and so forth for the years where population estimates exist. These are shown in table 4.3.

These figures can now be related to estimates for the overall productivity of the woodland, of which there was about 14,000 hectares, as measured by Kieser in 1682. If overall the annual average increment was about $2–3 \, m^3$ per hectare, then the *Forstamt* could have produced $28,000–42,000 \, m^3$ *per annum*. We are very much at the mercy of the margins for error here: but this would struggle to cover the demand for domestic fuel during the period. However, much of the woodland was not rigorously exploited. If, at most, 1 per cent of the ducal woodlands were felled in any one year, we might estimate that, if that wood were managed on a thirty-year cutting cycle, over two-thirds of those 2,300 hectares were never effectively used for firewood. Similarly, large areas of the monastic woodlands do not seem to have been used for sales beyond the *Holzgaab* accorded to subjects of those monasteries.

Table 4.3 is based upon estimates of demand and productivity having removed from the area of the woodland about 3,000 hectares that do not seem to have been open to regular exploitation for fuel. The range is still very large, of course, but nevertheless provides us with some benchmarks.

[115] Cited in Troeltsch, *Die Calwer Zeughandlungskompagnie*, p. 234.
[116] Gleitsmann, 'Und immer wieder', p. 202; Allmann, *Der Wald*, pp. 55–6.
[117] See Introduction.

Table 4.3 *Demand and supply of firewood in the* Forstamt *Leonberg, 1545–1700*

Year	Population (thousands)	Demand (1 m³ stacked)	Demand (1.85 m³ stacked)	Supply (2 m³ per ha stacked)	Supply (4 m³ per ha stacked)
1545	24	24	44.4	21.8	43.7
1598	27	27	50.0	21.8	43.7
1634	35	35	64.8	21.8	43.7
1655	14	14	25.9	21.8	43.7
1676	20	20	37.0	21.8	43.7
1700	27	27	50.0	21.8	43.7

We must remember that supply and demand were not evenly spread over the region. At the low estimates of demand and supply, the *Forstamt* would have been unable to supply itself by the 1540s. At the lower rate of demand, but higher rate of woodland productivity, problems would have been emerging by at least the 1620s. At the higher estimate for demand, even the higher rate of productivity would have struggled to supply the *Forstamt* by the 1540s. It has been argued above that yields appear to have been somewhat higher in the sixteenth century than at any later point, and by 1700 yield levels were probably closer to 2 m³ than 4 m³ per hectare. Shortages never seem to have emerged in the west of the *Forstamt*, but imports were necessary for much of the east, centre and north of the region by at least 1583. Certainly, as will be discussed further in chapter 5, the region probably ceased to be self-sufficient in firewood at some point between the 1540s and 1590s, and again by the end of the seventeenth century after more 'favourable' circumstances brought about by the Thirty Years' war.

Wood on the land – fencing and vineyards

Wood was not only a standing element in the landscape; it was used, literally, to stake out claims and foster particular uses. Fences and hurdles either protected large tracts from the attention of grazing animals, divided the fields from the commons or demarcated smaller gardens and orchards. The open-field system of course meant that fencing was still relatively scarce, and forestry officials were clearly reluctant, from the evidence of the account books, to grant wood for these purposes. Indeed the lack of fencing was another of the labour-saving implications of this system. Other 'woody' material such as very young switches were also used to bind sheaves and were collected in their tens of thousands before harvest time.

However, fencing receives relatively few mentions in the sources, perhaps as a use whose importance is too self-evident, whilst being far less important than fuel. The ducal woods in the Botnanger ward were apparently 'severely lightened' by grants of wood for cartwrights and fence-posts in 1583, and the wooden palisade that surrounded Renningen was replaced by a stone wall in the late sixteenth century.[118] Disputes over the fences that surrounded the cultivated fields to protect them from the invasive attentions of woodland-dwelling beasts such as boar and deer bring this form of wood consumption most frequently to our attention, but the overall demand is rather difficult to quantify. These game fences were regulated by the forest ordinances, though more with the intention of protecting the game from injury than preserving wood, or indeed, crops. A map of the Stuttgarter forest of 1678 shows them as being made of high fenceposts with cross-slats, rather than being palisades.[119] They could be a considerable length. Rutesheim requested nearly seven kilometres in 1573, and a group of settlements in the centre of the *Forstamt* some thirty-three kilometres in 1581.[120] Although, as with much construction, there was a preference for using old, rather decrepit trees, the numbers needed were considerable. Four oaks provided 200 fenceposts for the ducal sheep station at Bergheim in 1603; seventy years later, six healthier specimens, 900 posts.[121] But with dozens of kilometres of large-scale fencing, often seven or eight feet high, we must suppose that hundreds of trees were required. These, however, were long-lasting features and indeed were permitted only after extensive wrangling with the authorities. In 1607 the forester estimated that simply the work of fencing of Weissach and Flacht's fields would take ten to twenty years. Taken as a component of annual demand, fencing must have been only a very small proportion.[122]

A more regularised demand was probably that for vineyard poles, used to stake the vines. Bietigheim bought 200,000 poles *per annum* around 1570.[123] The two Ingersheims received some eighty-six cartloads of

---

[118] HStAS A59 Bü 13a; A572 Bü 69.
[119] Württembergischen Geschichts- und Altertumsverein, *Stuttgart im Spiegel*, p. 119.
[120] HStAS A227 Bü 1125 and 1133.   [121] HStAS A368 Bü 13.
[122] HStAS A227 Bü 1150.
[123] STABB Bh B540. This amounts to 600–700 stakes per *morgen*, when the total number of vinestocks per *morgen* appears to have been 3,000–4,000; although some authors give a much higher figure for the number of stakes, implying multiple stakes per vinestock. This practice was also followed in the *Amt* Brackenheim. Döbele-Carlesso, *Weinbau*, pp. 54, 131, 199.

wood for the thirty-six hectares of vineyard leased by the Duke of Württemberg there.[124] Vineyard poles were generally small, up to seven foot long but no more than an inch square at the sharp end, according to an ordinance of 1552.[125] However, were Bietigheim's practice imitated across the *Forstamt*, the demand for poles would have been very substantial, maybe as much as a third of the demand for firewood across the region by 1630, and probably a higher proportion before. These figures may conceal overlaps. It is difficult to believe that poles would simply be discarded. They may well, like the old vines themselves, have gone onto the fire on replacement. Indeed, the timing of the drawing of the stakes, November, would fit very well this being the 'heating' season. Bietigheim was getting its vineyard poles, cut from pines, from rafters operating out of the Black Forest as early as 1570, and this may have provided a significant stimulus to the development of that trade.

Artisanal wood consumption

As has been emphasised so many times, wood provided the medium of most aspects of material culture in the 'wooden age'. This could be directly as provided by those workers who fashioned the very means of everyday life, whether builders, carpenters and joiners, cartwrights, coopers, glaziers, joiners, rakemakers, saddlers, saltpeterers or woodturners. Others required wood to process their goods, such as blacksmiths and other kinds of smith, bakers and barber-surgeons. The prevalence of such artisanal labour in the region is difficult to assess before the early eighteenth century, when tax lists provide detailed occupational data for several of the *Ämter*, and a valuation of their economic activity. What this might mean in terms of wood consumed is harder to assess, as we do not know the turnover rates of goods. It is clear that much of the artisanal work involved old materials and the patching up of gear and buildings, rather than the manufacture or use of new materials.

Those who fashioned wood directly as part of their labour seem to have accounted for a relatively small amount of demand. The cartwright was the most ubiquitous of these, whose work was described in the handicrafts ordinance of 1579. Only smaller villages had no cartwright in the 1720s, and it appears to be the most geographically widespread trade in the account books. They made wagons and carts, working on wheels, axles,

---

[124] STABB Bh A1678.

[125] This was in fact a slight lengthening on a previous order of 1540. That such matters were legislated for shows the importance of the trade in stakes. 200,000 poles amounts to about 226 m^3 of solid timber. Reyscher, *SWG*, Bd.XII, pp. 134–5, 826.

'ladders' (the frame of cross-pieces attached to the side of the wagon to allow loads to be piled up), harrows, sledges for hauling manure, mill-frames, and the poles, beds and bodies of vehicles.[126] Perhaps even more important were ploughs, although only a small minority of households owned either a plough or a wagon, and they were probably replaced only rarely. In 1585–6, only 30 fl. was spent by cartwrights on buying wood out of the ducal woodlands, nearly all on naves (wheelhubs) and spokes, the parts most likely to wear out or break.[127] This is a miserly sum, even if much of the wood was obtained from communal woodlands. New products, in fact, were a very considerable investment, mostly for the iron that they contained. Local practice, however, did not seem to assist durability. Naves were made out of oak, occasionally beech, and in one instance birch – not the most hard-wearing of woods.[128] Recycling and combating wear and tear seems to have been the stock-in-trade of these craftsmen.

Assessing the turnover of barrels is almost impossible for cooping, a widespread trade as one would expect in a wine-producing region. Relatively large numbers of coopers congregated in the towns: nine in Bietigheim in 1736, five in Markgröningen and five in Leonberg in the 1720s. Leonberg had no less than twelve in 1568 and nine in 1575 at the height of the wine trade. Even villages with fairly small acreages of vineyard, such as Rutesheim or Hirschlanden, also had a cooper in the 1720s, although these were considerably poorer than their urban counter-parts, as was the case with most artisanal trades.[129] Indeed, Michael Bilfinger, the 'castle-cooper' of Leonberg who provided the storage for sharecropped and tithed wine, was one of the richest men of the town in the early seventeenth century.[130] It is likely, however, that the innkeepers who stored wine or other drinks aimed for a high turnover and had a relatively small number of barrels and casks, and purchases of wood for hoops or barrel-staves appear to be quite small. In years of very abundant harvests, there were not enough barrels to store all of the wine. The Renningen account-books of the 1560s show coopers coming over ten miles, from Ditzingen and Markgröningen, to obtain particular trees for their barrels.[131]

Carpenters and joiners appear frequently too, as one would expect. Indeed, it is something of a surprise that there is a group of settlements in the centre of the *Forstamt*, around the valley of the Glems, that had no carpenters in the 1720s. Carpenters did the rougher, bulkier work of the

[126] HStAS A58 Bü 26; A261 Bü 1004, 1134, 1635; STABB A1952.
[127] HStAS A302 Bd. 7221.   [128] HStAS A302 Bds. 7221–35.
[129] HStAS A261 Bü 1004, 1134, 1635; A572 Bü 37b; STABB A1952; Trugenberger, 'Der Leonberger Raum', p. 89; Trugenberger, *Zwischen Schloß und Vorstadt*, Prosopographie.
[130] Trugenberger, *Zwischen Schloß und Vorstadt*, Prosopographie.
[131] HStAS A227 Bü 1122; Glauser, 'Wein, Wirt, Gewinn 1580'.

building trade, while joiners dealt with interiors. Urban settlements had several carpenters, as did a few of the larger villages that may have made some money in trading wood – Renningen, Malmsheim and Rutesheim – in the 1720s.[132] Joiners appear a little less frequently. Carpenters were included in the governmental handicrafts ordinance of 1579 but got their own in 1590, partly on government suspicion of shoddy work.[133] There was often a 'municipal' or 'communal' carpenter who assessed building needs and grants out of the communal woodland and performed the basic shaping work, in Renningen, receiving the left-overs as part-payment.[134] Joiners appeared purchasing beech, oak, birch, aspen and pine. Finer ware, such as chairs, tables, bowls and beakers, was the province of woodturners, but these appeared far less frequently, limited to Leonberg, Bietigheim, and the city of Stuttgart. Their demand for trees – oak, beech, birch, aspen, ash, alder, cherry and sycamore – amounted to only a handful of trees in any year.[135]

Larger consumers were those who used wood as fuel as part of their trade. The leading bulk buyers of the seventeenth century were saltpeterers who obtained their wood at knock-down prices to cheapen the manufacture of gunpowder in the century of iron. In the years where books survived, sales at knock-down prices to saltpeterers peaked at 427 m^3 in 1680, still an insignificant amount on a regional scale even if the producers were buying up large amounts of wood outside of the ducal woodlands.[136]

Out of the array of wood-burning trades, ranging across smiths (black-, weapon-, gold-, copper-, lock-), bakers, barber-surgeons, brickmakers, cutlers, dyers, potters, founders, innkeepers and stove-setters, it is the bakers, barber-surgeons and smiths that stand out. Bakers very frequently appear as purchasers of wood in account books, and no village was without at least one, if not several, in the 1720s. Markgröningen had no less than twenty, Bietigheim fifteen, and Leonberg a more modest seven.[137] For baking, the ovens would be fired, often using fairly small diameter wood or old vinestocks, the ashes swept out, and the dough would then be set in, with an adjacent slower-burning wood-fire keeping the heat.[138] Sometimes a communal bakery was leased out, with the commune overseeing both upkeep of the capital, and setting prices. In addition to his *Gaabholz*, for example, the communal baker of Warmbronn was permitted just over 20 m^3 and 300 faggots of additional firewood at a special low price.[139] Communal baking was far more efficient in terms of wood

---

[132] HStAS A261 Bü 1004, 1134, 1635; STABB Bh A1952.   [133] HStAS A58 Bü 26.
[134] HStAS A572 Bü 69.   [135] HStAS A302 Bds. 7221–35.
[136] HStAS A302 Bd. 7222 and 7231.
[137] HStAS A261 Bü 1004, 1134, 1635; STABB Bh A1952.
[138] Roeck, *Bäcker*, pp. 153 and 183.   [139] HStAS A572 Bü 56.

use than home-baking or a scattering of bakeries, and when Gerlingen faced deterioration of its woodlands in 1612, foresters suggested repeatedly at *Vogt-Gerichten* that a solution would be the construction of a communal bakery.[140] If *all* of the grain needs of the region were consumed as bread (and much may have been consumed in other forms, such as gruel), statistics from Bavaria suggest that the wood consumed could have been very high indeed. Around 1600, the figure would have stood at around $9,000\,\mathrm{m}^3$, and would have been set to rise up until 1630. Even a much smaller figure would have helped to tip the region into a wood-supply deficit, compounded by the fact that the scarcity of wood was not reflected in the price of bread because of favourable grants to bakers. It is no surprise to read in 1583 of Eberdingen, where 'they have to give over the year to the baker and barber about 100 wagons of firewood; it is a great harm to their woodlands'.[141]

Barber-surgeons may seem unlikely consumers of wood, but their work stretched beyond cutting hair, trimming beards and shaving to general medical work and dentistry, and before the Thirty Years War, to stewardship of the village bath-house.[142] Thereafter this institution seems to have gone into something of a decline in the more rural districts of the *Amt* Leonberg, but in the 1720s, Leonberg could still boast four, Markgröningen five, Bietigheim four, and even a populous village like Gerlingen four.[143] Wood was required for heating water. In the autumn of 1565, when the barber of Renningen, Veit Humel, went to the ducal authorities claiming the right to free offcuts from timber-felling denied him by village authorities, he claimed that he needed thirty fathoms a year plus faggots to run the baths on Wednesdays and Saturdays. The *Vogt* compromised at half a fathom a week, but this still meant that in total perhaps $100\,\mathrm{m}^3$ *per annum* was consumed by the bath-house, and as late as the early eighteenth century, barber-surgeons may have required up to $2,000\,\mathrm{m}^3$ *per annum* for fuel.[144]

---

[140] HStAS A227 Bü 1154.

[141] These figures are based on calculations of the requirements of baking in Augsburg bakeries taken from Roeck, and utilise some of the price series from Elsas. Augsburg bakeries might be expected to be more efficient than those in this region as they operated on a larger scale, but the estimate is almost certainly too large because of the use of alternative fuels such as vinestocks and broom for firing the ovens. Roeck, *Bäcker*, p. 180; Elsas, *Umriß einer Geschichte der Preise und Löhne*; HStAS A59 Bü 13a.

[142] See Sander, *Handwerkschirugen*.

[143] HStAS A261 Bü 1004, 1134, 1635; STABB A1952.

[144] HStAS A227 Bü 1122. Surprisingly, a shortage of wood for the bath-house is given as one reason for its decline in the 1470s in Bietigheim! In 1550, the newly leased bath-house provided a bath – without a bathing robe – for 4 hlr, or a tenth of a labourer's daily wage, to an adult male. The establishment also provided massage and bleeding. STABB Bh B545 Bd. 2; B594.

This is probably rather more, in fact, than was used by blacksmiths. The everyday work of these individuals, who like bakers were to be found in every village in the 1720s and probably throughout the period, was maintenance rather than manufacture, and in some cases to act as a horse-doctor.[145] The largest part of a year's work was taken up shoeing and re-shoeing horses. Items such as ploughshares, pitchforks, scythes, sickles and shovels (if of iron) had to be imported from elsewhere. It is something of a mystery that charcoalers received only two mentions in local records.[146] It may be that the trade left no records, but as charcoal tends not to travel well and was probably made locally if required, it seems that demand was rather low. Other smiths, such as nail- or locksmiths, seem to have been confined to a few of the towns, and perhaps acted as petty iron traders as much as artisans.[147]

Potters, working on kilns and stoves, and tilemakers, manufacturing tiles, bricks and lime, operated on a larger scale. Potters were only town-based in the early eighteenth century and ceramics were probably for the most part imported. Tilemakers could be found in Leonberg, Bietigheim, Zuffenhausen, Markgröningen and Tiefenbronn just inside Baden. In the last, the four hectares of woodland set aside for both the tilemaker, and the baker and barber-surgeon is not suggestive of a huge demand, though one more marked than any other local trade.[148] Tanners required the bark of oaks for their trade, and indeed it was a stipulation of the forest ordinance of 1567 that bark should be stripped before felling for these purposes. The forest warden of Feuerbach in 1612 found himself in hot water for having failed to do so, but how widespread this practice really was is impossible to tell.[149] Tanners could be found in all the larger towns and Ditzingen, but like other trades who required wood, such as saddlers for saddle-frames, or butchers for their work-banks, demand was insignificant in relation to the productive powers of the forest.[150]

Building

Buildings were primarily made of wood, despite the efforts of ducal building ordinances to encourage the use of stone for lower storeys. The wood

---

[145] HStAS A261 Bü 1004, 1134, 1635; STABB A1952.
[146] HStAS A572 Bü 17; StAM Spitalrechnungen H73. In the first a witness in court in 1481 described some Eltingers attempting to buy wood for charcoaling from Leonberg in 1475. In the second wood was sold for charcoal by the hospital of Markgröningen, possibly to the town tilemaker.
[147] HStAS A261 Bü 1004, 1134, 1635; STABB A1952.
[148] HStAS A261 Bü 1004, 1134, 1635; STABB A1952; HStAS A368 Bü 5, 56.
[149] HStAS A227 Bü 1154.
[150] HStAS A261 Bü 1004, 1134, 1635; STABB A1952; HStAS A302 Bds. 7221–35.

Table 4.4 *Estimated number of buildings in the* Forstamt *Leonberg,*
1525–1700

Date	Estimated no. of *Bürger*	Estimated no. of buildings
1525	3,900	4,680
1545	5,300	6,360
1598	6,000	7,200
1634	7,800	9,400
1700	6,000	7,200

ranged from great blocks that formed a foundation, to large spars and rafters
for half-timbering, and the smaller cross-beams and wattle that filled the
gaps. Half-timbering was the regional fashion. We are in a position to
estimate the numbers of buildings in the *Forstamt* in the early 1630s,
1650s and in the 1730s, as tax returns from those years record their number.
In 1629–34, data from thirty-two settlements shows that 4,543 *Bürger* and
widows had 5,523 buildings at their disposal.[151] At this 'rate' of about 1.2
buildings per *Bürger* the actual number of buildings in the *Forstamt* would
have been about 9,400. We can thus extrapolate for the estimated populations over the period, although there is, of course, no guarantee that such a
ratio remained stable. In fact, it varied regionally, with urban centres in
particular having fewer buildings per *Bürger*, and as partitioning of houses
increased as the population grew, the ratio was undoubtedly somewhat
higher in the first half of the sixteenth century. Limited evidence suggests
that there were rather fewer buildings per household in the early eighteenth
century than a century earlier – which of course says nothing about the
size of those buildings. The extent of destruction in periods of warfare,
especially outside of the larger towns, meant that major reconstruction
was necessary (though possibly using old timbers). This also implies that
the number of buildings probably also fell with the decline in population. As
late as 1707, Eglosheim lost thirty buildings to French troops quartered
there. The small town of Hoheneck still only had twenty-one inhabitable
buildings after the Thirty Years' war in 1672, and this before the French
invasion.[152]

These somewhat speculative figures give a clear enough indication of
the rising demand for timber irrespective of the rate of replacement. But
how much wood did a 'building' require? This, to be precise, would need

[151] HStAS A261 Bü 727, 891, 1126, 1470, 1634.
[152] HStAS A261 Bü 1003, 1004; Burckhardt, *Eglosheim*, p. 155; Stein, Bolay and Felden,
'Die Katastrophe', p. 119.

to take both construction techniques and the species of tree involved into account. The first half of the sixteenth century saw the abandonment in south-west Germany of pillar-supported roofing employing a large, single frame, and a move towards separate frame construction for each storey, increasing the number of two-storey buildings.[153] Jutta Hoffmann's work on the whole of Baden-Württemberg has shown an increased propensity to use pine in construction, with oak ceasing to be the wood used for over half of building timbers around 1550.[154] Fir seems to have been used rather more than pine out of the *Forstamt* woodlands, and was also increasingly imported up until the Thirty Years' war. Generally speaking, rather more of such coniferous trees would be used in building than if oak or beech trees were used for similar work.

Estimates of the needs of construction can be derived both from the work of researchers on historical buildings, and grants by communes or ducal officials recorded in account books and court records. For example, 150 oak and fir trees were required for the new barn in Höfingen in 1544; four oaks were used by the steward of the ducal sheep station at Bergheim for a new kitchen in 1586; and before reducing the allowance in the 1580s, Renningen allowed '7, 8 or 10 trunks' to be cut for building. Glattbachers were restricted to sixteen firs for a barn or house, and 'enough' (*zimblich*) large timbers, presumably of oak. Leonbergers got twenty to thirty trees in 1583 and had to buy anything else from the rafters.[155] Olivia Hochstrasser has noted grants for buildings to peasants in Hohenzollern, south of Württemberg. These allowed for ten to forty-five *stumpen* for a barn, and thirty for a small house or cottage. A *stumpen* usually designates an old decrepit trunk. Bergheim recorded similar figures in the 1580s, with thirty-two oaks for a new house and eight for a pig sty.[156] Thirty oaks were allowed for the construction of buildings at the other end of Germany, in the *Amt* Schwalenberg in Lippe around 1600, and twenty to sixty tree trunks in an outline ordinance for the Harz region in 1654.[157] We have already seen that sales of timber for building out of both ducal woodlands across the seventeenth century and Renningen's woodlands in the 1560s appear to have been rather small. Certainly the latter suggests that peasants did not buy much timber

---

[153] See Gromer, *Bäuerlichen Hausbaus*; Eitzen, 'Zur Geschichte des südwestdeutschen Hausbaues'; Hochstrasser, *Ein Haus und seine Menschen*, p. 19.

[154] Hoffmann, 'Jahrringchronologien', p. 98.

[155] HStAS A368 Bü 23; A302 Bd. 7221; A572 Bü 69; A368L Bü 90; A59 Bü 13a.

[156] HStAS A368 Bü 13; Hochstrasser, *Ein Haus und seine Menschen*, p. 44.

[157] Schäfer, '*Ein Gespenst geht um*', p. 21; Steinsiek, *Nachhaltigkeit auf Zeit*, p. 146; see the similar figures for quite extensive house building in northern Germany in Timm, *Waldnutzung*, pp. 74–6.

beyond that permitted to them *gratis* out of communal woodlands.[158] If as little as thirty trees were required 'per building', then the 5,000 or so acquired between 1525 and 1630 would have needed a supply of around 1,500 trees *per annum*. At the 'staddle-setting' rate stipulated in the forest ordinances, this equates to felling around thirty hectares a year, assuming some fifty-one trees per hectare. A well-stocked century-old stand of beech trees without external disturbance can contain 400 trees, although this certainly was not matched in the region at this time.[159] At a rate of 0.002 per cent of the wooded acreage being felled *per annum*, we can see how easily this demand, in theory, could have been met. Indeed, a substantially higher demand would not be expected to make any kind of a significant impact, even if buildings were replaced or extended far more often than the oldest surviving house in Gerlingen today. That was built in 1417–18 and had its gable replaced in 1707.[160] Yet the 'right' timbers for particular buildings were clearly in short supply by the middle of the sixteenth century in some areas of the *Forstamt*. Building timber was being imported from the Black Forest via Bietigheim in the fifteenth century. In 1520 the Habsburg garrison on Asperg got its firewood from local woodlands and its building timber from the Enz rafters who landed at Bissingen. In the 1540s and 1550s ducal projects imported very large amounts of timber into the region. Sawmills at Vaihingen an der Enz and Bietigheim assisted the processing of this supply.[161] However, such shortages were no impediment, it seems, to building. The villages with the highest number of buildings *per capita* were in the timber-scarce east of the *Forstamt*.

A balance of forces?

Much of the analysis in this chapter is necessarily speculative, but the estimates of wood supply and consumption allow broad parameters to be set that are solidly founded on the data to hand. This demonstrates at the very least that it is possible to move beyond anecdote and the value-laden claims of competing interests in assessing the state of the early modern woodlands. The woodlands of the *Forstamt* Leonberg were clearly areas where the interests of those seeking pasture, whether for beasts of the chase or domestic herds, played a large part in dictating the form and management of the woodland. As described in chapter 3, government did not stint on initiatives to enhance the productivity of the woodland, but

---

[158] HStAS A302 Bds. 7221–35; A227 Bü 1122.
[159] Assmann, *The principles of forest yield study*, p. 85.
[160] Stadt Gerlingen, *Gerlingen*, p. 64.
[161] See chapter 5. HStAS J1 Nr. 141g; STABB Bh B 2; see also Scheifele, 'Alte Sagemühle'.

there is little sign of these being vigorously implemented. Yet they certainly had some, regionally circumscribed, effect. What evidence we have suggests yield decline during the latter part of the sixteenth century and in the early eighteenth century, and possibly more dramatic falls during the periods of the seventeenth century when the region was ravaged by warfare. Nevertheless, carefully managed underwood yields *could* be impressive. Although demand for poles for artisanal activity or building was fairly limited, and in theory well within the capacity of the localities to produce, staddles and standards were not densely set, but also not consumed locally at any great rate either. From an early point in the sixteenth century, imports became the norm for some parts of the *Forstamt*.

While there is significant margin for error in estimates of consumption levels, the cumulative effect of demand for firewood, largely for domestic purposes but also for baking and bathing, would have been pushing the limits of even a fairly productive forestry regime by the 1540s. Calculations here would suggest an annual consumption of at the very least $70,000 \, m^3$ of stacked cordwood for fuel and agricultural purposes being required around 1600.[162] Underwood production is unlikely to have topped $40,000 \, m^3$ on the most optimistic estimate. Imports were certainly necessary for the region, taken as a whole, by the 1580s, and probably some time before this, not just because of local bottlenecks, although some localities could subsist on local supplies. In fact, such is the gap between these two figures, one suspects that the poorer sections of the population were going short on firewood, reducing the demand figure. Given the relative medium-term stability of the population over the second half of the sixteenth century, an earlier date is perhaps more reasonable for the beginnings of importation.

Thus there was a wood shortage, in the sense that the necessary supplies could not be obtained locally, in some parts of the region by the middle of the sixteenth century. Nevertheless, while peasants understood well the need to set up coppicing cycles, protect woods from grazing animals, and to set aside and sow trees to provide timber, there is very little sign of 'adaptation' to local conditions. If there was any response to increasing shortage, it was nearly always to cut allowances or increase prices. Thus even an agrarian regime that was attuned to a certain 'ecology' and the need for flexibility showed very little ability to adapt to any notional 'carrying capacity'. There is no strong evidence of either the acreage of woodland, or the regime to which it was subject, altering

---

[162] This would assume around $45,000 \, m^3$ for domestic firewood, $15,000 \, m^3$ for vineyard stakes, and $10,000 \, m^3$ for bakers, tilemakers, barber-surgeons and blacksmiths.

radically across the entire period. Despite the expansion of population, the late fifteenth and sixteenth centuries were not a great age of clearance to assist the expansion of arable fields and vineyards, although some clearance did go on.

Did this end up, however, with crisis as increased demand clawed at an inelastic supply of resources? There were assuredly problems, which were not only the effects of histrionic rhetoric. But whether a 'crisis' existed depended on whether one had access to or an entitlement to wood, whether through the medium of rights accorded to the poor gatherers of deadwood, recipients of the *Holzgaab* or reliance on purchases in the market. It should be clear by now that the market must have had a significant impact on the supply of all kinds of wood throughout the period. It is to the operation of, and arguments about, forms of entitlement in access to wood that the next chapter is devoted.

5 The two ecologies

In the 'Wooden Age' nearly everything involved wood at some point in its production.[1] There was no iron without charcoal or wood for pit-props and pickaxe handles, no glass or soap without potash, no transport of anything above a minimal bulk without carts, sledges, wagons and rivercraft. The previous three chapters have identified the kinds of wood that people needed, the uses to which woodland was generally put, and the manner in which such flows were regulated. This chapter will develop these themes further, with two areas particularly in mind. One is the spatial distribution of the production and consumption of wood, the form of exchange involved, and the identification of what ecologists would call 'sources' (points of origin) and 'sinks' (points of consumption) of the resource.[2] Tracing these patterns over time will allow us to address questions of the nature of economic development, and the causes of landscape and environmental change. Understanding these processes, however, requires more than the mapping of material flows. It is also essential to comprehend how people thought about such movements and exchanges in a world strongly shaped by both institutional imperatives, and a straightforward fear of suffering, illness and mortality. In the cold winter of 1743, for example, the ducal authorities attempted to enforce the mandatory limit of two 'wood days' for cutting and collection in the *Vorstwald* of Bietigheim. But the snow lay deep on the ground that December, and local authorities objected. How could elderly people with no horses or carts get their desperately needed firewood in the time allotted? Many issues were involved here. The elderly received a free grant of wood from the commune, and presumably could not afford to purchase their supplies on the market. Nor did the town provide it for them by purchase or paying labourers to cut and haul it, although in

---

[1] The expression comes from Sombart. Sombart, *Der moderne Kapitalismus*, Bd. II.2, p. 1138.
[2] On these terms, see Forman, *Land mosaics*, p. 39.

Leonberg, for example, the infirm could have their wood cut for them.[3] The ducal authorities wished to protect the wood reserves, but also limit the potential for crime and poaching by making supervision of cutting easier. The bad weather made everything more fraught, indeed, this came after a run of bad years including the spectacular, once-in-a-millennium, cold of 1740.[4] Movement and flow of resources was governed in the end by the legitimacy accorded by the populace or the authorities to a particular way of doing things, and thus an understanding of notions of how resources should be justly allocated is crucial to understanding how they actually were obtained. If people did not get what they thought they should, they often stole it; an attitude that peaked in the often exceptionally bitter 'forest wars' of the early nineteenth century that left bad blood between foresters and peasants for many decades afterwards.[5]

This chapter will thus proceed by examining the form of resource flows, embracing imports and exports, types of exchange, and the significant issue of accounting for wood 'bound-up' in an already processed form in materials that were imported to the region such as iron or salt. The second half of the chapter will focus on how people thought about and managed these flows, the claims made and entitlements allotted to resources, whether legal or extra-legal. Together these sections will provide a quantifiable survey of flows, of potential disturbance and change, and the idioms through which institutions and individuals contested access to resources: in short, an ecology of wood use.

Markets and the 'natural economy'

In the Introduction to this volume, the frequently made distinction between the 'market' and the 'natural economy' was outlined. Elements of both market exchange, and direct allocation or appropriation for immediate use, can easily be found in the society described in the previous four chapters. The society described appears to be 'mixed', or if one views the early modern period as a move from a 'natural economy' dominated by feudal extra-economic coercion of peasants by lords, to a market-orientated capitalist economy underpinned by the legal guarantees of the state, to be 'transitional'. According to these explanatory tools, early modern Württemberg is neither one thing nor the other, but a tug of war expressed in social tension and conflict. The temptation is to ascribe to 'peasants' as a group a strong propensity for operating with in-kind, use-value-based

---

[3] HStAS A557 Bü 91. Leonberger practices are detailed in StAL Bürgermeisterrechnungen.
[4] On 1740, see Glaser, *Klimageschichte Mitteleuropas*, p. 180; Post, *Food shortage*.
[5] On these see Schmidt, *Der Wald in Deutschland*, pp. 118–19, 164–6.

exchange, and a pattern of conservative regulation orientated around immediately available resources and the local climate. 'The peasant plans for the round of time', as F. G. Bailey has put it.[6] The heralds of capitalist society, such as entrepreneurs, commercial farmers or rootless, migrant labourers, by way of contrast, wish to break down regulation and exclusive rights, demand flexible and easily transferable wages and profits, and wish to break the intimate connection between reproduction and locality.

However, although Württemberger villages were rife with 'in-kind' exchange, of grain, wine, labour and wood, it is not obvious that by any means all of this exchange was predicated on 'use values'. This is hardly surprising given that, as with many parts of Germany, only a minority could have subsisted from their own landholdings.[7] The fact that the central government regularly legislated to remove middlemen and ensure that exchanges of all of the above materials were only to be conducted with immediate use in mind suggests that much of the population, and obviously so those dependent on viticulture, had different ideas. The inhabitants of Botnang were not renowned as wood-thieves in the early seventeenth century solely because they had only a small communal wood and needed it for the local bleaching industry. They, as with peasants all over Germany, were selling it in the local urban market (Stuttgart) and wanted the cash. Similarly within households different members sought to accumulate their own shares of wealth (the proceeds of female dowries were always maintained in legal separation from those of the husband) and set their own consumption priorities, leading to conflict.[8] Capital accumulation itself was often achieved through judicious marital arrangements and during the eighteenth century the increasingly endogamous behaviour of wealthy farmers. These families still nevertheless treasured the 'traditional' economy that could keep their costs down by providing cheap labour and the flexibility to pay in kind when prices were depressed.[9] Such transactions can hardly be viewed as the 'impersonal' development of supposedly voluntary market exchange.

---

[6] Bailey, 'The peasant view of the bad life', p. 315.
[7] See chapter 2. Though we could posit the existence of a 'peasant sector' of largely subsistence farmers who nevertheless do not dominate the economy, in the manner of Daniel Thorner. In fact, there is strong evidence for the prevalence of a 'natural economy' in the production of grain, and given the general tendency of grain producers to come from the wealthier half of the community, a disproportionate political influence relative to their numbers. Thorner, 'Peasant economy', pp. 203–4; Warde, 'Subsistence, sales and the state', Economic History Review (2006); discussion in Holenstein, *Bauern zwischen Bauernkrieg und Dreissigjährigem Krieg*, pp. 45–7.
[8] Sabean, *Property*, pp. 163–207.
[9] Ibid., pp. 412–3; Maisch, *Notdürftiger Unterhalt*, pp. 218–19, 322; Fertig, *Lokales Leben*, p. 357.

Differentiated land markets could develop, organised around lordly restrictions (such as the maintenance of distinct tenancies or limits on mortgaging), the requirements of inter-generational transfer, the use of land as collateral in credit relationships, demand for land from urban or commercial investors, and the agricultural conjuncture.[10] Thus it is simultaneously the case that only some of these relations can realistically be considered part of a 'natural economy', but that many aspects of the commercial world saw their market structures predicated upon 'natural' roots. Not least among these was the domination of the grain market in Württemberg by state and religious institutions who could sell cheaply thanks to their in-kind rent receipts from the peasantry.[11] The often analytically useful distinction of 'natural' and 'market' certainly breaks down on a society level and often does not greatly assist with comprehending the nature of individual transactions.

The two ecologies

The framework employed here will not be that of the 'natural' and the 'market' economy. Instead, I propose a model of 'two ecologies' as another way of viewing things, not necessarily as a substitute, but as a different perspective. I will call these two ecologies the 'territorial' and the 'transformational'. The aim is not to describe complete 'systems'[12] or 'economies' or patterns of behaviour, but the operations that give rise to social and environmental structures.

A 'territorial ecology' tends to reinforce the integrity and functioning of a given process specifically located in space. An example of this is the ban on straw, dung or wood being taken out of a village *Markung* and the biomass thus being lost to the inhabitants, a matter of concern when biomass is difficult to replace. We do not have to decide whether the imperative behind such a rule is due to environmental concerns, recognising the fragility of the existing balance of the agrarian system, or economic concerns, where a lord might not wish his or her capital assets to be diminished. Such distinctions could probably never be decided on in any case, but what such a rule does express is the idea of an ecology functioning within a specific territory that should be able to reproduce

---

[10] Brakensiek, 'Grund und Boden'.

[11] This has been an important argument for some Marxist historians as to why peasants only had minimal incentive to invest in agriculture. See Brenner, 'Agrarian class structure', pp. 31, 232; Warde, 'Subsistence, sales and the state'.

[12] Ecologists still debate whether a concept so entrenched as the 'ecosystem' really exists. For a defence of ecosystem approaches in the natural and social sciences, see Moran, *The ecosystem concept*; Ellen, *Environment, subsistence and system*.

itself. It is not unlike some models of the 'natural economy' or the idea of running the world according to 'the round of time'.

Yet one could equally say that all businesses function around that 'round of time' that is the investment cycle. Most patterned behaviour provides a certain guarantee of repeatability. A territorial ecology was also underway in the scientific forestry management of the nineteenth century. The forester-economist Pfeil, for example, saw the aim of forestry as producing cutting cycles that maintained the capital value of the woodland stock.[13] The 'territory' of this strategy was determined by the economy at large, of course, because of fluctuations in the value of land, wood and interest rates. But at the same time this model implied sustainable management of the wood resource, without pre-empting, because the economy as a whole is unpredictable, what amount of wood should be harvested each year in the long term. Nineteenth-century forestry may have implied monocultures and biodiversity decline now seen as environmental 'bads', and certainly the exclusion of traditional peasant rights to graze and obtain stall-litter, but it was potentially quite sustainable on its own terms and frequently aimed to be so.[14] The 'territorial ecology' implies a repeatable set of actions happening at a particular place. It is a process that reinforces the 'integrity' of a particular way of doing things.[15]

The 'transformational ecology', put bluntly, does not. Eventually it must result in the disturbance of local processes; it is a problem generator. Wood shortages for one village demand imports that may upset the perceived just allocation of natural resources among the inhabitants. This might be because the rich are better able to pay for the imports and hence in the eyes of the poorer inhabitants they cannot really value their freely allocated *Gaabholz* to the degree to which the poor do. Freely and equally allocated *Gaabholz* hence becomes a generator of inequality. At the same time the exporting region is losing biomass, and possibly becoming more vulnerable to market fluctuations and soil erosion even as the locals enjoy the profits of the transaction. Such transformatory flows thus tend to undermine attempts at territorialisation and the integrity of ways of doing things. Yet 'transformations' do not have to occur on a large scale or as a result of commercialisation. In the long term an attempt to maintain a sustainable system of grazing animals in woodland to provide manure for the fields may in fact be removing biomass and nutrients to the fields and the village

---

[13] Rubner, *Forstgeschichte*, p. 126.
[14] Though only too often such forestry cultures have proven vulnerable to storms or pest infestations, or unexpected nutrient deficiencies.
[15] This is a version of the homeostatic model which implies a tendency towards the integrity of a certain way of functioning, rather than the existence of any 'equilibrium'. On this point, see Viazzo, *Upland communities*, pp. 34–5.

environs in a manner that will impoverish and change the previously existing woodland. Thus the territory of the carefully managed open-field system with woodland pasture is in fact a site of micro-scale local transformation. We cannot assume that sustainable intent translates into sustainable practice. On perhaps a more familiar scale, population growth may lead to stress on local common lands, limitations on users, and exclusions of newcomers, that will generate a transformatory flow of migrants elsewhere. In other words, the defence of particular territories can generate transformations in other places.

Such problems belong to the political as well as the more traditionally ecological schema of things. Semi-subsistent village communities will require goods such as iron, salt, clothing and ceramics from elsewhere, trading via urban centres. The transformatory flows generated between localities across the whole territory overseen by the government may result in disturbance and environmental degradation in centres of production, raising costs. What appeared to be locally sustainable systems were in fact reliant on flows causing transformations elsewhere. The answer to this problem might be to raise overall productivity via specialisation and technological change. Thus the entire previous agrarian system is undermined, even though a village-level 'territorial ecology' with a high degree of sustainability appeared to dominate over most of the polity's constituent units. Eventually, changes of this kind may undermine local ways of doing things and allow a more integrated economy to develop, shifting the spatial scale at which the system is relatively self-sufficient, or aims to be self-sufficient, to the polity as a whole. It was of course very unlikely that any polity really could be self-sufficient, and self-sufficiency was not universally seen as being desirable. The changes that permitted this shift in scale often took the form in the nineteenth century (and in some regions of north-western Europe, earlier) of the dissolution of the three-field system, abolition of woodland grazing and privatisation and enclosure of common lands. Thus, to describe a lengthy and complex process simply, village communities became integrated into a new 'territory' at the level of the polity, with the priority now to monitor the flows of exchange over international or interstate borders rather than at the level of the village as an agricultural unit. In fact, this explains much of the efforts of mercantilist and cameralist states throughout the early modern period. Apart from the scale on which they operated, it is not clear that they saw the world much differently from the producers of village by-laws.

Clearly the economies of long-distance traders and states can become territorial themselves even when they are locally experienced as transformatory. Grand planners and entrepreneurs like predictability and trustworthiness to ease decision-making. Hence the tendency for social and economic networks, and flows of resources, to develop their own inertia in turn, and Marx's law of the diminishing rate of profit to take hold.[16] Capitalism – or the search for greater capital accumulation – will then tend to force transformatory flows in areas of least resistance, with innovative technologies, development of new consumer tastes, conquest of new markets, political attacks on regulation, and exploitation of new resources. Yet it would be wrong to see transformations as pertaining just to the modern capitalist order, or indeed the realm of human decision-making. Transformations may be unintended, and they may be the result of 'natural processes' whether triggered by or independent of human behaviour. Equally, we must remember that transformations start out from the basis of particular territorial frameworks, and more often an amalgam of competing territorial frameworks.

It is clear that every action or process can be potentially transformatory or territorial at the same time. It is to some degree a matter of perspective, which is not the same as saying it is arbitrary. Every action or process has thus a tendency to generate problems whilst attempting to present a solution. The advantages of such a conceptual schema is that it demands recognition of this flux from the very beginning. It attempts to isolate the specific functions of particular material flows or actions in their precise context. It can work across scales and helps us think about human and environmental processes. Whilst abstract, almost 'empty' in its substance, such a schema allows us to think quite precisely about cause, intention and effect, whether 'territorial' or 'transformatory', identifying systematic conflict and disturbance without presupposing attitudes or approaches that belong to particular social actors ('peasants', 'the state') or material processes. It is also a way of thinking about both the social and the spatial order, as, in Robert Dodgshons' words:

A patchwork of incomplete adjustments, each orientated towards a particular conjunction of market circumstances, some – like anciently-formed rocks – bearing the mark of past magnetic north, but all bearing testimony to the innate tendency of markets to turn eventually.[17]

Ecologies of wood supply

As detailed in the previous chapter, the majority of wood felled was used for fuel. In many cases, this wood was obtained directly from communal woodlands from free-wood grants to all *Bürger*. Households cut wood for their own use, and while there is some evidence by the early eighteenth

---

[16] Dodgshon, *Society in time and space.*   [17] Dodgshon, *The European past*, p. 317.

century of the quality deteriorating in some cases, most fuel needs appear to have been met in this way in settlements that owned communal woodland.

However, only about three-fifths of settlements in the region had communal woodland, and relatively few households outside of that owned private woodland. Sometimes such private holdings were quite substantial but more often they were insufficient even to supply one household with firewood for a year. However, as private woodland covered at least 5 per cent of the wooded area, and was owned by perhaps 5–10 per cent of the households of the district, it might be locally significant.[18] In the north-west of the district villagers often had cutting rights in the woodlands of the monastery of Maulbronn, but such sources did not exist in the east.[19] Here, the peasants without communal woodland must have bought their wood from elsewhere. The distribution of property indicates that these purchases must have occurred from the beginning of the period, but by the 1580s at the latest, population expansion meant that wood was being imported over relatively large distances. Equally, there were always a few households in villages who either did not have access to sufficient supplies from the *Holzgaab* to fulfil their basic needs, or who desired particular types of wood for their handicraft. These households could either obtain it through buying elsewhere, or trading within the settlement. At least two-fifths of villages, then, and a much higher proportion of the population, were not ensconced in a 'natural economy' of wood use, but had to earn cash to be able to purchase it elsewhere. This is particularly the case for those who bought imports from the region or wood from the ducal forestry administration, as these transactions were certainly not in kind.

Evidence from the 1580s gives some indication of the extent of the wood market. In the *Amt* Leonberg itself, we have seen that communes could make substantial proportions of their income from selling wood. Rutesheim for example sold enough wood to supply the needs of an entire other village.[20] Generally the sums however were rather smaller, and sales were more prevalent within communities that already had fairly generous free-wood allowances. In Gebersheim one was permitted to sell wood within the commune 'as expensive as one can' in the 1590s, but the statutes of Leonberg from 1582 (at the latest) prohibit any sales of the *Gaabholz*.[21] The later years of the sixteenth century saw some poor men

---

[18] See chapter 2. There seems to have been an expectation that these were largely used for supply of the household's own needs, something explicitly mentioned in the case of Bietigheim, which had quite extensive private woodlands. HStAS A59 Bü 13a.
[19] HStAS A368L Bü 90; A59 Bü 13a.
[20] HStAS A572 Bü 45.   [21] HStAS A584 Bd. 832; A572 Bü 41.

being fined for this offence. Although Leonbergers could petition the authorities to buy any amount of wood out of the communal woodland, they were not allowed to buy more than 10 *Klafter* from another *Bürger*.[22] This was a rather substantial amount. As this did not pertain to wood being alienated from the *Markung*, and was a transaction internal to the town, it may have been an attempt to limit 'superfluity' in consumption or even reduce fire hazards. It could be the case, as in Höfingen from at least 1593, that no wood could be alienated from the *Markung* without the approval of the authorities, including wood that had been bought. In theory, all wood, whether obtained freely or through purchase, was to be for one's 'own use and householding'. Communal authorities thus kept a tight grip on a system strongly orientated towards household reproduction. But it was not an entirely 'natural economy', because in the case of building timbers, for example, villagers were only given the main timbers of the structure *gratis* and had to purchase the rest with cash.[23]

Communes themselves were happy to sell to outsiders. The majority of the sales from communal woodland were of timbers for building or renovation. Renningen for example made seventy-three such sales between 1563 and 1567, against about forty sales of firewood. Not all of these were local and some were specifically to artisans for their trade, such as coopers or cartwrights. Some of these artisans came from as far afield as Markgröningen.[24] A similar picture emerges from sales from the communal woodland of Höfingen some 140 years later. In 1697–8 the commune sold twenty-eight oaks, thirteen to two buyers from Canstatt and three to the shepherd and *Schultheiß* of Zuffenhausen. In 1703–4, a total of fifty-three oaks were sold, this time mostly to locals but a fair few to nearby Leonberg.[25] In the years 1630–6, the commune of Gebersheim recorded no less than 298 sales, mostly of small oaks and other timbers probably intended for building. Many buyers were local but a fair proportion came from Ditzingen, Hirschlanden or Leonberg.[26] These snippets of information demonstrate that communes had no difficulties in selling their wood, and that craftsmen could travel considerable distances to get the tree they wanted.

These figures suggest that the ducal woodlands, which for example saw 156 transactions in the year 1585–6, may have accounted for a fairly small proportion of overall sales, especially of timber.[27] The situation however

---

[22] HStAS A572 Bü 41; Trugenberger, *Zwischen Schloß und Vorstadt*, p. 44.
[23] StAL Höfingen Fleckenlagerbuch 1593.   [24] HStAS A227 Bü 1122.
[25] StAL Bürgermeisterrechnungen Höfingen 1697–8, 1703–4.
[26] HStAS A584 Bds. 1–11.
[27] HStAS A302 Bd. 7221. Some of these transactions conceal multiple buyers, however.

was clearly strongly regionally differentiated, both in patterns of overall demand and specifically in regard to the product required. The pattern of sales recorded in the account books of the ducal forest administration was predominately from the more wooded south and west to the less wooded north and east.[28] Also, perhaps surprisingly, even those settlements with limited access to other woodlands in the vicinity do not seem to have purchased consistently over time from ducal woodlands. This implies the relative significance of communal woodlands and rafters importing from upland forests in a wider market.

However, it is difficult to discern demand at the level of the individual purchaser.[29] Over half of those purchasers that can be identified from account books, both ducal and communal, purchased as part of a group, and the records do not permit us to see their precise share of the purchase. Often communes, or groups of named individuals from one settlement buying up wood from ducal foresters, were allocated wood from a single woodland that lay some distance away. This was because of the process of bidding for wood to the forester in August who would presumably meet all the petitioners from one village at one time. Although the buyer is often recorded as the 'settlement' (*Flecken*), 'citizenry' (*Bürgerschaft*), or 'inhabitants' (*Inwohnerschaft*) it is unclear whether this was a collective purchase or simply the aggregation of individual bids. In some cases it may have been an institutional purchase by the commune that was then divided up among *Bürger* in a process not unlike the allocation of the *Gaabholz* itself. More often, however, the forestry official simply did not bother to record all of the purchasers' names. Where these groups are disaggregated in the record the numbers involved are usually small, a handful of persons per settlement. The relatively limited number of purchasers also suggests that these might also have special characteristics. Often individual buyers were those with unusual demands, or who were

---

[28] The average size of purchase increased after the Thirty Years' war, it seems because the much smaller market was taken up by a larger share of bulk buyers, especially the saltpeterers who settled in Feuerbach, Eltingen and briefly Kornwestheim. Stuttgart always provided a steady market, for the most part to wealthier officials in the ducal government, and after the War, Canstatt appears as a frequent purchaser, probably because of disruption to the flow of rafted wood down the Neckar. HStAS A302 Bds. 7221–35.

[29] The following discussion draws on a database of 1,956 purchases where the purchaser is identified, drawn from communal and ducal account books between 1563 and 1691. Of these, 690 were purchasers of cordwood, 557 of wood by area, and 421 bought faggots. Inevitably it is easier to identify officials and the wealthier so one must exercise caution in interpreting these results. They also represent of course only a limited sample of the wood market.

not part of the usual system of acquiring free allocations of wood.[30] Both rich and poor bought wood from ducal woodlands, but can be identified in too small numbers to draw any conclusions as to the ability of each group to make purchases. The small numbers of Leonbergers recorded as buying wood in the late 1580s through to 1610 are generally from wealthy families or wood-related trades – a cooper, baker, innkeepers (with farms), or from the wealthier trading families.[31] The sum of evidence suggests that the poorer sections of the populace were limited to the *Gaabholz* or quite probably small amounts bought from rafters and communally organised purchases. Their complaints (as we shall see) about the inability to buy in wood had a basis in fact.

The market for mature oaks from ducal woodlands was equally limited. Only millers appear frequently as purchasers, as one would expect given the wear and tear on their equipment. Most sales were probably for patching up buildings, with some used for artisanal work. The average purchase recorded was 2.6 trees but the mode only one.[32] However, while operating on a similar scale of transaction, the account books of Gebersheim and Höfingen suggest that in the centre of the region around the Glems, there was a strong preference to buy from communal woodlands. This may have come in part from accessibility, but also because fewer institutional barriers (such as the requirement to bid for wood before the St Bartholomew's day report in August) created an incentive to go to the communes.

By 1583, it is clear, as illustrated in map 5.1, a swathe of the *Forstamt* lying near the Enz, around the Glems and in the east of the region had to 'import' wood, at least from outside of the *Markung*. In the bulk of these settlements firewood was imported from outside of the district altogether. This came along the Enz in the case of the settlements around the Glems valley, but further east, from rafts brought down the river Murr from the Reichenberger forest.[33] The purchases may have been organised to a large degree by communal authorities, as they had already been for many years before 1582, according to a report from Markgröningen.[34] This trade

---

[30] Such men might include forest wardens, pastors (8 per cent of those buying wood by area and 5 per cent of those buying cordwood), *Schultheißen* and *Bürgermeister* (whether as a function of their office or their usual relative wealth), schoolmasters (4 per cent of those buying wood by area), innkeepers, saltpeterers (after the war, and buying only cordwood), and bakers (predominately buying wood by area, for which they were 7 per cent of purchasers). See notes 28 and 29 for source.

[31] Based on data from ducal and municipal account books. HStAS A302 Bds. 7221–3; StAL Bürgermeisterrechnungen 1589–94.

[32] This is from 257 purchases where the size of an individual's purchase can be discerned. Millers were involved in 16 per cent of transactions. HStAS A302 Bds. 7221–35.

[33] HStAS A59 Bü 13a.   [34] HStAS A348 Bü 6.

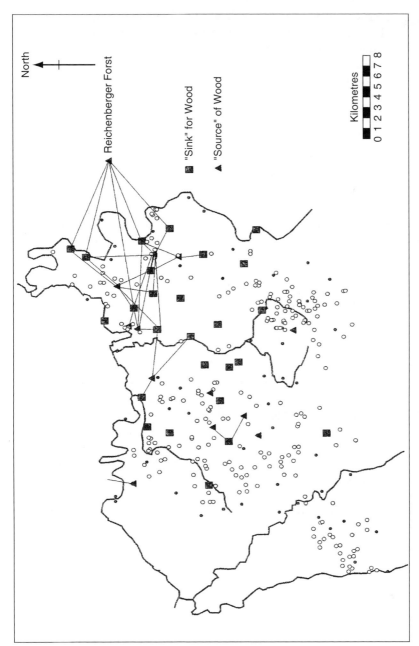

North

Reichenberger Forst

■ "Sink" for Wood

▲ "Source" of Wood

Kilometres

0 1 2 3 4 5 6 7 8

Map 5.1 Supply of firewood, 1583

undoubtedly started earlier for building timber than other products, though demand for it was less pressing. Bietigheim was an important transhipment point. In the 1540s it sent wagonloads of timber as far afield as Münchingen or Zazenhausen. These were occasional purchases by named individuals, largely it seems via men in Bietigheim who acted as their agents and presumably took a cut out of the deal. The toll ordinance 1605 anticipated similar practices.[35]

Rafting: bulk transport in the wood age

By far the most effective way to transport wood was to let nature take the weight and go by water. The region was well served in this regard, bounded by the Enz to the north, the Neckar with its tributary the Murr to the east and the Würm and Nagold to the west. The Enz, Nagold and Würm flowed into each other at Pforzheim, capital of the Margraves of Baden-Durlach, and from here the wealth of the Black Forest flowed towards Besigheim and the Neckar. This trade was borne by a race of hardy men, rafters who spent long weeks on the river and lived cramped into their own quarter of Au down by the riverside in Pforzheim. Exposure to the damp and chill could take its toll. As early as 1501, the ordinance on rafting by the Markgraf limited rafting from Easter to St Gall's day (16 October) 'so no harm is caused to [the rafters] on the water on account of cold and winter.'[36]

The wood came from the largely deciduous or mixed woods in the valley of the Murr above Backnang, the Black Forest highlands beyond Pforzheim, or down the Neckar itself, carefully shipped past Stuttgart's grain mills at Berg. The lower reaches of the Nagold and Würm were probably also a minor source, ruled by Baden, the Lords of Gemmingen and the (Württemberger) monastery of Hirsau. More significant was the Württemberger territory around the headwaters of the Enz, deep in the Black Forest and centred on the town of Neuenberg. On these high reaches of the river, wood was carted by peasants to sites where it was bound into rafts with rope or willow wands. Alternatively, trunks were simply cast into the streams to float downstream. At collection points where the waters became deeper and wider the timbers were collected

---

[35] STABB BhB B 1–8 Bürgermeisterrechnungen; HStAS A17 Bü 42.
[36] 'Inen auf dem wasser keltin und wynters halb nit schade erwachsen.' If we believe the ordinance, of course. This also conveniently restricted trade and was objected to by two or three of the allegedly poorest Württemberger rafters who operated from further upriver. In the rafting ordinance for the Nagold of 1623, similar time restrictions are given, but allegedly in this case to protect the fisheries. Scheifele, *Als die Wälder*, p. 342; Reyscher, *SWG*, Bd. XVI, p. 488.

and bound together into larger rafts, usually in the spring or early autumn. These rivulets could rarely generate the flow unaided and the process was assisted by artificial means. Dams were built against which the trunks collected, to be suddenly released in a torrent of water. In more placid stretches a series of weirs provided the necessary impetus, providing fishing grounds with channels for the rafts. Trunks often broke loose and damaged banks, bridges, gangplanks, and other obstructions in the water, a perennial cause for complaint. This also gave rise to competition for space, especially with the weirs of fishermen and millers. Although channels for rafts were constructed along the Enz as early as the fourteenth century, such problems delayed rafting along the Nagold until the early seventeenth century. These methods also may have accentuated the effects of tremendously damaging flash floods, which dashed great trunks and rocks against any barrier in their way. It was the aftermath of such a catastrophic flood on 27 December 1587 that prompted the Württemberger Rafting ordinance of 1588.[37]

Upstream of Pforzheim, the rafters were local farmers who made much of their living from the bounty of the woods. The trade became increasingly attractive, and government ordinances complained of men abandoning the fields for the wood trade in the Black Forest in 1552.[38] The men of the Pforzheim rafters' guild dominated the downstream trade at this time, as is clear by the accounts of the district of Neuenberg in 1524–5.[39] The 'master rafters' of Pforzheim were barred from cutting wood themselves, although some owned sawmills. They seem to have numbered around twenty-five, though participation in their Easter parade was limited to twenty-four. By 1610 some sixty men were employed altogether.[40] At numerous points downstream the rafts were required to pull in at various toll-points (not, it seems, always diligently overseen) and towns and villages had wood pounds where the timber could be stored and dried for use. The pounds were sometimes overseen by a municipal officer. Bietigheim had a sawmill from at least 1524.[41] Although sales could be managed *en route* it is clear that there was much advanced ordering, with the system operating on credit as the rafters themselves could not pay their suppliers until they had returned from their seaward journey. By 1623 at the latest, the trade on the upper

[37] HStAS A58 Bü 5a; Reyscher, *SWG*, Bd. XVI, pp. 485–7. See also Hagel, *Mensch und Wasser*, pp. 82–92.
[38] Reyscher, *SWG*, Bd. XVI, pp. 63–5.
[39] HStAS A58 Bü 5a. Men explicitly noted as 'of Pforzheim' paid over half of the rafting toll to the *Kellerei* of Neuenberg. HStAS A302 Bd. 9198.
[40] Scheifele, *Als die Wälder*, pp. 52, 91, 340–3; Gothein, *Pforzheims Vergangenheit*, p. 21.
[41] HStAS A17 Bü 42; A206 Bü 2054; STABB Bh B544, O/628.

Enz was in the hands of a state-appointed Württemberger wood factor who advanced grain and money to the local peasantry, against wood supplied each spring, reversing the previous credit relationship. The woodcutters became subject to prices set by the factor.[42]

Rafting on the Enz went back at least as far as 1342, when a treaty, instigated by the major transhipment point on the Neckar of the Imperial city of Heilbronn, was signed between the Markgraf of Baden and the Graf of Württemberg.[43] This mentions tolls all along the river, suggestive of a long-established trade. As early as 1383 we hear of timber for church-building in Mainz being bought from the *Schultheiß* of Pforzheim, and men from the adjacent region of Hirsau and Kieselbronn sold wood in Köln in the fifteenth century. Tolls on parts of the Nagold were collected in this period too, and after Baden promulgated a rafters' ordinance in 1501, the Markgraf's chief steward appealed to Württemberg to do the same.[44] However, Württemberg had to wait until 1552 for large-scale regulation of the trade, and the promise made then of a rafting ordinance was only fulfilled, and only for the Enz, in 1588. Fines were levied for damage to weirs, or for the failure to maintain them. Rafters were barred from other trades (presumably creating a monopoly for full-timers), the timing of the rafting was fixed and a prohibition established on staying in any place for more than four nights. Local officials were to oversee the unbinding and sale of rafts. The last two regulations were presumably to ensure a fair and equitable distribution of products, especially for down-stream communities, and to prevent the operation of middlemen. Above Pforzheim, the ordinance also attempted to enforce the use of sawmills lying in Württemberger territory.[45] The trade was eventually halted by the Thirty Years' war. Although 40 per cent of the Neuenberg toll was paid by just two men in 1524–5, it seems that the Enz rafters were a tight-knit and relatively egalitarian community.[46] This was to change later in the seventeenth century.

The war brought its typical devastation, with the weirs blocked up at Pforzheim after the burning of the town in 1645. However, it was demand from far beyond the region of the *Forstamt* and its environs that spurred the trade again. Dutch demand, primarily for conifers but also for oak, prompted exports from the district of Wildbad from the 1670s, and Liebenzell in the mid-1680s. These exports expanded on a vast scale

[42] Reyscher *SWG*, Bd. XVI, pp. 488–9. The establishment of a monopoly was suggested in 1613 in a letter from the Duke to the forester of Altensteig. HStAS A551 Bü 70.
[43] Scheifele, *Als die Wälder*, p. 53.   [44] Ibid., pp. 66, 72–3, 74; HStAS A58 Bü 5.
[45] Reyscher, *SWG*, Bd. XII, pp. 233–5; HStAS A58 Bü 5a.   [46] HStAS A302 Bd. 9198.

from the 1690s. Contacts were initially maintained between the Duke and
Dutch entrepreneurs, but from 1711 a private company was formed that
had the ducal woodlands at its disposal. This trade, passing down the Enz to
the Neckar, and on the other side of the Black Forest watershed, the Murg
to the Rhine and eventually to the Low Countries, would result in massive
and unsustainable rates of timber felling later in the century.[47]

Wood had been floated down the Neckar from the higher reaches
beyond Horb since at least a 1458 treaty between Württemberg, the
governors of the Austrian patrimony, and the imperial city of Esslingen.
Much of this trade was aimed at Stuttgart and found its terminus at
Berg. A further treaty between the Pfalzgraf, Graf of Württemberg and
Heilbronn, permitted rafting down the Murr in 1469. Duke Ulrich gave
the privilege to run this trade to a private monopoly, initially the *Vogt* of
Bottwar, until it was bought up by the town of Marbach, which ran the
business via a municipal rafting master. By the 1580s this trade supplied a
group of villages north-east of a line between Tamm, Asperg and Oßweil
with firewood.[48]

Much of the wood arrived sawn or prepared for use at mills in the Black
Forest.[49] The 1605 table of tolls on the Enz at Dürrmenz gives a selection
of such uses. There were bedsteads, boards for the manufacture of the
same, barrel staves and bottoms of various sizes, smoothed boards,
beams, rafters, crossbeams and other parts for half-timbering and roofing, planks, slats, window-frames, tables, posts, poles, vine stakes and
firewood. Oak and pine are the most frequently mentioned kinds of
wood. Downriver at Heidelberg, resin, wheelrims, hubs and spokes are
recorded as arriving. The precise extent of the trade, however, is difficult
to gauge. In theory, one only paid tolls to Württemberg once, and judging
by complaints about the negligence of tollmen, perhaps not all. The rafter
would obtain a receipt from the first toll station encountered which could
be amended as the occasion demanded, and goods were sold off, as one
proceeded downstream. As there are no complete series of toll receipts we
cannot definitely establish the scale of operations.[50]

However, the records of the toll station of Besigheim, at the confluence
of the Enz and Neckar, suggest a volume of wood passing by and out of
the *Forstamt* at approximately 15,000 m^3 in 1609–10, rising to about

---

[47] The development of the trade is apparent in the income of the forestry districts remitted
to the treasury. See HStAS A256. On the development of the trade, see Ebeling,
'Organisationsformen'; on over-exploitation, Schmidt, *Der Wald in Deutschland*,
pp. 216–7.
[48] HStAS A58 Bü 5a, Hagel, *Mensch und Wasser*, p. 82; HStAS A59 Bü 13a.
[49] On the development of the mills, see Scheifele, 'Alte Sägemühlen'.
[50] HStAS A17 Bü 42; A58 Bü 5a; Scheifele, *Als die Wälder*, p. 66.

20,000 m^3 in 1619–20 before falling off.[51] The toll at Bissingen, probably the main landing point for the east of the district, received payments for perhaps as much as 8,000 m^3 of wood being landed or shipped past in 1619–20. The same year, the Bietigheim tolls suggest some 5,000 m^3 of wood was shipped by, a reduction on the figure of 11,500 m^3 in 1599–1600. The short-lived monopoly trade of the 1710s based at Wildbad was much larger. In 1715 it shifted no less than 14,000 tree trunks, 51,000 beams, 292,000 boards and 158,000 laths, amounting to at the very least 50,000 m^3 and more likely twice that figure.[52] As these trades were largely run on credit we can see that the capital sums required for investment could be enormous, encouraging a concentration of ownership in the distribution process. It is rather difficult to know what all these figures add up to. They are themselves only rough estimates as volumes were never actually measured, and it is not clear how much double-counting or evasion went on. However, the data from three toll stations alone suggests traffic amounting to 33,000 m^3 in 1619–20. In 1629–30, where the information is supplemented by the Vaihingen a.d. Enz toll the total is nearly 30,000 m^3.[53] Although the accounts of the municipal 'wood masters' of Bietigheim do not survive, by 1620 they permanently held a balance of at least 2,000 fl. and regularly provided an annual surplus to the town of several hundred *gulden*. In other words, their profit alone amounted to the value of over 1,000 m^3 of firewood. In theory the masters of Pforzheim, who by no means monopolised the trade, were permitted to raft some 25,000 m^3 annually during the sixteenth century.[54]

---

[51] In the year 1609–10, toll was paid on 74,975 'pieces' (usually boards), and 218 'sawn blocks' (each amounting to 6.5 'pieces'). These figures were up to 98,120 pieces and 197 sawn blocks ten years later, but back down to 60,280 and 244 respectively in 1629–30. A decade later, amid the chaos of war, some 21,045 pieces and 175 sawn blocks paid toll, itself no mean achievement in these times. The figures in cubic metres of solid timber provided here are based on a rule of thumb that a 'piece' is equivalent to a standard deal which was 18 feet long, 5.35 inches deep and 13 inches wide (a Württemberger inch was 2.39 cm). A deal was thus 0.2 m. Using this, tolls either paid in kind (such as 2 or 3 deals per 100 passing, as in Bietigheim and Vaihingen) or cash (a set amount for the equivalent of a set number of deals) can be used to calculate the overall volume of trade. If anything, this method may underestimate the volume. The value of a sawn block was consistently equivalent to the value of 6.5 pieces in the Besigheim toll. See note 53.

[52] Ebeling, 'Organisationsformen', pp. 88–9. The same method has been used to roughly estimate the volume in solid timber of this trade using volume estimates of the middling sized tree-trunks, beams and boards in toll ordinances.

[53] HStAS A302 Bds. 886, 887, 888, 987, 988, 989, 8161, 8162, 13559. This still lacks data from tolls upstream of Pforzheim and those on the Enz at Dürrmenz and Oberriexingen.

[54] STABB Bh B 7. The Pforzheim calculation assumes that a '*Bort*' is roughly equivalent to a 'piece' or deal as the standard unit trans-shipped. Pforzheimer masters could ship 5,000 *Bort* each year. Scheifele, *Als die Wälder*, p. 342.

The accounts of the forester of Wildbad in the Black Forest, although only recording a small part of the overall trade, indicate clearly what was in demand: building timber, pine posts for staking vines, and sawn boards and deals which might be used for interiors or barrel-making. The ducal forester in the much less densely populated *Forstamt* of Wildbad earned between three and seven times more from sales of building timber than his colleague in Leonberg. In the late sixteenth century, oak timbers cost perhaps 15 per cent of the Leonberger average value in Wildbad, and conifers a tenth. Firewood was at most a quarter of the average price found in the *Forstamt* Leonberg, but even cheaper relative to the cost in the north-east part of the district bounded by the Enz and most easily supplied by the rafters.[55] We can see communities such as Markgröningen buying this wood up, especially for the ducally controlled business of wine production.[56] Stakes for vineyards were on sale in Bietigheim in the late fifteenth century, and it was clearly a major component of the trade around 1600.[57] Pinewood sold for use as fuel in the district of Wildbad alone probably amounted to several thousand cubic metres, and it is likely that a high proportion of this found its way downstream into the north and east of the *Forstamt* Leonberg. This gives a rough measure of how much was imported. The price differentials were not so steep in the later seventeenth century, probably due to a combination of lower demand in the lowlands of Württemberg, but higher demand from distant customers for Black Forest timber.[58]

Thus the rafting trade, initially for building timbers, began in the fourteenth century, continued throughout the fifteenth century, and was a major part of the region's wood economy by the latter part of the sixteenth century. The scale of the trade hinted at in the scattered evidence cited above would indeed seem to plug the rather large gap between local demand and supply that the previous chapter has shown to have been present in the *Forstamt* Leonberg by the second half of the sixteenth century. From at least 1500 Markgröningen fetched its wood from a narrow strip of meadowland sandwiched against the Enz between steep banks near Enzweihingen and Oberriexingen. By 1600 this had become liable to flooding, whether from erosion or the increased precipitation of these years we cannot tell. Dragging wood from the river was damaging the valuable hay, and local farmers worried

---

[55] HStAS A302 Bds. 7221, 14553–7.
[56] See the district accounts, HStAS A302 Bds. 8161–4.   [57] STABB Bh B539, 540.
[58] On top of these flows we must remember the direct transfers within the administration, for example between ducal woodlands in the Black Forest and 'sinks' such as the fortress of Asperg that received 1,308 beech and fir trees in 1590, or 200 cords of firewood in 1613. HStAS A551 Bü 70; A302 Bd. 14554.

that it would be washed away altogether. One night in November 1600, a group of eight fishermen detached the rafts belonging to Hans Jacob Bueb of Pforzheim. The wood, destined for Asperg and Markgröningen's tilemaker, was ruined. The protagonists claimed that it was in the past two decades that the flow of building wood had been supplemented by firewood for the tilemakers, dyer, bakers and barber of Markgröningen. This is another indicator of when imports began to play a major role not just in construction, but fulfilling the everyday heating needs of the populace and artisanal work.[59]

'Sink' or 'source'? The *Forstamt* and the wider world

We have seen clearly enough that direct imports of wood became increasingly important during the sixteenth and early seventeenth centuries. Numerous everyday objects and materials also had to be imported from elsewhere. The inhabitants of the *Forstamt* Leonberg, therefore, exploited the resources of far distant producing regions on a daily basis, and every single rural region of Germany belonged to the ecology of these centres of production. Iron, ceramics, copper, glass, gunpowder and salt all consumed large amounts of wood in their production, and all were imported. We do not, unfortunately, really know enough about the consumption of these goods to provide anything other than the most approximate calculations. Even where marriage or death inventories are available to allow us to assess household possessions, we often know little about the turnover rates of these goods, their size or provenance. However, estimates can be made, indeed, the greater the level of aggregation across regions, the more likely it is that the errors are not too great, because large flows are easier to trace than small.

Iron played a vital role in the agrarian economy. Cartwheels, ploughshares, harrows, chains, spades, scythes, sickles, knives, axes, nails, bolts, pitchforks, firearms, andirons, hinges, locks and, of course, horseshoes all necessitated iron. Large items like wagons could use considerable quantities. To shoe the ninety horses that the prosperous village of Kornwestheim held in this era would use about 168 kg of iron per year. Ironworks were very variable in their efficiency and might use anything between $50\,m^3$ and $100\,m^3$ of solid timber per tonne of iron in this period.[60] So for the horseshoes (not including the nails),

---

[59] HStAS A206 Bü 2054.
[60] Based on the weight of a middling-sized horseshoe that cost 10 *Pfennig* in 1579 in the handicrafts ordinance. This assumes a single annual shoeing of all four hooves. Estimates of the fuel consumption involved in iron production vary very greatly, partly because of

Kornwestheim had $8\,m^3$–$16\,m^3$ of wood embodied in horseshoes each year. The *Amt* of Leonberg had 536 horses according to a report of 1708,[61] or a tonne of iron in horseshoes, and the *Forstamt* probably three times this amount. We can come at this problem from the opposite direction. In the late sixteenth century, the German-speaking lands produced around 30,000 tonnes of iron each year.[62] Some of this was exported, so if we simply assume that the district of Leonberg consumed a share of this iron roughly proportionate to its share in the German-speaking population, we get a fairly crude, but useful ceiling of local iron consumption during this period. The 30,000 people of the region were less than two thousandths of central Europe's 16.2 million inhabitants around 1600.[63] This suggests a ceiling on iron consumption of 55 tonnes, or 1.8 kg *per capita* – the annual shoeing of a horse per person.[64] Somewhat more iron was produced by 1700, but given exports, *per capita* consumption is unlikely to have been any larger. Around 1700 *per capita* consumption in England was about 8 kg.[65]

Iron importation to the *Forstamt* may have accounted for as much as $5,000\,m^3$ of wood each year at the end of the sixteenth century, not a trivial amount when set against up to $50,000\,m^3$ for domestic heating. It was less than for baking but more than the barber-surgeons used. We are accustomed to thinking in this way for the sphere of influence of cities and their consumers, but 95 per cent of Germans lived in small towns and the countryside.[66] It was the cumulative effect of this demand that put pressure on the 'source' regions and ecologies of iron-producing regions. Domestic iron production in Württemberg was a ducal monopoly between the 1550s and 1607, centred on the works in Christophstal, but most finished wares came from other territories. Schwäbisch Gmünd produced scythes, Rottweil sickles and knives until destroyed by a siege

---

the variable quality of the ore, level of processing and efficiency of furnaces. Thus this is only a very approximate estimate, drawing on several secondary sources. HStAS A58 Bü 26; Sieglerschmidt, 'Wandlung des Energieeinsatzes'; Mantel, *Forstgeschichte*, p. 439–41; Sieglerschmidt, 'Landscapes'; Dipper, *Deutsche Geschichte*, p. 38; Held, 'Blei und Holz', pp. 85–109; Schmidt, *Der Wald in Deutschland*, pp. 81, 133.

[61] HStAS A368L Bü 136.

[62] See the evaluations in Kellenbenz, 'Europäisches Eisen'. Note that Kellenbenz gives a mistaken, and far too low, figure for the amount of wood needed to process the iron.

[63] On the population of the German-speaking lands, see Bardet and Dupâquier, *Histoire des populations*, p. 519.

[64] This is not out of line with Braudel's estimate of 1 kg iron *per capita* being consumed in Europe in the early sixteenth century.

[65] German *per capita* consumption was around 4 kg by 1800. Henning, *Handbuch*, p. 837; English estimate calculated from figures in Chartres, *Internal trade*, p. 34.

[66] Scott, *Society and economy*, p. 64. This takes 5,000 as the cut-off point for being an 'urban centre'.

in 1643. Other metals like copper came from further afield, from the Tyrol or the smelters of Thuringia who on occasion imported their ore from even further away in Slovakia.[67]

Glass and soap, though small in bulk, consumed vast amounts of wood in their production through their use of potash. This made up something like three-quarters of the glass, and along with the fuel required in production meant that a single kilo of glass could embody $1 \, \text{m}^3 - 3 \, \text{m}^3$ of solid wood. Thus producing just 2 kg of glass could require a hectare of sustainably managed oak coppice! Most local glassware probably originated in the highlands to the north-east of the Neckar, though fine work came from pedlars distributing the glass of Bohemia or products of the famed glassmaking quarter of Venice.[68] Small towns had two to three glaziers by the early eighteenth century, and they were also present in a few villages. Estimates of glass consumption are difficult to come by, especially before the late eighteenth century. However, some glaziers could make a good enough living out of the trade (with assessed incomes of 100 fl. or more in Leonberg in 1730). Consumption levels by the mid-eighteenth century cannot have fallen far below about 0.05 kg *per capita*. This may be a tiny amount, but would still see $3,000 \, \text{m}^3$ of solid wood 'imported' into the region in the shape of glass at early seventeenth- or early eighteenth-century population levels.[69]

Salt was also famously a product that demanded huge quantities of wood for its processing, encouraging early experimentation with coal as a fuel. It was an everyday staple required for the preservation of foodstuffs, and used in some manufacturing processes such as the tanning of leather. Local demand for salt is rather easier to assess than for other products, because its distribution was usually a monopoly overseen by the local authorities and accounted for in some detail. Duke Eberhard Ludwig demanded detailed information on salt distribution from every *Vogt* in 1710, allowing us to identify the main routes of transit across the *Forstamt*. Bietigheim got its supplies from Schwäbisch Hall to the north-east, while Calw, Canstatt, Hirsau, Markgröningen and Vaihingen a.d. Enz dealt with Bavarian towns.

---

[67] Gutram, 'Eisengewinnung'.

[68] Gleitsmann, 'Aspekte der Ressourcenpolitik', p. 56; Greiner, *Die Glashütten*, pp. 4–6, 42, 49; Gai, 'La produzione del vetro'; Fritz, *Stadt und Kloster*, p. 203.

[69] HStAS A261 Bü 1134. If 2–3 million cubic metres of timber were consumed per year in glassworks in the eighteenth century, this implies, at the lower end of the scale, a production of around 1,000 tonnes of glass with a population of 17.5 million in 1750. Thus a low estimate of consumption in 1750 would be 0.05 kg per person. If the region had around fifteen glaziers, who may have worked primarily on windows while tableware was imported, this would imply that they dealt with well under 100 kg of glass each in any given year. Dipper, *Deutsche Geschichte*, p. 38.

Leonberg and Merklingen obtained salt from Stuttgart at this point, doubtless an intermediary for Bavarian supplies. Account books from Leonberg itself dating back to 1542 show that while sources varied, the great majority of the district's salt came from Bavaria. Although in typical dirigiste fashion, Duke Friedrich had sought local supplies through shafts bored near Marbach and Canstatt in the 1590s, he had no success. The production of the salt imports, centred on boiling brine and extracting the salt crystals in a continuous process lasting days or weeks, consumed enormous quantities of wood, as did the packing of the end product.[70]

The salt was bought in blocks of about 65 kg and sold on in small measures. The method of calculating a standard *per capita* consumption level without accounting for fluctuations over time has been employed several times in this book and is a useful tool of estimation when other data is lacking. The consumption of salt in the district of Leonberg, however, adds a cautionary note to this method. Figure 5.1 indicates clearly that aggregate consumption could vary considerably over time.

Around 10 tonnes were purchased and sold each year in the 1540s. This total rose to over 30 tonnes in the late 1570s and early 1580s, before falling back to less than 20 tonnes by the end of the century. A brief resurgence before the Thirty Years' war was eclipsed by a further fall to around 10 tonnes again by 1630. In the late 1650s the 'salt master' of Leonberg sold around 15 tonnes each year, but by the 1670s this figure had fallen to under 10 tonnes, a level maintained into the early eighteenth century.[71] However, purchases remained somewhat higher, allowing the town to build up reserves. This pattern is not closely related to population change. Benchmark population figures in the 1540s, 1590s, 1650s, 1670s and 1700s allow us to roughly estimate *per capita* consumption rates, displayed in table 5.1.

The table shows clearly that the population varied their *per capita* consumption of even a good as basic as salt according to circumstances, and by a factor of over three. The best explanation for such startling variation is in the wine trade, as the fluctuations follow quite closely, although in a somewhat exaggerated fashion, fluctuations in wine income. It is well known that the salt trade relied on wine exports to Bavaria. The crucial and catastrophic year for the wine harvest, 1586–7, also saw a fall

---

[70] Although run as a monopoly controlled by the *Amtstädte*, smaller settlements could buy themselves out of this arrangement if they so chose, though there is no evidence of this occurring. StAL Salzrechnungen; Stadtmuseum Leonberg, *Das Leonberger Salzhaus*, p. 4; Carlé, 'Die Salinenversuche'; Piasecki, *Das deutsche Salinwesen*, pp. 58, 80, 82, 193.
[71] StAL Salzrechnungen.

Table 5.1 *Estimated* per capita *salt consumption in the* Amt *Leonberg*

Year	Estimated Consumption (kg)
1545	1.5
1584	3.9
1598	2.0
1629	0.8
1655	3.1
1676	0.9
1700	1.0

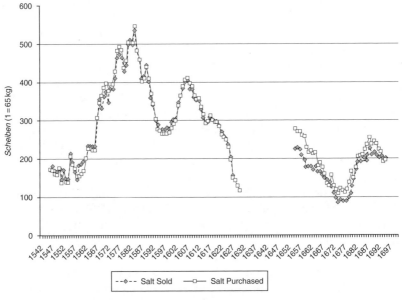

Source: StAL Salzrechnungen 1542–1700.

Figure 5.1 Salt trade of the *Amt* Leonberg, 1542–1700 (nine year moving averages)

of a third in salt imports, from which consumption levels were never to recover. Estimates of the amount of firewood required to produce salt vary considerably, not least because the amount varied from saltworks to saltworks. Very roughly, however, we can reckon that these figures translate into about 600 m³–700 m³ of wood embodied in salt being imported for the inhabitants of the *Forstamt* around 1600, nearly twice this much in the 1580s, but only half the 1598 figure a century later.[72]

We could carry on producing such figures, not forgetting precious metals, copper for Leonberg's coppersmith, tin for Leonberg's tinsmith, ceramics of all kinds, and so on. But they would not add much to the more general point being made here. What we can be sure about is that the region required several thousand 'extra' cubic metres of solid timber per year to go into those products that it was incapable, for the most part, of producing locally. Equally, the local ecology had to ensure that some sort of flow went in the opposite direction, whether of material goods or precious metals that fleetingly passed by and moved on to lands where they were higher valued. But one could not obtain coins for nothing, of course. At its most basic, whether the *Forstamt* was a net 'sink' or 'source' of biomass depended on the relative prices for the goods it could produce and those it needed to import. This brings us to the 'classic' manner of taking the measure of markets, stock and flows: through prices.

Prices, 'real prices' and the cost of obtaining wood

One would expect that as a commodity became scarcer relative to demand, it became more expensive, and as it became more plentiful relative to demand, it became cheaper. This is exactly what happened with wood in early modern Württemberg. However, understanding the nature and scale of such price changes is rather less simple. It is often difficult to tell what prices do or do not include (the cost of a raw material, of labour, of seasoning, or to cover capital depreciation, transport and transaction costs). Equally, there were privileged buyers who might get things on the cheap, such as the saltpeterers provided for from ducal forests during the seventeenth century. For these reasons we must also indicate, when giving an early modern price, where, why and for whom the transaction occurred.

Furthermore, we must be sensitive to what is being sold. A fathom (*Klafter*) of wood was a measure of rather variable quality depending on the tree species involved, the size or diameter of the branches, how well it had been stacked, how long it had being lying in the forest, and so on. All these kinds of assessments could be taken in within the blink of an eye by the seasoned purchaser, and incorporated into the final price, but remain

---

[72] Estimates even given within the same article can vary considerably, and not always with comment! Dipper, *Deutsche Geschichte*, p. 38; Gleitsmann, 'Aspekte der Ressourcenpolitik', p. 51; Mantel, *Forstgeschichte*, p. 444; Witthoft, 'Energy and large-scale industries', pp. 301, 303. Estimates vary from $10\,m^3$ to $22\,m^3$ being consumed per tonne of salt produced. I have used Arnold's figures for the largest Bavarian saltworks at Reichenhall between 1503 and 1619.

entirely beyond our reach. Fortunately, records of transactions from institutions, small town markets or sales from particular woodlands show a high degree of consistency in pricing for firewood. However, the problem is immediately clear in relation to larger timbers: how big is an oak tree? Account books demonstrate various ways of describing the different sizes and quality of timber, but none of them are fine-grained enough, as we try and trace price changes over time, to allow us to be sure how much timber of what quality was really being exchanged. We must always remain wary to the possibility that the quality of the commodity, not its relative scarcity, is what is changing – if these are ever really independent of each other.

In Renningen in the 1560s a fathom cost between 0.2 fl. and 0.6 fl.; the former price almost certainly represents the cost of the raw material, and the latter includes the costs of cutting and transporting the wood to the buyer.[73] Similarly, the poor chest of Leonberg was charged between 0.3 fl. and 0.5 fl., probably recognising the same distinction in how the wood was obtained. Prices in the 1570s seem not to have been much different – just over 0.3 fl. for the wood itself, uncut, but over 0.6 fl. for a pre-prepared fathom. Out in the west of the district, at Möttlingen, pre-cut fathoms were being sold for 0.4 fl. around 1570. By 1580 uncut wood in Leonberg cost 0.36 fl. per fathom and the price jumped to 0.53 fl. in 1590. By 1613 a fathom of cut wood cost 1.5 fl. and a fathom of uncut wood 0.8 fl. in Leonberg. Similar prices were paid in Gebersheim in the 1620s and 1630s. This represents up to a trebling between the 1560s and 1610s. In contrast, a fathom could already cost 2 fl. in Bietigheim by 1605. At the end of the seventeenth century, firewood in Leonberg cost about the same as it had in the 1560s.[74]

From 1585–6 we have the occasional survival of ducal forest account books that provide much larger samples of purchase prices. Averaged across the district as a whole, a fathom cost 0.78 fl. in that first year, between 1605 and 1620 was around 1.1 fl., and was nearly 1.3 fl. by 1630. The value of firewood, as we would expect, fell, to under 0.6 fl. in 1650, and only reached 1 fl. again in 1680.[75] Thereafter the price was fairly steady until the early eighteenth century. There do not seem to be any distinctions between the price of wood sold from ducally owned or any other kind of woodlands. In this regard the market was not structured by institutional privilege. In ducal woodlands, wood (largely uncut or unprepared) rose in price by around two-thirds between the mid-1580s and

---

[73] HStAS A227 Bü 1122.
[74] StAL Armenkastenrechnungen; Bürgermeisterrechnungen; HStAS A227 Bü 1126; A572 Bü 25; A584 Bds. 1–11; STABB B Bh B221 Armenkastenrechnungen 1605/6.
[75] HStAS A302 Bds. 7221–35.

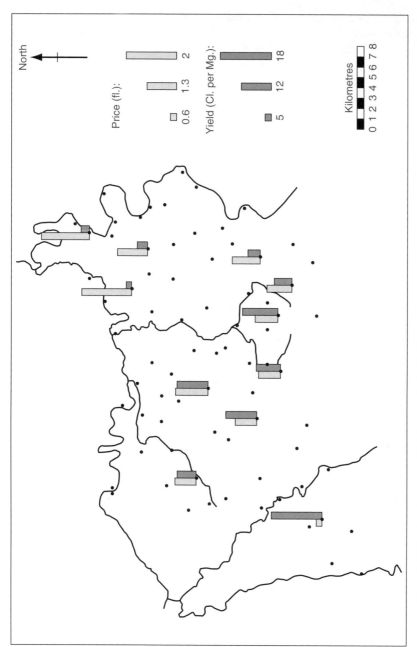

Map 5.2 Wood prices and yields by ward, 1603–04

early seventeenth century. From the somewhat laconic and scattered evidence it seems that the most dramatic rise in price of firewood took place, roughly speaking, in the last two decades of the sixteenth century and right at the beginning of the seventeenth century. It is this point in time that appears to show evidence of decline in yields from various sources in the *Forstamt*, as well as, in some instances, the rise of a firewood rafting trade. Given that population appears to have been fairly static, if not declining, during these decades, it must be presumed that supply, not demand, was undergoing change, though we cannot rule out entirely the effects of more numerous cold years on firewood demand.

It is also clear that firewood pricing was strongly regionally differentiated. This is clear enough from roughly comparing local prices, but in most years it is rather difficult to tell to what extent the variations are 'compositional'. That is, whether they reflect the quality of the wood being sold, or the need for a quick bulk sale (when, for example, ducal foresters wanted to sell the lop and top from felled mature timber), rather than local relationships of supply and demand. However, the pattern seems adequately displayed by looking at the prices from various forest wards paid in the accounting year 1603–4 in comparison with other data (see map 5.2). The region of high prices (predominately in the north-east of the *Forstamt*) tallies well with the region of short cutting cycles, low yields and extensive imports. A shorter cutting cycle implies an intensification of management taking advantage of stronger growth when trees or rods are young, bringing a higher marginal return (though not necessarily marginal profit, given that labour inputs may be high). The implication is that local management strategies are responding to a relative shortage of wood in the zone of higher prices. However, the shorter cutting cycle applies across woodlands irrespective of the purposes to which the wood will be put, or indeed its ownership. The shorter cycle cannot then, for the most part, be an attempt to increase revenue, but rather simply to increase available supplies. This strategy was not able to compensate for the higher demand, of course, because prices remained high despite the more intensive management.

Larger timbers show similar price trends, although the 'meaning' of the price is even more subject to the variations in the product and compositional effects in the sampling. Oaks from ducal woodlands seem to have cost on average about 0.9 fl. in the mid-1580s, and rose in value to over 1.62 fl. in 1610, but became no more expensive thereafter.[76] Birch was

---

[76] This may be because of average size of tree felled was declining, of course. While the rise from the 1580s is significant it is not as dramatic as that for firewood, indicating possibly again that mature timber shortages had emerged much earlier.

always cheaper than oak, and beech more expensive. Coniferous trees were cheap at less than 0.6 fl. each in the mid-1580s and even less, 0.4 fl., in the 1610s and 1620s. This decline may reflect competition from rafters, but equally a decline in the size of trees felled, especially as they all came from the west of the *Forstamt*. Prices of oaks at the end of the seventeenth century appear to be roughly similar to those around 1620, and relatively stable over several decades.[77]

So far we have been preoccupied with nominal prices of wood. However, economists often prefer to talk in terms of 'real prices' or at least set the price against some other store of value whose importance is universally recognised. This is because while wood prices increased, other prices (such as for labour, i.e. wages, or for food, or for wine, or for housing) might have been rising even faster. The *relative* price of wood compared to other costs is what would have impressed contemporaries. Equally, monetary change may have devalued the currency, so apparent changes in the nominal price of wood may not reflect increasing relative scarcity at all. The preferred way of assessing 'real' prices is against the value of silver at a specific point in time, or grain. Here I will compare it with the price of grain and wine. The value of money itself certainly had an impact on the value of wood, as in the dramatic inflation cased by debasement in the years 1622–3. However, most of the economy ran on credit or exchange in kind, and the overall readiness to supply credit, and the fortunes of the agricultural economy, would probably have more influence locally on the effective demand for wood than the state of the currency. However, if you wanted to buy wood off the rafters or the ducal government, it does seem that cash in hand was the only way.

Because food was obviously so central to households, and took up a large share of the budget, grain prices are often used as an index of general price change. However, we must add a number of caveats here. As populations grew, and as the demand for foodstuffs (though by no means particular foodstuffs) was quite inelastic, food prices could gallop ahead of the rest of the economy, as clearly occurred in the 'long sixteenth century'. This did not necessarily mean that people felt other goods to be becoming cheaper, however. This might be the case if one switched income between food and fuel, and fuel began to seem the cheaper option. But one might equally argue that if the budget available for other goods was being squeezed because of the necessity of spending more on grain, then one might become even more sensitive to small fluctuations in the prices of those goods, too. If there are no cheaper

---

[77] HStAS A302 Bds. 7221–35; StAL Höfingen Bürgermeisterrechnungen 1697–8, 1703–4.

substitutes for essential goods then minor price rises, even if that good (wood in this case) is becoming relatively cheaper than another (like grain), will still hurt. The ending of rapid price rises in wood in the 1610s may be because high grain prices and the uncertainty generated by warfare depressed demand for wood, an 'income effect' as economists would say.[78]

Everything got more expensive, but it is likely that wood increased in price at least as much as bread grains, between the 1560s and 1620s. Firewood almost tripled in price, while grain roughly doubled, as indicated in figure 5.2. But grain prices were far more variable. After the war, grain in turn became expensive relative to wood but wood recovered its late sixteenth-century value by the early 1680s. Wine became cheaper relative to wood at the end of the 'long sixteenth century'. But more important than this was probably the fact that wine incomes overall declined as harvest sizes shrank. As a consequence, for the hard-up vinedresser wood must have become an even more precious commodity. Yet how one was affected by all these changes basically depended on one's access to a free grant of communal wood, or put another way, one's dependency on the market for fuel. I will return to this issue, but suffice to say that in the latter part of the sixteenth century and early seventeenth century, wood was probably becoming more expensive relative to other commodities that agricultural producers could sell in this economy, and at the same time, local yields of wood were dwindling.

A final aspect of this is labour. Part of the labour of getting wood to market was, of course, through transport, and we have already seen that moving wood by water was far cheaper than doing so on land. This will be considered in its own right in the subsequent section. With regard to getting the wood into useable form, however, people had to fell the tree and hack it or saw it into a size that could be put in a stove, or erected as a fencepost or stake. They could either do it themselves, or pay someone else. If the labour costs of preparing the wood lagged behind the cost of the wood itself, or if labour costs to process wood became cheaper relative to other uses to which household labour might be put, there would be an increasing incentive for people simply to go out and buy the wood

---

[78] We must also remember that often people did not always buy grain; they bought bread, which fluctuates in price less than the raw material from which it was made. Unfortunately records of large-scale loaf sales tend to come in years of high prices, so they are not a very reliable guide to trends over time. Loaves valued by the poor chest of Leonberg and given out as doles roughly trebled in price between the mid-1560s and 1628–9, implying a more rapid increase than the price of bread grain, which seems to have doubled at most. This would be peculiar, and may be to do with the size and grain mix of the loaves. StAL Armenkastenrechnungen.

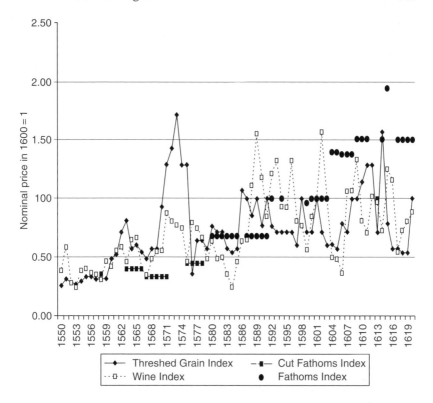

Source: StAL Armenkastenrechnungen; Bürgermeisterrechnungen; HStAS A227
Bü 1126; A572 Bü 25; A584 Bds.1-11; STABB B Bh B221 Armenkastenrechnungen
1605/6; Salzmann, *Weinbau und Wienhandel*, pp.90–5; Ginschopff, *Chronica*.

Figure 5.2 Relative price indices of basic goods near Leonberg,
1550–1620[a]
[a] Although historians frequently employ moving averages to describe
price changes, this has not been done in this case as it would present an
unrealistic view of the situation facing purchasers of wood. One of the
main challenges was the frequent rapid fluctuation in relative prices and
incomes from different sources.

pre-prepared rather than cut it. In some places people like pastors and
schoolmasters did not receive free wood allowances from the *Holzgaab*
but an apparently high propensity to buy probably came from a desire to
avoid the drudgery of wood chopping as well as a need to heat larger
dwellings and schoolrooms.

Anecdotal evidence, and records of people caught performing work
illegally (usually stealing) suggest that all members of the household

could be involved in one way or another in processing wood.[79] Children often accompanied adults on woodcutting expeditions, and both men and women were active in the woodland. Women however appear to have been primarily involved in cutting grass for fodder and taking small diameter greenwood or deadwood, as well as bearing this back to the village. Although women were present when larger timbers or branches were cut, they do not seem to have been so by themselves. Only men were paid for actual woodcutting, and only men appear doing especially heavy work such as cutting up old stumps. When these kinds of labour were paid the daily male wage appears to have been around 0.13–0.16 fl. in the 1560s in Bietigheim. This seems to have been a fairly steady rate throughout the late sixteenth century across the east of the region. More precisely, ducal authorities paid 0.12–0.13 fl. for cutting and stacking a fathom of wood up until around 1610, while Leonberg paid 0.12 fl. in 1571 but 0.12–0.15 fl. in the late 1580s and 1590s. Cutting barrel-hoops or switches was about 0.2 fl. per day in Leonberg in 1590.[80] By the 1610s payments of 0.17–0.18 fl. appear in the Leonberg area. The real inflation in wage rates came in the 1620s, pushed up to around 0.3 fl. by 1631 and 0.4 fl. per fathom by 1640. The wages for cutting a fathom of wood paid out by the hospital of Markgröningen were around 0.12 fl. up until the early 1570s when they rose to 0.15–0.16 fl. until at least the century's end. By the 1620s they, like those of Leonberg, stood at around 0.33 fl.[81] In a period when firewood prices seem to have at least trebled (1560s to the late 1620s), wages lagged behind a small amount, and much of their rise came late in the period. In the 1560s the actual cutting would add about 40 per cent to the value of firewood. 'Sticky' wages meant this figure had fallen to as little as 11 per cent by 1610, though it may have recovered to over a fifth of the value of the raw material by 1630. Thus as wood became more expensive the premium paid for the preparatory work was clearly falling.

[79] The list of 'miscreants' comes from Gebersheim (twenty-nine cases, 1628–32), Bietigheim (forty-seven cases, 1588–1648), Botnang (1596–7, thirty-nine cases) and the account books of the ducal forest administration (1585–1640, ninety-seven cases). HStAS A302 Bds. 7221–6; A227 Bü 1152; A584 Bds. 1–6; STABB Bh A1678.

[80] The daily wage of a journeyman was set (including food, during the winter when woodcutting would be done) at about 0.25 fl. in Leonberg. Day labour on woodcutting seems therefore relatively poorly paid. However, the journeymen's wages seem to be at the top of the scale for more menial work, as Ogilvie puts them at 0.18–0.26 fl. per day over most of the seventeenth and eighteenth centuries. Weavers in the 1590s however earned only around 0.13 fl. per day. Maisch follows eighteenth-century government ordinances in setting journeymen's wages at 0.37 fl. per day. A572 Bü 41; Ogilvie, *State corporatism*, pp. 93, 114–15; Maisch, *Notdürftiger Unterhalt*, pp. 46–7.

[81] HStAS A302 Bds. 7221–6; A572 Bü 41; A58 Bü 26; StAL Bürgermeisterrechnungen; STABB Bh B 1–6; StAM Spitalrechnungen H19–62.

Pricing landscapes: the cost of transport

Prices conveyed the relative scarcity of the raw material, the cost of extracting and preparing it, and, of course, the cost of getting it to the point of consumption. There was a point at which one would expect the local market price to settle, where it seemed better to put some of one's own labour into processing the wood rather than paying someone else to do it and bring it to you. The further one transported the wood, especially from regions of readily available timber, the smaller the wood component of the cost became. To take a late example, the price of rafted timber arriving at Freudenstadt on the Upper Kinzig in the Black Forest (still close to the sources of supply) comprised about 40 per cent for the raw material, 6 per cent for felling, 21 per cent for carting over land, and 23 per cent for rafting, with some other incremental processing and toll costs.[82]

If these conditions held in early modern Württemberg, we should find that combining the costs of raw material, labour and transport, we can come to a fit with the prices paid for pre-prepared wood in local markets. With the rafting trade, where larger investors and middlemen operated, one would assume a small amount of profit-taking too. If an integrated regional market was in operation, the variations in these should explain how far people were prepared to go to obtain wood, or put another way, their propensity to pay for people to bring it to them.[83] If such a model does not fit, it would seem that other, institutional factors or other demands on time at critical periods of the year determined the manner in which people made their purchases.

Carting, from the 1560s (Bietigheim), the 1580s and 1590s (Leonberg) and 1605 (ducal account books, Stuttgart), appears to have cost about 0.07 fl.–0.08 fl. per kilometre. Before the inflationary years of the 1540s onwards, the rate was perhaps half this.[84] Obviously there were variations around this price and transporting tree trunks rather than stacked wood cost almost twice as much. This gives a couple of rules, however rough the calculation. Like 'pure' labour, carting became relatively cheaper in relation to the price of the raw material as the 'long sixteenth century' progressed. Secondly, at the end of the sixteenth century, in most parts of the region wood doubled in price if it was taken seven kilometres over land. This impression fits well with the figures we have for the wage and carting rates from Leonberg outlined

---

[82] Ebeling, 'Organizationsformen', from Barth, p. 97; though Barth has got his sums wrong.
[83] There is of course a particular danger in this kind of analysis in filling in the gaps by deriving costs from residuals left over when other costs have been deducted from the market price, thus creating circularity in the argument.
[84] HStAS A302 Bds. 7221–6; A348 Bü 1; StAL Bürgermeisterrechnungen; STABB Bh B 1–6; B 221; A 2161.

above. A fathom cost 0.5 fl. uncut in the woods and up to 1 fl. in the town after being pre-prepared and carted about five kilometres into town.[85]

At this kind of expense it is clear why there was strong regional variation in prices. Around 1630 wood from Mönßheim or Rutesheim could be bought at only a little over half of the price of that in the north-east of the *Forstamt* or near Stuttgart, but when one added carting costs of 15–20 km it simply did not pay to tap into these reserves. The latter regions could thus bear the cost of buying rafted wood where 85–95 per cent of the cost could be for transport. The hospital of Markgröningen bought wood from the rafters at Bissingen for around 3 fl. per fathom in the late 1590s, wood that could be purchased for as little as 0.07–0.14 fl. upriver in the Black Forest, before any processing. It could actually be obtained for somewhat less than this out of neighbouring ducal or communal woodlands, were the authorities prepared to sell it.[86] However, this may not have been the case, and undoubtedly further transaction costs would have been incurred in finding a willing local seller. The costs for carting wood locally may appear lower than they might have been if there had been more demand for carting services, simply because people never paid for the cost of carting at more expensive times of the year when there were other demands for haulage. If they could avoid it, people avoided the potentially heavy burden of carting costs. Indeed, across the whole period, areas of wood sold by ducal foresters to be cut by the purchaser were on average only just over four kilometres from the homes of the buyers, and the modal distance was a mere two kilometres. It does not seem that increased wood prices encouraged people to become more adventurous as transportation took up a lower proportion of the total cost. On the contrary, average distances travelled to obtain wood tended to diminish from the 1580s right on until the 1670s (from 6 to 2.4 kilometres).[87] This stands as a corrective to those who think increased market dependence

---

[85] We might note that this made wood by weight more expensive to transport overland than the famously expensive transport of coal in seventeenth-century England, where the Newcastle price was added again by 6–8 miles of overland transport in Cambridgeshire. Coal however had more calorific value as a heat source than wood, so it is in fact what one would expect if wood was primarily used as fuel. Hatcher, *The history of the British coal industry*, p. 13; Allen, 'Was there a timber crisis', p. 471.

[86] These calculations are based on sales from ducal woodlands in the forest of Wildberg, and the costs in the wards of Enzweihingen and Ingersheim of buying, cutting and carting wood to Markgröningen in 1585–6. HStAS A302 Bds. 7221–2, 14553–4; StAM Spitalrechnungen H51–3.

[87] These distances are subject of course to compositional effects in purchasing and the decisions of the ducal foresters to allocate wood from particular woodlands. For most villages the number of purchases is not large enough to establish a trend, and for others the distance travelled remains very constant. Changes appear to be most clearly associated with a group of settlements along the valley of the Glems relatively distant from

means more mobility. It seems likely that people were more inclined to have wood brought long distances *to them* via the rafting trade, and generally tried to minimise the cost of carting.

The higher cost of transporting larger tree trunks made it relatively more expensive to bring oak trees overland, and transporting coniferous trees was more expensive still relative to their value. It is thus not surprising that from ducal woodlands at least, the market for conifers was limited to where they were prevalent in the south-west of the region, and that an attraction for imported rafted wood developed much earlier in the building sector than elsewhere. Indeed, those areas with easy access to the Enz, although relatively speaking short on mature timber themselves, actually ended up having more buildings per head of population than elsewhere. On average, people only went three to four kilometres to buy oaks out of ducal and communal woodlands up until the second half of the seventeenth century. Timber, of course, still required carting overland once it reached the offloading points at Bissingen or Bietigheim. Given that oak prices were rising faster than those of conifers, it is easily explicable why people increasingly made the switch to using pine deals and spars in construction once the rafting trade was established. Smaller sawn wood, of course, was not as cumbersome to transport as larger beams and trunks. This supply from the upper reaches of the Enz set the pace of pricing, the trade encouraged further by the ever-higher prices that could be fetched at Heidelberg or Heilbronn. An inquiry into opening up the Nagold in the 1550s noted that they had to set the tolls to be competitive with the prices of the Enz rafters.[88]

In unusual cases people were prepared to travel over twenty kilometres to obtain the wood they wanted, so there does not seem to have been a very large information restriction on getting hold of reserves. Indeed, the process of applying to ducal foresters for allocations of wood in the summer before they were cut may have assisted buyers in finding relatively distant reserves. However, people wanted to buy close to home, and it seems that the relative costs of carting and rafting provide an explanation for the patterns of marketing observed.

ducal woodland, along with the compositional effect of settlements choosing whether or not to bid for ducal wood. The latter however is presumably influenced by their ease at obtaining supplies elsewhere, as purchasers could choose to get their wood elsewhere if they wished. Distances are measured as the crow flies and rounded to kilometres. I have tended to round numbers up to reflect that the 'real' distance travelled will always be longer. Although there is a decline in the average distances travelled to obtain areas of wood to be cut, this is not true for sales of fathoms that generally took place at 5–7 kilometres distance across the period. The longer distances may reflect the more specialised quality of some of these sales to wealthier consumers of wood and artisans. After the Thirty Years' War, saltpeterers and buyers from Canstatt and Stuttgart are prominent customers. HStAS A302 Bds. 7221–35.

[88] HStAS A58 Bü 5a.

The ecology of wood use

By integrating all these flows of resources, whether within the village *Markung*, between settlements, or obtained as direct imports or as pre-processed goods, we can come to an understanding of its ecology and the processes that underpinned its dynamics. There have been various attempts to understand, at different scales, the flows or 'social metabolism' of pre-industrial societies, exemplified in recent years in Europe by the work of Christian Pfister and several Austrian scholars.[89] These have often been conducted on the settlement level and show evidence of strong continuities, a 'territorial economy' as I have called it. However, there is rarely detailed examination of imports of iron and salt and other consumer products; nor the markets that have to exist to purchase commercial products; nor the importance of factors such as emigration in 'sustaining' the local ecology. Here I will seek to extend these models, discounting for now factors such as demographic change, and concentrate on the ecology of wood use.

Here we encounter scale issues again. Does a 'region' have an ecology, or a village, or even a 'household'? Certainly the use of the *Forstamt* as an administrative region provides very arbitrary boundaries. Here I will build from the *Markung* up. This was the most immediate scale of regulation in many cases. We must remember that the free *Gaabholz* provided by many communes, along with further sales from communal woodlands, remained the primary source of fuel and timber. Both the regulators of communal property and the enforcers of state law operated first and foremost at the village level.[90]

From the beginning of our period the region as a whole imported building timber from rafters, and precious raw materials, commodities or manufactures such as salt, iron equipment, glass and ceramics from elsewhere. As the sixteenth century progressed it is likely that such dependencies increased, along with the growing import of vineyard stakes that must have had to keep pace with the expansion of vineyards. In this period we can also identify a number of settlements, such as Markgröningen, Groß Ingersheim or Kornwestheim that had no very substantial woodland of any kind. They were therefore dependent on at least intra-regional transfers from late medieval times.

---

[89] Pfister, *Das Klima der Schweiz*, Winiwarter and Sonnlechner, *Der soziale Metabolismus*, Projektgruppe Umweltgeschichte, *Kulturlandschaftsforschung*.

[90] This is based on aggregating the estimates of communal woodland yields and local demand from fifty-three settlements, and remains of course a very rough estimate.

We can attempt to build up an overall 'balance' around 1600, for which there are population estimates for the entire region. This is at the heart of the period where firewood prices appear to have been rising fairly rapidly and the importation of all kinds of wood was reaching a large scale. I have taken a reasonably generous estimate of 3 m^3 (stacked) per hectare each year being produced in all woodlands, and assumed generously again that it was efficiently used. If we then estimate a (low) *per capita* annual consumption figure of 1 m^3, an assessment of likely flows within or between *Markungen* can be made. On this basis, only a minority of settlements (41 per cent) could have satisfied even their firewood needs from the *Gaabholz*, or indeed from any form of distribution of the product of communal woodlands. The greatest shortages lay in the centre of the region and in the north and east of the *Forstamt*, a picture that concurs entirely with that drawn by the forester Philip Roßach in his report of 1583. Although some settlements also had private woodlands they would · only have been able to ameliorate conditions significantly in a few cases, and nowhere could they overcome the basic shortage.[91] Even on this basis, then, only a minority of the settlements can be considered potentially 'closed' communities by 1600. Village authorities were faced with the choice of either keeping the amount of *Gaabholz* allocated per household low, forcing all to buy additional wood, or alternatively being more generous but excluding some from access to it altogether.

A large number of villagers were thus faced with the prospect of buying wood, which could either be imported to the region or obtained from communes enjoying local surpluses, ducal woodlands or the nobility. Such transactions all implied biomass transfers, whether to obtain cash or during exchange in kind. The sum involved was large, some 15,000 m^3 of cordwood, or the equivalent of at least 5,000 hectares of sustainably managed woodland.

One can see why settlements were keen to implement rules that forbade the export of wood, straw or dung from their *Markungen*, and in some cases even barred its sale within communities. Communities operated a limited 'territorial strategy' that combined, where possible, a communal wood used for the *Holzgaab* and for sales, along with extensive grazing in the woodland which also transferred biomass to the fields. About two-thirds of communities could operate in this fashion. Yet this apparently village-based 'territorial' strategy is in part illusory, because if we treat the 'territory' as the

---

[91] Opportunities to sell may have been limited. A fragment of a document from 1698 states that even private woodowners could not sell or even use building timber without explicit permission from the forester, although there is no sign of this being enforced. HStAS A59 Bü 35a.

Markung, it is clear in many cases that biomass flows were crossing its jurisdictional boundaries to a major extent long before 1600. This local strategy was hedged by an economy of importing wood from elsewhere to such an extent that it seems unreasonable ever to talk of subsistent or autarkic communities when it came to supplies of fuel or building material. Yet transport was expensive, and communities did not generally seek supplies from great distances. As a consequence, much of the deficit was probably largely made up by imports to the region from proximate regions with access to cheap supplies. Some of the more remotely sited supplies within the *Forstamt* were thus actually exploited to an extent far under that which their natural regeneration could have supported. Even at peak points in supply, no more than $6,000 \, \text{m}^3$ of wood seems to have been sold in any one year out of ducal woodland. Ducal woodland provided, nevertheless, a stabilising element, precisely because this pressure was far within its productive capabilities, although the pressure to supply settlements from relatively near at hand meant that exploitation was unevenly distributed. The question is whether these intra-regional transfers, combined with other sales and imports, constituted a larger and sustainably managed 'territory' which could satisfy regional demand, or whether local imbalances of supply and demand were forcing it towards ecological transformation.

In 1600 it seems reasonable to suppose that at the very least some $10,000 \, \text{m}^3$ of wood was being removed from the rafting trade down the Enz, and being used as fuel, construction timber and vineyard stakes. To get a 'real' picture of flows, we should add another $6,000 \, \text{m}^3$ embodied in materials such as iron, glass and salt. As with salt, it may be the case that the levels of imports were heavily dependent on the ability to pay with the proceeds of the local economy. In other words, the ability to convert flows of biomass or nutrients into cash. The fact that the salt trade was so clearly dependent on wine exports suggests that in this regard, local flexibility was limited. Overall, the products of the region that could be used to obtain imports were grain, livestock, wine and cloth. Although some of these transactions could take place in kind, it is convenient to convert these flows into cash equivalents as this was, in the end, how contemporaries evaluated transactions. The wood must have cost at the very least 3,000 fl., but probably more. The salt costs were much higher, partly because, as shown in figure 5.3, the price of salt steadily increased from the late 1560s. By the 1610s it was twice as high, and by the end of the 1620s almost three times as high as in the 1560s. Unlike other products, salt did not become cheaper after the war, but continued to become more expensive. As the cost of fuel was a major component of the price of salt costs (along with transport), this appears to indicate that wood in the source regions of the eastern

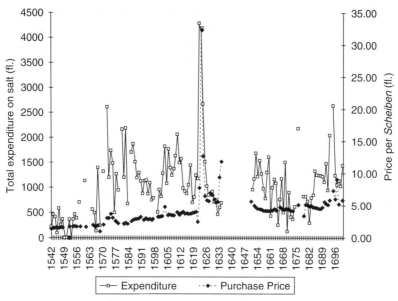

Source: StAL Salzrechnungen.

Figure 5.3 Salt price and expenditure on salt in the *Amt* Leonberg, 1542–1700

Alps was becoming progressively more expensive and that the war did not ameliorate this situation. The district of Leonberg probably consumed about one third of the region's salt. Thus the overall burden for the *Forstamt* was about 6,000 fl. at the height of demand, and 3,000–4,000 fl. each year in the early seventeenth century.[92] Given the much smaller amount of wood embodied in salt than was received as direct imports, the much greater cost of salt illustrates again the weight of transport costs in this economy.[93] Iron cost perhaps between 2,000 and 3,000 fl. *per annum*, and glass probably much less.[94] The wood embodied in the last two came

---

[92] StAL Salzrechnungen.

[93] Even within southern Germany where, as Scott notes, good transport links, especially by water, were crucial to commercial success. Scott, *Society and economy*, p. 24.

[94] This is a rough estimate based on the price of iron embodied in horseshoes and a *per capita* consumption of 1.8 kg *per capita per annum*. As making horseshoes was fairly cheap labour this will underestimate the price of most iron products, but 1.8 kg *per capita* consumption is at the high end of probable levels. Glass prices are not available for the region, but as the early eighteenth-century income of glaziers for *all* their work cannot have much exceeded 1,000 fl., the cost of glass itself must have been much less than this.

rather cheap by local standards.[95] All told the local ecology had to pay out at the very least 11,000 fl. to avoid having to produce more wood locally (and, of course, to import the iron and salt to be processed). In the year of the population survey, 1598, this could have been obtained by exporting 1,100 *Eimer* of wine, or about 3,200 hectolitres. In other words, it took roughly the gross product of 160 hectares of poorer-yielding vineyard to keep an ecological 'balance'. This may have represented the *net* output of over a quarter of the region's vineyards. However, the maximum sum of estimated demand presented in chapter 4, some 70,000 m^3, compared with a likely maximum of woodland output of some 40,000 m^3, suggests that the level of direct wood imports could have been as much as three times higher.[96]

It made sense. A hectare of vineyard produced far and away more income than a hectare of woodland, so it was undoubtedly worth tearing down the trees and staking out the vines, even if one generated more demand for wood in doing so. Although they were demanding of manure, providing an incentive to keep livestock numbers high and inhibit woodland growth, there is little evidence, though studies are almost completely lacking, of the expansion of vineyards causing ecological degradation. In this regard the mood of the authorities to inhibit, by and large, the expansion of vineyards into the woodland was misplaced. Vineyards were more productive than woodland and wine could be transported at far less cost than wood, so why not produce wine and buy in wood or products which used large quantities of wood in their making?

The ducal authorities, however, were not solely concerned to keep things local, and to encourage a *Markung*-based territorial ecology whether by restricting the expansion of vineyards or ordering export bans, tolls and the exclusion of middlemen. Without the co-ordination involved in selling wood from the large areas of ducal woodland overseen by the forester, or having the jurisdictional clout to remove impediments to the rafting trade, such an economy never could have arisen. The jurisdictional fragmentation and plethora of tolls in south-western Germany in the pre-industrial periods tends to blind scholars to moments when states assisted in market co-ordination and development. In this case the agreements between Württemberg, Baden and Heilbronn from

---

[95] This is especially after allowing for the deduction of tolls, as imported iron paid no less than 10 d. toll per pound, perhaps doubling its price! However, most iron would have been either already processed into manufactured goods, or before 1607, from the ducal monopoly in Christophstal.

[96] The taxation assessments of the eighteenth century took costs of cultivation as being two-thirds of the value of production, implying in this case the net return of 480 hectares, if they are to be believed. Reyscher, *SWG*, Bd. XVII, p. 360.

1342 onwards, and the investment in locks and weirs to regulate the rivers and avoid fishponds and mills, were crucial in establishing a new territorial ecology based on trade flows.[97]

This sometimes conscious attitude is exemplified in a Württemberger report on rafting in 1583. It noted the 'great wasting (*Abgang*) of the woodlands, and shortage of wood in all lands'. However, there were also great stores of wood lying in the Black Forest that frequently rotted unused and went to waste, by which many people could earn a living and thereby prevent 'present and future wood shortages'. The latter were being expressed in the 'ever more persistent inflation, that more and more oppresses the poor people as time passes'. Yet part of the solution, to open the Nagold to rafting, had already failed in the 1560s on account of those who for their 'private benefit' (*privat nutz*) wanted to protect weirs and fishponds and hindered the 'work for the common good' (*gemein nutzig werckh*). The Nagold would not be opened up until the first half of the seventeenth century.[98]

At the beginning of the period there were already two well-established ecologies of wood use, but they were two symbiotic ecologies. The territory of the *Markung* circumscribed one. The other was comprised of shifting wider trade links between the villages of the region and beyond. Increasingly the territory of trade became more important, though in volume of flow still behind local movements. But neither could exist without the other. Trade required the largely agricultural products that were sustained by the management of the *Markung* and transfer of biomass from the woodland to the field. In turn, the rewards of trade brought salt, iron, wood and other products to the villages and small towns of central Württemberg. This system appears to have been very stable locally in the two centuries under observation. Its cost to the region, of at the very least 11,000 fl., may seem low when set against a probable regional income of around one million *gulden per annum* in the early eighteenth century, or a tax bill (much of which stayed in the region) of 45,000 to 60,000 fl.[99] However, we have seen that importing wood, or products embodying wood, took a large slice of the *net* income of the most important money-spinner, viticulture. Equally, salt consumption was clearly highly sensitive to fluctuations in purchasing power. Money values do not, of course, tell the whole story in any case. More telling perhaps is the fact that around 1600 approximately 6,700 hectares at the very least would have been needed to produce all of the wood embodied in imports

---

[97] See also Epstein, *Freedom and growth.*   [98] HStAS A58a Bü 5.
[99] Based on a *per capita* income of around 36 fl. and a *per capita* tax bill of 1.5–2 fl. See chapter 2.

to the *Forstamt*, half again of the actual woodland area.[100] Such a local transformation was perhaps not impossible to imagine, but why do so when it was clearly cheaper to buy the material from elsewhere?

Yet trade could have a transformatory effect in the long term through the integration of the local world into increasing dependency on the larger development of trade flows. Such a dependency was almost invisible at the local level because the very point of much of the trade was to keep things the same and avoid the radical reconfiguration of local relations that would have been required without the ability to import and export. The trading system was already in place in the late medieval period, and thus was not a creation of pressure on resources at a regional level during the sixteenth century. However, because of the extraordinary cost of transporting wood overland, rafting became an increasingly attractive source of raw material when wood prices began to rise. Equally, the terms of trade and the ability to import via water from regions where wood was extremely cheap provided no incentive to radically alter the local system of agro-forestry combining grazing and wood production.

The social dynamics of ecological change

Those who enjoyed more favourable terms of trade or who operated as the conductors of the flows of resources were in a strong position to accumulate wealth and capital. Key to this process were those merchants able to dominate the long and expensive transport routes for salt, wine and manu-factured goods across southern Germany.[101] Equally, benefits came to those who had strong and extensive property rights to the raw material – to the woodland. In this sense commercialisation, 'the market', and the cash economy were indeed key to long-term change. Most important of all was the ability to operate on credit, as all of the significant trades, such as wood rafting, wine and salt, operated on this basis. With high transport costs and limited demand in any one locality, only those who could enjoy significant economies of scale by the size of their trade could compete effectively across large market areas.[102] Yet transformation was not, in itself, a

---

[100] On the assumption of around 20,000 m³ being imported (50 per cent from wood, 25 per cent from iron, 15 per cent from glass, and the rest from salt and miscellaneous goods such as ceramics). Buying this wood thus cost around 1.87 fl. for a fathom equivalent, although the costs for iron or salt of course include the labour, capital equipment and raw material as well as the wood, so the real price for the wood component would have been quite a bit lower. In other words, by early seventeenth-century prices, trade was a good deal.

[101] Certainly it was those with storage facilities in the wine trade that were able to profit, rarely the direct producers. Döbele-Carlesso, *Weinbau*, pp. 296–7.

[102] See Grantham cited in Hoppenbrouwers and van Zanden, 'Restyling the transition', p. 23.

product of 'exchange relations' based on cash superseding relationships based on exchange in kind for immediate use. The most important fact in developing this ecology and determining who benefitted from it, at least in regard to wood, was the uneven distribution of the resource and the right to exploit it. In other words, while a cash economy clearly could assist accumulation, the balance of property rights was the key to power. Both the ecology of the *Markung* and that of trade were a mix of 'natural' and market relationships. Hence the dominance of the early modern era by two phenomena essential to facilitate such exchanges: 'state formation' and the 'merchant capitalist'. But it was not these phenomena that had the only hand in shaping either the management of, or claims to, resources. Nor were flows of resources simply a function of relative prices, because they clearly still moved within a tightly defined institutional framework. And the institutional framework was the result of politics, both at the village level, the district level, and through the intervention of central government. We should not isolate our understanding of how material flows operated from the manner in which they were experienced, conceived and justified. The discussion must now move from considering flows of resources to the actions and claims of people.

Disputes over the *Gaabholz*

People were present everywhere as agents in the ecologies outlined above. The farmers, linen weavers and vinedressers of the region experienced profit or privation in a direct form from their ability to obtain wood. Privation came in with chill or a habitation in cramped, subdivided and often rented dwellings that marked one out from the wealthy home-owner. The vinedresser with an acre of vineyard could rejoice little in the favourable terms of trade that allowed the salt and iron to flow. Vinedressers sold their wine or their labour to wealthier landowners and traders who shifted their products on to profitable markets. The same landowners, traders and middlemen were best placed to bring in the necessities of fuel, timber, iron and salt, whether through inter- or intra-regional exchange. Without the means to directly market their product on any scale both the woodcutter and the vinedresser got the worst terms at either end of the flows of transactions. The unequal entitlement to resources generated different temptations depending on where one stood in the economic order, and brought tension in its wake.

We have seen that one of the most important consequences of member-ship of the village or town commune could be the free allocation of wood from communal woodlands. This could be a considerable buffer against the vagaries of two constraints. One was the weather that left grape harvests more unpredictable than any other. The other was fluctuation in demand for wood or the products that the peasants sold (itself often not independent of weather conditions, of course), both in the shorter and longer term. In the face of such uncertainty the *Holzgaab* gave guaranteed and cheap access (not entirely free, for as a *Bürger* one still had responsibilities) to resources. Access to communal woodland could guarantee a degree of warmth in the home. Another strategy for the poor, however, even where it was illegal, was to sell *Gaabholz* in desperate times. Thus did the poor Leonberger coppersmith Hans Zier in 1584 'because he is poor', or in 1587 the once mason, then swineherd Conrad Haaf, father to nine children, regular debtor and (as his widow after him) recipient of alms. Leonberg prosecuted and imprisoned five men for the offence in 1596, another hard year with a meagre grape harvest. Similarly, authorities complained that this was a frequent phenomenon in Flacht in 1619.[103]

However, simple 'misuse' of the *Gaabholz* was not the only difficulty that arose with its distribution. The wood was allocated among social groups who had both clearly discrepant needs for wood, and the ability to obtain it. It provided a redistributory impulse into an unequal society, mediated via public institutions. Dissatisfaction could arise over the nature of this redistribution, which came to a head in a series of disputes across the region in the latter part of the sixteenth century, as prices rose and yields declined. The unfolding of these disputes provides a window into how people thought resources should be allocated more generally, how it was felt the authorities should act, and what underpinned the legitimacy of their actions. In other words, we can see how different social groups defended the integrity of the territory that they wished to occupy, and how they responded to transformatory pressures. There is direct evidence of legal proceedings from Münchingen (1559), Renningen (1581, 1602–5), Magstadt (1580s), Feuerbach (1580s), Münklingen (1606), Zuffenhausen (1600s) and Heimerdingen (1619), with some evidence of recent contention from Höfingen (1593).[104] We are aware of these disputes, for the most part, because the disgruntled (and invariably poorer) set of litigants petitioned the supreme council to intervene in their favour. These disputes centred on the size of the *Gaabholz* allocation to each household. The poorer households tended to argue that everyone should get an equal share, irrespective of the size of the household or the economic enterprise that it ran. The rich, in contrast, argued that the amount of wood allotted should reflect the

---

[103] Trugenberger, *Zwischen Schloß und Vorstadt*, p. 44; HStAS A572 Bü 33 (index provided in StAL by Achim Landwehr); Schray, *Ortsgeschichte Flacht*, pp. 84–5.

[104] StAL Höfingen Fleckenlagerbuch 1593; StAR Nr B349; HStAS A572 Bü 69; Warde, 'Law'.

needs of the household that they ran, and consequently that they should get more.[105] This dispute could also spill over into an argument about the nature of the commune itself. The village institutions of the *Schultheiß* and *Gericht*, generally staffed by the wealthy, saw all authority residing in themselves with the backing of their ducal overlord. Communal regulations were solely the responsibility of these authorities. The poorer plaintiffs could argue in contrast that local authorities were only implementing rules that should be set by the commune as a whole, and expected this 'one *Bürger*, one vote' principle to be reflected in equal lots of wood.

We can see that these are not disputes between those who favoured a 'natural economy' and those able to purchase wood on 'the market', because nobody actually disputed that the wood should be granted to all *Bürger*.[106] What both sets of protagonists wished to preserve was the stability of their way of doing things, of their social and economic status, by keeping the grant that they received as high as possible, while attempting to minimise the need for flows that might transform their status for the worst. In the case of the poor this worst case might mean having to buy more wood. In the case of the rich it meant conceding the right to allocate local resources to all, rather than through the court that was prepared to translate their greater access to private property to a larger share of communal property.

Receipt of the *Gaabholz* rested on residence as a household head on one of the 'original' village farmsteads, a condition satisfied by nearly all households in this land of tightly nucleated settlements. In some cases this stipulation allowed for discrimination in the size of grants in two ways. Firstly, the number of lots of wood that went to each building or farmstead was restricted. For example, in the wood ordinance of Münklingen in 1587, each farmstead received one lot. If these had, 'as of old', been divided and contained two houses, then two lots were permitted, but if any further residences were built, the whole still only received two lots. Identical rules can be found elsewhere, such as from

---

[105] Such distinctions are typical throughout Europe at this time. Moor *et al.*, *The management of common land.*

[106] This situation was not mirrored everywhere in central Europe. The partible inheritance system of dividing old farmsteads in nucleated villages in this part of Württemberg meant that all *Bürger* had a residence on these farmsteads to which the rights were allocated. However, in areas where many were landless and had no property, and where property holding was the condition of communal membership, only a minority of the *inhabitants* had common rights of any kind. This situation had existed from medieval times in some places, but may have been a later development in others. Warde, 'Common rights'; Shaw-Taylor, 'Labourers, cows, common rights'; Shaw-Taylor, 'The management of common land'; Eliasson and Hamilton, '"Blifver ondt att förena sigh"', p. 49.

Höfingen in 1593. If there was one house but two 'hearths' within it, then each received one lot, but the upper limit remained two lots and further subdivision would not be rewarded with any more wood. The second method was to distinguish between farmers and vinedressers or day-labourers, one that made one's status in the production process more explicit. As the right consisted in the allocation of small areas of woodland to be cut by those receiving them, the commune simply assigned more vinedressers and labourers to each lot than farmers at a ratio of three to two, or four to three.[107]

As the sixteenth century advanced, the rise in population increased pressure on space and buildings. Increasingly, a poorer group became differentiated by the quality of their housing, a process familiar throughout Europe through variations on the term 'cotter'. Such social distancing, although by no means an entirely new phenomenon, had potential to be especially explosive when related to rights that were allocated by residence. This was, however, a complex process, as can be illustrated by the experience of Magstadt, a village lying immediately south of Renningen. Here the jurors of the village court complained that one of the leading proponents of an equal distribution of wood lots was one Hans Betzner, the village mayor, who only did so in order to rent out part of his house at a higher rate. The jurors reported that such partitioning had been going on for about forty years in the village, detailing eight farmsteads that had been divided among sixteen households. This had come about through a mixture of partible inheritance among brothers, and unauthorised building work to house a growing population or to rent out.[108]

The poorer group in these disputes, which went forward for arbitration to the supreme council in Stuttgart, would describe themselves as those without whole houses, or simply 'poor *Bürger*' or the 'inhabitants'. The counter-descriptions by the *Schultheiß* and jurors were not so generous. It was noted that the petitioners had only recently become *Bürger* in Münklingen (which may mean that they were immigrants, or young); in Zuffenhausen they were described as 'unholy', of 'little use' to the duke as taxpayers or providers of corvée labour, and simply as trouble-makers. Furthermore, they were immigrants and not 'children of the village's children'. In describing the rich group of wealthy tenant farmers in

---

[107] In Bietigheim, the dividing line was drawn between *Söldner* who were expected to provide corvée labour with their hands, and owners of draft animals. This was formally established as a divide between those who owned more or less than six acres of arable field, probably in the 1560s. The terms *Söldner* and *Weingartner* were used almost interchangeably. Warde, 'Law', pp. 189–90, 207; StAL Höfingen Fleckenlagerbuch 1593; STABB Bh B546.

[108] HStAS A227 Bü 483.

Möglingen, the *Vogt* of Markgröningen noted that they were the 'notable' (*Ehrbar*) of the village and essentially identical with the local officials. They had used this position to gain precedence in choosing which lots of wood to cut and to permit the cutting of switches to bind sheaves, a practice theoretically against the forest ordinances. The latter fact was used against them by the poor. The wealthier tenant farmers argued in turn that the poor (in this case cotters owing only hand corvée labour, or *Söldner*) had little land (and thus presumably were of less value as taxpayers) and that they were usually in the farmers' employ.[109]

It is notable that the poorer petitioners, who gained most from the 'natural economy' of the *Holzgaab*, generally had rather little to say about the actual state of the woodland. They simply wanted to secure the rights to it. Hans Jungaberlin of Münklingen simply stated that there was 'enough' wood for his, as the jurors described it, 'small ramshackle lean-to'. In this settlement, jurors had rather more to say, not about the present state of their woodland (though the ducal forester thought it in a bad way when consulted), but the future. The 1587 Münklingen wood ordinance had been made, they stated, to prevent the further partitioning of buildings, higher demand for wood, and the subsequent degradation of the woodland. A similar reason was given by Magstadt's authorities in 1564. In Zuffenhausen authorities claimed that the rush to partition houses to gain rental income if wood lots were given out freely would increase the risk of that perennial early modern hazard, fire. In 1619, the officials of Heimerdingen argued that they had a 'modest store' of wood and thus giving out a full lot to all households would be 'unbearable'.[110]

Of course, the future state of the woodland was not an immediate issue for the poor, because their wishes could be met as much by *reducing* the lots given to the rich as expanding those given to the poor. But unusually in Münchingen it was the lawyer representing the *Söldner* who condemned the damaging activity of cutting switches and acknowledged that population growth was restricting the *per capita* share of wood being allotted from the communal woodland. It was thus the poorer group expressing fears of the 'ruination and shortage of wood', '... not only for themselves, but much more for their descendants'.[111] A form of 'ecological' argument was not necessarily, then, the property of any particular social group, but

---

[109] Warde, 'Law' p. 194. [110] Ibid., p. 195.
[111] Tantalisingly, the latter phrase is used by Noé Meurer in the first ever book published on forestry in Germany. Meurer served on the supreme council until 1557, two years before the Möglingen case. It would be an important service to determine whether this expression was common currency or had its origins – along with other arguments employed in this case – from Meurer and his colleagues. Meurer, *Jag und Forstrecht*, p. 5.

raised by those, rich or poor, who sought to restrict the woodcutting of others. As these arguments tended to stress *future* shortages, it is not clear to what extent these represent real difficulties, as opposed to the rhetoric likely to impress a government that had been promulgating ordinances since 1495 lamenting a 'great shortage of wood for fuel and building'.[112]

Such arguments were hardly innocent of other concerns of the time, over disorder and the perceived threat from the itinerant poor. Solutions provided by jurors demonstrate the desire to keep the commune exclusive by limiting rights. In addition, jurors such as those of Zuffenhausen gave voice to a social ranking which, whilst partly predicated upon measurable material status, also introduced notions of the 'use' and moral standing of their opponents. This could be supplemented by a hierarchy of *Bürger*, according to whether one was recently arrived or putatively of long-standing local pedigree. Thus whilst the story of future over-exploitation is utilised by various parties, the narratives in which we find it embedded can be rather different. That of village officials envisages more general problems of disorder. Poorer petitioners, however, focused on questions of justice and distribution of resources, feeling that discrimination was to their 'disadvantage'. Indeed, the lawyer for the Möglingen *Söldner* went further. 'Who can approve,' he declaimed, 'that such inequity should hold in a place, that a rich man who can well afford to purchase wood should take twelve wagonloads in one year from the place's common woodland.' The poor received one or two wagonloads. 'This would meet the approval of no-one.' The notion that economic justice dictated that households should always enjoy what they 'needed' was deeply embedded in the thought of the time.[113] Indeed, communal officials defended the practice of giving smaller lots of wood to certain households by arguing that this still covered household needs and did not necessitate the purchase of wood. Social, and in these cases spatial, differentiation among social groups, allowed interests to coalesce around their experiences of receiving wood lots. With rising population and rising wood prices both sides feared that a transformation could be triggered in which their previous forms of communal regulation and household economies became increasingly untenable.

The onus to resolve these disputes fell to the supreme council. They were not really greatly interested in the outcome of a matter that was considered

---

[112] HStAS A348 Bü 13. It may be that the argument about the future of the woodland of the *Söldner* of Möglingen originated with their lawyer, as it does not appear in their original petition in the same form; however, that first petition does express concern at the damage that the tenants were allegedly doing.

[113] HStAS A348 Bü 13. See Blickle, 'From subsistence to property'.

the responsibility of village courts. The basis by which the supreme council judged these petitions was strictly speaking the purely legal one of whether the village court had made the right decision according to local custom or its ability to alter custom so long as it was not in contravention of centrally promulgated ordinances. The supreme council was generally happy to affirm the judgement of the village court. Yet there was more to the response of the council than this. In the Zuffenhausen case, the councillors made inquiries as to how the neighbouring village of Feuerbach distributed the lots of wood, whose *Schultheiß* reported that an attempt to discriminate some twenty years earlier had failed. In Heimerdingen the supreme council ordered the *Vogt*, forester, *Schultheiß*, jurors and an *ad hoc* extra committee of members of the commune, the *Zusatz*, to arbitrate, although it was a task that the ducal officials found 'arduous'. The result was that there should be a limit of one lot of *Gaabholz* per farmstead, supplemented by a strict admonishment that houses should not be partitioned into three separate dwellings, a practice which in fact contravened the state building ordinance of 1565.[114] Petitioners in Magstadt objected that village officials had granted wood out for the partitioning of buildings and then only some time later barred householders from receiving a full lot of wood. In Münklingen, where interestingly a wood ordinance provided documentary 'proof' of the state of affairs from 1587, the reaction was harsher than anywhere else. Not only did the supreme council back the village authorities; it also instructed the *Vogt* to punish the petitioners to bring them 'to order'.[115]

The hopes of the petitioners were dashed, although not on the basis of the state supporting or imposing a particular distribution of wood. In Weilimdorf or Feuerbach, for example, we see non-discriminatory arrangements prevailing, even when some villagers wanted to introduce unequal shares.[116] Their problem was that the supreme council basically trusted the judgement of those men of 'standing' in the village court unless there was firm contrary evidence. In turn, those jurors and officials came to recognise the utility of having a written record of their position. It was precisely these men who *requested* that the *Vogt* and town notary of Leonberg record and approve their 'custom and rights', presumably at the annual court headed by the *Vogt*, in Münklingen in 1587. Similarly, on winning the case, the wealthy tenantry of Möglingen requested that they should receive a letter confirming the judgement in 1559.[117] What we witness here, in a matter not of immediate concern to the authorities, is the 'trickle-up' process of state formation which leads to central government becoming the authority of last resort. In doing so

---

[114] HStAS A227 Bü 1148 and 1427.   [115] HStAS A227 Bü 483 and 1149.
[116] HStAS A227 Bü 1148.   [117] HStAS A368 Bü 40; A348 Bü 13.

it underpinned both the judgements of the village court, and offered an avenue of redress to those who felt excluded by the court's proceedings. This also allowed the government to present itself as an arbitrating and neutral power which had the final say over matters concerning their subjects rather than being bound into a reciprocal relationship of obligation. As such, it could appear to be a party without interests that only had the best interests of all at heart.[118] At the same time, the written record gradually becomes a material isomorph of the web of legal rights, obligations and reciprocities that finds its final resting place in the ducal archive. We do not see the 'commune' emerging in opposition to 'feudalism' or the 'territorial state'. Rather, the state is called upon to affirm a particular vision of what the commune should be. In doing so, of course, the state was affirming, fairly unintentionally, a particular territorial ecology, a particular distribution of property rights and ability to exploit flows of resources and wealth. It could not really create or destroy these ecologies by itself; its transformatory power was simply not large enough. But it could facilitate certain kinds of solutions to disputes and in this case it tended to strengthen the hands of its traditional local agents, the larger property holders, the 'notables' of the villages and small towns.

Predictably, similar problems arose in the early eighteenth century. Renningen came to an agreement in 1581 after arbitration that those living on 'ancient farmsteads' enjoyed a full grant of *Gaabholz*, but that others who did not, or widows and those living in rented accommodation, would receive only one fathom. Those without a full grant made up nearly half of households at this point, when the local authorities considered the village to be 'highly overpopulated, and with building their woodland has become very exhausted'. (Although in 1594 more senior ducal officials thought there was 'enough building- and firewood'.) The Stuttgart government rejected complaints over this arrangement in 1605. By 1716 the situation had moved full circle: 'The population increases from day to day, and the woodland begins all the more to diminish.' This seems to have provoked a return to the perhaps abandoned previous practice of limiting many households to one fathom. However, the shift in turn brought expense as the commune paid for woodcutting to provide this cordwood. And despite all, the woodland was still 'somewhat ruined'. The court resolved to give those entitled to just one fathom half of a *Gaab* instead, a sure sign that the once generous grants of *Gaabholz* must have been in decline. But they did not want laxity in application of the rule to trouble them again. The judgement

---

[118] See Fuhrmann, Kümin and Würgler, 'Supplizierende Gemeinden', pp. 289 and 303; and Holenstein, 'Bittgesuche, Gesetze und Verwaltung', p. 357.

makes clear that whether 'the population grows or declines', grants of wood must always be made under the auspices of the court.[119]

Crime

If you did not possess property rights to sufficient wood, or the where-withal to buy it, you could just take it anyway. This went for all other woodland products too. This was clearly 'transformatory' in its redistributive effect, though like all notional crime, if it became commonplace then it become a new *status quo*. Indeed, just as wood was imported from elsewhere so that locally matters could stay as they were, crime was often an attempt to maintain stability, not undermine it. It also seems that the very economy of viticulture that allowed this region to import goods left its poorer members particularly vulnerable and prone to steal when times got hard. Years of disastrous grape harvests saw wood theft soar.

All of the official institutions were supposed to enforce the forest ordinances. Village courts similarly enforced their own rules of woodland management, but rarely recorded transgressions. Town courts (which doubled as courts for the *Amt*) are more promising sources, and ducal forest account books record transgressions where fines were levied, as part of these went into the forester's chest. A few cases appear in reports to the supreme council in Stuttgart, and the swearing of *Urfehden*, a kind of recognisance binding someone over to good behaviour, was recorded in the district up until around 1560. As with all crime, there is a 'dark figure' of unknown activity. We do not know why most people came to be prosecuted, although some were clearly caught 'green-fingered' in the woods.

Theft was by far the most frequently recorded crime, ranging in practice from illegally cutting greenwood to pilfering from someone else's wood-pile. (The latter offence was considered more serious in law.)[120] The majority of this theft consisted in actual cutting or felling of wood. However, the rates of crime recorded in ducal account books are very low indeed, doubtless a product of failure to oversee woodlands by the wardens, the use of local and unrecorded measures for dealing with miscreants, but also the very uneven distribution of the woodland itself. Much of it was not particularly accessible to large populations. Communal account books show much higher rates of transgressions.

[119] StAR Nr B349; 1602 Urthel- und Vertragsbuch; HStAS A206 Bü 1002.
[120] Observations are based on a sample of 256 offences in ducal and communal account books. HStAS A302 Bds. 7221–6, A227 Bü 1152; A584 Bds. 1–6; A572 Bü 33; STABB Bh A1678; Mantel, *Forstgeschichte*, p. 517.

Bietigheim recorded a mere two in each of 1619 and 1622, but ten in 1623 and eleven in 1624, involving twenty-three and eight persons respectively. Higher still were rates of presentment in Gebersheim in the late 1620s. Most of the records indicate little more than the name of the transgressor, the nature of the crime and their punishment. Certainly not all of these people were poor, because some had access to carts and wagons, and some also appear purchasing wood for their trade, such as bakers and smiths. Neither were they the very poorest, who could expect support from the poor chest.[121] However, when we hear the voices of those caught, sometimes moving virtually en masse to cut down green-wood, such as the Enzweihingers who invaded the Pulverdinger Holz in the mid-1570s, there is a common refrain. They stole out of desperate need, especially those, as was reported in October 1573, who could not afford to buy wood and would suffer greatly (or even die) from the winter cold. The very high grain prices of the early 1570s also squeezed budgets, leading the peasants to request the right to collect wood in ducal wood-land because of the 'extreme famine'.[122]

About 86 fl. was paid in fines to the ducal forester in 1585–6, 128 fl. in 1609–10, 144fl. in 1619–20 and 130 fl. in 1630–1. This does not represent any real increase given population rise over the same period. Fines paid to the ducal forester dropped as low as 33.5 fl. in 1679–80 but were back up to 137 fl. by the last year of the century. In the early 1690s cold weather and French invasion led to massive illegal woodcutting by those with the misfortune to have troops stationed nearby.[123] These movements to a large extent reflected population levels, but the early decades of the seventeenth century brought particular pressures, and some years stand out. In a report of April 1616 the forester Hans Ulrich Bauder singled out 1597, 1603 and 1612 as being difficult years. These were years of high poor relief expenditure too, but more particularly, were the years of catastrophically bad grape harvests. This loss of income clearly had important repercussions for those who were accustomed to purchasing their wood.[124]

In 1615, by Bauder's account not one of the worst years, a sudden frost destroyed countless vines after several years of dearth, cold winters and heavy, long-lying snow had hit incomes. The forest warden of Eglosheim, Jacob Mückhenfüß, reported gangs of 'ten or yet more' men crossing the frozen Neckar from neighbouring villages to plunder the

[121] There is no overlap between recipients of alms and bread doles in the 1620s in Leonberg and those prosecuted for wood theft, but some of those prosecuted had been forced to take loans of grain from the town granary in previous years. StAL Armenkastenrechnungen; A584 Bds. 1–6; STABB Bh A1678.
[122] HStAS A227 Bü 1124.   [123] HStAS A302 Bds. 7221–35.
[124] HStAS A227 Bü 1428.

nearby woods of the monastery of Bebenhausen. The monastic threshers who were sent to defend the property were told by the raiders that they would 'strike them to the ground'. When apprehended by the forest warden the erstwhile thieves were entirely unapologetic. They told him that he could do with them as he willed, as they had nothing, and if they were thrown into prison, their wives and children would have nothing to eat. At the same time, men, women and children from the villages around Stuttgart were going *en masse* into the forest to cut wood that they sold on the Stuttgart market. Most had 'neither corn, bread nor anything else'. Forest officials were met with swearing and threats, or more subtly were given false identities by those that they apprehended. The supreme council insisted on the full rigour of the law. Locals could 'curse and swear as they want'. The forester replied somewhat tartly that he had read the forest ordinances in all the local villages, to no avail. He presented Theiß Löfler as an exemplar, a man who 'gushed evil words', refused to surrender his axe to the forest warden, and replied that 'he could not bite away the wood with his teeth'. He declared himself 'a very poor fellow' and suggested that the warden turned a blind eye, but ended up in gaol.

The hills above Stuttgart, and especially the viticulture and bleaching centre of Botnang, had a long record of pilfering wood from the local forests where there was little communally owned property. A fifth of the entire population of Botnang were fined for wood theft in 1596–7, although Ulrich Bauder claimed in 1616 that only a tenth of those caught by the forester and his wardens ever appeared for their trial. The 'poorly paid warden' ran 'day and night' but received only abuse, a strong disincentive to enforce the rules. The forester and the wardens had virtually given up trying to fine anyone from Botnang or other nearby settlements. In 1619 the pattern was the same, with the forester estimating that eighty households (i.e. the entire village!) from Botnang earned their subsistence by selling wood in Stuttgart. To do otherwise was 'against their nature and custom', so that 'by night and fog no woodland was safe'. This district may have been exceptional, but a 'custom of disobedience' could clearly take root with a combination of poverty excluding people from the market, but avenues of market participation equally open to those prepared to acquire property by illegal means.

The sad case of Georg Meidelin concludes the story. He was heavily in debt having recently purchased horses, and he and his wife Barbara had not 'a shoe's width of wealth' between them. Coming along the road from Leonberg to Stuttgart, Georg was caught with a cartload of stolen wood. Although reprimanded, he took it to Stuttgart and sold it to a baker, from whom he received a princely 1.5 fl. Meidelin had the wood measured out in a back alley, commenting that he feared he would be seized by a ghost

out the front, and the wood was stored in the baker's cellar. No ghost but
the forest warden found it there, and a few days later the forester caught up
with him and Meidelin was gaoled. Three days later he dodged past a
gaoler who was bringing him a meal and fled both the gaol, and his wife,
who was left to lament that in Botnang stealing wood for subsistence was a
'universal thing' (gemein ding).[125]

Poaching

Poaching was a rather different kind of crime. It was not a crime of
subsistence; in contrast to theft, no poaching was prosecuted at all in
the hard years 1603–5, when other fines were extraordinarily high.
Regina Schulte has described a number of motivations for the illegal
pursuit of game, and a high degree of tolerance for the practice among
the peasantry. She lists simple assertion of masculinity, the thrill of the
chase, and the experience of conviviality (some operated in gangs) or
the indeed the loneliness of the stalker.[126] This list already indicates that
the form of poaching varied greatly, from the harvester who grabbed a
hare darting in front of his scythe or snared a hare in his vineyard, to the
nocturnal armed gang pitted against the forest warden. The practice
spanned social classes, as those who swore Urfehden were often reasonably prosperous. And were they so different from the nobility who per-
sisted in hunting over those areas where they had not been given formal
permission by the Duke?

As we have seen in chapter 3, efforts to prevent poaching (and preserve
game for the nobility and Duke) meant that the carrying of firearms in the
woods was entirely banned, and dogs were not allowed to run loose. Fines
for poaching were heavy and could take many years to pay off, along with a
four-week gaol sentence at one's own cost. The severity of these sentences
can be explained by the association of the right to hunt with lordly power
and honour, and hence poaching with treasonable intent. It was not unusual
for poachers to be scapegoated as a band of bogeymen who, in the official
eye, brought ruination on wives and children (though presumably only if
they got caught), and were also responsible for the murder of officials and
'persons unknown'.[127] They were even blamed for assassination attempts
on Duke Ulrich. There was hardly a secret league of poachers, of course,
but men out and about at night with firearms were automatically suspicious
in many ways.[128] But this view of the evils of poaching was not shared by the

[125] Ibid.   [126] Schulte, The village in court, pp. 121–77.
[127] Reyscher, SWG, Bd. II, pp. 96–8; Bd. XVI, pp. 51–5.
[128] Schindler, 'Nocturnal disturbances'.

wider populace. When the motivation for hunting could vary so much, why would it be so? There was repeat lone offender Stoffel Geylern of Botnang, who fled, abandoning his wife and children, when caught again in 1603. Then there was the entire population of Mönßheim who insisted on their right to catch birds within their *Markung* throughout the sixteenth century. Or there was the Lord Truchseßen of Höfingen, riding across the snows of January 1598 to a slaughter of hares after the forester himself had commented that a couple of hares wouldn't be missed. With such disparate experiences of illegal hunting, it is hardly surprising that people did not come to very firm conclusions about the morality of poaching.[129]

What it all meant for the 'common man'

Petitions, arbitration, trials, prices, reports – there is a welter of evidence as to the variable experience of those that inhabited the region. Certain types of crime and disputes over allocation indicate that some people had it hard. Using this data we can, however, come to a more refined position on how this influenced particular households. Generally speaking, those who received a *Gaabholz* had most, though not necessarily all, of their household needs covered. The basic construction timbers for buildings could also be provided out of communal woodlands. However, both the size of the communal grant and the number of timbers permitted became more limited in the latter part of the sixteenth century and early eighteenth century in at least some places. We would assume that this led to greater dependence on purchases, though it may also have presented villagers with an incentive to cut heating, limit the use of fencing, and partition houses rather than build new ones.

However, many households, especially in the east of the region, had no access to *Gaabholz*. As the population of these regions grew, they had the most potential to have a transformatory effect on the woodlands of importing regions, and were required to export something in exchange. We have seen that 'middling' households in the east of the region earned 2,000–3, 000 grams of silver each year by the early seventeenth century, and that wealthy villagers could earn at least twice that sum.[130] Around 1600 a fathom of cut, stacked timber delivered to the purchaser probably cost 1.5–2 fl. in the east of the region. This amounted to 30–40 grams of silver.[131] If most households required no more than about two fathoms of firewood per year, this made up no more than 4 per cent of

---

[129] HStAS A227 Bü 1143; A557 Bü 210; A302 Bd. 7222.
[130] See chapter 2.
[131] This is at a rate of 19.98 grams to the *gulden*, although this fell to 15.3 grams after 1608.

income for a middling household. Richer households probably had a larger consumption so the proportion of income spent on wood may have been roughly the same. A weaver, however, might earn only 800–900 grams of silver each year from weaving, and firewood would cost 10 per cent of income in this case, although weavers usually had some land too. Two fathoms of firewood could cost as much as twenty-three days' wages for those dependent on labour. Given the generally low level of income, obtaining firewood could thus become a real burden if food prices went up or the grape harvest allowed only low incomes from wine. Basic spelt consumption for a family of five could cost 700 grams of silver *before* processing costs to make bread.[132] There was little room for manœuvre. Obviously wood was easier to steal than food so it is not surprising that in years of bad harvests, which might be colder too, wood theft could soar. Equally, the 1620s, with rampant inflation, poor harvests and disease, saw high rates of theft. This was as much the case in communal woodlands as ducal ones: from 1620 Leonberg set Thursday as the day on which wood could be cut or collected in the communal wood to prevent theft, but this did not prevent a rising tide of offences lasting until 1624.[133] Later eighteenth-century surveys, when wood had become relatively more expensive, put the costs of heating and lighting at between 3 and 13 per cent of household income. Some surveys did not actually mention heating at all, though it is unclear whether this is because a communal *Holzgaab* was taken for granted, or because the poorest simply did not heat.[134]

Communal woodland was not costless. One paid taxes to the commune, and these maintained wardens. There could be corvée labour duties, such as the cutting of building timber required by the commune of Renningen.[135] However, none of these costs are likely to come anywhere near the cost of purchasing firewood, even when one factors in the cost of cutting the wood oneself. In other words, communal property was a considerable boon for the poor, both for firewood, and for grazing rights if they had livestock. And we must remember that these proportions of income devoted to wood are born of a society with much communal property. There is a possibility that wood could have been much cheaper if it had all been available on the open market with no communal

---

[132] The figures are based on previous estimates of prices of a fathom of wood (1.5–2 fl.) and daily wages (0.17–0.18 fl. per day) around 1600. Spelt consumption is set at 2.8 *Scheffel* per person, when a *Scheffel* would have cost 2.5 fl. around this time in Leonberg.

[133] StAL Gerichtsprotokollen Nr.4. 1574–1644.

[134] Troeltsch, *Die Calwer Zeughandlungskompagnie*, pp. 234–5, 239; Walter, *Die Kommerzialisierung*, pp. 118–19.

[135] HStAS A572 Bü 69.

restrictions, although the market demand might have pushed prices commensurately in the other direction. And peasants and labourers would have had to increase their cash income to pay for it.

Making sense

With a few exceptions, nearly everyone spoke the same language ('everyone' being those male voices with the privilege to be set down on paper) when it came to making claims on resources. There were two main ways of justifying claims and behaviour. Firstly, that one had a basic right (one might say a natural right) to subsistence, for which the lord of the land also had a responsibility. This idea was encapsulated in the concept of *Notdurft* (Latin *necessitas*) or 'need'.[136] Often grants of wood, or indeed the amount of wood that households were permitted to buy, were limited to this *Notdurft* which historians have sometimes interpreted as resting on the idea of a subsistence economy of autarkic households. However, it is clear that such a concept could be used very flexibly, and in fact households of all sizes defined their *Notdurft* relative to the size of the household economy rather than a basic unit of subsistence. Consequently, these notions could be employed by anybody, and it constituted a key part of the 'normal language'[137] of discussion about resources and rights. As well as the 'needs' of households one equally finds the services required to lords or communes being talked about in the same way.[138]

Opposed to *Notdurft* and also *nutz* (meaning 'use', 'utility' or 'advantage') were *Schaden* ('damage', 'injury' or 'loss') and *Nachteil* ('detriment' or 'disadvantage'). The nuances of use of these terms were many. A *Schaden* could be the shadow cast by a tree overhanging one's garden and inhibiting grass growth; or a tax (*Landschaden*), a cost incurred, an infringement of rights, a simple loss (like animals eating your crop), someone punching you, or a loss of the ability to acquire one's *Notdurft*. *Nachteil* could be an immediate misfortune to someone, or the threat of long-term degradation as when the supreme council ordered woodcutting in Renningen to proceed 'without detriment' to the woodland in a

---

[136] Blickle, 'From subsistence to property'.

[137] Richard Rorty terms a 'normal language' as 'that which is conducted within an agreed upon set of conventions as to what counts as a relevant contribution, what counts as answering a question, and what counts as having a good argument for that answer or a good criticism of it.' Rorty, *Philosophy and the mirror of nature*, p. 320.

[138] In fact, if there really was an 'Image of Limited Good' one could argue that the idea of each household receiving its recognised *Notdurft* out of a fixed supply of resources actually brought about a 'Pareto-optimal' situation.

dispute over the rights of the village barber in 1567.[139] All these terms appear very frequently in all kinds of records. There was no specialised language in which claims were made, but rather one that was open to all. However, this language did have a specific tenor. It emphasised the continuity or stability of pre-ordained economies and practices. It was, then, the expression of a 'territorial ecology'. However, this was not the same as being the expression of a subsistence or in-kind 'natural economy' for as we have seen, households could not be run entirely on this basis.

When people spoke of their 'need' or 'uses' they were rarely so crass as to justify their desires independently of a claim about the wider good. This brings us to the second primary way of claiming resource use – that it was for the 'common good' or 'common weal', the *gemein nutz*'. This was opposed to selfish appropriation of resources, or '*eigen nutz*'. In the forest ordinance of 1552, for example, one should not cut switches without supervision to one's *eigen nutz*; or the *Vogt* of Liebenzell condemned Württembergers taking wood from a disputed wood near Möttlingen in 1569 as an *aigen* undertaking against good neighbourliness.[140] Forestry officials engaged in petty corruption, or overstepping their jurisdiction, were being *aigennützlich*.[141] This concept was not always an evil, but as understood by the Lutheran theologian Ferrarius Montanus in 1533, 'each of the town-dwellers may work to their *eigen nutz* so long as it is not to the detriment of another'.[142] It was of course easy for the Duke to constantly refer to the *gemein nutz* to justify everything he did, for how could the needs of the father of the land differ from his people's? This was a world, however, where obedience from subjects was reciprocated with the provision of protection and welfare. Indeed, the ducal forest ordinances were not based on any 'forest law' that came (as jurists at the time thought) from hunting rights, but appeared as instructions to officials to ensure supplies of firewood and building timber in ordinances concerned with the general welfare of the population. The poor were thus also always accorded the right to collect dead wood in the woodlands to ensure their subsistence needs, although subject to limitations such as the days of the

---

[139] HStAS A227 Bü 1122.

[140] HStAS A227 Bü 1126. Reyscher, *SWG*, Bd. XVI, p. 46. This is not universally the case in central Europe during the sixteenth century, but praise of the principal of self-interest as being inherently good for the polity as a whole – in providing richer taxpayers, for example – is rare. See Schulze, 'Vom Gemeinnutz zum Eigennutz.'

[141] See HStAS A227 Bü 1147.

[142] 'Ieder aus der bürgerlichen geselschaft mag also sein eigen nutz schaffen/das es einen andern nit zu nachteil geschehe', cited in Landwehr, *Policey im Alltag*, p. 63.

week on which this could occur. The poor, and for that matter anyone else, could thus also claim that the maintenance of good order in the polity had to be fulfilled by ensuring that their needs were met – for the *gemein nutz*.

This linkage of order and access to resources means that it is difficult to distinguish 'economic' claims from those about the more general legitimacy of juridical or institutional practice. Assessing the validity of appeals to the *gemein nutz* or *Notdurft*, that could obviously express opposing interests or be contradictory, required the operation of correct legal procedure. Equally, however, the legitimacy of the legal procedure rested on the fact that *Notdurft* or the *gemein nutz*, however defined, were being effectively satisfied.[143] This conundrum meant that disputes over resources could very easily become disputes over the correct institutional framework in which to adjudicate them, and hence matters of state. This is precisely what occurred with the arguments over the allocation of the *Gaabholz*, a matter that eventually came to be determined by the supreme council as a result of appeals, rather than through its own intervention.

All of which helps shed light on the early modern preoccupation with custom or the 'good old law'.[144] Village regulation is often thought to have rested upon custom and the oral transmission of norms from generation to generation. This ties in with a conception of peasant society as relatively immobile, hedged within its environmental limits and beholden to the 'Image of Limited Good'. In this framework, resource management is thought to have settled into an unalterable system of checks and balances, guaranteeing both sustainable agriculture and the universal provision of subsistence in the face of permanent and absolute limits on available resources. 'Custom' hence becomes a backward-looking method of establishing and legitimising behaviourial and legal norms, as well as a guarantee of future reproduction.

Some of the claims to custom were extravagant. When the communal authorities of Münklingen had their new wood ordinance written out by the town notary of Leonberg in 1587 the practices recorded therein were claimed as being as 'old as the village' and 'how it was at all times previously held by them'.[145] A counter-claim by petitioners disputing these rules said their version was customary from a time 'beyond man's

---

[143] For contemporary arguments about the relationship between law and conscience or justice, see the citations in Strauss, *Law, resistance and the state*, pp. 13–14, 33.

[144] Schmauder, *Württemberg im Aufstand*, p. 175; Blickle, *Theorien kommunaler Ordnung*, p. 7; Freedman, *Images of the medieval peasant*, p. 285; Kelley, ' "Second Nature" '; Scribner, 'Communities and the nature of power'; Suter, *Der Schweizerische Bauernkrieg*.

[145] 'Wie es bey inen hievor jederzeitten gehallten werden.' HStAS A227 Bü 1149.

memory',[146] a variation on 'from time immemorial' that is frequently encountered in the sources. One did not have to be overly choosy about the claim so long as it worked. The more claims one could manage, the better. When the village ordinance of Gebersheim was recorded in 1594, their legitimacy was derived from the fact that they were 'as of old and from longer than man's memory, always and ever, the liberties, law and right' of the place.[147] Sometimes men's memory was given a specific time period, possibly as little as thirty years, although it could be stretched to one's grandfather's grandfather.[148] Although some of the claims made were undoubtedly fallacious, there is enough consistency in the forms used to suggest that people really were reproducing the products of oral testimony, even if exactitude about ages of interlocutors was rather hazy. This goes for officials too, as well as the peasantry. In 1573, for example, the forest warden of Malmstal had to establish the rights and wrongs of a case by testifying to the forester Jacob Harnisch what the prior forester Hans Mentzing had told him about the matter of regulating the fence designed to keep deer out of the fields of Weilimdorf. This was an entirely normal process within and without the administration, though friendlier than the systematic cuffing that Leonberger boys were given while beating the bounds of their *Markung* to assist in the memorisation of the information! Indeed, in 1578, again in Weilimdorf, the supreme council were impressed enough by the unanimity of opinion displayed by villagers to concede that they were *in possessione* of disputed rights, against the testimony of their own forest officials. The translation of a verbal 'from time immemorial' to the learned '*ultra memoriam hominum*' did not fundamentally alter the sentiment.[149] Nevertheless, the increasing 'tickle-up' of such cases to be adjudicated by central authorities, affirmed a particular version of local order and saw central government become the general authority of last resort.

However, it was generally recognised that something being customary did not justify it if it came into conflict with other standards that determined the proper ordering of society. Different people had different priorities, needs and ideas of stability. Even if a practice was established as 'customary', it by no means automatically enjoyed the force of law, for the linkage of custom and law was a type of claim that *could* be effective in directing norms, rather than the *determining* part of a putative system of

---

[146] 'Über menschen gedenckhen herkommen.' HStAS A227 Bü 1149. More generally on these issues, see Troßbach, ' "Mercks Baur" '.

[147] HStAS A584 Bd. 832.

[148] In 1550, jurist Justin Gobler allowed for a period of regular practice as short as a decade to establish custom. Strauss, *Law, resistance and the state*, pp. 100–1.

[149] HStAS A227 Bü 1130, 1132; A572 Bü 41.

'customary law'. The legal system was equally established on precepts other than the simple establishment of 'custom'. In the words of Otto Brunner, opinion rested more on the basis: 'It is not good because it is old, but old, because it is good.'[150] Even then the antiquity of custom was not a guarantee; as the tract *To the Assembly of Common Peasantry* stated in the Peasants' War of 1525, '. . . one does not speak of "custom", one speaks of "rightful customs". But when one has acted unjustly for a thousand years, that would ever be right for a single hour.'[151] As a consequence, the kind of arguments in which 'custom' emerged could be rather varied. It could be used as a defence against recent innovation, as was the case in the claims of Württemberger rebels in the 'Poor Conrad' rebellion of 1514. However, it could also be argued that long-established practices in fact offended another precept of justice that it was customary to uphold.[152]

It is hardly surprising that the village court jurors, those entrusted with the determination and enforcement of law in the village, tended to testify that their version of proper practice was 'customary', the 'old custom of the village'. In the disputes over the allocation of wood grants, the current '*Holzgaab* right' was said to reflect things that had been practised 'always and is customary'. The dissenters, the poorer and in their eyes disadvantaged men who petitioned against village court decisions, were left with two strategies. The first was to argue that a diminution of what the officials saw as discretionary grants to them was an offence against custom, 'the expropriation of customary use-rights', as E. P. Thompson puts it, which could result in them being 'rebellious in defence of custom'.[153] In Heimerdingen this took the form of pleading that practices were different thirty years ago. In Münklingen, dissenters used the strategy of appealing to a document that had supposedly guaranteed their rights in the matter for five hundred years as well as asserting that in any case local practice had been as they claimed 'from time immemorial'.[154] These cases illustrate the strategy of asserting a different version of custom from that of the village court, if possible providing some documentary evidence of the antiquity of such custom that would stand as irrefutable

---

[150] Brunner, 'Bermerkungen zu den Begriffen', p. 75; for a measured discussion of the relation of custom and law, see Poos and Bonfield, *Select Cases*.

[151] This is of course part of the early sixteenth-century argument between 'godly law' and 'custom', concepts that sometimes emerged in tandem, and sometimes opposed. Cited in Scott and Scribner, *The German peasants' war*, p. 274. See similar examples from England cited in Fox, *Oral and literate culture*, p. 279.

[152] Schmauder, *Württemberg im Aufstand*, p. 79. Also Strauss, *Law, resistance and the state*; Blickle, *From the communal Reformation*, pp. 13 and 150–61.

[153] Thompson, *Customs in common*, p. 9.   [154] HStAS A227 Bü 1149, 1427.

before the testimony of the jurors. The second strategy was followed at Möglingen. Here custom was simply not mentioned. Instead, the lawyer for the *Söldner* argued that regulatory power over the woodland was vested in the commune as a whole, not the court. Indeed, this could be a follow-up to the argument of 'custom' if it could be alleged that the jurors were not in fact upholding their role as defenders of the true custom.

It is in comparing these two accounts that we can perceive the pragmatic appropriation of concepts and arguments. In one place the *Schultheiß* and jurors argued both that they were upholding things as 'they had been maintained at every time before this', *and* that such measures were necessary for the preservation of wood supplies. In another, the poorer sorts maintained that they (as a majority in the commune) had the right to alter earlier practice to ensure wood supplies for their descendants, arguing at the same time that the current distribution of lots was manifestly unjust and intolerable.[155] In short, the poor were only 'litigious in defence of custom' so long as it could be harnessed to defend their idea of what the reciprocities around which the commune was built should be. Furthermore, peasants perceived custom as alterable, and made the kinds of distinctions that we would see as relating, respectively, to positive and natural law, whilst not being able to articulate them clearly because of a reliance on the legitimacy of 'custom'. It may be that pressure to articulate the legitimacy of local norms to a different audience in fact *generated* a search for the 'origins' of custom among parties to such disputes, causing later scholars both to lose sight of custom's strength (the ability to alter norms according to circumstance, unlike, for example, natural or divine law), and contemporaries to posit to themselves an 'original', more harmonious society from which custom derived.[156] As with the disputes over the allocation of communal resources and conduct of officials charted in Hesse by Robert von Friedeburg, the manner in which concepts were appropriated and employed belonged to a peasant politics, an intra-communal argument that nevertheless had to orient its rhetoric towards outside arbitrators. Unsurprisingly, the fact that numerous relatively autonomous communes existed could give rise to different outcomes depending on the immediate circumstances, even when, as in these cases, there tended to be two relatively easily defined opposing groups predicated on their entitlements to material goods. Equally unsurprisingly in this age, an

---

[155] HStAS A348 Bü 13.

[156] This opposes a commonly held view that 'godly', 'natural' and 'customary' law were never distinguished. For instance Suter, *Der schweizerische Bauernkrieg*, p. 413.

alliance of the already established holders of local office, and more senior ducal officials, tended to prevail in conflicts.[157] But even where a broad consensus was lacking, people attempted to copper-fasten their case in terms that were well understood. This was equally the case when the fault line of disagreement indeed fell between the ducal officials and villagers.

Gerlingen 1581: leading and misleading questions

State formation, often presented (above all for the seventeenth century) as the onward march of a determined and innovatory central government, often proceeded on a rather different basis and allowed a high degree of consensus about the terms of discussion. These terms in themselves, however, were flexible enough to allow both a reasoned defence of 'custom' by villagers, where they so wished, and a drive to change local practice on the part of officials in order to enhance the *gemein nutz*. A shared language did not make for harmony, but banal and everyday contestation. This is exemplified by a dispute over whether the villagers of Gerlingen in the early 1580s had to pay extra for the 'late' masting of pigs (that is, after the traditional date for the practice to end in the autumn).[158]

Although it is fairly clear that officials, especially supreme councillors out in the field, drew up and asked a stock set of questions of witnesses in each case, it is unusual for these to be provided for us. One of the fortunate examples in this respect is the dispute over Gerlingen's pannage rights that brought the forester, several councillors and the *Heimburg* and *Gericht* of the village together on 13 December 1581. The councillors engaged in the questioning were not only to acquire the opinion of the interlocutors, but establish what they had heard from others – showing some faith, perhaps, in 'collective' opinion-making beyond the testimony of the individuals present. They also had no less than five lists of questions drawn up to put to the Gerlingers.

Whilst to some degree masquerading as simple inquiries into the 'fact' of the matter, many of these were not, it seems, innocently phrased. The villagers were repeatedly asked questions which began 'If there were not . . .', or 'If it had not been customary that . . .', inviting assent on the assertion contained in the phrase. Much of the matter turned on why the rights claimed by the villagers for free, but that the councillors wanted to charge for, had not been recorded in the survey of 1556. The witnesses

[157] Friedeburg, '"Reiche", "geringe Leute" und "beambte"'.
[158] The discussion below is based on the case in HStAS A368 Bü 29.

were presented with two opposing propositions with which to agree or disagree. Firstly, that the forester and his warden had simply not wanted to acknowledge the rights claimed. Alternatively, if they had not been recorded (and the officials must have known this to be the case), 'if they were not therefore to conclude, that they consequently had no power or right to the "after-pannage", for otherwise they would have doubtless also have presented and had it recorded'.[159] The last list of questions was more pejorative. The officials enquired if this was in fact a *'gemein geschrei'*, a 'rumour' or 'stir' in the public domain, and how many people were 'making and causing' such a *'Sag'* (rumour, story).[160] In applying these terms the officials relegated the opinions expressed to a matter of peasant talk rather than entertaining the legitimacy of the rights, although they checked the villagers understanding by asking, 'What is called a *gemein geschrei* ...?' This was contrasted with the more wholesome *'Sag'*, as they asked if it was not the case that the *'gemeine sag'* in fact agreed that the rights claimed belonged to the Duke. This line was then condescendingly followed up by asking if the neighbouring settlements didn't accord the Duke the rights, and if not, which settlements had the rights that were being claimed for Gerlingen. If anyone at this point still asserted that these claims were correct, they were asked straight out if those who said so had a current or future personal interest in having these rights, and who was propagating these rumours (*'gemeine sag'*).

The witnesses did not, however, accept this approach. Virtually all agreed that the pannage claimed had been practised on and off for no payment, whilst Claus Lonhardt, and Jacob Schopff, directly contradicted the implication of the councillor's question by stating that the villagers did so by a legal right. Gall von Sachsenheim, forester some twenty-five years before, did not know the answers to many of the questions, though he did state that the warden at the time knew such things. He stated baldly that the fact that he received no money from the villagers was proof enough of their right to free after-pannage – not that he had failed to fulfil his duties. Villagers were quite happy to admit a personal interest in the matter – no dissembling there – but Michel Frieß added that he didn't want to damn his soul either, and so would speak the truth. Answers tended to the blunt and practical. Asked if the wild boar had eaten all the acorns, so that the forest officials never asked for a payment for the meagre left-over mast, Frieß replied that no one would

---

[159] HStAS A368 Bü 29. 'Und wann dem also, ob nicht darauß zuschließen, das Sie derwegen kheinen fuog oder recht deß Nachackerich haben, sonnsten wurden Sie es damalen ohnzweiffenlich auch dargethan und einschreiben lassen haben.'
[160] On these terms, see Sabean, *Power in the blood*, pp. 148–9, 179–80.

be so mad as to let their pigs run in a wood where there wasn't any pannage (this after stating that they had gone in with two or three hundred).

Jaus Winderer, a (by his account) sixty-seven year-old juror of the village court, equally said that he didn't believe anyone would drive their pigs into an 'empty heath'. He had been present when the *Renovator* recorded local rights in 1556, but as the official had not asked specifically about pannage, it appears that nobody mentioned it. The talk about the pannage was not a *Geschrei* but a *gemeine Sag* among everyone in the commune, and if the testimonies are anything to go by, there was a universal agreement on the issue. Three more points are of particular interest. He stated that if the rights had pertained to the Duke, then the forester would have prevented them being exercised for free by the Gerlingers. Was this 'optimistic' estimation of the power of the forester mendacious? Secondly, whilst admitting, as did others, the somewhat obvious interest that any inhabitant with pigs had in the outcome of the case, he stated that it had 'always been a *gemeiner nutz*' that he enjoyed what the woodland yielded. Finally, when asked if the practice of pannage had been 'customary' but had never in fact been a 'right' (*Gerechtigkeit*) he simply shook his head and asked what the question meant.

Jaus Winderer did not speak for everybody. His testimony above all, however, exemplifies the encounter of somewhat condescending officials, and locals. The councillors, who got out into the field to deal with this on a face-to-face basis, suspected that the claims stemmed from laziness on the part of officials at best, or possibly scurrilous self-interested rumour. The peasants did not beat about the bush in pointing out the practicalities of the situation. The latter were neither cowed, nor foolhardy in their answers. The repeated emphasis on the tolerance the foresters had always shown them, whilst perhaps talking up the expectation that the foresters fulfilled all of their duties, was a strong argument to present to the councillors who were, after all, reliant on the foresters and wardens above all else. Peasant witnesses turned an acknowledgement of their individual interests into an assertion of the practice or opinion of the commune as a whole. Finally, Jaus Winderer's confusion, at least as it appeared, over the difference between 'custom' (*Herkommen*) and 'right' in law (*Gerechtigkeit*) – himself a juror of the village court – sidestepped the rigorously procedural view of the councillors.[161] This does not mean that all custom was blithely taken to be law, or was unalterable, but that

---

[161] Although it was in itself compatible with the Justinian Code's view on the matter in Section 1.2.9 of the *Institutes*, Strauss, *Law, resistance and the state*, p. 100.

each was the underpinning of the other, and to separate them in such a way was nonsensical.

Faced with the overwhelming unanimity of testimony the officials in fact conceded the rights of the Gerlingers, though limiting them to two pigs each in the 'after-pannage'.[162] Much as the councillors attempted to posit a proper procedure, an order of fact that could be equated with the legal norms of the juridical training, the villagers remained determinedly resistant to their insinuations. Nevertheless, the legitimacy in the eyes of the state was finally vested in the supreme council's adjudication. There can be no doubt that in the long term, this process, whilst not 'one-way', was drawing the villagers more closely into the web of procedures of central government.[163]

Ecology and the state

The early modern state has been called many things: mercantilist, absolutist, cameralist, home of 'projects' or the agent of 'social discipline'. Many of these discussions, though often only tangentially related to each other by historians, turn around what one thinks about the ability of the state to expand its power to command the population and extract wealth from it. An implicit or explicit agenda is whether, firstly, the state acted as an innovator to attempt to transform social and economic relations to its advantage, and secondly, often in response to Marxist arguments, whether in doing do so it advanced the interests of particular groups within society. Obviously outcomes of such processes can be argued as being 'progressive' or 'reactionary' depending on one's understanding of such terms.

Chapter 3 has already examined how the state was engaged in an ongoing process of self-positing, argument and engagement within itself and with those formally outside of its structures (a group rather difficult to define given the broad range of office-holding in early modern Württemberg). Here I would like to bring these processes more explicitly into connection with economic development and ecological change. Most of the state's activity in relation to the management of the key resource, wood, attempted the same kind of 'territorialisation' familiar to any other resource users. People wished their rights to be cemented, and income flows (which in the case of something like after-pannage rights was as much to provide recognition of legal possession as a real money earner) to be secured. However, given competing claims, a

---

[162] HStAS A368 Bü 29.   [163] See Strauss, *Law, resistance and the state*, pp. 38–40.

generally inequitable distribution of wealth and access to resources, and ecological change (albeit fairly slow by modern standards), in practice the maintenance of territories, and indeed status, required changes and innovations in managing and justifying flows of resources. This could be recognised at all social levels. Through contesting territories, arose transformation, a process from which relative winners and losers could emerge.[164]

What marked the state out from other actors in these processes is perhaps the most obvious fact about it. It was concerned with the entire territory of the state, not just one part within it. This did not make ducal councillors, foresters or any other official equitable or reasonable in their dealings, but it defined a level of operation, and an ability to exercise power, through which interest groups (sometimes with the best intentions) sought security, prestige and influence. This fact, rather than any differences in language, ideology or means, set the state apart and gave it its peculiar role in economic development. It tended to aggrandise power because it could facilitate or marshal flows (and tax them) across a wider range of activity and on a wider spatial scale than virtually any other organisation. It could equally play the arbiter among other groups (within smaller territories, just as the Empire did to the princely states and imperial cities within it) because it transcended the territories over which subaltern groups and local elites struggled.[165]

The language of 'need', 'custom' and the 'common weal' was a spectacularly successful idiom with which to deal with these problems, enduring throughout the period. Everybody could legitimately have their say, and especially could articulate via custom the transmission of good practice among groups rooted in an ecology where transport was costly, and resources limited and vulnerable. But 'custom' and the desire to define a territory did not necessarily generate inertia. If 'custom' could not guarantee 'needs' being met then the 'common good' determined that this could be changed. Change itself was perfectly legitimate so long as it could convincingly be argued that it served the 'common good', and the world of 'custom' and that of innovation could co-exist, if not happily on

---

[164] This is clear where strategies such as peddling or long-term or seasonal migration brought clear changes of the local ecology in their wake, though often preserving aspects of the old. Troßbach, 'Beharrung und Wandel "als Argument"', p. 119. See also Ambrosoli, *The wild and the sown*, p. 11.

[165] Braddick's argument that the state is defined as being not central but 'more extensive than the locality' is useful here. He is surely right to be suspicious of a simple model of increasing 'centralisation' but the increased ability to 'co-ordinate' across a wide range of matters often went hand in hand with the oversight of a centralised decision-making process or locus of final authority. Cited in Hindle, *The state and social change*, p. 20.

every occasion. The sixteenth century would see the rapid expansion of the use of Roman Law principles, often in response to anomalies that had arisen among contradictory local customs and in a world where rulers happily enforced the 'good old law' alongside the new precepts of the *ius commune* espoused by jurist councillors.[166] Of course, sheer power and wealth could bypass the need to convince. Under Roman Law the state was also viewed as the only arbiter of what law should be, but in practice government still argued that it knew best what the 'common good' was, rather than simply making a procedural argument.[167] The state was certainly powerful and wealthy, though still exposed to any counter-currents and pressures, internal and external. It was also best placed, as the self-professed provider of solutions to problems that could not be resolved within more restricted milieu, to determine in what form the 'common good' was best served, whether for good or ill. Facilitation of market development by legal guarantees and removal of privilege, the upholding of privilege and restrictions on trade, redistribution of wealth through taxation, borrowing and bond sales, the provision of defence and the attracting of conflict through dynastic ambition, care of souls and the poor and the provision of schooling: all these and more were issues that exercised and engaged all Württembergers. In different contexts all of this and none of this seemed reasonable. In the wake of the search for 'equilibria', to use a term from economics, came transformation, conflict, but, equally, enduring patterns and inertia. Such a formulation stands as a corrective, one hopes, to less discriminating or more linear models of development.

---

[166] Strauss, *Law, resistance and the state*, pp. 52, 60–65, 85–6.
[167] Ibid., p. 244. See also Landwehr, 'Die Rhetorik'.

Conclusions

The conceptual framework that I have attempted to develop in this volume strives to be one adequate to the task of understanding how the state and the material world intersected, and to enable us to describe and explain what might be implied by early modern society living in the 'wooden age'. One hopes the reader has been convinced of the degree to which early modern history is intertwined with what is usually considered the realm of botanists or environmental scientists in a 'historical ecology'. The growth rates of plants to a large degree determined available energy supplies, setting the parameters for economic development. The high rate of friction of wooden surfaces against earthen or, very rarely, paved roads contributed to high transport costs and impeded exchange. The relatively lesser friction, and the continual downward surge born of gravity, gave a comparative advantage to those who could bear their wooden loads on waterways. These things have perhaps been so evident to historians, that they have rarely attempted to investigate their influence in depth or quantify the flows (ecology) or values (economy) of the resources involved. Yet were they any less worthy of detailed attention than rents, wages or profits, over which so much ink (if still not enough) has been spilt? Yet it should also be clear by now that the vegetation of a region, whether a river was navigable in any way or not, and so forth, is the product of human action and choices. As described in the introduction and chapter 1, historians approaching these interactions have often assumed that these choices represent an adaptation to the circumstances that people found themselves in. So much would be presumed for any vaguely rational creature, or simply implied by survival. However, it is quite another thing to imply that people adapt their actions to the *optimal* behaviour for their environment. Conversely, it could be argued that institutions and ecological forms ('environments', vegetation cover) persist for long periods of time precisely because people are not great optimisers, whether of income, yields, or energy conversion rates. Long duration cannot simply be taken as evidence of optimal behaviour.

What to analyse, and what we learn: households, communes, states

How we perceive early modern society often depends on the unit we take for analysis. The units listed below, and which have appeared repeatedly in this book, are not simply analytical constructs, but they were the creation of a particular set of power relations and institutions. *Households* are often seen through fiscal eyes, because they were the unit of taxation and, to some degree, inheritance. Nevertheless, it would be quite wrong to argue that households were the *product* of particular fiscal policies. The fiscal perspective is simply one way to view the multi-faceted household. The same goes for the institutions of the *commune* or the *state*. They meant different things to different people, and so the fact that the 'commune' was internally differentiated, or that the ideology of the '*ganzes Haus*', the co-ordinated and harmonious household unit, were idealised constructs, does not grant them any less real or concrete a role in social relations. Institutions were not simply projections of the interests of those who staffed them, but structured behaviour in their own right.[1]

What makes the units of the household, commune and state significant is not that they always took on a particular form but that they were the institutional framework by which expectations of reciprocity were generated. When, for example, Sebastian Löw of Leonberg claimed that he was not ill each morning from excessive drinking, but because of the lentils his wife cooked for his food, he was certainly not describing a model and harmonious household, but he was evoking an order of shared responsibility and tasks.[2] He may well have been getting unpleasantly large amounts of lentils to eat and it may have had something to do with his drinking – reciprocity in action. Clearly the dominant 'household' model of the time, by which the male had authority and by which taxation and communal benefits were apportioned, had very negative consequences for women.[3] Women were not completely powerless or passive in the face of this. They had separate rights to the property they brought to a marriage and contested their share of household income, as demonstrated for Württemberg by David Sabean and Sheilagh Ogilvie.[4]

---

[1] It is rather difficult to agree with Sreenivasan that the 'seamless conception of the German village community', has 'become a virtual orthodoxy'. One could, in fact, argue quite the contrary, as it is increasingly rare to find a study that does not emphasise the internal differentiation of communes. Sreenivasan, 'The social origins', p. 31.
[2] Landwehr, *Policey im Alltag*, p. 196.   [3] See Ogilvie, *A bitter living*.
[4] Sabean, *Property*; Ogilvie, *A bitter living*.

Yet, although there were plenty of people who remained unmarried, especially by the eighteenth century, the household as a fundamental organising unit remained unchallenged.[5] It was certainly a primary mechanism for the allocation of wood, as both communal grants and sales more generally were supposed to be limited to those required for household consumption. It seems that in earlier medieval centuries the household had been coterminous with the farmstead. The main allocation disputes seem to have arisen where subdivision of farmsteads and buildings pitted the claims of the household against those of the house, the building or building plot itself. At this point disputants began to argue about the wood that should be allocated on the basis of relative positions of households in relation to the economy of the whole commune.

It has not been the purpose of this book to describe how these institutions emerged, because for the most part they clearly existed in the late medieval period. Features of communal agriculture may well have been labour-saving measures introduced in periods of relative labour scarcity and slack population pressure that would have made the agreement necessary for institutional change correspondingly easier.[6] We do however need to explain why they endured. I have argued that once in place, the commune and the communal governance of economic affairs represented above all an avenue for the reduction of complexity in decision-making, especially in regard to the agricultural calendar. It was attractive, above all, for *organisational* reasons. This is not to say that it always offered the cheapest avenue for any single question or could not be a fundamental hindrance for individuals. Yet once established, and perhaps in part out of simple inertia, it became the dominant arena for public

---

[5] See the excellent discussion in Knotter, 'Problems of the "family economy"'. The persistence of the household unit down to the present should not disguise radical changes within it, and strongly divergent structures at every point in time. Löfgren usefully distinguishes households with 'centrifugal' tendencies (such as a family farm) and the 'centripetal' (orientated towards waged labour elsewhere) at either end of a continuum. Although we are now taxed largely on individual income and purchases, household income remains a consideration for welfare benefits and exemption from full liability for local taxation in the United Kingdom.

[6] Some authors, especially working on northern Germany, have associated strong communal institutions with collective agricultural arrangements, as communes were absent in enclosed coastal regions but prevailed in open-field regions. It is not clear however that these patterns were replicated elsewhere. England certainly had open-field arrangements and some collective determination of agriculture and land use via the manorial court, but did not have communal government as can be found in many parts of western Europe. Rheinheimer, *Die Dorfordnungen*, pp. 122–3; Lorenzen-Schmidt, 'Siedlungshistorische Aspetke'; Moor, Shaw-Taylor and Warde, *The management of common land*.

dispute resolution and resource allocation. Indeed, once established, it became very expensive, as struggles over enclosure demonstrated, to disentangle any of the web of communal governance. Given this, it would be astonishing if communes were not internally rather disputatious, as where else would people go to argue? To some degree this approach follows the argument made by Douglass North:

... the more easily others can affect the income flow from someone's assets without bearing the full cost of their action, the lower is the value of that asset. As a result, the maximization of an asset's value involves the ownership structure in which those parties who can influence the variability of particular attributes become residual claimants over those attributes. In effect they are then responsible for their actions and have an incentive to maximize the potential gains from exchange.[7]

This is certainly a plausible explanation for why woods might be communally owned, although of course far from all were. However, the explanation of the commune's role does not have to rest upon the defence of asset value, even if this explains why they would prevent alienation of goods from the *Markung*, limit commercial exploitation and regulate use rights. One could also make an ecological argument, or an egalitarian one, and we have seen in chapter 5 that people did precisely this. They did not need only one explanation for the importance of an institution like communal property holding, but imagined its benefits in many ways. Reducing friction and providing avenues for dispute resolution of course reduced costs (for some, at least) and helped secure the value of assets. But the commune also instilled a very broad idea of what constituted an asset, attached to the slippery notion of the '*gemein nutz*'. A scarcity of wood, for example, raises prices and thus can be seen to impinge on the assets of the population by increasing their living costs. This indirect effect, which early modern peasants were clearly keenly aware of, is only indirectly captured in North's formulation. The commune thus gave the opportunity for people to defend their livelihood, their *Nahrung* or *Notdurft*, even as it gave the village oligarchs a strong hand in allocating resources, sometimes in favour of themselves.[8] Everyone could have the hope of getting something from the commune, which is not to say that this always happened.[9] The greater the property holdings or regulatory power

---

[7] North, *Institutions*, p. 31.

[8] In that they found their own justifications for their actions more convincing than the claims of others. One might want to argue that their arguments about 'equality' and rights in the allocation of resources were fair. They are still frequently encountered today.

[9] This conclusion is in some ways, though not entirely, in contradiction to Sheilagh Ogilvie's very negative assessment of the institution and its long-term effects. The negative effects she suggests very probably loomed large in the lives of many, especially women.

of the commune, the more secure access to those assets might seem to those who had a stake in communal property. Once established, the commune also had a tendency, as a ready-made arena for dealing with resources, to attract all such disputes into its field of operation. Any diminution of the commune's powers could be represented as the victory of interest groups, and to be resisted.

I believe that a similar account can be given of the development of the state. This may explain why the idea of an institution evoking expectations of reciprocity and providing regulation on a certain scale of operation (i.e. central government) proved attractive to many, increasingly had demands placed upon it by the populace, and appears to have operated in a relatively consensual environment (indicated in part by the fact that people brought their disputes to it). It may have proved all the more attractive when incomes for most people were persistently low, and the risks of market dependency correspondingly high. Stefan Epstein has convincingly argued, indeed, that only the state could effectively provide the framework for trustworthy market transactions on a large scale and people may have viewed the commune in the same light when it came to local resource allocation. If communes were prone to dominance by local oligarchs, the state potentially provided a counterweight to their power, though by no means necessarily so.[10] Yet, at the same time, peasants violently opposed the state, or simply ignored its agents, in the case of particular issues where innovations that from the state's viewpoint seemed to make things 'simpler', less complex, or more effective, introduced unwanted disturbance into local conditions. There was, of course, a considerable incentive for the state to operate by co-opting communal institutions. The passage of these developments will now be traced in more chronological detail.

The pattern is set: late medieval antecedents, ca 1450–1540

In the second half of the fifteenth century it seems clear that the communally regulated three-field system of agriculture with communal

---

Nevertheless, her view of the impact of communal institutions is one sided. For every incidence where communes restricted movement, consumption choices, marriage rights or freedom to allocate labour (presumably raising costs), we can point to cheap access to property and collective labour-saving arrangements. While Ogilvie highlights, for example, the potential inefficiencies generated by the strict partible inheritance system that did not allow widows to 'pay' for their children's labour by promising differential inheritance shares, one could equally argue that partible inheritance guaranteed many women a share in property to which they otherwise might have no access. A balance sheet of these contradictory effects is yet to be drawn up. Ogilvie, *A bitter living*, pp. 332–4, 352.

[10] Epstein, *Freedom and growth*.

pasture was prevalent. Württemberg was a wine-exporting region, and sheep-raising was an important part of the economy of the Strohgäu. Woodland grazing was important and a matter for dispute between neighbouring communities. While there is relatively little known about the precise details of most of the wood economy, coppicing was present, if not generally systematically applied, in communal and ducal woodlands. Many communities, especially in the centre and east of what became the *Forstamt* Leonberg, did not have their own woods and presumably bought in supplies from elsewhere. This probably did not involve the purchase of firewood on any great scale, but timbers and stakes for vines were being rafted down the Enz in the late fifteenth century. The mighty oaks used to build Markgröningen's magnificent town hall in 1477, for example, have notches indicating that they had been bound into rafts at some point.[11] In other words, all the main material aspects of the later economy were already in place.

There was also a forestry administration, which seems to have had its roots in the fourteenth century. From at least the middle of the fifteenth century, lordly foresters and forest wardens became more numerous, but still had responsibility for overseeing only property owned directly by the *Graf* of Württemberg. Equally, the system of administrative districts headed by a *Vogt* and centred on a small town with a hinterland of villages was a creation of the fourteenth century. This was expanded as the territory of Württemberg grew, largely by purchase but at some points by conquest. In some cases new individual *Ämter* were founded, in others, older districts simply engrossed new possessions. None of the administrative innovations of the early modern period fundamentally altered this structure of governance. The written record of the activity of communal authorities and by-laws are largely a product of the sixteenth century, so we cannot be sure that their competence was equivalent in the earlier period. However, judging by the activities they are seen to engage in by the end of the fifteenth century (purchase and exchange of property, taking on of credit, some communal agriculture), they would seem to have been very similar.

The increased ambition of lordship evident at the end of the fifteenth century manifested itself in increased regulation and responsibility for these well-established bodies. In the case of 'forests', the state ordinance of 1495 did not seek to expand the competence of foresters as a claim to regal rights over uncultivated land or to particular types of resources, as was the case in some other parts of

---

[11] Petra Schad, personal communication.

Europe. The *Graf* Eberhard the Bearded could already claim those rights by virtue of being lord over the communes, and land-use change was already subject, in theory at least, to the scrutiny of the *Vogt*. Rather, an expressed fear of wood shortages enjoined the government to seek to regulate wood out of concern for the welfare of the population. This claim of a general right to legislate for such matters does not seem to have been disputed at any point and remained the cornerstone of all subsequent forestry legislation. What was at issue, especially given the rather vague terms of the first state ordinance, was the precise form that regulation would take. Communes and foresters would engage in a prolonged struggle over who had the first right to regulate common lands, and whether foresters should regulate communal cutting of communal woods, though there is little evidence that they made more than sporadic efforts in regard to the latter. Similarly, the expansion of the forestry administration's purview led very quickly to demands for clear limits to be placed on its activity, for the respect of ancient custom, and transparency and honesty in the foresters' dealings. These and other themes fed into unrest in 1514 and 1525. These were rebellions that gave vent to anger against the feudal order, the simple inequality of wealth in society, and religious idealism. They also, however, were the product of an era where the 'services' provided by the state did not seem sufficient to justify the increased vigour of its activity.[12] Perennial concerns like the depredations of game to the subject's crops also found expression in these rebellions and throughout the rest of the period. The theme of confrontations between the state and the 'people' was set. That wood regulation was a legitimate concern of government seems to have been widely recognised, but the terms of the regulation were not. This reflected increased vigour in state regulation across a range of economic activity, moral behaviour, bureaucrats, poor relief, and after the Reformation, schooling and religion.

---

[12] Over time, one would expect the village 'oligarchs' to become increasingly sympathetic to the state as they became more enmeshed in its functions, and the state proved itself to be responsive to their concerns. However, this could also be true for poorer groups who desired avenues of appeal over the heads of local authorities. The situation in 1525 is complicated by the very different kind of lordships from which rebels came. Sreenivasan suggests that in Ottobeuren, the war was begun by 'village oligarchs as a traditional form of landlord–tenant bargaining', but it seems unlikely that this could be a more general explanation for the course of the war unless we credit wealthy villagers with an extremely poor judgement of the consequences of their actions. Sreenivasan, 'The social origins', p. 52.

The age of disturbance, 1540–1618

The ordinance of 1540 constituted the first major piece of forestry legislation, and was the model of such practice up until the nineteenth century. Around the same time, it appears that ducal forest income began to
rise sharply, ahead of even a general European rise in prices (though not
of grain prices in Württemberg in a decade of favourable harvests). It is
likely that this reflected both the implementation of the ordinance and
increased market dependency for obtaining wood supplies on the part of
the peasantry. As population grew, though with considerable local fluctuations driven by epidemic, the levels of importation and biomass transfer also grew. At the same time as the Duchy became more integrated
both economically and administratively, however, regulation increasingly
reiterated or possibly even imposed a degree of 'localisation'. Trade and
the activities of middlemen were restricted. 'Need' (*Notdurft*) was a
widely articulated principle of resource allocation. The government
enforced once and for all limits on grazing herds, although, it seems, as
much in the context of disputes over grazing rights as pending ecological
disaster. The increased disturbance born of population growth, and
higher demands on the local biomass, were tackled by poor relief systems
that gave the whip hand to local oligarchs. Legislation sought to set
maximum prices locally at the same time as granting increasing guild
rights that presumably raised prices to maintain income levels. Wood
imports to the region increased. Despite tension and disputes over allocation of wood grants within communes, there is no *statistical* evidence of
increased wealth polarisation. The response to disturbance was largely to
try and keep things locally as they always had been, or as it was imagined
they always had been. At the same time dispute resolution and the
demands to resolve problems born of disturbance increasingly gave an
accepted regulatory role to the central authorities.

Repeated outbreaks of plague, dearth in the 1560s and 1570s and
climatic deterioration after the mid-1560s brought additional burdens.
The destruction of vines and lower wine production after 1586 appears
to have been especially damaging to Württemberg. By the end of the
century the purchasing power of the region was in decline as the need for
biomass imports grew. Trade probably declined from a high point when
the region flourished along with the general economy of southern
Germany in the first half of the sixteenth century. While there were rich
and poor within the Duchy, in comparison with the status of equivalent
social groups in Italy or north-western Europe, early seventeenth-
century Württembergers were probably quite poor, and they would

become poorer, relatively speaking, over time. Nevertheless, the society weathered the 'age of disturbance' remarkably intact.

Disturbance, in fact, appears to have left surprisingly few marks on the woodland ecology. Legislation was more likely to be enforced in areas that the forester frequented, or on ducal property. Communes succeeded in retaining their autonomy, and the stipulation that foresters should oversee cutting in communal woods was given up after 1608. Though foresters were still to ensure that the forest ordinances were followed on all property, direct management was limited to the oversight of communal finances more generally by other officials. Communes regulated their property, it seems, parallel to, rather than in response to, government ordinances. Grazing and firewood remained the paramount products of the woodlands. Despite communal and state regulation of building practice that explicitly took regard of increasing timber shortage, there is no evidence that the relative local availability of wood affected building practice, save for an increased use of imported pines.

Yet around 1600, there were signs of stress. Woodland yields were very probably in decline, at the same time as wine yields were falling sharply, and possibly grain yields too. Climate change played a role, but it is also likely that local ecologies were being over-exploited relative to the regime that had previously existed. Game numbers, a burden for the forest on top of the grazing of domesticated livestock, were probably at a high point. The very cold 1590s and early 1600s may also have pushed up demand for wood for heating. Certainly this is the period where wood prices appear to rise most rapidly, and local authorities express increasing concern about the state of their woodlands. Yet in the case of wood, imports could, as yet, cover the gap and be paid for. After 1618, catastrophe of a more immediate nature than long-term environmental degradation would characterise the next century.

The age of iron, 1618–1715

The resilience of the ecology and economy was demonstrated by their surviving epidemic and destruction on a huge scale, most notably during the Thirty Years' War, but also during the 1670s, 1680s and 1690s, and again during the War of Spanish Succession. The population, and presumably (though this has not been measured) the capital assets of the region, took a long time to recover, in the case of the former over a century. Communes, however, renewed and updated their destroyed or ill-remembered customs. The central state re-established its personnel and reinvigorated economic regulation, the education system and the military. Guild regulations were renewed, more ambitious and, it seems, applied with more rigour. Attempts to invigorate economic life, though with strong antecedents, especially in the reign of Friedrich (1593–1608), sought to encourage a favourable balance of trade. The profits of enterprise, however, as in the wood-rafting trade or indeed the worsted export industry, appear to have accrued to monopolistic factors or trading companies.

Despite the fall in population, there was little respite for the woodland. This was in part, presumably, because the disruption and destruction simply meant a reduced dependence on imports, although building timber which could not be plundered from abandoned dwellings must have been imported to a large extent soon after the Thirty Years' War. However, any lowered local demand because of a smaller population was counteracted by continued grazing pressure, and above all the depredations of wartime. Without a functioning forest administration and with communities under enormous fiscal pressure, it is not surprising that we hear of widespread supposedly irresponsible woodcutting. Consequently, the woodland of the 1680s appears to have been much like the woodland of the 1580s, and government sought to regulate it in much the same way without resorting to new legislation. Destructive this period may have been, but in some ways it constituted less of a disturbance, when we look at flows of biomass or resources, than the previous high-pressure regime of the end of the sixteenth and early seventeenth centuries. However, an overall economic, or indeed demographic, accounting of the effects of war in this period is still outstanding, notwithstanding suggestions of major longer-term influence by some historians.[13]

The Old World in the New World

Württemberg entered the eighteenth century with an economy and society much like that to be found a century earlier. This was not a society incapable of change or economic growth, as it saw slowly rising *per capita* consumption of goods, trade, and agricultural yields over the subsequent century.[14] That it was able to achieve this suggests that the wars may have had a considerable inhibiting effect. However, these changes in Württemberg's *ancien regime* would come in a considerably altered continental and global context. European trade generally was on the rise, driven especially by the economy of the 'Atlantic zone' stretching

---

[13] Bardet and Dupâquier, *Histoire des populations*, pp. 241–2, 253; Gutmann, *War and rural life*, pp. 108, 199.

[14] This is charted in most detail for Württemberg in Walter, *Die Kommerzialisierung von Landwirtschaft*.

from Lisbon to Hamburg and on into the Baltic trade. England's long rise and expanding levels of income were well under way, and the Netherlands had assumed continental economic pre-eminence. The causes of these developments are, of course, still much debated but undoubtedly colonial trade, relatively favourable demographic regimes governed by migration and shifts in marital behaviour, and a relatively benign climate and resource endowment relative to the rest of the continent, all played their part.

Württemberg enjoyed few of these advantages. Perhaps above all, trade remained enormously expensive. This was inhibited by institutional barriers, but probably for the most part simply the wear and tear of raw materials and, to express it in an ecological fashion, the enormous levels of friction endured by draught animals hauling traditional wagons and carts over poorly kept roads. Nearly all of Europe remained in the 'wooden age'. Perhaps only England had shifted to the larger part of its thermal energy being provided by coal, along with the long-standing Dutch use of peat.[15]

The late seventeenth- and eighteenth-century changes could and did impact on the heart of the Old World. However, Württemberg's institutional structures remained robust and the core of the communal economy was preserved. Yet this would have its ecological consequences, prefigured in events around 1600. Woodland yields began to decline, and by the 1760s appear to have reached extraordinarily low levels. Exports from the Black Forest region, both of firewood for adjacent lowlands, and timber for importing zones along the Rhine, stripped bare large parts of the uplands.[16] Livestock numbers rose inexorably along with the population, abandoning in the second half of the century the stinting limits set in the 1550s. Württemberg's agricultural economy was perhaps assisted by improved terms of trade for that sector as the century wore on, but by this time the major industrial regions of the continent enjoyed far higher agricultural productivity in their own right. Very extensive but poorly remunerated handicrafts, a degree of agricultural specialisation and weak proto-industry characterised the region into the nineteenth century.

This chronological survey has argued for strong continuities in Württemberger history and the experience of the inhabitants of the

---

[15] This matter remains contentious, and, amazingly, little researched. Given England's 6–7 per cent woodland cover it is extremely unlikely however that most thermal energy consumption was not derived from coal by 1700. Rackham, 'Forest history', p. 297; Rackham, *Trees and woodland*, p. 88; this is similar to the assertion of Hatcher, although his estimate of wood production is probably too high. Hatcher, *The history of the British coal industry*, p. 55.

[16] Schmidt, *Der Wald in Deutschland*, pp. 218–20.

Duchy over the early modern centuries. This continuity was certainly not born of a lack of dynamism in the region or an uneventful history. It was the product of an ecology that maintained its integrity on lowland areas such as the *Forstamt* Leonberg by the investment of its inhabitants in enduring communal and state institutions, and the basic parameters set by living in the 'wooden age' in this region of Europe. Indeed, continuity in property rights, resource allocation, landscape and environmental conditions is particularly striking when we look at that absolutely essential resource, wood. A full or even very partial accounting of the significance of relying on this basic resource has not yet been undertaken anywhere in Europe. Yet set in its ecological context, examining how people handled, managed, burned, transported, hacked at and neglected wood goes some way towards discovering the secret of the political economy that lay at the heart of the Old World. State formation and any mode of production have for their fundamental condition the integrity or disturbance of the ecologies that deliver their most basic resources. The constraints of a 'wooden world', of the need to acquire wooden goods, or items made using wood, on the use of the land and the expense of transport, and the progress of the institutions to hold economy and ecology together, go far towards explaining the robust but static experience of this particular 'organic economy' in the early modern age.

Bibliography

Manuscript sources

Hauptstaatsarchiv Stuttgart

A2	Regierungsakten der habsburgischen Regierung
A4	Statistik und Topographie
A8	Kabinettsakten
A17	Kanzleiakten
A28	Kriegsakten I
A34	Landschaftsbeschwerden
A44	Urfehden
A54a	Türkensteuer
A58	Landwirtschaft, Gewerbe, Handel
A58a	Berg Werke
A59	Forstsachen
A79	Zölle
A206	Oberrat: Ältere Ämterakten
A227	Oberrat: Forst, Jagd und Wald
A230	Oberrat: Präjudizialakten
A237	Oberrat: Ältere Repertorien
A237a	Oberrat: Ältere Repertorien
A248	Rentkammer
A256	Landschreiberei Rechnungen
A261	Steuereinschätzungakten
A302	Weltliche Rechnungsbücher
A303	Geistliche Rechnungsbücher
A314	Backnang Weltliche Verwaltung
A320	Bietigheim Weltliche Verwaltung
A348	Markgröningen Weltliche Verwaltung
A359	Hoheneck Weltliche Verwaltung
A368	Leonberg Weltliche Verwaltung
A368L	Leonberg Weltliche Verwaltung
A421	Wildbad Weltliche Verwaltung
A551	Forstamt Altensteig
A553	Forstamt Böblingen
A557	Forstamt Leonberg
A572	Stadt Leonberg

360   Bibliography

A583   Gemeinde Hemmingen
A584   Gemeinde Gebersheim
H101   Weltliche Lagerbücher
H107   Forstlagerbücher
J1   Allgemeine Sammlung von ungedruckten Schriften zur
            Landesgeschichte
L6   Materienreigstratur

Stadtarchiv Bietigheim-Bissingen

A1678   Waidgerechtigkeit und Waldnutzung
A1952   Vermögensteuer 1736
A2161   Armenkastenrechnungen
Bh B 1–8   Bürgermeisterrechnungen
Bh Bd.2   Annalbücher
Bh B221   Armenkastenrechnungen
Bh B539
Bh B540   Annalbuch
Bh B544   Annalbuch
Bh B545
Bh B546   Annalbuch
O/628

Stadtarchiv Leonberg

Armenconsignation
Armenkastenrechnungen
Bürgermeisterrechnungen
Extra Ordinari Contribution
Gerichtsprotokollen
Höfingen Bürgermeisterrechnungen
Höfingen Fleckenlagerbuch
Holzordnung
Salzrechnungen
Steuerbücher
Wald- und Holz Particularrechnungen

Stadtarchiv Markgröningen

Spitalrechnungen

Stadtarchiv Renninegn

Nr B252
Nr B349 Urteilsbuch
Urthel- und Vertragsbuch

Primary Works

Ginschopf, J., *Chronica/Oder Eygendtliche Beschreibung vieler Denckhwürdigen Geschichten/die sich im Fürstenthumb Württemberg/sonderlichen vmb Stutgart her zugetragen* ... (Durlach, 1631).

Grimm, J., *Weisthümer. Gesammelt von Jacob Grimm* (Göttingen, 1840–78).

Grosser, M., *Anleitung zu der Landwirtschaft*, ed. Schröder-Lembke, G. (Stuttgart, 1965).

Heresbach, C. von, *Foure bookes of husbandry* (London, 1577, reprinted in facsimile Amsterdam, 1971).

Kieser, A., *Alt-Württemberg in Ortsansichten und Landkarten, 1680–1687* (Stuttgart, 1985).

Kollnig, K., *Die Weistümer der Zenten Eberbach und Mosbach* (Stuttgart, 1985).

KSL, *Württembergische Gemeindestatistik* (Stuttgart, 1907).

Meurer, N., *Vom Forstlicher Oberherrligkeit unnd Gerechtigkeit* (Pforzheim, 1560). *Jag und Forstrecht. Das ist: Undericht Chur: und Fürstlicher Land, auch Graff und Herrschafften und anderen Obrigkeiten, Gebiet, von verhawung und widerhawung der Wäld und Gehöltz, Auch den Wildtbänen, Fischereyen, und was solchen anhangt, wie die nach Kesyerlichen und Fürslichem gemeinen Rechten Gebrauch und gelegenheit, in guter Ordnung zu halten, und in besser form anzurichten* (Frankfurt am Main, 1576).

Montaigne, M. de, *Essays* (Harmondsworth, 1958).

Reyscher, A. L., *Vollständige, historisch und kritisch bearbeitete Sammlung der württembergischen Gesetze*, 19 vols. (Stuttgart, Tübingen, 1825–41).

Schulz, T. (ed.), *Altwürttembergischer Lagerbücher aus der österreichischen Zeit. 1520–1534. V. Ämter Asperg, Bietigheim, Besigheim, Markgröningen, Leonberg und Vaihingen* (Stuttgart, 1989).

Steeb, J. B., *Von der Verbesserung der Kultur auf der Alp und den ihr aehnlichen Gegendendes Vaterlandes* (Stuttgart, 1792).

Thumbshirn, A. von, *Oeconomia*, ed. Schröder-Lembke, G. (Stuttgart, 1965).

Secondary Works

Abel, W., *Geschichte der deutschen Landwirtschaft vom frühen Mittelalter bis zum 19. Jahrhundert* (Stuttgart, 1962).
Massenarmut und Hungerkrisen im vorindustriellen Europa: Versuch einer Synopsis (Hamburg, 1974).
Agricultural fluctuations in Europe from the thirteenth to the twentieth centuries (London, 1980).

Abetz, K., *Bäuerliche Waldwirtschaft. Dargestellt an den Verhaltnissen in Baden* (Homburg, 1955).

Achilles, W., *Landwirtschaft in der frühen Neuzeit* (Munich, 1991).

Agnoletti, M., and Anderson, S. (eds.), *Methods and approaches in forest history* (Wallingford, 2000).

Allen, R. C., *Enclosure and the yeoman* (Oxford, 1992).
'The great divergence in European wages and prices from the Middle Ages to the First World War', *Explorations in Economic History* (2001), pp. 411–47.
'Progress and poverty in early modern Europe', *Economic History Review* (2003), pp. 403–43.
'Was there a timber crisis in early modern Europe?', in Cavaciocchi, S. (ed.), *Economia e energia secc. XIII–XVIII* (Florence, 2003), pp. 469–82.
Allmann, J., *Der Wald in der frühen Neuzeit: eine mentalitäts- und sozialgeschichtliche Untersuchung am Beispiel des Pfälzer Raumes 1500–1800* (Berlin, 1989).
Ambrosoli, M., *The wild and the sown: botany and agriculture in Western Europe: 1350–1850* (Cambridge, 1997).
Appuhn, K., 'Inventing nature: forests, forestry and state power in Renaissance Venice', *Journal of Modern History* (2000), pp. 861–89.
Assion, P., and Brednich, R. W., *Bauen und Wohnen im deutschen Südwesten: dörfliche Kultur vom 15. bis zum 19. Jahrhundert* (Stuttgart, 1984).
Assmann, E., *The principles of forest yield study. Studies in the organic production, structure, increment and yield of forest stands* (Oxford, 1970).
Bader, K. S., *Das mittelalterliche Dorf als Friedens- und Rechtsbereich* (Weimar, 1957).
Dorfgenossenschaft und Dorfgemeinde (Cologne, 1962).
Rechtsformen und Schichten der Liegenschaftsnutzung im mittelalterlichen Dorf (Wien, 1973).
Bailey, F. G., 'The peasant view of the bad life', in Shanin, T. (ed.), *Peasants and peasant societies; selected readings* (London, 1971), pp. 299–321.
Bailey, M., 'Sand into gold: the evolution of the foldcourse system in west Suffolk, 1200–1600', *Agricultural History Review* (1990), pp. 40–57.
Bardet, J.-P., and Dupâquier, J. (eds.), *Histoire des populations de l'Europe. I. Des origines aux prémices de la révolution démographique* (Poitiers, 1997).
Bavel, B. J. P. van, and Thoen, E. (eds.), *Land productivity and agro-systems in the North Sea area* (Turnhout, 1999).
Bayliss-Smith, T., *Ecology of agricultural systems* (Cambridge, 1982).
Beck, R., *Naturale Ökonomie. Unterfinning: bäuerliche Wirtschaft in einem oberbayerischen Dorf des frühen 18. Jahrhunderts* (Munich, 1986).
Unterfinning: ländliche Welt vor Anbruch der Moderne (Munich, 1993).
Below, S. von, and Breit, S., *Wald – von der Gottesgabe zum Privateigentum: gerichtliche Konflikte zwischen Landesherren und Untertanen um den Wald in der frühen Neuzeit* (Stuttgart, 1998).
Benning, S., 'Überfluß und Mangel oder Innenansicht einer Krise. Bietigheim zu Anfang des 18. Jahrhunderts', *Blätter zur Stadtgeschichte* (1989), pp. 99–122.
'Studien zur frühneuzeitlichen Seuchengeschichte Württembergs unter besonderer Berücksichtigung der Amtsstadt Bietigheim', Magister-Arbeit Universität Stuttgart (1997).
'Eine Stadt "… in höchstem Flor"? Struktuelle Aspekte der Stadtgeschichte Bietigheims im 16. Jahrhundert', in Kultur- und Sportamt der Stadt Bietigheim-Bissingen, Stadtmuseum Hornmoldhaus (eds.), *Himmelzeichen und Erdenwege. Johannes Carion (1499–1537) und Sebastian Hornmold (1500–81) in ihrer Zeit* (Ubstadt-Weiher, 1999), pp. 7–50.

Bentzien, U., *Bauernarbeit im Feudalismus: landwirtschaftliche Arbeitsgeräte und -verfahren in Deutschland von der Mitte des ersten Jahrtausends u. Z. bis um 1800* (Berlin, 1990).

Bernhardt, W., *Die Zentralbehörden des Herzogtums Wurttemberg und ihre Beamten, 1520–1629* (Stuttgart, 1972–3).

Blaikie, P. M., and Brookfield, H. (eds.), *Land degradation and society* (London, 1987).

Blanchard, I., 'International capital markets and their users, 1450–1750', in Prak, M. (ed.), *Early modern capitalism: economic and social change in Europe, 1400–1800* (London, 2001), pp. 107–24.

Blickle, P., *Deutsche Untertanen: ein Widerspruch* (Munich, 1981).

'Wem gehörte der Wald? Konflikte zwischen Bauern und Obrigkeiten um Nutzungs- und Eigentumsansprüche', *Zeitschrift für Württembergische Landesgeschichte* (1986), pp. 167–78.

From the communal Reformation to the revolution of the common man (Leiden, 1998).

Blickle, P. (ed.), *Theorien kommunaler Ordnung in Europa* (Munich, 1996).

Resistance, representation, and community (Oxford, 1997).

Blickle, R., 'From subsistence to property: traces of a fundamental change in early modern Bavaria', *Central European History* (1992), pp. 377–86.

Boelcke, W. A., 'Bäuerlicher Wohlstand in Württemberg Ende des 16. Jahrhunderts', in *Jahrbücher für Nationalökonomie und Statistik* (1964), pp. 241–80.

'Zur Entwicklung des bäuerlichen Kreditwesens in Württemberg vom späten Mittelalter bis zu Anfang des 17. Jahrhunderts', *Jahrbücher für Nationalökonomie und Statistik* (1964), pp. 319–58.

'Die Grundbesitzverhältnisse auf der Gemarkung Kornwestheim um 1365', in *HABW*, IX, 3.

Bois, G., *The crisis of feudalism: economy and society in eastern Normandy c. 1300–1550* (Cambridge, 1984).

Bork, H.-R., Bork, H., Dalchow, C., Faust, B., Piorr, H.-P., and Schatz, T., *Landschaftsentwicklung in Mitteleuropa. Wirkungen des Menschen auf Landschaften* (Gotha, 1998).

Braddick, M. J., *State formation in early modern England, c. 1550–1700* (Cambridge, 2000).

Brady, T. A., *Communities, politics, and Reformation in early modern Europe* (Leiden, 1998).

Brakensiek, S., *Agrarreform und ländliche Gesellschaft. Die Privatisierung der Marken in Nordwestdeutschland 1750–1850* (Paderborn, 1991).

'Grund und Boden – eine Ware? Ein Markt zwischen familialen Strategien und herrschaftlichen Kontrollen', in Prass, R., Schlumbohm, J., Béaur, G., and Duhamelle, C. (eds.), *Ländliche Gesellschaften in Deutschland und Frankreich 18.–19. Jahrhundert* (Göttingen, 2003), pp. 269–90.

Braudel, F., *The Mediterranean and the Mediterranean world in the age of Philip II* (London, 1975).

The wheels of commerce (London, 1982).

The perspective of the world (London, 1984).

The identity of France. Volume Two. People and production (London, 1990).

Braudel, F., and Spooner, F., 'Prices in Europe from, 1450 to 1750', in Rich, E. E., and Wilson, C. H. (eds.), *The Cambridge economic history of Europe. Vol IV. The economy of expanding Europe in the sixteenth and seventeenth centuries* (Cambridge, 1967), pp. 378–486.

Brenner, R., 'Agrarian class structure and economic development in pre-industrial Europe', in Aston, T. H., and Philpin, C. H. E., *The Brenner debate. Agrarian class structure and economic development in pre-industrial Europe* (Cambridge, 1985), pp. 10–63.

Brunner, O., 'Bermerkungen zu den Begriffen "Herrschaft" und "Legitimität" ', in Brunner, O., *Neue Wege der Verfassungs- und Sozialgeschichte* (Göttingen, 1968), pp. 64–79.

Buis, J., *Historia forestis: Nederlandse bosgeschiedenis*, 2 vols (Utrecht, 1985).

Bull, K.-O., 'Die durchschnittlichen Vermögen in den alt Württembergischen Städten und Dörfern um 1545 nach der Türkensteuerlisten', *Historischer Atlas von Baden-Württemberg* 12(1) (1975).

Bull-Reichenmiller, M., *'Beritten, beschriben und gerissen'. Georg Gadner und sein kartographisches Werk 1559–1602. Inventar und Begleitbuch zu einer Ausstellung im Hauptstaatsarchiv Stuttgart* (Stuttgart, 1996).

Burckhardt, H. (ed.), *Eglosheim. Ein Ort im Wandel der Jahrhunderte* (Ludwigsburg, 1999).

Bürgi, M., 'How terms shape forests; "Niederwald", "Mittelwald" and "Hochwald" and their interaction with forest development in the canton of Zurich, Switzerland', *Environment and History* 5 (1999), pp. 325–44.

Burke, P., *Popular culture in early modern Europe* (London, 1978).

Bütterlin, R., *Der Württembergische Staatshaushalt in der Zeit zwischen 1483 und 1648* (Tübingen, 1977).

Campbell, B. M. S., *English seigniorial agriculture, 1250–1450* (Cambridge, 2000).

Campbell, B. M. S., and Godoy, R. A., 'Commonfield agriculture: the Andes and medieval England compared', in D. W. Bromley (ed.), *Making the commons work: theory, practice and policy* (San Francisco, 1992), pp. 99–127.

Cancian, F., 'Economic behaviour in peasant communities', in Plattner, S. (ed.), *Economic anthropology* (Stanford, 1989), pp. 127–70.

Carlé, W., 'Die Salinenversuche im Herzogtum Württemberg', *Zeitschrift für württembergische Landesgeschichte* (1964), pp. 157–88.

Carsten, F. L., *Princes and parliaments in Germany, from the fifteenth to the eighteenth century* (Oxford, 1959).

Chartres, J., *Internal trade in England, 1500–1700* (London, 1977).

Chayanov, A. V., *A. V. Chayanov on the theory of peasant economy*, eds. Thorner, D., Kerblay, B., and Smith, R. E. F. (Homewood, 1966).

Christiansen, P. O., *A manorial world: lord, peasants and cultural distinctions on a Danish estate, 1750–1980* (Oxford, 1996).

Clasen, C. P., *Die Wiedertäufer im Herzogtum Württemberg und in benachbarten Herrschaften: Ausbreitung, Geisteswelt und Soziologie* (Stuttgart, 1965).

Collins, E. J. T., 'The wood-fuel economy of eighteenth-century England', in Cavaciocchi, S. (ed.), *L'uomo e la foresta sexx. XIII–XVIII* (Prato, 1996), pp. 1097–121.

Corvol, A., 'Les communautés d'habitants et l'approvisionement énergétique: les combustibles ligneux', in Cavaciocchi, S. (ed.), *Economia e energia secc. XIII–XVIII* (Florence, 2003), pp. 737–64.

Crafts, N. F. R., *British economic growth during the industrial revolution* (Oxford, 1985).

Cronon, W. (ed.), *Uncommon ground: toward reinventing nature* (New York, 1995).

Dehlinger, A., *Württembergs Staatswesen: in seiner geschichtlichen Entwicklung bis Heute* (Stuttgart, 1951–2).

Deleuze, G., *Bergsonism* (New York, 1988).

Delfort, R., and Walter, F., *Storia dell'ambiente europeo* (Bari, 2002).

Demélas, M.-D., and Vivier, N. (eds.), *Les propriétés collectives face aux attaques libérales (1750–1914)* (Rennes, 2003).

Dipper, C., *Deutsche Geschichte 1648–1789* (Frankfurt am Main, 1991).

Döbele-Carlesso, I., *Weinbau und Weinhandel in Württemberg in der frühen Neuzeit am Beispiel von Stadt und Amt Brackenheim* (Brackenheim, 1999).

Dodgshon, R. A., *The European past. Social evolution and spatial order* (Basingstoke, 1987).

Society in time and space: a geographical perspective on change (Cambridge, 1998).

Dornfeld, J., *Die Geschichte des Weinbaus in Schwaben: eine geschichtliche Darstellung des Weinbaues und des damit in verbindungstehenden Weinverkehrs in Schwaben von der ältesten bis auf die neueste Zeit* (Stuttgart, 1868).

Dülmen, R. van, *Kultur und Alltag in der frühen Neuzeit*, 3 vols. (Munich, 1990–4).

Duplessis, R., *Transitions to capitalism in early modern Europe* (Cambridge, 1997).

Ebeling, D., 'Organizationsformen des Holländerholzhandels im Schwarzwald während des 17. und 18. Jahrunderts', in Keweloh, H. W. (ed.), *Auf den Spuren der Flößer. Wirtschafts- und Sozialgeschichte eines Gewerbes* (Stuttgart, 1988), pp. 81–99.

Eckardt, H. W., *Herrschaftliche Jagd, bäuerliche Not und bürgerliche Kritik: zur Geschichte der fürstlichen und adligen Jagdprivilegien, vornehmlich im südwestdeutschen Raum* (Göttingen, 1976).

Eckhardt, E. A. *The Structure of plagues and pestilences in early modern Europe. Central Europe, 1560–1640* (Basel, 1996).

Eitzen, G., 'Zur Geschichte des südwestdeutschen Hausbaues im 15. und 16. Jahrhundert', *Zeitschrift für Volkskunde* (1963), pp. 1–38.

Eliasson, P., and Hamilton, G., '"Blifver ond att förena sigh" – nägra linjer i den svenska skogalagsstiftningen om utmark och skog', in Petterson, R. (ed.), *Skogshistorisk Forskning i Europa och Nordamerika. Vad är skoghistoria, hur har den skrivits och varför?* (Stockholm, 1999), pp. 47–106.

Eliasson, P., and Nilsson, S. G., 'Rättat efter skogarnes auftagende – en miljöhistorisk undersökning av den svenska eken under 1700- och 1800-talen', *Bebyggelsehistorisk tidskrift* (1999), pp. 33–64.

Ellen, R., *Environment, subsistence and system: the ecology of small-scale social formations* (Cambridge, 1982).

Ellis, F., *Peasant economics: farm households and agrarian development* (Cambridge, 1988).

Elsas, M. J., *Umriß einer Geschichte der Preise und Löhne in Deutschland: vom ausgehenden Mittelalter bis zum Beginn des neunzehnten Jahrhunderts* (Leiden, 1936).

Epperlein, S., *Waldnutzung, Waldstreitigkeiten und Waldschutz in Deutschland im hohen Mittelalter (2. Hälfte 11. Jahrhundert bis ausgehendes 14. Jahrhundert)* (Stuttgart, 1993).

Epstein, S. R., *Freedom and growth: the rise of states and markets in Europe, 1300–1750* (London, 2000).

Epstein, S. R. (ed.), *Town and country in Europe, 1300–1800* (Cambridge, 2001).

Ernst, C., *Den Wald entwicklen. Ein Politik- und Konfliktfeld in Hunsrück und Eifel im 18. Jahrhundert* (Munich, 2000).

Ernst, F., *Die wirtschaftliche Ausstattung der Universität Tübingen in ihren ersten Jahrzehnten (1477–1534)* (Stuttgart, 1929).

Ernst, V., 'Geschichte', in WSL (ed.), *Beschreibung des Oberamts Leonberg* (Stuttgart, 1930), pp. 252–434.

Ertman, T., *Birth of the leviathan: building states and regimes in medieval and early modern Europe* (Cambridge, 1997).

Evans, J., 'Coppice forestry – an overview', in Buckley, G. P. (ed.), *Ecology and management of coppice woodlands* (London, 1992), pp. 18–28.

Farr, I., '"Tradition" and the peasantry. On the modern historiography of rural Germany', in Evans, R. J., and Lee, W. R. (eds.), *The German peasantry* (London, 1986), pp. 1–36.

Fél, E., and Hofer, T., *Bäuerliche Denkweise in Wirtschaft und Haushalt; eine ethnographische Untersuchung über das ungarische Dorf Átány* (Göttingen, 1972).

Feldbauer, P., 'Lohnarbeit im österreichischen Weinbau. Zur sozialen Lage der niederösterreichischen Weingartenarbeiter des Mittelalters und der frühen Neuzeit', *Zeitschirft für Bayerische Landesgesichte* (1975), pp. 227–43.

Felden, H. (ed.), *Ortsbuch Hoheneck: Stadtteil von Ludwigsburg* (Neckarwestheim, 1983).

Fertig, G., *Lokales Leben, atlantische Welt: die Entscheidung zur Auswanderung vom Rhein nach Nordamerika im 18. Jahrhundert* (Osnarbrück, 2000).

Filzer, P., *Die Flora Wüttembergs in lhren Beziehungen zu Klima und Boden* (Karlsruhe, 1982).

Forman, R. T. T., *Land mosaics: the ecology of landscapes and regions* (Cambridge, 1995).

Forstliche Standortskartierung Baden-Württemberg (Neufassung Stand, 1996).

Foster, G., 'Peasant society and the image of limited good', *American Anthropologist* (1965), pp. 293–315.

Foucault, M., *Power/knowledge: selected interviews and other writings, 1972–1977* (Brighton, 1986).

Fox, A., *Oral and literate culture in England* (Oxford, 2000).

Freedman, P., *Images of the medieval peasant* (Stanford, 1999).

Frey, S., *Das württembergische Hofgericht (1460–1618)* (Stuttgart, 1989).

Friedeburg, R. von, '"Reiche", "geringe Leute" und "beambte": Dörfliche "Faktionen", gemeindliche Partizipation und Landherrschaft, 1648–1806', *Zeitschrift für historische Forschung* 23 (1996), pp. 219–65.

Ländliche Gesellschaft und Obrigkeit. Gemeindeprotest und politische Mobilisierung im 18. und 19. Jahrhundert (Göttingen 1997).

Fritz, G., *Stadt und Kloster Murrhardt im Spätmittelalter und in der Reformationszeit* (Sigmaringen, 1990).

Fuhrmann, R., 'Amtsbeschwerden, Landtagsgravamina und Supplikationen in Württemberg zwischen 1550 und 1629', in Blickle, P. (ed.), *Gemeinde und Staat im alten Europa* (München, 1998), pp. 69–147.

Fuhrmann, R., Kümin, B., and Würgler, A., 'Supplizierende Gemeinden. Aspekte einer vergleichenden Quellenbetrachtung', in Blickle, P. (ed.), *Gemeinde und Staat im alten Europa* (München, 1998), pp. 267–323.

Fulbrook, M., *Piety and politics: religion and the rise of absolutism in England, Württemberg and Prussia* (Cambridge, 1983).

Fussell, G. E. (ed.), *Robert Loder's farm accounts 1610–1620*, Camden Third Series (1936).

Gai, S., 'La produzione del vetro preindustriale in Germania sud-occidentale stato della ricerca e prospettive', http://192.167.112.135/NewPages/COLLANE/TESTIQDS/vetro/Intro.rtf.

Gaisberg-Schöckingen, Freiherr F. von, *Schöckingen* (Ditzingen-Schöckingen, 1983).

Geisel, T., 'Chaos, randomness and dimension', *Nature* (1982), pp. 322–3.

Gemeinde Münchingen (ed.), *Heimatbuch Münchingen* (Korntal-Münchingen, 1973).

Gemeinde Rutesheim (ed.), *Heimatbuch Rutesheim* (1970).

Gemeindeverwaltung Benningen am Neckar, *Benningen am Neckar* (Benningen, 1979).

Gestrich, A., *'Aufwiegler, Rebellen, saubere Buben': Alltag in Botnang; Geschichte eines Stuttgarter Stadtteils* (Stuttgart, 2000).

Glaser, R., *Klimarekonstruktion für Mainfranken, Bauland und Odenwald anhand direkter und indirekter Witterungsdaten seit 1500* (Stuttgart, 1991).

Glaser, R., *Klimageschichte Mitteleuropas: 1000 Jahre Wetter, Klima, Katastrophen* (Darmstadt, 2001).

Glaser, R., and Schenk, W., 'Einflüßgrößen auf die Anbau- und Ertragsverhältnisse des Ackerlandes im frühneuzeitlichen Mainfranken – Forschungsstand, Ergebnisse und offene Fragen', *Mainfränkisches Jahrbuch* (1988), pp. 43–69.

Glauser, F., 'Wein, Wirt, Gewinn 1580. Wirteeinkommen am Beispiel der schwerizschen Kleinstadt Sursee', in Beyer, H. C. (ed.), *Gastfreundschaft, Taverne und Gasthaus im Mittelalter* (Munich, 1983), pp. 205–20.

Gleitsmann, R.-J., 'Aspekte der Ressourcenpolitik in historischer Sicht', *Scripta Mercaturae* (1981), pp. 33–89.

'Und immer wieder starben die Wälder; Ökosystem Wald, Waldnutzung und Energiewirtschaft in der Geschichte', in Calliess, J., Rüsen, J., and Striegnitz, M. (eds.), *Mensch und Umwelt in der Geschichte* (Pfaffenweiler, 1989), pp. 175–204.

Gorbonzoon, P., *Rienck Hemmema. Rekenbook off memoriael* (Grins, 1956).

Gothein, E., *Pforzheims Vergangenheit. Ein Beitrag zur deutschen Städte- und Gewerbegeschichte* (Leipzig, 1889).

Göttmann, F., *Getreidemarkt am Bodensee. Raum – Wirtschaft – Politik – Gesellschaft (1650–1810)* (St Katharinen, 1991).

Grantham, G., 'Contra Ricardo: on the macroeconomics of pre-industrial economies', *European Review of Economic History* (1999), pp. 199–232.

368   Bibliography

Grees, H., *Ländliche Unterschichten und ländliche Siedlung in Ostschwaben* (Tübingen, 1985).

Greiner, K., *Die Glashütten in Württemberg* (Wiesbaden, 1971).

Gromer, J., *Über die Entwicklung des bäuerlichen Hausbaus in Württemberg* (Tübingen, 2000).

Grove, A. T., and Rackham, O., *The nature of Mediterranean Europe: an ecological history* (New Haven, 2001).

Grube, W., 'Dorfgemeinde und Amtsversammlung in Altwürttemberg', *Zeitschrift für Württembergische Landesgeschichte* (1954), pp. 194–291.

Der Stuttgarter Landtag, 1457–1957; von den Landständen zum demokratischen Parlament (Stuttgart, 1957).

Günther, R., *Der Arnsberger Wald im Mittelalter. Forstgeschichte als Verfassungsgeschichte* (Münster, 1994).

Gutmann, M. P., *War and rural life in the early modern Low Countries* (Princeton, 1980).

Gutram, P., 'Eisengewinnung und Eisenverarbeitung in südwestdeutschen Raum von 1500 bis 1650', in Kellenbenz, H. (ed.), *Schwerpunkte der Eisengewinnung und Eisenverarbeitung in Europea 1500–1650* (Cologne, 1974), pp. 204–32.

Hagel, J. (ed.), *Stuttgart im Spiegel alter Karten und Pläne* (Stuttgart, 1984).

Mensch und Wasser in der Geschichte. Dokumente zu Umwelt, Technik und Alltag vom 16. bis zum 19. Jahrhundert (Stuttgart, 1989).

Hagen, W., *Ordinary Prussians: Brandenburg Junkers and villagers, 1500–1840* (Cambridge, 2002).

Hahn, H., *Die deutschen Weinbaugebiete* (Bonn, 1956).

Hale, J., *War and society in renaissance Europe 1450–1620* (Stroud, 1998).

Hammersley, G., 'The charcoal iron industry and its fuel', *Economic History Review* (1973), pp. 593–613.

Hardin, G., 'The tragedy of the commons', *Science* (1968), pp. 1243–8.

Harris, T. (ed.), *The politics of the excluded, c. 1500–1850* (Basingstoke, 2001).

Harrison, M., 'The peasant mode of production in the work of A. V. Chayanov', *Journal of Peasant Studies* (1977), pp. 323–35.

Hart, C., *Practical forestry for the agent and surveyor* (Stroud, 1991).

Hatcher, J., *The history of the British coal industry. Towards the age of coal* (Oxford, 1993).

'The emergence of a mineral-based energy economy in England, c.1500–c.1850', in Cavaciocchi, S. (ed.), *Economia e energia secc. XIII–XVIII* (Florence, 2003), pp. 483–504.

Hauff, D., *Zur Geschichte der Forstgesetzgebung und Forstorganisation des Herzogtums Württemberg im 16. Jahrhundert* (Stuttgart, 1977).

Held, W., 'Blei und Holz für den Saalfelder Bergbau in der Mitte des 16. Jahrhunderts', in Westermann, E. (ed.), *Bergbaureviere als Verbrauchszentrum* (Stuttgart, 1997), pp. 85–109.

Henning, F.-W., *Handbuch der Wirtschafts- und Sozialgeschichte Deutschlands. Bd. 1. Deutsche Wirtschafts- und Sozialgeschichte im Mittelalter und in der frühen Neuzeit* (Cologne, 1989).

Herrmann, K., 'Die deutsche Weinwirtschaft während des Zweiten Weltkrieges', *Zeitschrift für Agrargeschichte und Agrarsoziologie* (1980), pp. 157–81.

Hess, R.-D., *Familien- und Erbrecht im württembergischen Landrecht von 1555, unter besonderer Berücksichtigung des älteren württembergischen Rechts* (Stuttgart, 1968).

Hindle, S., *The state and social change in early modern England* (Basingstoke, 2000).

Hippel, W. von, *Die Bauernbefreiung im Königreich Württemberg* (Boppard am Rhein, 1977).

'Bevölkerung und Wirtschaft im Zeitalter des 30 jährigen Krieges', *Zeitschrift für historische Forschung* (1978), pp. 413–48.

'Historische Statistik des Herzogtums Württemberg vom 15/16. bis zum 18/19. Jahrhundert', in Diederich, N., Hölder, E., and Kunz, A. (eds.), *Historische Statistik in der Bundesrepublik Deutschland* (Stuttgart, 1990), pp. 52–64.

Hochstrasser, O., *Ein Haus und seine Menschen 1549–1989. Ein Versuch zum Verhältnis von Mikroforschung und Sozialgeschichte* (Tübingen, 1993).

Hofacker, H. G., 'Die Epoche von 1648 bis 1800', in *Leonberg. Eine altwürttembergische Stadt und ihre Gemeinden im Wandel der Geschichte* (Stuttgart, 1992), pp. 127–55.

Hoffmann, J., 'Aufbau und Auswertung von Jahrringchronologien zur Erforschung von historischen Waldzuständen und –entwicklungen', in Schenk, W. (ed.), *Aufbau und Auswertung 'langer Reihen' zur Erforschung von historischen Waldzuständen und – entwicklungen* (Tübingen, 1999), pp. 91–101.

Hohkamp, M., *Herrschaft in der Herrschaft. Die vorderösterrichische Obervögten Triberg von 1737 bis 1780* (Göttingen, 1998).

Holenstein, A., *Bauern zwischen Bauernkrieg und Dreissigjährigen Krieg* (Munich, 1996).

'Bittgesuche, Gesetze und Verwaltung. Zur Praxis "guter Policey" in Gemeinde und Staat des Ancien Régime am Beispiel der Markgrafschaft Baden (-Durlach)', in Blickle, P., *Gemeinde und Staat im Alten Europa* (Munich, 1998), pp. 325–57.

Hollstein, E., *Mitteleuropäische Eichenchronologie: Trierer dendrochronologische Forschungen zur Archaeologie und Kunst-geschichte* (Mainz am Rhein, 1980).

Hopcroft, R. L., *Regions, institutions, and agrarian change in European history* (Ann Arbor, 1999).

Hoppenbrouwers, P., and Zanden, J. L. van, *Peasants into farmers?: the transformation of rural economy and society in the Low Countries (Middle Ages – 19th century) in light of the Brenner debate* (Turnhout, 2001).

Hornberger, T., *Die kulturgeographische Bedeutung der Wanderschäferei in Süddeutschland: süddeutsche Transhumanz* (Remagen, 1959).

Hornstein, F. von, *Wald und Mensch. Waldgeschichte des Alpenvorlandes Deutschlands, Österreichs und der Schweiz* (Ravensburg, 1951).

Hoskins, W. G., *The making of the English landscape* (London, 1955).

Hughes, J. D., *An environmental history of the world: humankind's changing role in the community of life* (London, 2001).

Imhof, A. E., *Die verlorene Welten* (Muncih, 1984).

Isermeyer, H., *Ländliche Gesellschaft Württembergs im Umbruch: ein Beitrag zur politischen und sozialen Geschichte während der ersten Hälfte des neunzehnten Jahrhunderts: dargestellt am Beispiel des Oberamts Vaihingen/Enz* (Stuttgart, 1992).

James, N. D. G., *A history of English forestry* (Oxford, 1980).

Jänichen, H., *Beiträge zur Wirtschaftsgesichte des schwäbischen Dorfes* (Stuttgart, 1970).

Jeggle, U., *Kiebingen – eine Heimatgeschichte* (Tübingen, 1977).

Kaschuba, W., 'Kommunalismus als sozialer, "common sense"', in Blickle, P. (ed.), *Landgemeinde und Stadtgemeinde. Ein struktureller Vergleich* (Munich, 1991), pp. 78–86.

Kaschuba, W., and Lipp, C., *Dörfliches Überleben: zur Geschichte materieller und sozialer Reproduktion ländlicher Gesellschaft im 19. und frühen 20. Jahrhundert* (Tübingen, 1982).

Keitel, C., *Herrschaft über Land und Leute: Leibherrschaft und Territorialisierung in Württemberg 1246–1593* (Leinfeld-Echterdingen, 2000).

Kellenbenz, H., 'Europäisches Eisen-Produktion -Verarbeitung -Handel (Vom Ende des Mittelalters bis ins 18. Jahrhundert', in Kellenbenz, H. (ed.), *Schwerpunkte der Eisengewinnung und Eisenverarbeitung in Europea 1500–1650* (Cologne, 1974), pp. 397–452.

Kelley, D., '"Second nature": the idea of custom in European law, society and culture', in Grafton, A., and Blair, A. (eds.), *The transmission of culture in early modern Europe* (Philadelphia, 1990), pp. 131–61.

Kieß, R., *Die Rolle der Forsten im Aufbau des württembergischen Territoriums bis ins 16. Jahrhundert* (Stuttgart, 1958).

Kießling, R., 'Markets and marketing, town and country' in Scribner, B. (ed.), *Germany – a social and economic history, Vol. I: 1450–1630* (London 1995), pp. 145–79.

Kirby, K. J., and Watkins, C. (eds.), *The ecological history of European forests* (Wallingford, 1998).

Kjaergaard, T., *The Danish Revolution 1500–1800: an ecohistorical interpretation* (Cambridge, 1994).

Klein, U., and Raff, A., *Die Württembergischen Münzen. Vol I, 1693–1797* (Stuttgart, 1992).

Die Württembergischen Münzen von 1374–1693 (Stuttgart, 1993).

Kleinschmidt, E., 'Klima und Witterung', in WSL (ed.), *Beschreibung des Oberamts Leonberg* (Stuttgart, 1930), pp. 48–88.

Knapp, T., *Gesammelte Beiträge zur Rechts- und Wirtschaftsgeschichte vornehmlich des deutschen Bauernstandes* (Tübingen, 1902).

Knöller, K., *Unser Dürrmenz-Mühlacker: ein Ortsbuch für Haus und Schule* (Dürrmenz-Mühlacker, 1928).

Knotter, A., 'Problems of the "family economy". Peasant economy, domestic production and labour markets in pre-industrial Europe', in Prak, M. (ed.), *Early modern capitalism* (London 2000), pp. 135–60.

Königlichen-statistischen-topographischen Bureau, *Beschreibung des Oberamts Leonberg* (Stuttgart, 1852).

Küster, H.-J., *Geschichte der Landschaft in Mitteleuropa. Von der Eiszeit bis zur Gegenwart* (Munich, 1995).

Ladurie, E. Le Roy, *The peasants of Languedoc* (Urbana, 1974).

Landsteiner, E., 'The crisis of wine production in late sixteenth-century central Europe: climatic causes and economic consequences', *Climatic Change* (1999), pp. 323–34.

Landwehr, A., 'Finanzen, Rechte und Faktionen – eine herzogliche Untersuchungskommission in Leonberg 1755/56', in Stadt Archiv Leonberg, *Streifzüge durch 750 Jahre Leonberger Stadtsgeschichte* (Leonberg, 2000), pp. 87–111.

Policey im Alltag: die Implementation frühneuzeitlicher Policeyordnungen in Leonberg (Frankfurt am Main, 2000).

Landwehr, A., 'Die Rhetorik der "Guten Policey"', *Zeitschrift für Historische Forschung* (2003), pp. 251–87.

Langdon, J., 'The Use of Animal Power from 1200 to 1800', in Cavaciocchi, S. (ed.), *Economia e energia secc. XIII–XVIII* (Florence, 2003), pp. 213–22.

Langton, J., and Höppe, G., *Peasantry to capitalism: Western Östergötland in the nineteenth century* (Cambridge,1994).

Leibundgut, H., *Der Wald in der Kulturlandschaft. Bedeutung, Funktion und Wirkungen des waldes auf die Umwelt des Menschen* (Stuttgart, 1985).

Lenk, H., 'Bemerkungen zur Methodologie der Systemanalyse für die Umweltforschung', in Lübbe, H., and Ströker, E. (eds.), *Ökologische Probleme im kulturellen Wandel* (Munich, 1986), pp. 28–34.

Löfgren, O., 'Peasant ecotypes. Problems in the comparative study of ecological adaptation', *Ethnologia Scandinavica* (1976), pp. 100–15.

Lorenzen-Schmidt, K., 'Siedlungshistorische Aspetke der Allmenden und Markgenossenshaften in Spätmittelalter und frühe Neuzeit', in Meiners, U., and Rösener, W. (eds.), *Allmenden und Marken vom Mittelalter bis zur Neuzeit* (Cloppenburg 2004), pp. 101–14.

Lüdtke, A., 'Introduction. What is the history of everyday life and who are its practitoners?', in Lüdtke, A., *The history of everyday life* (Princeton, 1995).

Luhmann, N., *Social systems* (Stanford, 1995).

Maisch, A., *Notdürftiger Unterhalt und gehörige Schranken: Lebensbedingungen und Lebensstile in württembergischen Dörfern der frühen Neuzeit* (Stuttgart, 1992).

Malanima, P., 'The energy basis for early modern growth, 1650–1820', in Prak, M., *Early modern capitalism: economic and social change in Europe, 1400–1800* (London, 2001), pp. 51–68.

'Il Produtto', in *L'Economia italiana. Dalla crescita medievale alla crescita contemporanea* (Bologna, 2002).

'Measuring the Italian economy 1300–1861', *Rivista di Storia Economica* (2003), pp. 265–95.

Mantel, K., *Forstgeschichte des 16. Jahrhunderts unter dem Einfluss der Forstordnungen und Noe Meurers* (Hamburg, 1980).

Marcus, K. H., *The politics of power: elites of an early modern state in Germany* (Mainz, 2000).

Marx, K., 'Peasantry as a class', in Shanin, T. (ed.), *Peasants and peasant societies; selected readings* (London, 1971), pp. 229–37.

Marx, K., and Engels, F., *The communist manifesto* (London, 1967).

Mathieu, J., *Bauern und Bären: eine Geschichte des Unterengadins von 1650 bis 1800* (Chur, 1987).

Maurer, H.-M., 'Bauernkrieg', *HABW*, VI, II.

McCloskey, D., 'The open fields of England: rent, risk, and the rate of interest, 1300–1815,' in Galenson, D. W. (ed.), *Markets in History: Economic studies of the past* (Cambridge, 1989), pp. 5–51.

Medick, H., *Weben und Überleben in Laichingen 1650–1900: Lokalgeschichte als allgemeine Geschichte* (Göttingen, 1996).

Medio, A., *Chaotic dynamics: theory and applications to economics* (Cambridge, 1992).

Mensching, H. G., 'Ökosystem-Zerstörung in vorindustrieller Zeit', in Lübbe, H., and Ströker, E. (eds.), *Ökologische Probleme im kulturellen Wandel* (Munich, 1986), pp. 15–27.

Mertens, D., 'Württemberg', in Schaab, M., and Schwarzmaier, H. (eds.) *Handbuch der Württembergischen Geschichte Bd.2. Die Territorien im Alten Reich* (Stuttgart, 1995), pp. 1–163.

Metz, R., *Geld, Währung und Preisentwicklung: der Niederrheinraum im europäischen Vergleich, 1350–1800* (Frankfurt am Main, 1990).

Midelfort, H. C., *Witch hunting in Southwestern Germany, 1562–1684* (Stanford, 1972).

Militzer, S., *Bedingungen und Ergebnisse des Getreidebaues ernestinischer Güter in Thüringen im 16. Jahrhundert. Eine agrarhistorische Studie unter besonderer Berüksichtigung der Produktion in den Vorwerker des Amtes Weimar* (Frankfurt am Main, 1993).

Milonakis, D., 'Commodity production and price formation before capitalism: a value theoretic approach', *Journal of Peasant Studies* (1995), pp. 327–55.

Mone, F.-J., 'Beiträge zur Weingeschichte', *Zeitschrift für die Geschichte des Oberrheins* (1862), pp. 29–45.

Moor, M. de, Shaw-Taylor, L., and Warde, P. (eds.), *The management of common land in north west Europe, c.1500–1850* (Turnhout, 2002).

Moran, E. F., *The ecosystem concept in anthropology* (Epping, 1984).

Moreno, D., and Poggi, G. 'Storia delle risorse boschive nelle montagne mediterranee: modelli di interpretazione per le produzioni foraggere in regime consuetudinario', in Cavaciocchi, S. (ed.), *L'uomo e la foresta secc. XIII–XVIII* (Prato, 1996), pp. 635–53.

Muldrew, C., *The economy of obligation: the culture of credit and social relations in early modern England* (Basingstoke, 1998).

Mulliez, Jacques, 'Du blé, "Mal nécessaire". Réflexions sur les progrès de l'agriculture, 1750–1850', in *Revue d'histoire moderne et contemporaine* (1979).

Münch, P., 'The growth of the modern state', in Ogilvie, S. C. (ed.), *Germany: a new social and economic history. Vol. II, 1630–1800* (London, 1996), pp. 196–232.

Myllyntaus, T., and Saikko, M. (eds.), *Encountering the past in nature: essays in environmental history* (Athens, OH, 2001).

Nef, J., *The rise of the British coal industry* (London, 1932).

Netting, R., *Balancing on an Alp: ecological change and continuity in a Swiss mountain community* (Cambridge, 1981).

Newman E. I., and Harvey, P. D., 'Did soil fertility decline in medieval English farms? Evidence from Cuxham, Oxfordshire, 1320–1340', *Agricultural History Review* (1997), pp. 119–36.

Niklaus, S., 'Dreißigjähriger Krieg', *HABW*, VI, II.

North, D. C., *Institutions, institutional change and economic performance* (Cambridge, 1990).

North, D. C., and Thomas, P. P., *The rise of the western world: a new economic history* (Cambridge, 1973).

North, M., 'Lohnarbeit und Fronarbeit in der ostpreußischen Landwirtschaft vom 16. bis zum 18. Jahrhundert', *Zeitschrift für Agrargeschichte und Agrarsoziologie* (1988), pp. 11–32.

Oestreich, G., *Geist und Gestalt des frühmodernen Staates: Ausgewählte Aufsätze* (Berlin, 1969).

Ogilvie, S. C., 'Germany and the seventeenth-century crisis', in Parker, G., and Smith, L. M. (eds.), *The general crisis of the seventeenth century* (London, 1997).

State corporatism and proto-industry: the Württemberg Black Forest, 1580–1797 (Cambridge, 1997).

'The economic world of the Bohemian serf: economic concepts, preferences and constraints on the estate of Friedland, 1583–1692', *Economic History Review* (2001), pp. 430–53.

A bitter living: women, markets, and social capital in early modern Germany (Oxford, 2003).

Ostrom, E., *Governing the commons: the evolution of institutions for collective action* (Cambridge, 1990).

Özmucur, S., and Pamuk, S., 'Real wages and standards of living in the Ottoman Empire, 1489–1914', *The Journal of Economic History* (2002), pp. 293–321.

Petterson, R. (ed.), *Skogshistorisk Forskning i Europa och Nordamerika. Vad är skoghistoria, hur har den skrivits och varför?* (Stockholm, 1999).

Pfister, C., *Klimageschichte der Schweiz 1525–1860. Das Klima der Schweiz von 1525–1860 und seine Bedeutung in der Geschichte von Bevölkerung und Landwirtschaft* (Bern, 1984).

Bevölkerung, Klima und Agrarmodernisierung 1525–1860. Das Klima der Schweiz von 1525–1860 und seine Bedeutung in der Geschichte von Bevölkerung und Landwirtschaft (Bern, 1985).

Pfister, Forstmeister, *Der Leonberger Stadtwald* (Leonberg, 1939).

Piasecki, P., *Das deutsche Salinwesen 1550–1850* (Idstein, 1987).

Polanyi, K., *The great transformation* (Boston, 1967).

Post, J. D., *Food shortage, climatic variability, and epidemic disease in pre-industrial Europe* (Ithaca and London, 1985).

Pratt, J. C., *The rationality of rural life: economic and cultural change in Tuscany* (Chur, 1994).

Prigogine, I., and Stengers, I., *Order out of chaos: man's new dialogue with nature* (London, 1984).

Projektgruppe Umweltgeschichte, *Kulturlandschaftsforschung: historische Entwicklung von Wechselwirkungen zwischen Gesellschaft und Natur* (Vienna, 2000), CD–ROM.

Rackham, O., *Trees and woodland in the British landscape* (London, 1976).

'Forest history of countries without much forest; questions of conservation and savanna', in Cavaciocchi, S. (ed.), *L'uomo e la foresta secc. XIII–XVIII* (Prato, 1996), pp. 297–326.

Radkau, J., 'Zur angeblichen Energiekrise des 18. Jahrhunderts' *Vierteljahrschrift für Sozials- und Wirtschaftsgeschichte* (1986), pp. 1–73.

'Wood and forestry in German history. In quest of an environmental approach', *Environment and History* (1996), pp. 63–76.

'Das Rätsel der städtischen Brennholzversorgung im "hölzernen Zeitalter"', in Schott, D. (ed.), *Energie und Stadt in Europea. Von der vorindustriellen 'Holznot' bis zur Ölkrise der 1970er Jahre* (Stuttgart, 1997), pp. 43–75.

Natur und Macht. Weltgeschichte der Umwelt (Munich, 2002).

Raeff, M., *The well-ordered police state: social and institutional change through law in the Germanies and Russia, 1600–1800* (New Haven, 1983).

Regnath, R. J., 'Die Stadt auf dem Lande – spätmittelalterliches Wirtschaftsleben in Leonberg zwischen Landwirtschaft und Handwerk betrachtet anhand der altwürttembergischen Lagerbücher', in Stadt Archiv Leonberg, *Streifzüge durch 750 Jahre Leonberger Stadtsgeschichte* (Leonberg, 2000), pp. 23–53.

Rheinheimer, M., *Die Dorfordnungen im Herzogtum Schleswig: Dorf und Obrigkeit in der frühen Neuzeit. Bd.1.* (Stuttgart, 1999).

Robisheaux, T., *Rural society and the search for order in early modern Germany* (Cambridge, 1989).

Roeck, B., *Bäcker, Brot und Getreide in Augsburg 1600–1650* (Stuttgart, 1987).

Rorty, R., *Philosophy and the mirror of nature* (Oxford, 1980).

Rublack, U., 'Frühneuzeitliche Staatlichkeit und lokale Herrschaftspraxis in Württemberg', *Zeitschrift für Historische Forschung* (1997), pp. 1–30.

'State-formation, gender, and the experience of governance in early modern Württemberg', in Rublack, U. (ed.), *Gender in early modern German history* (Cambridge, 2002), pp. 200–17.

Rubner, H., *Forstgeschichte im Zeitalter der industriellen Revolution* (Berlin, 1967).

Sabean, D. W., 'The social background to the Peasants' War of 1525 in southern Upper Swabia', University of Wisconsin Ph.D. Thesis (1969).

Power in the blood: popular culture and village discourse in early modern Germany (Cambridge, 1984).

Property, production, and family in Neckarhausen, 1700–1870 (Cambridge, 1990).

Kinship in Neckarhausen, 1700–1870 (Cambridge, 1998).

Salzmann, E., *Weinbau und Weinhandel in der Reichsstadt Eßlingen bis zu deren Übergang an Württemberg* (Stuttgart, 1930).

Sander, S., *Handwerkschirurgen. Sozialgescichte einer verdrängten Berufsgruppe* (Göttingen, 1989).

Sauer, P., 'Not und Armut in den Dörfern des mittleren Neckarraums in vorindustrieller Zeit', *Zeitschrift für württembergische Landesgeschichte* (1982), pp. 131–49.

Schaab, M., 'Das Waldeigentum im Nordschwarzwald und in der nördlichen Ortenau', *HABW*, IX, 5.

Schäfer, I., *'Ein Gespenst geht um.' Politik mit der Holznot in Lippe 1750–1850. Eine Regionalstudie zur Wald- und Technikgeschichte* (Detmold, 1992).

Scheifele, M., 'Alte Sägemühle im Enz-Nagold-Gebeit', *Zeitschrift für württembergische Landesgeschichte* (1994), pp. 143–77.

Als die Wälder auf Reisen gingen. Wald-Holz-Flößerei in der Wirtschaftsgeschichte des Enz-Nagold-Gebietes (Karlsruhe, 1996).

Schenk, W., 'Viticulture in Franconia along the River Main – human and natural influences since 700 AD', *Journal of Wine Research* (1992), pp. 185–203.

'Eichelmastdaten aus 350 Jahren für Mainfranken – Probleme der Erfassung und Ansätze für umweltgeschichtliche Interpretationen', *Allgemeine Forst- und Jagdzeitung* (1994), pp. 122–32.

Waldnutzung, Waldzustand und regionale Entwicklung in vorindustrieller Zeit im mittleren Deutschland: historisch-geographische Beiträge zur Erforschung von Kulturlandschaften in Mainfranken und Nordhessen (Stuttgart, 1996).

'Möglichkeiten und Begrenzungen des Aufbaus und der Auswertung, "Langer Reihen" aus Archivalien für die Erfassung vorindustrieller Waldzustände und – entwicklungen, diskutiert an frühneuzeitlichen Rechnungsbeständen aus dem mittleren Deuschland', in Schenk, W. (ed.), *Aufbau und Auswertung "langer Reihen" zur Erforschung von historischen Waldzuständen und –entwicklungen* (Tübingen, 1999), pp. 3–22.

Schilling, H., *Konfessionskonflikt und Staatsbildung: eine Fallstudie über das Verhältnis von religiösem und sozialem Wandel in der Frühneuzeit am Beispiel der Grafschaft Lippe* (Gütersloh, 1980).

Schindler, N., 'Nocturnal disturbances: on the social history of the night in the early modern period', in Schindler, N., *Rebellion, community and custom in early modern Germany* (Cambridge, 2002), pp. 193–235.

Schlenker, G., and Müller, S. (eds.), 'Erläuterungen zur Karte der regionalen Gliederung von Baden-Württemberg, I. Teil', *Mitteilungen des Vereins für forstliche Standortskunde und Forstpflanzenzüchtung* (Stuttgart, 1973).

Schlitte, B., *Die Zusammenlegung der Grundstücke in ihrer volkswirthschaftlichen Bedeutung und Durchführung*, 3 vols. (Leipzig, 1886).

Schlögl, R., *Bauern, Krieg und Staat: oberbayerische Bauernwirtschaft u. frühmoderner Staat im 17. Jahrhundert* (Göttingen, 1988).

Schlumbohm, J., *Lebensläufe, Familien, Höfe: die Bauern und Heuerleute des Osnabrückischen Kirchspiels Belm in proto-industrieller Zeit, 1650–1860* (Göttingen, 1994).

'Gesetze, die nicht durchgesetzt werden – ein Strukturmerkmal des frühneuzeitlichen Staates?' *Gescichte und Gesellschaft* (1997), pp. 647–63.

Schmauder, A., *Württemberg im Aufstand. Der arme Konrad, 1514* (Leinfelden-Echterdingen, 1998).

Schmidt, U. E., *Der Wald in Deutschland im 18. und 19. Jahrhundert* (Saarbrücken, 2002).

Schofield, R., 'Family structure, demographic behaviour, and economic growth', in Walter, J., and Schofield, R. (eds.), *Famine, disease and the social order in early modern society* (Cambridge, 1989), pp. 279–304.

Schray, W., *Ortsgeschichte Flacht* (Ulm, 1980).

Schröder, K.-H., *Weinbau und Siedlung in Württemberg* (Remagen, 1953).

Schulte, R., *The village in court. Arson, infanticide, and poaching in the court records of Upper Bavaria, 1848–1910* (Cambridge, 1994).

Schulze, W., 'Vom Gemeinnutz zum Eigennutz', *Historische Zeitschrift* (1986), pp. 591–625.

Schüttenhelm, J., *Der Geldumlauf in südwestdeutschen Raum von Riedlinger Münzvertrag 1423 bis zur ersten Kipperzeit 1618. Eine statistische Münzfundanalyse unter Anwendung der elektronischen Datenverarbeitung* (Stuttgart, 1987).

Scott, J. C., *Seeing like a state. How certain schemes to improve the human condition have failed* (London, 1998).

Scott, T., *Regional identity and economic change. The upper Rhine, 1450–1600* (Oxford, 1997).

Society and economy in Germany, 1300–1600 (Basingstoke, 2002).

Scott, T. (ed.), *The peasantries of Europe from the fourteenth to the eighteenth centuries* (Harlow, 1998).

Scott, T., and Scribner, R. W., *The German Peasants' War: a history in documents* (London, 1991).

Scribner, B., 'Communities and the nature of power', in Scribner, B. (ed.), *Germany. A new social and economic history. Vol. I. 1450–1630* (London, 1996), pp. 291–325.

Scribner, R. W. 'Police and the territorial state in sixteenth-century Württemberg', in Kouri, E. I., and Scott, T. (eds.), *Politics and society in Reformation Europe* (London, 1987), pp. 103–20.

Shaw-Taylor, L., 'Labourers, cows, common rights and parliamentary enclosure: the evidence of contemporary comment c. 1760–1810', *Past and Present* (2001).

The management of common land in the lowlands of southern England, c. 1500–c. 1850', in Moor, M. de, Shaw-Taylor, L., and Warde, P. (eds.), *The management of common land in north west Europe, c.1500–1850* (Turnhout, 2002), pp. 59–85.

Shiel, R., 'Improving soil fertility in the pre-fertiliser era,' in Bruce M. S. Campbell and Mark Overton (eds.), *Land, labour, and livestock: historical studies in European agricultural productivity* (Manchester, 1991), pp. 51–77.

Sieferle, R.-P., 'The energy system – a basic concept of environmental history', in Brimblecombe, P., and Pfister, C. (eds.), *The silent countdown. Essays in European environmental history* (London, 1990), pp. 9–20.

The subterranean forest. Energy systems and the Industrial Revolution (Cambridge, 2001).

Sieglerschmidt, J., 'Social and economic landscapes', in Ogilvie, S. C. (ed.), *Germany: a new social and economic history. Vol II. 1630–1800* (London, 1996), pp. 1–38.

'Wandlungen des Energieeinsatzes in Mitteleuropa in der Frühneuzeit', in Schenk, W. (ed.), *Aufbau und Auswertung 'langer Reihen' zur Erforschung von historischen Waldzuständen und –entwicklungen* (Tübingen, 1999), pp. 47–89.

Siemann, W. (ed.), *Umweltgeschichte. Themen und Perspektiven* (Munich, 2003).

Simmons, I. G., *Environmental history: a concise introduction* (Oxford, 1993).

Simon, T., *Grundherrschaft und Vogtei: eine Strukturanalyse spätmittelalterlicher und frühneuzeitlicher Herrschaftsbildung* (Frankfurt am Main, 1993).

Skipp, V., *Crisis and developments: an ecological case study of the forest of Arden, 1570–1674* (Cambridge, 1978).

Slicher van Bath, B. H. *The agrarian history of western Europe 500–1850* (London, 1959).

Slicher van Bath, B., 'Robert Loder en Renck Hemmema', in Slicher van Bath, B., *Bijdragen tot de agrarische geschiedenis* (Utrecht, 1978).

Smil, V., *Energy in world history* (Boulder, 1994).

Söderberg, J., and Myrdal, J., *Agrarian economy of sixteenth-century Sweden* (Stockholm, 2002).

Sombart, W., *Der moderne Kapitalismus*, 5th edn, Bd. II (München, 1922).

Soll, W., *Die staatliche Wirtschaftspolitik im 17. und 18. Jahrhundert* (Tübingen, 1934).

Sörlin, S., *Naturkontraktet: om naturumgängets idéhistoria* (Stockholm, 1991).

Sreenivasan, G., 'The social origins of the peasants' war in Upper Swabia', *Past and Present* (2001), pp. 30–66.

The peasants of Ottobeuren, 1487–1726: a rural society in early modern Europe (Cambridge, 2004).

Stadt Gerlingen, *Gerlingen, 797–1997* (Gerlingen, 1997).

Stadt Heimsheim (ed.), *Heimsheim: einst und Heute* (Heimsheim, 1992).

Stadtmuseum Leonberg, *Das Leonberger Salzhaus. Salz und Salzhandel im Oberamt* (Leonberg, 1996).

Stein, R., and Felden, H., 'Die Plünderungen in der Kriegen Ludwigs XIV', *Ortsbuch Hoheneck: Stadtteil von Ludwigsburg* (Neckarwestheim, 1983), pp. 120–2.

Stein, R., Bolay, T., and Felden, H., 'Die Katastrophe des Dreißigjährigen Krieges', in Felden, H. (ed.), *Ortsbuch Hoheneck: Stadtteil von Ludwigsburg* (Neckarwestheim, 1983), pp. 116–19.

Steinsiek, P. -M., *Nachhaltigkeit auf Zeit. Waldschutz im Westharz vor 1800* (Münster, 1999).

Steward, J., *Theory of culture change; the methodology of multilinear evolution* (Urbana, 1955).

Evolution and ecology: essays on social transformation (Urbana, 1977).

Stieglitz, L. von, *Zünfte in Württemberg: Regeln und Zeichen altwürttembergischer Zünfte vom 16. bis zum 19. Jahrhundert* (Ulm, 2000).

Straub, A., *Das badische Oberland im 18. Jahrhundert: die Transformation einer bäuerlichen Gesellschaft vor der Industrialisierung* (Husum, 1977).

Strauss, G., *Law, resistance, and the state: the opposition to Roman law in Reformation Germany* (Princeton, 1986).

Stuart, K., *Defiled trades and social outcasts: honor and ritual pollution in early modern Germany* (Cambridge, 1999).

Suter, A., *Der schweizerische Bauernkrieg von 1653. Politische Sozialgeschichte – Sozialgeschichte eines politischen Ereignisses* (Tübingen, 1997).

Tack, G., Bremt, P. van den, and Hermy, M., *Bossen van Vlaanderen. Een historische ecologie* (Leuven, 1993).

Thompson, E. P., *Customs in common* (London, 1991).

Thorner, D., 'Peasant economy as a category in economic history', in Shanin, T. (ed.), *Peasants and peasant societies* (London, 1971), pp. 202–18.

Tilly, C., *Coercion, capital, and European states, AD 990–1992* (Oxford, 1992).

Timm, A., *Die Waldnutzung in Nordwestdeutschland im Spiegel der Weistümer; einleitende Untersuchungen über die Umgestaltung des Stadt-Land-Verhältnisses im Spätmittelalter* (Cologne, 1960).

Troeltsch, W., *Die Calwer Zeughandlungskompagnie und ihre Arbeiter* (Jena, 1897).

Trossbach, W., 'Beharrung und Wandel, "als Argument". Bauern in der Agrargesellschaft des 18. Jahrhunderts', in Trossbach, W., and Zimmermann, C. (eds.), *Agrargeschichte: Positionen und Perspektiven* (Stuttgart, 1998), pp. 107–36.

'"Mercks Baur": Annäherung an die Struktur von Erinnerung und Überlieferung in ländlichen Gesellschaft (vorwiegend zweite Hälfte des 16. Jahrhunderts), in Rösener, W. (ed.), *Kommunikation in der ländlichen Gesellschaft vom Mittelalter bis zur Moderne* (Göttingen, 2000), pp. 209–40.

Trugenberger, V., *Zwischen Schloß und Vorstadt: Sozialgeschichte der Stadt Leonberg im 16. Jahrhundert* (Vaihingen/Enz, 1984).

'Malmsheim und Renningen im Zeitalter der Glaubensspaltung', in *Renningen und Malmsheim. Eine Stadt und ihre Geschichte* (Stuttgart, 1991), pp. 115–52.

'Der Leonberger Raum an der Wende vom Mittelalter zur Neuzeit', in *Leonberg. Eine altwürttembergische Stadt und ihre Gemeinden im Wandel der Geschichte* (Stuttgart, 1992), pp. 83–120.

'"Die Magd bey dem Knecht angetroffen." Gesinde im Strohgäu in der frühen Neuzeit', *Ludwigsburger Geschichtsblätter* (1999), pp. 37–73.

'"Von wegen des Unbaws von Grund uff von Newem erbawen" – Eltinger Häusergeschichte(n) des 15. und 16. Jahrhunderts in Spiegel archivalischer Quellen', unpublished paper (2002).

Ulbrich, C., 'Agrarverfassung und bäuerlicher Widerstand im Oberrheingebiet', *Zeitschrift für Agrargescichte und Agrarsoziologie* (1982), pp. 149–67.

Vann, J. A., *The making of a state: Württemberg, 1593–1793* (Ithaca, 1984).

Vera, F., *Metaforen voor de wildernis. Eik, hazelaar, rund en paard* (The Hague, 1997).

Viazzo, P., *Upland communities: environment, population and social structure in the Alps since the sixteenth century* (Cambridge, 1989).

Vries, J. de, *The economy of Europe in an age of crisis 1600–1750* (Cambridge, 1976).

Wall, R., 'Some implications of the earnings, income and expenditure patterns of married women in populations in the past', in Henderson, J., and Wall, R. (ed.), *Poor women and children in the European past* (London, 1994), pp. 312–35.

Wallerstein, I., *The modern world-system I.* (New York, 1974).

The modern world-system II. (New York, 1980).

Walter, R., *Die Kommerzialisierung von Landwirtschaft und Gewerbe in Württemberg (1750–1850)* (St Katharinen, 1990).

Warde, P., 'Common rights and common lands in south-west Germany, 1500–1800', in Moor, M. de, Shaw-Taylor, L., and Warde, P. (eds.), *The management of common land in north west Europe ca. 1500–1850* (Turnhout, 2002), pp. 195–224.

'Law, the "commune", and the distribution of resources in early modern German state formation', *Continuity and Change* (2002), pp. 183–211.

'Forests, energy and politics in the early modern German states', in Cavaciocchi, S. (ed.), *Economia e energia secc.* XIII–XVIII (Prato, 2003), pp. 585–97.

'Recording regulation: the context of by-laws and their relation to resource scarcity in early modern Germany', unpublished Paper given at European Social Science and History Conference, Berlin, 26 March 2004.

'Sources of welfare support in early modern Württemberg', unpublished paper (2004).

'Subsistence and sales: the peasant economy of Württemberg in the early seventeenth century', *Economic History Review* (2006).

Watkins, C. (ed.), *European woods and forests: studies in cultural history* (Wallingford, 1998).

Weidner, K., *Die Anfänge einer staatlichen Wirtschaftspolitik in Württemberg* (Stuttgart, 1931).

Weiss, 'Mountain forest policy in Austria: a historical policy analysis on regulating a natural resource', *Environment and History* (2001), pp. 335–55.

Weitprecht, O., 'Schreckentage aus dem 30jährigen Krieg', unpublished manuscript provided courtesy of Volker Trugenberger.

Westra, L., *An environmental proposal for ethics: the principle of integrity* (Lanham, 1994).

Williams, M., *Deforesting the earth. From prehistory to global crisis* (Chicago, 2003).

Wilson, P. H., *War, state and society in Württemberg, 1677–1793* (Cambridge, 1995). *Absolutism in central Europe* (London, 2000).

Winiwarter, V., 'Landwirtschaft, Natur und ländliche Gesellschaft im Umbruch. Eine umwelthistorische Perspektive zur Agrarmodernisierung', in Ditt, K., Gundermann, R., and Rüße, N. (eds.), *Agrarmodernisierung und öklogische Folgen. Westfalen vom 18. bis zum 20. Jahrhundert* (Paderborn, 2001), pp. 733–67.

Winiwarter, V., and Sonnlechner, C., *Der soziale Metabolismus der vorindustriellen Landwirtschaft in Europa* (Stuttgart, 2001).

Wittfogel, K. A., *Oriental despotism. A comparative study of total power* (New Haven, 1957).

Witthoft, H., 'Energy and large-scale industries (1330–1800)', in Cavaciocchi, S. (ed.), *Economia e energia secc. XIII–XVIII* (Florence, 2003), pp. 293–304.

Wolf, A., 'Simplicity and universality in the transition to chaos', *Nature* (1983), pp. 182–3.

Woronoff, D. (ed.), *Forges et forêts: recherches sur la consommation proto-industrielle de bois* (Paris, 1990).

Worster, D., *Rivers of empire: water, aridity, and the growth of the American West* (New York, 1985).

'Transformations of the earth: toward an agroecological perspective in history', *Journal of American History* (1990), pp. 1087–106.

The wealth of nature. Environmental history and the ecological imagination. (Oxford, 1994).

Wright, W. J., *Capitalism, the state, and the Lutheran Reformation: sixteenth-century Hesse* (Athens, 1988).

Wrightson, K., and Levine, D., *Poverty and piety in an English village: Terling, 1525–1700* (Oxford, 1995).

Wrigley, E. A., 'Urban growth and agricultural change: England and the Continent in the early modern period', *Journal of Interdisciplinary History* (1985), pp. 683–728.

'The classical economists and the Industrial Revolution', in Wrigley, E. A., *People, cities and wealth* (Oxford, 1987), pp. 21–45.

Continuity, chance and change. The character of the industrial revolution in England (Cambridge, 1988).

'Energy constraints and pre-industrial economies', in Cavaciocchi, S. (ed.), *Economia e energia secc. XIII–XVIII* (Florence, 2003), pp. 156–72.

Württembergischen Geschichts- und Altertumsverein, *Stuttgart im Spiegel alter Karten und Pläne* (Stuttgart, 1984).

Zanden, J. L. van, *The rise and decline of Holland's economy: merchant capitalism and the labour market* (Manchester, 1993).

'Early modern economic growth: a survey of the European economy, 1500–1800' in Prak, M. (ed.), *Early modern capitalism* (London 2000), pp. 69–87.

Index

accounting 59, 169–70, 196, 218
  account books 78–9, 81, 111, 151, 152,
    155–6, 163, 170, 188–9, 190, 197,
    204, 212, 228, 231–2, 235, 238,
    251–5, 259, 266, 268, 270, 272, 276,
    289, 290, 301, 304, 310, 311, 329
adaptability, thesis of 16–18
agriculture 11, 12, 18, 31, 35, 37, 52, 76,
    91–8, 99, 116, 118–20, 127–8, 129–30,
    141, 226–7, 263, 278, 283, 349, 357
  collective management of 15–16, 20, 24,
    54–6, 57, 58, 60–2, 65–8, 74–5, 80–3, 86,
    93, 98, 105, 152–4, 163, 349, 351, 352
  importance in economy 134–8, 143–6,
    149–50
  productivity in 17–18, 91, 95, 98, 99,
    356–7; see also grain, yields per hectare
Allen, Bob 59, 140
Alsace 94
Amsterdam 139–41
Annales School 10
annuities 127, 135
anthropology 10, 15, 35
Antwerp 114, 141
arable 8, 84–5, 92–8, 103, 135–7, 143–6
  extent of 44–52, 64, 68, 71, 74, 92–5,
    104, 118–20, 131, 226, 279
  forms of cultivation 56–66, 86, 125, 156
artisans 60, 91, 98, 116–30, 134–7,
    141–4, 149; see also handicrafts
  numbers of 120–30
  using wood 204, 263, 270–4, 278, 287,
    288, 290
Asperg 30, 48, 107, 184, 206, 257, 277,
    295, 297, 298
auditing 169–70
Augsburg 114, 140–1, 273
Aurich 45, 47, 48, 50, 111, 122

Backnang 58, 292
Baden 2, 64, 108, 183, 206, 231, 274,
    292–4, 318

Bader, Karl Siegfried 58
Bailey, F. G. 282
bailiff, see Schultheiß
bakers 6, 41, 42, 117, 127–8, 141, 150, 270,
    272–4, 278, 290, 298, 299, 330, 331
barbers 127, 154–6, 270, 272–3, 274, 278,
    298, 299, 336; see also bathhouses
barns 34, 41–2, 144, 195, 224, 276
bast 79
bathhouses 41, 150, 154–5, 273; see also
  barbers
Bauer, see farmers
Bavaria 16, 59, 91, 129, 150, 273, 300–1
beans 57
Bebenhausen
Beck, Rainer 16, 59, 129, 137
begging 97, 210
Beisitzer 150
Benning, Stefan 28, 29
Benningen 108
Bergheim 48, 269, 276
Bernhardt, Walter 170
Besigheim 292, 295
Beutelsbach 200
Bietigheim 28, 43, 45, 48, 60, 68, 71, 80,
    82–3, 110, 126, 128, 129, 130, 143,
    194, 222–3, 238, 240, 249, 260,
    269–70, 271, 273, 277, 280, 287, 292,
    293, 296–7, 300, 304, 310, 311, 313,
    324, 329
biomass, transfer of 53–5, 85, 92, 283, 284,
    303, 315–19, 354–6
Bissingen 45, 48, 108–10, 238, 277, 296,
    312, 313
Black Forest 5, 8, 33, 73, 75, 108, 117, 129,
    177, 182, 215, 231, 232, 244, 270,
    277, 292–7, 311–12, 319, 357
blacksmiths 41, 127, 128, 150, 212,
    270, 274; see also smiths
bleaching 282
Böblingen 27, 91, 171, 202, 206
Boelcke, Willi 265

Cambridge Studies in Population, Economy and Society in Past Time